THEOLOGY, SCIENCE AND LIFE

THEOLOGY, SCIENCE AND LIFE

Carmody Grey

t&tclark

LONDON • NEW YORK • OXFORD • NEW DELHI • SYDNEY

T&T CLARK
Bloomsbury Publishing Plc
50 Bedford Square, London, WC1B 3DP, UK
1385 Broadway, New York, NY 10018, USA
29 Earlsfort Terrace, Dublin 2, Ireland

BLOOMSBURY, T&T CLARK and the T&T Clark logo are trademarks of
Bloomsbury Publishing Plc

First published in Great Britain 2023
Paperback edition published 2024

Cover image: Greens87/istockphoto

A catalogue record for this book is available from the British Library.

Library of Congress Cataloging-in-Publication Data
Names: Grey, Carmody T. S., author.
Title: Theology, science, and life / Carmody T.S. Grey.
Description: London ; New York : T&T Clark, 2022. | Series: Religion and
the university | Includes bibliographical references and index. |
Identifiers: LCCN 2022027050 (print) | LCCN 2022027051 (ebook) | ISBN
9780567708489 (hardback) | ISBN 9780567708533 (paperback) | ISBN
9780567708496 (pdf) | ISBN 9780567708526 (epub)
Subjects: LCSH: Religion and science. | Biology–Religious
aspects–Christianity. | Milbank, John. | Jonas, Hans, 1903-1993. |
Philosophical theology. | Radicalism–Religious aspects–Christianity.
Classification: LCC BL240.3 .G746 2022 (print) | LCC BL240.3 (ebook) |
DDC 261.5/5–dc23/eng20221028
LC record available at https://lccn.loc.gov/2022027050
LC ebook record available at https://lccn.loc.gov/2022027051

ISBN: HB: 978-0-5677-0848-9
       PB: 978-0-5677-0853-3
       ePDF: 978-0-5677-0849-6
       ePUB: 978-0-5677-0852-6

Typeset by Deanta Global Publishing Services, Chennai, India

To find out more about our authors and books visit www .bloomsbury .com and
sign up for our newsletters.

DEDICATION AND ACKNOWLEDGEMENTS

Gavin D'Costa, who supervised the research which seeded this book, has been a meticulous reader, an incisive critic, a wise guide and, above all, an unfailingly generous friend. He has been an example to me in every way, personally and professionally.

Without Simon Oliver, this work would never have begun. He has been instrumental to my intellectual development in so many ways, not least in being the first one to bring Hans Jonas to my attention. His support, encouragement and example made this book possible.

My parents Jan and Rupert, and my sisters Katherine and Rose, are my highest inspiration, my wonder and my joy. Without their shining example and unfathomable love for me, I could not have taken a single step on this path. This book is dedicated to them.

CONTENTS

INTRODUCTION

Ask now the beasts, and they shall teach thee;
and the fowls of the air, and they shall tell thee:
Or speak to the earth, and it shall teach thee:
and the fishes of the sea shall declare unto thee.

– Job 12.7-9

The nondogmatic thinker will not suppress the testimony of life.

– Hans Jonas

This book is motivated by two ambitions for Christian theology. First, that it should call time on its apologetic and accommodationist approach to the natural sciences, recovering its sense of itself as the 'science', the true knowledge, of everything there is. Second, that it should have something to say about 'life' – not just human life but life itself – which can stand as the strongest kind of rebuke to the human violation of the biosphere and the life it supports.

Christian theology needs to frame the value not just of human life but of organic life altogether, and to do so not as indifferent to biological, ecological and environmental sciences but precisely within, through and for them. To be for life, on the side of life, Christian communities must express and act from a total solidarity of the living. What has been undertaken here brings theology only to the threshold of that framing. Laying the groundwork proved labour enough for one book. But it is hoped that, at the very least, a mandate for the task has been set forth.

We live in an age which has justly been named 'the age of biology'.[1] As physics sought to be *the* authoritative discourse in the nineteenth and twentieth centuries, biology now claims the same hegemony. It represents not just a 'scientific' but also a cultural discourse, which pervades contemporary self-understanding. The present study challenges this perceived monopoly by arguing that the notion of life itself

---

1. Stephen Toulmin prophesied that the second half of the twentieth century would be 'the age of biology' (*The New York Review*, 31 December 1964, https://www.nybooks.com/articles/1964/12/31/the-age-of-biology/, accessed 14 April 2022). Arguably, however, it is the twenty-first century which will claim that honour in the end. Jeremy Rifkin, 'This is the Age of Biology', *The Guardian*, 28 July 2001; James Stavridis, 'The Dawning of the Age of Biology', *The Financial Times*, 19 January 2014.

exceeds 'biological' boundaries as conventionally conceived. Rather, the organic must be seen as moral and spiritual 'all the way down'. Life is an intrinsically theological notion and needs theological unpacking to make any kind of sense.

To accomplish these ends, the book forms and defends two theses. Firstly, biology is a kind of theology: its discourse and its object cannot be determined as securely immanent. Secondly, theology is a kind of biology: it is a story about life which cannot be confined to 'religious' subject matter but pervades every disciplinary space. These theses are critically derived from the thought of John Milbank (Parts I and II) and put to work on and with the philosophical biology of Hans Jonas (Part III).

The first two chapters outline Milbank's claim that theology properly exercises 'mastery' over the disciplines and explains his conception of reason as continuous with faith. Chapter 3 argues that, despite appearances, Milbank does not undermine scientific knowing, but elevates it, while mandating a critical mode for Christian theology in its approach to the disciplines. Engaging an interlocutor sharing many of Milbank's concerns, Michael Hanby, Chapter 4 clarifies and refines the agenda for Christian theology in relation to the sciences. Chapter 5 proposes that Christian theology's account of organic life will be a vitalism: a story of life as epistemically and ontologically uncontainable. Chapter 6 examines the philosophical biology of Hans Jonas, enabling the final chapter to propose that Christian theology, the true metaphysics of life, is voiced in Jonas's philosophical biology but also prophetically disrupts it with its own narrative of peace.

Why John Milbank? Simply put, because he has so consistently contested the modern compartmentalization of theology. His *Theology and Social Theory* set out to 'disrupt' the cultural environment of academic specialisms,[2] holding that there is 'nothing in nature which the light of faith might not re-interpret and indeed no true nature which has *not* been transfigured by faith'.[3] What follows is a critical examination, development and selective deployment of Milbank's thought, rather than comprising a study of him *in se*. To do so, book's first part explores the philosophical rationale which underlies his claim for theology's mastery. In the second part, the conception of knowledge as intrinsically theological which underlies this programme is critiqued. The third and final part tests and refines this conception of theology by applying it to what is perhaps theology's most confident contemporary interlocutor: biology. If knowledge is intrinsically theological, we

---

2. Fergus Kerr, 'Simplicity Itself: Milbank's Thesis', *New Blackfriars* 73 (1992): 305–10, 305.

3. John Milbank, 'The Theological Critique of Philosophy in Hamann and Jacobi', in *Radical Orthodoxy: A New Theology*, ed. John Milbank, Catherine Pickstock and Graham Ward (London: Routledge, 1999), 21–37, 30. The two central moments of Milbank's thought are here evident: the transformation of knowledge and reason by faith and nature's own transfiguration by grace. The first corresponds broadly to the project of *Theology and Social Theory* (henceforward *TST*) as a critique of secular knowledges; the second is more apparent in Milbank's later work which develops a greater focus on ontology.

should be able to see this in the dominant knowledge of our age. Ultimately, I aim to demonstrate that life science and its object, 'life', are inescapably theological. They testify to their own impatience of scientistic circumscription. I argue this from theology's point of view, via Milbank, and also from biology's point of view, via Hans Jonas.

The methodological issues raised by this kind of project are considerable, since it involves a foray into what seems to be territory far outside the competence of a theologian. Both theologians and scientists might find such audacity doubtful at best. Far from being a failing, however, this audacity not only warranted but is also one of the marks of theological authenticity insofar as it follows from theology's understanding of the uncircumscribability of the whole created order as participating in God.[4] Theology's in-depth engagement with 'other disciplines' is on this view not audacious in the sense of foolhardy or unjustified, since it does not constitute a 'stepping outside' of theology's own subject matter. It does draw attention to 'the massive intellectual demands of doing theology', insofar as it calls the theologian to be proficient in a wide range of intellectual enquiries and subject matters.[5] In a study which aims to engage with life science, these exigencies are particularly acutely felt, and the book hopes to testify to 'just how demanding and varied [theology] is', while also attempting to bear out the claim that theology's unlimited ambitions are 'warranted' by its inherent scope: to read the whole created order as mediating God.[6]

Engaging John Milbank

The diversity and range of Milbank's oeuvre makes summary challenging. Not only is his style often opaque but also he moves without hesitation across a wide range of topics and areas of expertise. 'To describe Milbank's work as "dense" is an understatement.'[7] He is not a systematic theologian, and outlining his overall vision requires drawing from many different moments in his thought. The purpose here is not to offer a study of Milbank's theology but to give a critical account of his agenda for theology in relation to the disciplines, to refine that agenda and then to carry it forward in relation to the life sciences and the question of the character of life itself. For this reason, Part I offers a thematic summary, rather than attempting

---

4. 'It is striking that it has taken somebody whose primary scholarly background is not theology (at least, as classically conceived) to catalyze and crystallize ideas so widely disseminated as those of Radical Orthodoxy' (David Grummett, 'Radical Orthodoxy', www .research.ed.ac.uk/portal/files/14269984/radical_orthodoxy.docx, accessed 9 May 2017).

5. Simon Oliver, 'Radical Orthodoxy: A Conversation', in *The Radical Orthodoxy Reader*, ed. John Milbank and Simon Oliver (London: Routledge, 2009), 47.

6. Oliver, 'Radical Orthodoxy: A Conversation', 47.

7. William Meyer, *Metaphysics and the Future of Theology* (Eugene, OR: Pickwick, 2010), 407.

to trace the development of Milbank's thought in toto. The first chapter attempts to clarify the position he stakes out as it is relevant to the engagement pursued in the following chapters. The focus is principally on *Theology and Social Theory* as programmatic of a distinctive vision of theology's engagement with the disciplines.

Insofar as this is not a critical study of Milbank in himself, it does not aim either to assess or to justify his project as a whole. In particular, it does not assess Milbank's use of particular figures who are lynchpins in his project, such as Nicholas of Cusa and Maurice Blondel. A lack of critical commentary on such uses should *not* be taken as an argument from silence in defence of Milbank's reading of these figures, though the critical examination of theological method in Chapter 3 is meant partially as a cautious comment on their legitimacy *in principle*. The concern here is not to probe the accuracy or comprehensiveness of any particular use of texts but to see what emerges on the logic of Milbank's construction of theology. The reinforcement provided by Milbank's heroes and the foil provided by his villains take their place within a grand narrative which does not call for justification from anywhere outside itself. It makes its readings according to its own *mythos*. I am here tackling that approach in itself and in general, not the credibility of Milbank's specific recruitments of individual players in the story.

Nor, importantly, does the book directly take up the comparative question about Milbank's attribution of exclusive primacy to Christianity in the wider context of religious pluralism, though the reader will glimpse, in the narrative shape of Christianity as Milbank sees it, the sort of defence that would be undertaken on behalf of his claim.[8] The criticisms which bear on the use made of Milbank here are those which concern his conceptions of reason and knowledge, and of the theological agenda in relation to other disciplines. The hope is to test Milbank's thought through a particular application. In this sense, while not a critique of Milbank as such, it is a *critical* enquiry, because the case of the life sciences offers an opportunity to scrutinize and refine Milbank's understanding of theology by putting it into practice.[9]

As has been clearly recognized, not without frustration, by some of his readers,[10] Milbank has deliberately put his position beyond external refutation. The significance of this is dealt with at length in Part II. As well as assessing whether this is acceptable in principle, there is a place for accepting the terms of

---

8. The claim for Christianity's uniqueness is total and uncompromising: '[Christianity] is also *uniquely* different . . . Christianity is unique in refusing ultimate reality to all conflictual phenomena' (*TST*, 262). Milbank's provocative foray into the arena of religious pluralism will likely convince only those already 'on board'; 'The End of Dialogue', in *Christian Uniqueness Reconsidered: The Myth of a Pluralistic Theology of Religions*, ed. Gavin D'Costa (New York: Maryknoll, 1998), 174–91.

9. Additionally, one of my purposes in Chapter 4 is to show how Hanby in particular represents an opportunity to respond to some of the criticisms made of Milbank's theology.

10. E.g. Graham Ward, 'John Milbank's Divina Commedia', *New Blackfriars* 73 (1992): 311–18.

the challenge and putting this vision of theology through its paces by application, rather than by an attempt at dialectical adjudication which would have difficulty finding a purchase on the target. The hope is that this method gives a stronger sense of a position thinking itself through, rather than being externally assessed. I attempt at least partially to justify this approach in the performance of it, adverting to the method again at relevant points.

To raise in advance an obvious worry: it may appear that this will render suspiciously invisible my own authorial voice. But the close focus on Milbank's thought in the first half of this book, where the platform for the engagement of the second half is developed, is deliberately intended as a cue to the reader: I am not intending to make normative pronouncements of my own but to test-drive a conception of theology that seems to me to have mileage in it. I openly state at the outset that *I am unsure whether Milbank's position is the 'right' one.* But I think it compelling enough to do some thoughtful work as if it were, not least because it offers a particularly powerful account of what it means for a position to be 'right'. Milbank invites one to narrate a view and see how its narration fares in the doing of it, and if I have presumed anything, it is simply that it is worth the effort of applying his own method to himself, and thence to the question 'What is life?' This is necessarily a sympathetic process in that it assumes that Milbank's approach is credible enough to make the exercise helpful. If the following examination achieves nothing else, I hope that that assumption at least can be borne out. I don't intend to foreclose the viability or urgency of an external interrogation of Milbank's project. I do mean, though, to draw to the attention of any such critique that it must be ready to pit against Milbank its own account of what it could mean for anyone to be 'right' about anything.

Milbank's thought is part of a movement in late twentieth- and early twenty-first-century philosophy and theology which challenges secularism and liberalism, rejects a purely apologetic role for theology and reasserts its prophetic role in relation to the contemporary academic, political and social scene.[11] Leading voices include Stanley Hauerwas, George Lindbeck, Alasdair MacIntyre and Charles Taylor, embracing both Protestant and Catholic perspectives and covering areas as diverse as narrative theology, postliberal theology, virtue ethics and political philosophy. The strands in this development are unified by a critical relationship to Enlightenment traditions of universal rationality. All seek in some way to go beyond the early twentieth-century stalemate between Barthian neo-Orthodoxy and a Harnack-style capitulation to secular liberalism, by exploring anew the church (Hauerwas), the nature of doctrine (Lindbeck), the traditioned character of reason (MacIntyre) and the origins of secularism and individualism (Taylor). The influence on Milbank of the early twentieth-century *nouvelle théologie* in Roman Catholic theology is considerable, in its emphasis on the overcoming of a secular/

---

11. The most succinct overview is Simon Oliver, 'Radical Orthodoxy', in *The Encyclopaedia of the Philosophy of Religion*, ed. Charles Taliaferro and Stewart Goetz (Oxford: Wiley-Blackwell, 2021).

profane, natural/supernatural dichotomy, so reinstating theology's responsibility to deal with the whole world and not simply with the content of revealed faith. Milbank's critique of secular reason is part of this broader picture of an energetic re-examination of the standing of religious faith and theological reflection in relation to reason and the public square.[12] But he would locate himself also in a longer history, a 'counter-Enlightenment' tradition in which the cold regard of a disembodied rationality is challenged by the appreciation of reason as embodied, traditioned and sensory, a flag carried in Milbank's genealogy by the critics of Kant – Jacobi, Hamann, Herder and Kierkegaard.

In this developing history, the movement associated with Milbank, 'Radical Orthodoxy', 'emerged out of John Milbank's dissatisfaction with modern theology's acceptance of its fate . . . as innocuous and irrelevant'.[13] Exemplifying the recovery of theological nerve which Milbank has called for, it is a 'theologic' whose ambition is to participate decisively in *all* knowledge:

> [Radical Orthodoxy] mediates politics, ethics, philosophy and aesthetics without becoming correlationist and accommodating the modern spirit. . . . [It] makes possible a theological knowledge that must then mediate all other forms of knowledge. . . . [It] avoids the false pathos of humility that characterizes modern theology.[14]

Pugnaciously asserting theology's 'mastery' of the disciplines, *Theology and Social Theory* threw down the gauntlet to theologians. It attempted to demonstrate theology's mastery of social science, a discipline which in modernity has posed a particular challenge to the credibility of traditional theological discourse. This book takes up the gauntlet in relation to what is, today, another forbidding sparring partner: the sciences of life. Can theology be 'master' even of biology in the twenty-first century?

---

12. See Shakespeare's account of this broader picture, where he considers Radical Orthodoxy's future; *Radical Orthodoxy*, 32–5.

13. Stephen Long, 'Radical Orthodoxy', in *The Cambridge Companion to Postmodern Theology*, ed. Kevin J. Vanhoozer (Cambridge: Cambridge University Press, 2003), 126–46, 130. (Note, however, Smith's record of a communication with Graham Ward who argued that Radical Orthodoxy can be traced to his own work prior to *Theology and Social Theory*.)

14. Long, 'Radical Orthodoxy', 144. To be distinguished from the true and fitting humility 'before God and our task', as Oliver specifies; 'Radical Orthodoxy: A Conversation', 28–48, 47 (first published in Rupert Shortt, *God's Advocates: Christian Thinkers in Conversation* (London: Darton, Longman & Todd, 2005), 103–25).

Part I

THEOLOGY

Part I explores Milbank's understanding of theology as intrinsic to the character of reason itself so that to it there can be no 'outside'. It examines how, for Milbank, forms of thought can resist that character of reason and so become illegitimately theological, calling for disruption and critique. It also explains why, for Milbank, truthful theology is defined as coincident with peace. The discussion in Part I focuses on outlining and clarifying Milbank's thought in relation to these issues; critical discussion and application is undertaken in the following chapters. Chapter 1 explains his critique of social science and looks at its implications for natural science, and considers Milbank's redefinition of 'nature'. Chapter 2 considers the key elements of Milbank's Christian alternative to secular reason and raises the question of the status of 'truth' in Milbank's vision.

Chapter 1

REFUSING CONFINEMENT

THE NATURE OF THEOLOGY

Milbank's conception of theology: An overview

The unity in Milbank's diverse engagements stems from a conviction that Christianity is 'an entire coherent intellectual vision' which makes a difference to everything, not a set of propositions or attitudes which are tacked on to non-religious foundations.[1] As the elaboration and explication of Christian orthodoxy, theology has something to say about the whole of reality, because reality just is participation in God. In *Theology and Social Theory: Beyond Secular Reason*, Milbank both justifies and enacts this conception of theology.[2]

> [*Theology and Social Theory*] is calling into question the idea that the right way forward, if you're relating theology to other disciplines, is to see [the disciplines] as having their particular areas of expertise, and theology as having its own discrete sphere of competence, and then to bring them together.[3]

On this view, theology would be one compartment of knowledge among many, which lines up with other discourses to make a contribution in its turn, but with no pre-eminent constitution or role. That would imply that 'knowledge' and 'reason' are intrinsically atheological or pre-theological notions, existing in a fundamental plane which hovers below all disciplines equally. This universal discourse of autonomous reason would be 'pure', unconditioned by the insights of any one discipline. Its autonomy would guarantee perfect neutrality which, it is supposed, is what constitutes reason's trustworthiness. This quintessentially modern conception of reason supposes that the most rational mind is the disembodied, un-situated and unbiased subject who presumes nothing. Accepting such an autonomous

---

1. Oliver, 'Radical Orthodoxy: A Conversation', 29.
2. *Theology and Social Theory: Beyond Secular Reason* (Oxford: Blackwell, 2006). This study has used the revised second edition. The first edition was published in 1991 (Edinburgh: T&T Clark).
3. Oliver, 'Radical Orthodoxy: A Conversation', 30.

reason is tantamount to admitting that 'God' is a supplementary hypothesis within a pre-existent fundamental discourse, rather than the source and ground of reason itself. By accepting a discourse-independent rationality, theology is co-opted by a secular reason and in this way brings about its own dissolution as a discipline.

Against this concept of reason, Milbank argues that theology must be committed to holding that all reason is illumination by the divine *logos*, and all knowledge is participation in the knowledge of God, regardless of whether the reason or knowledge in question is 'religious' or 'spiritual'. This leads to a reassessment of reason's relationship to desire, feeling and beauty, a relationship which was problematized by the Enlightenment's dualism of (limited, partial) subjectivity and (transparent, unbiased) objectivity. In Milbank's vision, the creation of categories of the 'religious', the 'spiritual' or the 'theological' as definable departments of human life and understanding is the heresy of secularism, which idolatrously supposes that there is a reserve of created territory which can be coherently imagined apart from its participation in God. Linked to such compartmentalization is the definition of reason as a faculty whose purity depends on its being untainted by feeling, desire, embodiment or faith. The religious, the spiritual and the theological become bounded categories within existence as a whole, rendering theological enquiry and religious activity a sort of hobby, an optional special interest. 'Reason' becomes a self-standing and self-justifying 'epistemological' category which excludes the aesthetic and the erotic. Against this, Milbank maintains that there is no reason apart from faith, and no definable department of life or knowledge which can be isolated as 'the theological'. Reason is an erotic and aesthetic movement which is a response to the desirability of the Good. If the theological concerns the whole of existence and is intrinsic in every act of knowing, it 'doesn't have its own special subject matter; it's much more a question of the way in which the epiphany of God makes a difference to everything'.[4] Not being a specialism, theology cannot be limited to select 'topics' which fall within its subject-specific concerns. Rather *all* topics are amenable to theological reading and beg theological interrogation and critique, and every use of reason is implicitly theological.

Practically speaking, therefore, theology does not make 'some absolutely distinct contribution . . . to social and political understanding', or any other kind of understanding.[5] Rather it makes a 'disruptive difference' to all discourses, at every level of those discourses.[6] This 'difference' is not confined to the addition of supernatural information or interpretation but extends to the deep structures and methods of those discourses and their modes of understanding. This already constitutes a strong critique of the project undertaken by some theologians in the dialogue with natural sciences over the past half-century to distinguish a discrete contribution which theology can make, while carefully circumscribing the area

4. Oliver, 'Radical Orthodoxy: A Conversation', 30.

5. Milbank, *TST*, 241.

6. John Milbank, *The Word Made Strange: Theology, Language and Culture* (Oxford: Blackwell, 1997), 3 (henceforward *WMS*).

which is to be left to science – a division of labour in knowledge production.[7] It is just this division of labour which Milbank's conception of theology disallows. Once theology makes a discretely delimitable contribution, it soon makes no contribution at all. Rather than being positioned *by* the disciplines, theology positions them; rather than placing itself in the story told by other discourses, theology tells the story. For Milbank, theology 'absorbs and makes possible all other discourses . . . completely and without reserve'.[8]

Milbank's metaphysics, which foregrounds participation of creatures in God and mediation of God by creatures, expresses the ontological aspect which is the counterpart of the cognitive aspect just outlined. A metaphysics of participated transcendence expresses the impossibility of any separation of creatures from God, cognitively or ontologically. Milbank's distinctive twist to the premodern ontology of participation is to radicalize it through an appropriation of the postmodern engagement with language and time: human action mediates God, including all human acts of knowing and enquiring. In this scheme, immanence is *never* indifferent to transcendence, even formally. But a symmetry appears here. A metaphysics of participation, and the mediation of God by the creature, equally means that transcendence is not indifferent to immanence, for immanence is not 'outside' transcendence. Transcendence and immanence cannot be externally demarcated, and there is no unmediated knowledge of God for us as creatures: every creature is a 'speaking' of God, and revelation is therefore not bounded by the apparently 'religious'.

> [W]hile insisting that no human discourse has any 'secular' or 'scientific' autonomy in relation to theology, I seek to recognise equally that theology has no 'proper' subject matter, since God is not an object of our knowledge, and is not immediately accessible. Instead, theology must always speak 'also' about the creation, and therefore always 'also' in the tones of human discourses about being, nature, society, language and so forth.[9]

What is below refers to what is above, and what is above to what is below. We know God in any and every creature, and our knowledge of creatures really is our knowing of God:

> The divine creation is always 'a speaking to the creature through the creature' . . . 'revelation' *adds nothing* to 'creation', for the latter is precisely revelatory. Since God is genuinely transcendent and not a mere higher transcendental

---

7. As for example the well-known 'NOMA hypothesis' put forward by Stephen Jay Gould; see, for example, *Rocks of Ages: Science and Religion in the Fullness of Life* (New York: Ballantine, 1999).

8. Gavin Hyman, *The Predicament of Postmodern Theology: Radical Orthodoxy or Nihilist Textualism?* (London: Westminster John Knox, 2001), 4.

9. Milbank, *WMS*, 3.

reality within the same order as us, he never confronts the creature in an 'I-Thou' relation but always addresses the creature – from the beginning and always – *as* the expressive self of this and other creatures.[10]

Crucially, therefore, 'our knowledge of God, since it is analogically mediated, is *always* and *only* given through a shift in our understanding of the things of this world.'[11] Theology is never indifferent to any enquiry into creatures, and it expresses its own understanding of God by adopting a certain way of speaking about this world.[12] It does not simply have a license to enquire into other disciplines; it has a mandate to do so, not just generically but to the finest level of detail; it must be concerned with their methodologies, their subject matters. The consequences for theology's interactions with the sciences are considerable.[13] This and the following chapter do not attempt a comprehensive mapping of Milbank's oeuvre but selectively follow relevant trajectories, with the ultimate interest of exploring what this mandate means with regard to life science and its object, life (Part III).

Theology's critique of the disciplines

In this chapter, *Theology and Social Theory* (henceforward *TST*) is examined with a principal focus on its applicability to the sciences. Though 'natural science' is not the explicit focus of *TST*, Milbank's unmasking of social theory amounts to a general assault on the possibility of 'natural science' conceived as a self-grounding explanatory account of the world.

One purpose of Milbank's interrogation in *TST* is to demonstrate that the social-scientific analysis of society in the modern period, which claims to find it explicable in purely natural terms, does not operate in terms of a universal, autonomous reason. At the same time Milbank counters the Enlightenment attempt to contain theology by relegating it to consideration of 'the religious' as a clearly demarcated sphere within the more basic category of the social. This represents the first plank of his programmatic disdain for traditional disciplinary

10. Milbank is here quoting Johan Georg Hamann, one of the heroes of the Christian 'countermodernity' he defends (*WMS*, 74, italics original). '[R]eligion is about mediation. Ironically so, because it is about the divine; but because the divine is never directly available, religion must instead be about how the divine is indirectly manifest' (John Milbank, 'Culture, Nature and Mediation', http://blogs.ssrc.org/tif/2010/12/01/culture-nature-mediation/, accessed 6 June 2017).

11. Milbank, 'Foreword', 13; italics original.

12. See Simon Oliver, 'Introducing Radical Orthodoxy', in The Radical Orthodoxy Reader, ed. Simon Oliver and John Milbank (London: Routledge, 2009), 20.

13. To anticipate the discussion of Part II, the assumption that this picture calls for theology to 'tell the sciences what to do' is unwarranted; this conception of theology does not have to be 'theocratic'.

boundaries, enacting his disruption of 'the cultural environment of academic specialisms'.[14] By pronouncing judgement on social theory, Milbank equally pronounces judgement on all 'scientific' quests for a category more basic than the religious. In the current model of self-contained academic fields, every discipline finds a place for the religious within its own supposedly universal terms: the biological, the psychological, the historical, the anthropological, etc. But theology, holding to the unity of knowledge as participation in God's knowledge and reason as illumination by the divine *logos*, contests this positioning; nature is always graced; reason is always already suffused with faith.

Milbank introduces *TST* as a diagnosis of modern theology as pathological. Its pathos is 'a fatal disease': 'false humility'.[15] He defines this confinement in a specifically disciplinary context: theology's false humility is the condition of accepting itself to be merely a discourse within discourses. Human beings necessarily construe their knowledge in terms of 'an ultimate organising logic' and this necessity 'cannot be wished away'.[16] If theology accepts that this ultimate organizing logic is settled by discourses other than the Christian narrative of creation and redemption, theology itself will always be expressive of a narrative more fundamental than its own. The solution is to restore 'the possibility of theology as a meta-discourse', a discourse which 'seeks to position, qualify or criticise other discourses'.[17] The discourse which positions modern theology is modernity's myth of an autonomous, self-grounding secular reason which emerges grandly and inevitably from the shadows of religious belief. Milbank identifies two symptoms of theology's disease:

> Either it idolatrously connects knowledge of God with some particular immanent field of knowledge – 'ultimate' cosmological causes, or 'ultimate' psychological and subjective needs. Or else it is confined to intimations of a sublimity beyond representation, so functioning to confirm negatively the questionable idea of an autonomous secular realm, completely transparent to rational understanding.[18]

These represent 'confinements' of theological reasoning because 'God' is pigeonholed in a particular department of immanence, or hived off into an inaccessible transcendence, condemning theology either to parasitism or to pious irrelevance.

TST contests this positioning in relation to one field in particular, the social sciences. Through a critical discussion of the history of social theory, Milbank challenges the assumption that there is a way of analysing society and human life which can 'explain' religion in non-religious terms by considering it as an

---

14. Kerr, 'Simplicity Itself', 305.
15. Milbank, *TST*, 1.
16. Milbank, *TST*, 1.
17. Milbank, *TST*, 1.
18. Milbank, *TST*, 1.

expression of some 'natural' or given substratum. It pursues a comprehensive critique of the possibility of a neutral, suppositionless social-scientific discourse from which commitments which go beyond the allegedly obvious or demonstrable have been purged, which can then be used to unmask religious beliefs and practices as expressions of some more fundamental human predisposition or structure. This critique of secular reason is grounded in a crucial admission to the most characteristic insight of late modernity: the constructed character of all knowledges.

> theology has rightly become aware of the (absolute) degree to which it is a contingent historical construct emerging from, and reacting back upon, particular social practices conjoined with particular semiotic and figural codings. . . . my entire case is constructed from a complete *concession* as to this state of affairs.[19]

Thus Milbank is not seeking to position theology *over against* postmodernity's anti-foundationalist, constructivist and historicist analysis of discourses. *TST* claims for theology the status of a 'master discourse'[20] *not* as an exemption from this condition but rather as overcoming the opposition between the true and the constructed. This tells against the root notion of secularism, which is that human making marks an area of autonomy, and in this way liberates discourses from nihilist dissolution.[21]

The critique of social science

TST adopts an 'archaeological' or 'genetic' approach to demonstrate the non-secular origins of secular social theories. Its purpose is precisely to expose 'the genesis of the main forms of secular reason, in such a fashion as to unearth the arbitrary moments in the construction of their logic'.[22] The argument is that the key notions of social theory are theologically constituted from within, in that they participate covertly in a theological narrative. Examining the fathers of social theory, from Malebranche through Durkheim, Marx and Weber, disinterring the inherited theologies they express, Milbank argues that the supposedly scientific notions employed by these theorists, such as 'society', are in fact doing illicit

---

19. Milbank, *TST*, 1–2.

20. Milbank, *TST*, 6.

21. Brendan Triffett is too quick to label *TST* as fundamentally a redescription of secularism ('Plurally Possessed: Gift and Participation in the Theo-ontology of John Milbank', PhD diss., University of Tasmania, 2011, 3). This is surely not the greatest distinctive of the work, being at least as much an achievement of other authors; peace, I shall argue, is rather the real heart of *TST*.

22. Milbank, *TST*, 3.

theological work. This work is illicit because unadmitted, and also because the theologies it embodies are heretical, and so are susceptible of Christian exposure and critique. Social theory's fundamental concepts, principally the concept of 'the social', are question-begging, and not self-evidently 'natural' and *a priori*. Particularly important for pursuing a further engagement with the natural sciences is Milbank's interrogation of the categories of cause, function and explanation with which social science analyses the human. (Milbank's treatment of natural science becomes our more explicit focus in section 'Explanation in "social" and "natural" science'.) In Milbank's view these concepts, along with the reifications of social phenomena on which social theory is based, are themselves instances of construction, and not a transparent base from which other constructions, such as 'the religious', could be exposed. Social science requires a 'virtually religious faith' in the truth of these concepts in order to be able to produce its 'explanations' of religion and religious behaviour. The 'explanations' they generate are simply secularizing redescriptions which add nothing except the occlusion of their own failure to 'explain'.[23]

In a critical analysis of the origins of political theory, Milbank argues that it is parasitic on the idea of 'secularity' as a realm of pure power. The secular arose as a 'positive institution', not simply as the inevitable stripping away of a question-begging and unnecessary religious superstructure. Milbank's genealogy of the origins of modernity is well-known and has been competently summarized by others, so only a brief overview is offered here.[24]

An understanding of 'nature' as theoretically separable from the regime of the supernatural, sponsored by the Scotist theory of the univocity of being and associated epistemologies of representation, underpinned the invention of 'the secular', 'the political' and 'the state'. These notions had to be imagined through a theological narrative which posited a sphere of purely formal autonomous

---

23. Milbank, *TST*, 259.

24. See, for example, Hyman, *Predicament*, 32–8, and James K. A. Smith, *Introducing Radical Orthodoxy: Mapping a Post-Secular Theology* (Grand Rapids, MI: Baker, 2004), 87–124. Considered as a historical claim, the location of the sources of modernity in a theological shift during the fourteenth century is not specific to Milbank or Radical Orthodoxy. The idea that mediaeval scholasticism moved away from the analogical ontology of Thomas Aquinas and towards a Scotist concept of univocity of being was proposed by Eric Alliez, *Capital Times: Tales from the Conquest of Time*, trans. Georges Van Den Abbeele (Minneapolis: University of Minnesota Press, 1996); William Placher, *The Domestication of Transcendence: How Modern Thinking About God Went Wrong* (Louisville, KY: Westminster John Knox Press, 1996); and Hans Urs von Balthasar, Milbank cites *The Glory of the Lord: A Theological Aesthetics V: The Realm of Metaphysics in the Modern Age*, trans. O. Davies et al. (Edinburgh: T&T Clark, 1991) B.1, 'The Parting of the Ways', 9–48. It can be consistently defended without necessarily regarding this development as a 'wrong turn', a heretical move which calls for theological correction (Hyman suggests that this is the position of Michel de Certeau (*Predicament*, 33)).

power 'independent' of, and theoretically construable apart from, the divine.[25] This move originated in nominalist voluntarism which conceived a gulf between God's *potentia ordinata*, his declared will, and his *potentia absoluta*, or infinite and absolute power, instituting arbitrary power as the defining characteristic of the divine action.[26] The Scotist claim that being is univocal between God and creatures broke the chain of analogy, causing the divine to retreat into an inscrutable darkness and fuelling the idea of God's power as an arbitrary infinitude. The interpretation of divine action as power cooperated with the notion of being as univocal to sponsor a notion of divine and immanent causation as competing on a single plane of being.[27] The collapse of the mediaeval hierarchy of primary and secondary causalities, which could not be conceived to compete because they did not operate on the same ontological level, led to immanent and transcendent causation being conceived as alternatives; created and uncreated causal explanation became a zero-sum game. Natural causes were those which were identifiable and measurable by human beings, and supernatural causation was understood to mean direct, unmediated divine intervention which overwhelms or bypasses created causality. With the conception of causation as univocal power, modernity invented the idea of the incompatibility of transcendent and immanent and, eventually, a compartmentalization of nature and grace.[28] Modernity and postmodernity, as the inevitable consequence of a deracinated reason, are therefore Christian heresies. An adequate response requires theological retrieval and renewal.

The assertion of the autonomy of the human sphere, which is the invention of the secular, grounds social theory as an investigation of society and politics in purely 'natural' terms. In a nominalist account of the will, the meaning and being of objects is arbitrarily given by a divine *fiat* which bears no relation to intrinsic natures or characters of created things. The idea of a will with no responsibility to given structures makes possible a conception of the state as the contractual cooperation of individuals whose privacy is defined as *dominium*, the sphere of the arbitrary exercise of personal right.[29] Hobbesian and Machiavellian political science see society as organized around the control of the inevitably resulting conflict, by means of contractual agreements or through state coercion. Here liberalism, or individual right, colludes with totalitarianism, or the controlling role of the state, in the ideology of 'original violence' in which the play of power is the governing narrative of both nature and culture, making conflict pervasive and fundamental.

25. Milbank, *TST*, 10.

26. Milbank, *TST*, 15.

27. But see Thomas Williams, 'The Doctrine of Univocity is True and Salutary', *Modern Theology* 21, no. 4 (2005): 575–85, who argues that the Radical Orthodox reading of Scotus wrongly interprets his doctrine of univocity as an ontological thesis, whereas in fact it is semantic.

28. Milbank, *TST*, 241.

29. Milbank, *TST*, 13, 16.

In Milbank's analysis, Comte's positivism and Durkheim's analysis of society rely on theological traditions and are narratively constituted rather than dialectically established. Positivism belonged first in social theory, where it expressed the founding of social science on irreducible social facts, not only the individual but also the 'social whole' or 'social organism'; 'the "social" did not have to be deduced . . . it was merely given, in all its unfathomable finitude'.[30] Positivism accepted this social object as a given and sought explanation of other human phenomena in relation to this *datum*.[31] This positivist tradition, for which the social is fundamentally an ahistorical reality, is in Milbank's analysis in continuity with the French tradition of 'social theology' which posited God as the immediate cause of social reality, as in de Bonald's and de Maistre's analysis of society as directly created and revealed by God; the notions of the 'positive' and the 'social fact' first come about as distinctly theological theses.[32] Comtean positivism performs a naturalistic reversal of de Bonald's theological explanation of society: the social fact, rather than divine power, is granted ultimacy. This leaves 'intact the metaphysical framework in which the reversal occurs' and retains the dualism of 'irreducible social whole over . . . constituent parts', with the association of the totality with the necessary reign of religion.[33] The cohesion of this social whole is maintained by sacrifice, with evident theological debts. As positivism was secularized, it gradually became viewed as a 'scientific' translation of the Kantian critique, a rigorous application to the social of Kant's epistemology.[34] In the new sociological analysis, the always-prior framework of society means that the knowing of the individual is relative to its social environment, which is the true 'given' in relation to which other explanations occur. In this way the social and biological explanations of individual behaviours pursued by Comte found a natural ally in the Kantian rejection of transcendent metaphysics; knowledge as environmentally determined is considered to erase transcendence.[35] The elevation of the social to an *a priori* thus reinforced the new hegemony of the fabricated status of human knowing. We know only the social and the human; knowledge beyond this is ungrounded speculation. This led to the association of social science with the rejection of theology and metaphysics, as expressed in Durkheim.[36]

This brief genealogy indicates the kind of reasoning Milbank uses to challenge the foundations of a social-scientific analysis. Acknowledging the way in which the

---

30. Milbank, *TST*, 51.

31. Milbank means the term 'positivism' 'in its historical complexity and ambiguity and never . . . anachronistically – except where appropriate – in the mere sense of scientific or "logical" positivism' (*TST*, xii).

32. Milbank, *TST*, 52.

33. Milbank, *TST*, 62.

34. Milbank, *TST*, 65.

35. Milbank, *TST*, 65.

36. 'Comte and Durkheim have succeeded in instilling in us the illusion that sociological critique . . . "finitizes" and humanizes religion' (Milbank, *TST*, 66).

socially and culturally relative character of practices and beliefs became apparent, he denies the secularizing conclusion. The linguistic and cultural construction of knowledge only leads to a denial of transcendence if one assumes against the mediating possibilities of linguistic and cultural structures. In other words, it spells naturalism only if one assumes *a priori* that the fabricated is coterminous with the 'purely' (i.e. immanently considered) human.

Against the circumscription of reason

At this point one of the major constructive programmes of *TST* comes into play: to challenge Kantian epistemology's assumption against mediation.[37] The Kantian critique of metaphysics which the early social theorists absorbed supposed that one can set fixed boundaries to knowledge. But this requires that one can 'round upon' the finite as an object and list the categories which organize finite knowledge. Such a rounding constitutes an illicit claim to transcendent knowledge, because only from a vantage point outside the finite could there be a total knowing of the finite and its bounds. '[A Kantian] scheme suppresses the fact that, since no such boundaries can be clearly identified without a contradictory crossing over to their other side, all human discourses have to cope with *aporias* that arise from the irreducibly indeterminable nature of things with which human beings are confronted.'[38] In Milbank's treatment, this confusion raises its head whenever certain immanent facts are hypostasized and raised to the status of absolute givens, such as Comte's or Durkheim's 'social whole'.[39] Just as Kant transcendentalized the categories of knowing, Comte and Durkheim suppose that 'one can "round upon" society as a finite object, and give an exhaustive inventory, valid for all time, of the essential categorical determinants for human social existence'.[40]

Against this, Milbank contends that the conditionedness of our knowing wholly rules out the possibility of categories that are securely either *a priori* or *a posteriori*.

---

37. Milbank's reading of Kant has been subject to withering critique by Paul Janz ('Radical Orthodoxy and the New Culture of Obscurantism'). It has already been said that, for this project, the accuracy or otherwise of Milbank's use of a particular source is not decisive; what is important is whether his understanding of knowledge and reason promotes a poor reading of sources in principle, a question which occupies Chapter 3. For what it's worth, though, it's arguable that Janz's correction of Milbank's reading of Kant does not substantially change the way in which Milbank uses Kant in this respect, not least because in *TST* he is more interested in the way Kant was absorbed and put to use in social science. Chapter 3 returns to other aspects of Janz's critique.

38. John Milbank, 'Faith, Reason and Imagination: The Study of Theology and Philosophy in the Twenty-First Century', http://theologyphilosophycentre.co.uk/papers/Milbank_StudyofTheologyandPhilosophyinthe21stCentury.pdf, accessed 24 June 2014, 7.

39. Milbank, *TST*, 66.

40. Milbank, *TST*, 66.

If we cannot exhaustively determine the limits of finitude, we cannot know where our knowledge 'stops'. Transcendental categories 'can only justify themselves as a kind of "conjecture" about the transcendent, and the relation of this transcendence to finitude'.[41] Smuggling in transcendental social categories, social science does not succeed in circumscribing finitude but simply replaces the former religious givens with equally question-begging 'scientific' ones. Modern sociology continues and expands this Kantian programme of providing 'an exhaustive inventory of the essential aspects of our (social) finitude' in a way which excludes any theological or metaphysical account of this finitude, or speculative extension of our knowledge of finitude towards a possible infinite.[42] This circumscription of the knowable, as an attempt to establish 'a once-for-all representation of finitude', is a form of 'policing the sublime' insofar as it attempts to confine thought within a prison of pure immanence. The idea of limit is always ontologically laden.[43]

The impossibility of circumscribing finitude, a theme to which Milbank frequently returns and which anticipates his use of Blondel, is essential for his project with respect to language, culture and the material world (Chapter 2 returns to this). The traditional doctrine of analogy stands against just such a circumscription, and so a retrieval of analogy ontologically conceived as a metaphysics of participation is essential to an overcoming of problematically 'modern' theology which has accepted an *a priori* confinement.[44] Wittgenstein, whose philosophy of language would otherwise seem hospitable to the kind of work Milbank wants to do, is found wanting on just these grounds: he tries to determine in advance what cannot be said.[45] The alternative, a fuller doctrine of analogy supported by a higher place given

---

41. Milbank, *TST*, 66.

42. Milbank, *TST*, 66.

43. This important issue arises again below. David Schindler explores the ontology of limit in a Thomist key in 'The Given As Gift: Creation and Disciplinary Abstraction in Science', *Communio* 38 (2011): 52–102: 'This idea of limit, even if intended to be only disciplinary in nature, will inevitably carry some tacit conception of what lies beyond the entity's limit, some tacit conception, that is, of the relation of x to non-x, and just so far some conception also of both x and non-x. . . . the assumption that the idea of limit can be originally empty of or neutral toward ontology already embeds a hidden ontology itself, one that is rightly termed mechanistic' (55–6).

44. See Milbank, *WMS*, Chapter 1, in which he defends the *via eminentiae* against Kantian transcendentalism.

45. It is 'the general problem of Wittgenstein's linguistified Kantianism and finitism, which tends to regard the grammatical rules of religious, as of other discourses (however obscure these may be), as marking out transcendental bounds for correct reasoning which cannot be speculatively transgressed', when in fact, 'a *really* rigorous linguistic analysis – as has been shown all the way from Plato to Derrida – tends to augment rather than to reduce the speculative unboundedness of our discourse'. John Milbank, 'Faith, Reason and the Imagination: The Study of Theology and Philosophy in the 21st Century' (theologyphilosophycentre.co.uk) 7.

to linguistic mediation as intrinsically analogical, means that there is no good reason to suppose that the stories we tell, and the cultural objects we move among, do not, in some uncertifiable and indemonstrable way (because the stories and cultures are inescapable and could never be assessed from outside), reflect, approach or participate in reality itself. Below we see how this grounds the high estimation of speculation and conjecture which Milbank needs to support his conception of metaphysics. If there are no secure grounds for drawing a clear boundary between finite knowledge and transcendent knowledge, the modern sociological critique of religion as explicable in 'purely' natural, immanent terms is void insofar as it is parasitic on such a boundary. Milbank's continuation of the *nouvelle théologie* project is evident: finitude, 'nature', can never be 'pure' in the sense of securely immanent. The boundaries of the 'natural' sciences, carefully policed by an ontological naturalism, are here in view: 'nature' cannot be defined or isolated in the way such a policing presupposes. How one could develop a coherent account of natural science in the absence of such isolability is an important metaphysical and epistemological question consequent upon Milbank's claim which occupies Part II.

Instead of undertaking the counteroffensive of challenging social-scientific accounts of the human, contemporary theology has in Milbank's view hastened to a rapprochement with sociological explanations of religion. Frequently it has done this by taking refuge in an inexplicable 'remainder' which constitutes the real core of faith.[46] This is an accommodationism which presumes the validity of the sociological critique and accepts whatever corner of 'inexplicability' remains to it. For example, the neo-orthodox response of locating religious content in an ineffable revealed realm which wholly transcends the social and the cultural simply buys into sociology's 'ownership' of the immanently human. Rather, Milbank suggests, theology should interrogate the sense of 'explanation' that is being presupposed and contest the settled picture of what is 'natural' which such accounts necessarily rely on. It should mount its own meta-critique against social-scientific explanation, demonstrating its secret perpetuation of theological narratives and exposing the impossibility of sociological 'explanation' tout court. By buying into the key explanatory terms of such discourses, whether social or (we shall argue) biological, theology accepts a level of explanation more basic than its own and so seals its own irrelevance. Milbank instead reclaims social science's terms and places them in a theological frame, to the extent that, at the end of *TST*, he states quite simply that social science can only be done by and in the community of the church.[47]

---

46. Theologians 'seek to limit the scope of [sociological] suspicion by staking out a dimension to religion or theology which must remain irreducible. A sensibly critical faith is supposed to admit fully the critical claims of sociology (as indeed of Marxism and Freudianism) as a propaedeutic to the explication of a more genuine religious remainder'. Milbank, *TST*, 101.

47. This study touches on Milbank's use of 'the church' only where it illuminates present concerns; this is not meant to elide the real concerns arising from his ecclesiology. Some critics' hesitations are mentioned later.

Explanation in 'social' and 'natural' science

For Milbank, the *nouvelle théologie*'s defence of the inseparability of nature and grace is theologically decisive. Although the concept of 'nature' is not explicitly the central focus of *TST*, the book can be read as an extended critique of the idea of nature as a stable, constant and external reference point for thought, and of those cognate categories which play the same role in other disciplines. Milbank is targeting 'naturalisms' in the sense of those projects of thought which claim to base themselves on 'nature', where 'nature' is a transparent starting point which is self-evident and equally accessible to all: 'secular reason' would in this sense be a supreme naturalism.[48] He contests the idea of a self-explanatory 'nature' if it is understood to refer to a realm that can be discussed (even formally) apart from grace, as a heresy which cooperates with the Enlightenment's project to establish a sphere of self-contained immanence which corresponds to the realm of 'pure' reason uncontaminated by baseless faith.[49] Problematically 'modern' theology accepts the idea that that which is baseless cannot be credible and so attempts to justify faith with reference to something putatively fundamental, obvious and universal: 'reason' or 'nature'. The countermodern alternative is to show the equal baselessness of reason and faith, and so to clarify reason as but a species of faith and faith as a species of reason. The same logic applies to nature, which, admitted or not, is the supposedly given set of facts or states of affairs which modern 'natural' sciences take as normative. Milbank's analysis is meant to reveal the non-availability of 'nature' in the sense which secular reason intends, rendering culture, religion and all allegedly 'constructed' realities no more question-begging, no less 'natural', than anything else.

'Explanation' in secular reason and science is naturalistic in the sense of operating as an attempt to give an account of a phenomenon in terms of something more basic. In the life sciences, that which is to be 'explained' is life; life sciences go behind it to look for something in terms of which it can be exhaustively accounted for, begging the same questions as notions of 'pure' reason or 'pure' nature. Where sociology is concerned, the unavailability of a 'natural' substratum or prehistory in relation to which reason could isolate the social makes its ambition to 'explain' culture unrealizable. In Milbank's treatment, liberalism, positivism and sociology are all grappling with an irresolvable antinomy which undermines their attempts to generate a settled scientific definition of the human: they cannot negotiate the *aporia* which results from holding both that humans construct culture and society and that culture and society construct the human. Sociology tries to get around

---

48. The picture of secularism as a naturalism has been amplified by Charles Taylor, whose 'naturalization thesis' captures the sense that secularism regards religious belief as a question-begging superstructure built on an obvious and universal set of givens. Charles Taylor, *A Secular Age* (Cambridge, MA: Harvard University Press, 2007), especially Chapter 1.

49. John Milbank, *The Suspended Middle: Henri de Lubac and the Debate Concerning the Supernatural* (Grand Rapids, MI: Eerdmans, 2005), details his approach to this theme.

this by invoking ideas of the naturally given structures of society. Liberalism in contrast begins with the individual as the fundamental fact. But 'the antinomy itself is fundamental'[50] and is impossible to resolve in the terms of secular reason. Thus the claim to discover a *most basic* category is bogus. The social sciences require a category of the natural as the incontestable basis in light of which the 'social', the 'religious', the 'economic' or the 'political' can be exposed for analysis. But the *aporia* of human construction of society/social construction of the human is pervasive.[51] This polarization begs the question of the origin or given which constitutes the starting point for social science.[52] It is impossible to separate the social from the religious, the economic or the political.

This state of affairs undermines the possibility of 'social science' as an ultimate account of the human and points rather to an ultimacy of narration: 'the antinomy can only be mediated by narration.'[53] Modern sociology in fact contains its own covert narrative: a liberal narrative of progress informed by Protestantism, the Enlightenment and capitalist economics.[54] This belies its attempt at a 'would-be rational account of universal history'.[55] What is problematic in the inheritance of modernity is the notion that there is an ahistorical reason which is self-grounding and self-transparent, separable from understanding, language and culture. Far from being a 'science' in the positivist sense of starting with universal and irreducible givens, social theories are simply narrations of the human, readings of social

50. 'One cannot . . . commence a "science" with either the social whole, or the individual act – there can be neither a positive, nor a liberal science. But nor can there be some mixture of the two, because both the social and the individual contribution are entirely contingent, and constantly being modified, the one by the other.' Milbank, *TST*, 70–1.

51. There cannot, for example (against Weber), be a dualism between external historical event and internal intention or consciousness. History cannot be split into the 'objective' and scientifically analysable reality of economics and politics and the subjective and hidden force of agents' inner lives and motivations – the 'factual' and real versus the irreal and evaluative.

Alan Thomson sees this paradox of the origin as the fundamental insight Milbank derives from Vico, driving his conception of culture which itself is the heart of Milbank's theological project: '[H]istory has been made by human beings, and the origin which this points to has the unsurpassable character of a tautologous statement of the problematic – human beginnings are *human* beginnings, the origin of culture is cultural, the transition to history consists in the human making of language' (Alan Thomson, *Culture in a Post-Secular Context: Theological Possibilities in Milbank, Barth, and Bediako* (Eugene, OR: Pickwick Publications, 2014), 100, quoting Milbank's doctoral thesis, italics original). History and culture simply cannot be got behind, and every discipline has to reckon with this state of affairs.

52. Milbank, *TST*, 74.

53. Milbank, *TST*, 74.

54. Milbank, *TST*, 76.

55. Milbank *TST*, 76.

phenomena in the light of a particular history; they cannot get back to 'nature' as a clear starting point which could generate a universal consensus. In his later development of this theme, Milbank considers early modern theories of the origin of language, arguing that Hamann, Herder, Vico and others placed metaphor at the origin and in this way made it impossible 'to appeal to a basic, universal natural norm that will still be a human norm'.[56] This underlines his contention that religion cannot be 'got behind' in the sense in which modern critiques of religion implicitly suppose, for '[i]f metaphor is fundamental, then religion ceases to be a mystery *in addition* to the mystery of humanity itself'.[57]

Marx too, for Milbank, problematically accepts the idea of a 'natural', free and non-religious condition of human beings, onto which religious fictions are slowly grafted through the operation of power relations. Marx correctly realizes that capitalism is a human fiction driven by an invented 'language of commodities'.[58] But his imagination of an alternative perpetuates the illusion that there is such a thing as a non-narrative, non-fictional human reality and that there is a reason that could be extricated from such fictions. Capitalism is no more or less 'rational' than any other story.[59] '[R]eligious logic is no more nor less strange than cultural logic in general; this allows one to go on to recognise that the "critique of religion" is an impossible venture.'[60]

In sum then, there can only be a sociology if the modes of human association are explained, but this explanation would have to be in reference to some normative mode of association, which could never be identified in purely 'natural' terms.[61] Sociological explanation is supposed to 'transcend historiographical narration of deeds, purposes and uses', but this contains the illegitimate Kantian claim to round upon the finite and to have atemporal access to the total 'finite range of social possibilities'.[62] It is always implicitly universal and so claims exemption from the historical and an escape from narrative, even where this is explicitly denied.

Milbank's denial of permanent human 'facts' such as the social whole and his claim for narrative as the most basic way of giving an account of things amount to an assertion of the inexplicability of cultural existence.[63] To say that narrative is the most basic form of giving an account of the world is to deny the possibility of a fixed and inert way-things-are which could be identified outside the terms of any one story. 'There *is* no pre-textual genesis: social genesis itself is an "enacted" process of reading and writing.'[64] 'Nature' therefore only has purchase as a term

---

56. Milbank, *WMS*, 106.
57. Milbank, *WMS*, 106.
58. Milbank, *TST*, 186.
59. Milbank, *TST*, 186.
60. Milbank, *TST*, 188.
61. Milbank, *TST*, 226.
62. Milbank, *TST*, 112.
63. Milbank, *TST*, 140.
64. Milbank, *TST*, 115, italics original.

within a contestable story. For Milbank that is the story of grace. In the same way 'faith' is the story outside of which 'reason' cannot be meaningfully employed.

Insofar as natural science trades on problematic ideas of reason, nature and explanation, it falls within the scope of the same critique. '[N]atural science itself possesses no privileged access to truth and cannot, purely on its own account, build up a realist ontology. Its "truth" is merely that of instrumental control.'[65] Instrumental control is inescapably cultural insofar as goals for which instruments are sought are culturally determined.

Milbank critiques explanation in its modes of 'cause' and 'function' as concepts employed pervasively by modern science in ways which make an implicit claim to universality and atemporality, and so represent an attempt to escape from narrative into a given nature. 'Cause' and 'function' are always metaphysical; when used naturalistically (in the ontological sense) they are question-begging. In the case of 'cause', for example, it is impossible fully to 'account for' a succeeding event exclusively in the terms of what precedes it 'without a reduction of the specificity of the later event.'[66] To the extent that a 'cause' is not identical with an 'effect', it is not an exhaustive category for the 'explanation' of it; if framed as a complete explanation, it fails to capture the relation between events.[67] This is also true of explanation in terms of 'function', which, although it appears to supply new explanations, is always reducible to narrative form; it is just 'a mode of narrative redescription.'[68] Functional analyses have to be narrated as sequences of connections, which constitute redescriptions motivated by a certain kind of suspicion. Furthermore, equations of the type 'When *a* occurs, so does *b*' always amount to inductive correlations where causal priority is impossible to establish precisely because social explanations founder on the starting point of explanation: is the social phenomenon a function of the belief or the belief a function of the social phenomenon?

> [E]xplanation is scarcely an appropriate term for any theoretical proposal, as it implies that the prior and the original is the adequate source of what it engenders. . . . The adequate explanation of . . . anything whatsoever, means merely its representational repetition, a *narration* of text or thing which identifies causes as occasions taken serious notice of by later events.[69]

---

65. Milbank, *TST*, 259.

66. Milbank, *TST*, 84; he criticizes Weber for failing to grasp just this point.

67. Milbank pursues a fuller elaboration of this critique in the context of an approbatory interpretation of Hume in 'Hume Versus Kant: Faith, Reason and Feeling', *Modern Theology* 27, no. 2 (2011): 276–97 (republished as 'What Lacks Is Feeling: Hume Versus Kant and Habermas', in *Faithful Reading: New Essays in Theology in Honour of Fergus Kerr OP*, ed. Simon Oliver, Karen Kilby, and Thomas O'Loughlin (London: T&T Clark, 2012), Chapter 1).

68. Milbank, *TST*, 111.

69. Milbank, *TST*, 267.

To say 'causation' or 'function' just is to say 'meaning', because it is a mode of something being regarded as *significant* in the sense of having some standing or interest or point from the perspective of a later or subordinate event.[70] In this sense semantics has no purchase outside of culture. Further, because we are unable to identify a 'pure, self-contained and original cause', the notion never obtains an absolute purchase.[71] Explanation assumes 'punctiliar facts' or 'discrete meanings', but it is just these isolable units of value or signification that we cannot have.[72] Recent attempts to rescue sociology from this empiricist fantasy of beginning from isolated observations fail because they still try to hypostasize causal processes 'behind, underneath or before phenomena'.[73] Textuality is the inescapable mode of human knowing; narration is a more basic category than explanation and cannot be got behind, for going behind narration is always simply the institution of another narrative. It is for these kinds of reasons that, for Milbank, science simply 'cannot explain'; 'the finding of causes' is 'a matter of redefinition and redescription'.[74] It does not follow, to anticipate our discussion below, that such redefinition or redescription is not illuminating or critical, but simply that 'explanation' in a naturalist sense is a misunderstanding of what science does.

Milbank also argues that science's positivist aspirations are undermined by the narrative mediation of natural scientific knowledge which emerges from, and presumes, modern stories about the human transformation of nature. Early theorists of science, such as Mersenne and Bacon, were interested in technological or operational knowledge, the harnessing of nature to human ends, so underlining that true knowledge is the knowledge of artifice.[75] '[W]e only apprehend nature as part of the narrative of our own lives' and the specification of our purposes.[76] To this presence of the narrative of our own purposes is added the inductive character of scientific knowledge, in which what is 'true' is simply that which goes on happening: 'scientific theories and experiments are themselves repeatable narratives.'[77] Accordingly, observation language and theory language in natural science cannot be separated, because scientific hypothesizing, theorizing and experimentation are reciprocally constituting. A theory is itself a kind of imagined experiment, and experimentation begins by formulating data in a certain way, so theories and experiments do not float free of one another. Situated as we are in the

---

70. Milbank, *TST*, 267.

71. 'As there is no pure, self-contained original cause that we are aware of, what we know first and last is simply a sequence, and the "causal" relationship of a first element to a second is in fact necessary even to define the first element: who is the father but he who has a son, the chieftain but he who is obeyed.' Milbank, *TST*, 267.

72. Milbank, *TST*, 267.

73. Milbank, *TST*, 276.

74. Milbank, *TST*, 123.

75. Milbank, *TST*, 269.

76. Milbank, *TST*, 270.

77. Milbank, *TST*, 271.

midst of the text, neither once-for-all verification nor once-for-all falsification is possible, undermining attempts by Popper, Lakatos and others to find science in a pre-experimental account of human knowing.[78] Experiments only make sense as part of the narration of experimentation in general.[79]

This identification of a pervasive diachronicity is central to Milbank's account of science, illuminating its unavoidably speculative and conjectural character. Experiments are never free-standing, isolated events but are always represented in relation to past scientific practice and prospective hypothetical extensions. Theories never pertain only to a specific experimental event but always embody a drive to some bigger, more comprehensive account of reality itself.[80] In this sense, the experimental method is driven by the fantasy of a total experiment, one which could 'test' the whole of reality.[81] This fantasy is a speculative necessity, because of science's drive towards a conception of the whole; in lieu of such an experiment, science inevitably employs '"pre-scientific", speculative natural histories' which tell a story of the whole, within which alone the open-ended stories of experimental progress can be situated.[82] Being thus placed in the midst of narratives and unable to circumscribe finitude, the performance of an experiment on 'everything' is not possible; science cannot reach experimentally or analytically to ultimate origins and causes.[83]

---

78. 'Even if, like Lakatos, one says that the long-term success of a research programme measures truth, this definitive "success" still implies that other research programmes have been once and for all defeated, and this can only mean falsified by a "reality" apprehended apart from the theoretical conception' (Milbank, *TST*, 270–1).

79. '[B]y contrast to mere positivism, a pragmatist approach accepts that modern science has already theorized internally its peculiar specificity, simply by concentrating on experimental knowledge' (Milbank, *TST*, 271).

80. Theories do appear to 'hover free' of experiments. But this is 'not because a theory embodies hypotheses conceived independently of the setting up of experiments . . . but because theory articulates, beyond the individual experiment, an always necessary surplus drive towards a bigger, general experiment on all reality. . . . This widest level of theory also takes a narrative form, as natural history, and as the narration of the history of experimentation; showing how one experiment builds on another, how one negates another, how a previous theoretical account of a set of experiments can be replaced by another account, which also takes into consideration experimental results which appear to conflict with the first account' (Milbank, *TST*, 271).

81. Milbank, *TST*, 271.

82. Milbank, *TST*, 271.

83. The notion of a scientific 'test' always contains a necessary counterpoint, that which something is tested against or in comparison to which its distinctive points or workings or processes become apparent (hence the idea of a 'control' for every experiment). In this sense the scientific enterprise is doomed not to have a *total* knowledge, since experimental testing of the totality is incoherent; it 'can never be accomplished, without reproducing that reality' (Milbank, *TST*, 271).

The following chapters consider in more depth the question of whether Milbank is overall undermining or supportive of science. Briefly, however, insofar as his assessment of all knowledge as fabricated allows him to elevate its mediative character, this account of scientific knowledge is *not* – in his terms – a pessimistic assessment of natural science's capabilities. Nor does it constitute an anti-realist philosophy of science, since he does not accept a contest between the true and the constructed. Although he admits that modern science is founded on an *epoché* with regard to realism,[84] the 'instrumentalism' or 'operationalism' which he defends does not preclude what he calls 'a realist habit of mind', in the sense that speculation about the totality is an indispensable aspect of scientific thinking.[85] Speculation is not an idle 'contemplative luxury' but actually 'alters and delimits just what we try to do', his example being that if we think of the cosmos as a machine we are likely to instrumentally or operationally mechanize the world, either by the way we picture it experimentally and hypothetically or by producing actual machines, as in the industrial revolution.[86] This understanding of natural science as inherently speculative is of a piece with his argument that speculative metaphysics is indispensable to even the most common-sense approach to the world, supported by his adoption of a Cusan model of conjecture as the mode of intellectual assent to God (see Section 3e). As alternatives based on subject-centred epistemology and buying into substance-based ontologies, both realism and anti-realism in philosophy of science need to be overcome. Neither does justice to the reciprocity between mind and world, nor to the realist orientation of human making or *poesis* which sees all knowledge as a fabrication whose *telos* is the real itself. Instead of realism or anti-realism, Milbank speaks of 'theological objectivism', where there is no being that is not analogically the being of God, whose reality defeats the modernist dualism of subject and object, mind and world.

The next chapter returns to the character and plausibility of this 'objectivism'. It addresses Milbank's view of human understanding as a form of cultural making or *poesis* which reaches speculatively beyond itself, supporting the necessarily metaphysical character of scientific language. Even our ordinary language has implications beyond the immanent, exceeding its immediate object in ways we cannot determine. Since it cannot be established that human judgement is confined to the finite, our categories of understanding, which include causation, are not securely immanent, opening the notion of exhaustive causal closure to question.[87] Teleology can no longer be rejected because it belongs merely to our 'subjective'

---

84. 'The rule of objective, publicly undeniable knowledge is gained at the price of the foregoing, by science, of ontological ambitions' (Milbank, *TST*, 270).

85. Milbank, *TST*, 270.

86. Milbank, *TST*, 270.

87. The role of 'closed world structures' has also been examined by Charles Taylor, who exposes their role in contemporary non-belief. He summarizes this concept in outline in 'Closed World Structures', in Mark Wrathall ed., *Religion After Metaphysics* (Cambridge: Cambridge University Press, 2003), 47–68.

apparatus of understanding; there is no *a priori* reason to favour mechanical causation over teleology, since the boundary between mind and reality is not definable.[88] Calling on the premodern idea of primary and secondary causality, Milbank contests 'cause' as a univocal concept: it is better explicated in terms of 'influence' on diverse ontological levels; efficient and material causality do not exhaust the range of causal 'explanation'. The notions of causation and explanation need to be radicalized so as to embrace the erasure of finite circumscription.

'Nature' and 'culture'

How, in Milbank's treatment, are 'natural' and 'social' science related? The idea that human behaviour is less predictable than that of inert or non-conscious 'natural' bodies would seem to be the more humanizing conclusion which better protects freedom. The types of social science which most strenuously apply the methods of the natural sciences to human social or psychological phenomena, such as behaviourism, tend to be those theology resists most strongly, because of the deterministic or reductionistic conception of the human they imply. The traditional division of *Geisteswissenschaften* and *Naturwissenschaften* promotes this sharp distinction between human and natural objects. But it is important for Milbank's project that this typology be resisted. Setting culture as a sphere somehow over against nature, or as requiring exemption from merely material causation in order to preserve the human as a sphere of freedom, problematically implies an incompatibility between spirit and matter or between causation and freedom. It is the whole created sphere that needs to be liberated for freedom in its very createdness, just as, in the modern period, it was claimed entirely for negative freedom defined as autonomy. It is just this recognition we find motivating the philosophical biology of Hans Jonas in Part III: sundering nature and culture, human and animal, brings about the loss of both.

In a characteristically contrary move, Milbank suggests a reversal of the usual nature-culture epistemic ordering. Drawing on Vico and the Renaissance theorists of human making, he holds that culture is more knowable than nature; *verum est quia factum*.[89] In his example, our knowing would be more incomprehensibly disturbed if the people of Great Britain woke up tomorrow speaking Urdu than

---

88. Milbank, *TST*, 152.

89. For Vico, culture is more knowable than nature because human beings have made culture, and what we have made, we can know. Thomson takes the view that Milbank's appropriation of this insight is the determinative force in his whole oeuvre: '[C]ontrary to appearances Milbank cannot be properly understood without attending to his understanding of culture . . . he offers a poetic cultural theology that exerts a powerful subterranean influence on his entire corpus'; although this overriding preoccupation becomes fully apparent only in *WMS* and more recently in *Being Reconciled*, in fact it 'was *always already* informing his entire theological project' (Thomson, *Culture*, Chapter 3, italics original).

it would be if the sun were to be diverted from its course: '[P]redictions about human society are more secure than predictions about nature.'[90] What might seem, counterintuitively, to be an invitation to a deterministic behaviourism functions instead to overcome our received picture of inert and predictable matter and pure immaterial spirit. (Anticipating the concerns of Part III, the concept of 'life' instantiates this, for it cannot be confined to either nature or culture and so can be used to narrate their mutuality.) Milbank links the predictability of the cultural sphere instead to the notion of habit, which for him is also the key term in explicating 'life'.

The ubiquity of cultural mediation and the impossibility of an ahistorical access to an inertly given nature make for a fundamental convergence of natural and social science in Milbank's understanding. He observes a problematic version of this convergence at the origin of modernity, which invented 'nature' as 'a sealed-off totality' described by an arbitrary, positivistic conception of natural law based on the *conatus*, or drive to self-preservation, of every creature, which was supposed by the inventors of political science to be 'the universal hermeneutic key' which unlocks nature and society alike.[91] Nature is brought into modernity's voluntaristic conception of autonomy defined in terms of a sphere of legal governance. But the significance of this convergence is transformed if the modern attribution of autonomy to this sphere, as the sphere of the *factum*, is contested. Modernity's admission of nature into the realm of the fabricated need not spell nature as sealed-off totality – quite the opposite.[92] Contesting secularism as a naturalism, and inheriting the *nouvelle théologie*'s agenda to articulate a sound concept of nature, what is Milbank's own account of 'nature'?

Nature according to Milbank

Given his account of the ubiquity of cultural mediation, Milbank's assertion of the superior knowability of culture tends to a more radical claim: stated minimally, nature is knowable only insofar as it is cultural, only insofar as it becomes cultural

---

90. Milbank, *TST*, 272.

91. Milbank, *TST*, 10.

92. '*Nature* is supposed to be given and fixed and to run according to immutable laws, while *culture* is supposed to be entirely mutable and to pursue no pre-assigned ends whatsoever. Yet today we realise that there may be nothing fixed about nature and that her supposed "laws" may merely apply to certain regional natural republics within a more fundamental sea of chaos. Moreover, we have discovered that there may be no intrinsic limit to our capacity to transform also the physical world for good or ill. Nature, too, it seems, turns out to be cultural. But on the other hand, if that is the case, then our cultural reality is conversely entirely natural – it exhibits, as it were, on the surface of the earth, a strange fusion of nature's capacity both for unpredictable fluidity and for the imposition of order' ('Faith, Reason and Imagination', 19–20).

for us; maximally, there simply is no nature apart from culture, apart from narration.[93] This conclusion is implicit in his observation of the antinomy of the human and the social which so troubles, and eventually defeats, social science: do we construct society, or does society construct us? The antinomy can be restated in terms of nature and culture, with natural science as its target: is culture natural? Or is nature cultural? For Milbank culture is inexplicable, in the sense of 'explanation' which he polemically excludes. To the extent that natural science seeks such an explanation for 'nature', it illegitimately seeks an absolute beginning, a vantage point for a total account of things. It is this inexplicability of nature, culture and the human that theology alone, which is narration and not explanation, is equipped to address – a narration which, because it accepts the paradox of origin and yet does not constitute this paradox as a defeat for thought, can find this inexplicability to be not an arrest for knowing but an invitation.[94]

Narrative is 'the way the world happens to us', not just the so-called 'cultural' world but the 'natural' world as well. Milbank's welcome of Deleuze's emphasis on 'surface' as the location of meaning, with the associated rejection of a dichotomy between interior intention and exterior action, is important in his repudiation of the customary division between the natural and cultural worlds. The emphasis on 'surface' is a counter to the Kantian/Cartesian location of meaning in a supposed

---

93. In *The Suspended Middle* Milbank explores this theme in light of de Lubac's doctrine of nature and grace: '[F]or de Lubac all created nature was in some sense orientated to human nature' and so the 'paradoxical structure' of nature/supernature 'even extended to the constitution of all finite beings as such' (5). De Lubac 'saw the paradox of grace as equally the paradox of culture and of human history' (56). He also parses this nature-culture continuity in terms of a Humean 'sympathy' ('Hume's human "sympathy" remains (extraordinarily enough) a kind of "occult" sympathy, in continuity with the inscrutable binding powers within nature. . . . By historical derivation "sympathy" in Platonic, Stoic and Hermetic thought meant the secret power that binds together the cosmos, the body and human society' (Milbank, 'Hume Versus Kant', 278)). The Proclean lineage of Neoplatonism also 'invites . . . consideration of the irreducibly obscure "sympathies" that must obtain between mind and matter if mind is spiritual and yet the two are able to interact with each other' ('Afterword', in *The Radical Orthodoxy Reader*, ed. John Milbank (London: Routledge, 2009), 267–404, 383).

94. Although for Milbank Christian theology is uniquely able to address this paradox meaningfully, he regards 'religion', as opposed to secular reason or social science, as being capable of living with it constructively rather than denying it or drawing a blank. 'Such an admission requires on the part of secular thought a nihilist courage, whereas, it is much easier for religious societies to own up to the contingency and singularity of their fundamental choices, for religions themselves acknowledge that these are not fully explicable, but wrapped up in mystery and the requirements of "faith". Just at the point of their greatest obscurity, where they most seem to invite a scientific suspicion, religions are more realistic about the inexplicable character of cultural existence than science normally dares to be' (*TST*, 140).

pristine interior of the subject, a conscious intention. Milbank emphatically rejects the location of intentions in a projected interior, seeing this as part of a modernist dualism of subject/object, interior/exterior, language/world: 'What makes an action is *not* the presence of a "human" or a "cultural" motive or "internal" reason . . . what matters is the objective surface presence of a teleological ordering.'[95] This is reminiscent of Blondel's account of action as that which can never be inviolably 'our own' but always exceeds and escapes us, which is examined below. Further, it indicates the dissolution of metaphysical dualism which is so central to the vitalism explored in Part III.

Rejecting a notion of mind as an inviolable interiority, and holding that 'story' does not belong to a mental projection onto the world, but is the form of the world itself, changes our conception of the world of supposedly inanimate or 'non-human' phenomena. Identification of objects at all requires a narrative, and our stories are not stories only because they are 'about' human beings; natural objects too have stories and are characters: 'narrative is simply the mode in which the entirety of reality presents itself to us: without the story of the tree, there is no distinguishable, abiding tree.'[96] Echoing Deleuze, Milbank says that entities and sequences, or 'facts and motions', always present themselves as meanings: 'it is only *as* meaning (or as semiotic articulation) that one encounters energies and forces for change at work.'[97] It is not an elimination of nature in favour of culture in a way which would render human beings the unilateral makers of meaning but is rather the establishment of a total reciprocity between these terms. The antinomy is pervasive: it is no more the case that humans invent nature than it is that nature invents the human. 'It is *not at all* that our teleological reading of trees is anthropomorphic; for it is equally true that our teleological, or intentional reading of our own actions is dendromorphic.' There is 'no special "human" sphere of narrative action'.[98]

A transformation of the meaning of 'nature' is being suggested which goes beyond the polemical rejection of naturalism.[99] It is not 'naturalism' per se that is

95. Milbank, *TST*, 362.
96. Milbank, *TST*, 362.
97. Milbank, *TST*, 362.
98. Milbank, *TST*, 362. He continues: 'Instead, the question about what the whole of nature should look like, how even it would like to appear, impresses itself through all our apprehensions.'
99. Milbank expands on the theme of the presence of intention and subjectivity in nature particularly in the context of his discussion of gift, where he rejects a dualism of active agent and passive object; 'things' are *gifts* rather than *givens* and thus are dynamic and not static inert realities: 'In *my* dramatic therefore, "things" are equally, or perhaps more the primary players than are persons – although both these categories are fundamentally disturbed in their usual meanings. . . . If one sees only objects, then one misapprehends and fails to recognise true natures' (John Milbank, *Being Reconciled: Ontology and Pardon* (London: Routledge, 2003), x–xi). We make the world up and the world makes us up.

rejected but the 'nature' that contemporary scientific naturalism trades on; with his propensity to transform terms by bringing them into theological ownership, Milbank might properly be said to be defending a naturalism of his own, one which expresses a metaphysics of participated transcendence supported by a doctrine of analogy. 'Nature' is a mediation of transcendence and is not finitely circumscribable; the exchange of predicates between finite and infinite cannot be *a priori* excluded. Nature has to be taken as an epiphany of supernature; we might say, borrowing another's phrase, that supernature is the real nature.[100] However, as discussed in the next chapter, for Milbank this account of nature is narratively constituted, not dialectically established, and so is inseparable from an account of human making or *poesis* as participation in divine making.[101] This does not mean that nature is 'invented' by human beings, since the notion of invention problematically implies a non-invented substratum in relation to which the invention can be defined as constructed: 'fiction' is not, in Milbank's terms, the opposite of 'reality'. It is only within an always-particular constructed account that criteria for the identification of 'naturalness' or 'rationality' are available. The next chapter elaborates just how we are to give an account of rationality, by considering Milbank's narrative-specific 'theological reason' in detail.

Theology is a biology: Reclaiming 'life'

Reviewing this chapter in light of the overall concerns of this study, the shape of the central question emerges clearly. The point of Milbank's analysis of social

'[W]e do not think merely with our brains but also with our bodies and with our environment. . . . [C]onsciousness somehow "reaches out to things" . . . Is not me thinking the tree as the tree where the tree is, also me being really moved by the tree in an ontological dimension of emotion in which the tree is situated alongside myself?' ('Hume Versus Kant', 287).

Milbank's attribution of a distinctive kind of subjectivity and sentience to material things reverses the 'turn to the subject': we are not *merely* subjects who make the world, in which case we would find no meaning except the meaning that we ourselves projected; we are *also* ourselves the objects of the world's making. The 'modern' epistemology of representation is inverted: as our poetic actions escape our intentions, we are met by meanings 'out there' in the fabric of the world so that it is not only that we make representations of the world, but the world also re-presents us: 'we make signs, and signs make us' (*WMS*, 2). The subject is not trapped in a world of her own groundless invention but always already drawn out of herself by the world's making of her – which nevertheless is inseparable from her own habitual activity of imagining and storytelling. The local, particular and material conditions of our lives participate with us in a shared and mutually constitutive *poesis*.

100. Conor Cunningham, 'Natura Pura, the Invention of the Anti-Christ: A Week with No Sabbath', *Communio* 37 (2010): 243–54.

101. Ontology responds to and enquires into narrative, in which 'ontological questioning is always already begun' (Milbank, *TST*, 390).

science is not that reductions of the religious to the social are unachievable; that would concede too much. Rather he is suggesting that there is nothing more basic to which the religious could be reduced. There is no 'nature' which is a blank substrate for grace and no knowing which is more 'fundamental' than theology. The true knowledge of anything is always theological. To the question, 'What is 'sociology', the true science of society?', Milbank answers: it is theology.[102]

Discussions of religious beliefs or practices in the public square frequently dwell on the biological 'function' or 'origin' of religious belief. Biological categories, like sociological ones, control and confine the phenomenon of religion in explanatory terms which trade on an immanent reading of nature and the identification of a supposedly 'basic' level of discourse. Academic and public forums are littered with attempts to identify this most basic level with biology.[103] Edward Wilson's 'sociobiology' is exemplary in its attempt to bridge the gap between biological and sociological accounts of the human, with the language of 'most basic' operative in its programmatic definition: 'the systematic study of the biological basis of all social behaviour'.[104] What would it look like to perform the same exercise for biology as Milbank performs for sociology?[105] It could not mean importing a 'spiritual'

---

102. Opening the final chapter of *TST*, Milbank summarizes: 'The foregoing eleven chapters of criticism were but preludes to an assertion: of theology as itself a social science, and the queen of the sciences for the inhabitants of the *altera civitas*, on pilgrimage through this temporary world' (*TST*, 382). Notably, Milbank is presenting an 'assertion', not an 'argument'.

103. Daniel Dennett, *From Bacteria to Bach and Back: The Evolution of Minds* (London: Allen Lane, 2017), is the most recent contribution from the 'New Atheists', energetically pursuing a Darwinist account of culture for a popular audience. Dawkins is pursuing a project for a new higher education curriculum which 'places evolution at the centre'; 'evolution will become the new classics' (British Humanist Award acceptance speech, https://www.youtube.com/watch?v=BkPoDnLgdco, accessed 4 March 2019). Sociologists and anthropologists have adopted the enterprise in partnership with biology; see, for example, Pascal Boyer, *Religion Explained: The Evolutionary Origins of Religious Thought* (New York: Basic Books, 2001). (The project is not monolithic, however; Richard Dawkins is at loggerheads with Wilson's concept of 'multilevel selection'; 'The Descent of Edward Wilson', review of *The Social Conquest of Earth*, by E. O. Wilson, *Prospect*, June 2012, http://www.prospectmagazine.co.uk/magazine/edward-wilson-social-conquest-earth -evolutionary-errors-origin, accessed 4 March 2019.)

104. E. O. Wilson, *Sociobiology: The New Synthesis* (Cambridge, MA: Harvard University Press, 1975), 4.

105. Milbank explains exactly what he expects Christianity to 'do' with sociology. '[T]he claim here is not that theology, conceived in a broadly traditional fashion, can now add to its competence certain new, "social" pronouncements. On the contrary, the claim is that all theology has to reconceive itself as a kind of "Christian sociology". . . . The task of such a theology is not apologetic, nor even simply argument. Rather it is to tell again the Christian *mythos*, pronounce again the Christian *logos*, and call again for Christian *praxis* in a manner

interpretation of the biological that hovers over the organic realm and gives it an optional freight of added meaning. Nor could it mean an attempt to find areas of complement or overlap, as though theology and biology meet in a neutral space of explanation and together come up with an account of the whole. This would be to hand over the territory of the organic to a hegemony of an autonomous biological discourse, with theology proffering attributions of 'religious' or moral content. Rather, the organic needs to be actively read, interpreted, understood, and accounted for – by theology – *as* organic; as living. The claim that there is nothing self-containedly 'natural' to which 'life' could be reduced, that there is no 'outside' to theology's domain, must be articulated in the most concrete way possible, or risk betraying theology's unrestricted scope. Theologians keep faith with their regard of each creature as a mediation of God by practising an infinite interest in the living organism itself, and by a 'science', a knowing, of the organism in a certain key, for 'the visible things refer always to the invisible, the invisible things refer always back to the visible'.[106] This is an intractable manifesto, and unfinishable one: Christianity 'requires, as a full exercise of reason . . . infinite exact study of the natural world'.[107]

Milbank argues in *TST* that theology is a necessarily a sociology, *the* sociology. It owns 'society'. Can theology also be a biology, *the* biology? Can it own 'life'? The necessity of this undertaking is pressing on Milbank's logic, since theology is the true science of everything; and yet the questions it presents are even more perplexing than those which arise in the case of sociology. Theologians are hardly going to open laboratories. Looking to the philosophical biology of Hans Jonas for inspiration as to how such an enterprise might go, Part III explores how theology might speak in the tones of biology, while simultaneously, in the shortcomings of Jonas's account, showing how biological 'facts' illustrate the insufficiency of purely immanent accounts of the living. But the methodological issues are legion; more content needs to be given to the way theology construes the work of knowing the world, and the protests against Milbank's programme need to be heard and given purchase. Consequently Chapter 2 considers Milbank's proposed alternative to secular reason, and Chapter 3 tests and scrutinizes his programme for theology. In light of all this, Chapter 4 attempts a normative account of theology's relationship with 'the disciplines'.

that restores their freshness and originality. It must articulate Christian difference in such a fashion as to make it strange' (*TST*, 383). Milbank's insistence on the inseparability of 'nature' and 'culture', and his denial of the mute externality usually attributed to the non-human realm, underlines the implicatedness of the biological in any such 'telling again' of the Christian *mythos*, *logos*, etc., for the Christian narrative has no less to say about 'life' than it does about the human.

106. Quoting Maximus the Confessor; John Milbank, 'Life, or Gift and Glissando', *Radical Orthodoxy: Theology, Philosophy, Politics* 1 (2012): 121–51, 146.

107. John Milbank, 'The New Divide: Romantic Versus Classical Orthodoxy', *Modern Theology* 26, no. 1 (2010): 26–38, 30.

Chapter 2

THEOLOGICAL REASON

THE STORY OF PEACE

If a 'secular' reason is rejected, what is a 'theological' reason? Minimally, that form of thought which is specified by the narrative of creation, redemption and sanctification which is Christianity. Theology is simply the reasoning of the narrative of peace.

In this chapter, that narrative reasoning is further explored so as to establish the content, for Milbank, of the alternative to secular reason. Our question about theology's relationship with the disciplines is here served by clarifying Milbank's conception of theological reason itself. This provides a robust platform for the following chapter to pursue its implications for theology's relationship with the disciplines and the nature of scientific knowing.

Theological reason: Narrating peace

There is a natural suspicion that Milbank's claims about narrative are hidden claims for a new universal reason, a rationality of narrative which pretends to be specific while smuggling in universality once more. But Milbank is *not* recommending narrative *in general*; he is recommending the Christian narrative as the only adequate one.[1] All criteria for true and false reason, like criteria for the correct specification of 'nature', are tradition-specific.[2] It is not tradition-specificity per se that he defends; rather, one tradition alone is defensible. Here the distinctive content of the theological reason defended by Milbank comes into play:

1. 'Christianity starts to appear – even "objectively" – as not just different, but as *the* difference from all other cultural systems, which it exposes as threatened by incipient nihilism. However, it is only at the ontological level, where theology articulates (always provisionally) the framework of reference implicit in Christian story and action, that this 'total' difference is fully clarified, along with its ineradicable ties to non-provable belief.' Milbank, *TST*, 383; italics original.

2. Milbank, *TST*, 348.

the Christian narrative is to be preferred because it alone is capable of peacefully mediating difference.

For Milbank, difference is ontologically ultimate:

> the absolute uniqueness of every individual, which follows from its necessarily unique position in a series (so that nothing can be exactly repeated), makes difference ontologically ultimate and worthy of the highest valuation.[3]

What Christian theology *makes of* difference is the key to Milbank's thought. In his account, Christianity actually '*is* the coding of transcendental difference as peace'.[4] This is what chiefly distinguishes his account from that of other authors who share a fundamental concern with story.[5] It is this which not only justifies but actually constitutes theology's 'mastery': it alone fully affirms the peaceful cohabitation of narratives. Theology is therefore 'master' in a somewhat ironic sense, because it evacuates the term of violent domination.[6] This is what makes it capable of being the 'meta-narrative', the narrative which embraces all stories: it refuses the translation of difference into violence, because in its narrative of God's *free* creation of the cosmos from nothing and God's call of creation to a harmonious conviviality, reality is construed as fundamentally peaceful. Conflict has no ultimate reality; it is purely privative.[7] In this story, origin and destination are characterized above all by their lack of rivalry, the absolute priority of gratuitous donation. Diversity here cannot be conflictual. Narratives are allowed to be themselves without being swallowed by one another. For there is, in the ultimate perspective, no incompatibility between difference. Milbank therefore defends '*the most radical imaginable modern pluralism*', which is 'that positive differences, insofar as they

---

3. Milbank, *TST*, 422.

4. Milbank, *TST*, 6; italics added.

5. Cf. Charles Taylor: 'Because we cannot but orient ourselves to the good, and thus determine our place relative to it and hence determine the direction of our lives, we must inescapably understand our lives in narrative form, as a "quest." But one could perhaps start from another point: because we have to determine our place in relation to the good, therefore we cannot be without an orientation to it, and hence must see our life in story. From whichever direction, I see these conditions as connected facets of the same reality, inescapable structural requirements of human agency' (*Sources of the Self* (Cambridge, MA: Harvard University Press, 1989), 51–2). But for Taylor, critical reason still plays a crucial role, and so the manner in which he defends the Christian story is quite different to Milbank. In fact it has not escaped notice that Taylor's defence of Christianity's narrative specifically is quite muted (John Haffner, 'Post-Metaphysical Faith in the Philosophy of Charles Taylor', MA Thesis, Queen's University Ontario, 1998, 28ff). This perhaps points up the particular strength of Milbank's evaluation of Christianity's narrative, which is unashamedly both partisan and evangelical.

6. It seeks to recover 'the concealed text of an original peaceful creation beneath the palimpsest of the negative distortion of *dominium*.' Milbank, *TST*, 423.

7. Milbank, *TST*, 262.

are all instances of the Good (a condition which of course will never be perfectly fulfilled in fallen time), must for that reason analogically concur'.[8]

The mastery of theology is therefore not a mastering of discourses in their difference but the peaceful construal of this difference as transcendent harmony. 'Mastery', then, has a quite different meaning in the theological narrative, allowing Milbank paradoxically to identify, for theology alone, mastery and non-mastery: 'This is why it is so important to reassert theology as a master discourse; theology, alone, remains the discourse of non-mastery'.[9] This is the driving force of the critique of secular reason, which is deplorable precisely in its conflictual reading of difference. Recognizing 'no original violence', Christianity acknowledges only 'a harmonic peace' as the truly real. This peace is not forced consensus – 'the reduction to the self-identical' – but 'the sociality of harmonious difference'; violence is merely 'a secondary willed intrusion upon this possible infinite order (which is actual for God)'.[10] Though Christianity's peace is 'beyond the circumscribing power of any totalizing reason', it is precisely not arbitrary; rather it exposes the 'non-necessity of supposing, like the Nietzscheans, that difference, non-totalization and indeterminancy [*sic*] of meaning necessarily imply arbitrariness and violence'.[11]

For Milbank, peace is first of all narratively specified. In affirming an analogical ontology of peace, Christianity alone escapes nihilism, but 'this ontology is not dialectically established, but is rather implied in narratives about divine creation and redemption'.[12] For him as for Augustine and Nietzsche, the genealogical language of origin frames the most basic reality in relation to which all else is to be construed. Nicholas Lash eloquently summarizes *TST*: 'both [Nietzsche and Augustine] described the way things really are in tales concerning how things are "*in principio*"'; for Nietzsche, in the beginning 'is violence, the struggle for mastery, the will to power'; for Augustine,

> in that *absolute* beginning 'out of nothing' from which all things came, is peacefulness, pure gift for the possibility of all things healing into peace. Pride and violence, mastery and antagonism, are subsequent intrusions, the darkening of the world, our refusal of reality, our denial of peace. What we call Christianity is the dramatized announcement, the enacted word, that, nevertheless, peace will be – in the end, as it was in the beginning.[13]

---

8. Milbank, *TST*, xvi.

9. Milbank, *TST*, 6.

10. Milbank, *TST*, 5–6.

11. Milbank, *TST*, 6. 'By exposing the critical non-necessity of the reading of reality as conflictual . . . an alternative possibility of reading reality as of itself peaceful is gradually opened to view' (*TST*, 297).

12. Milbank, *TST*, 262.

13. Nicholas Lash, 'Not Exactly Politics or Power?' *Modern Theology* 8, no. 4 (1992): 353–64, 354–5; indeed, '*The Genealogy of Morals* is a kind of *Civitas Dei* written back to front' (Milbank, *TST*, 391).

David Burrell glosses Milbank: 'Everything turns on the account we give of "in the beginning".'[14]

> What distinguishes Christianity from the others is the life and death of a Jesus who expressly appeals to what it was like 'from the beginning' (Mt 19:8), and whose resurrection discloses 'the concealed text of an original peaceful creation'.[15]

For (Milbank's) pagan and the postmodern alike, there is in the last analysis *only* power, conflict and violence, and so difference is read fundamentally in terms of rivalry and incompatibility.[16] For Christianity, 'in the beginning' is the gratuitous gift of being – unrivalrous, uncoerced, with no substrate or rationale beyond itself. *Creatio ex nihilo* indicates quite simply that 'peace is essential', 'violence . . . an unnecessary intrusion', claims that cannot be 'demonstrated' but simply 'follow' as 'an explication of the doctrine of creation'.[17] In the free creation of the world from nothing, all that is is bookended by peace, originary and eschatological.[18] This is Milbank's most abiding concern and the defining content of his Christianity. It defines the opposition of the two cities which shapes his metanarrative. Without a peace 'in the beginning', a peace founded on the originary gift-character of creation itself, the only peace the *civitas terrena* can achieve is a peace of 'mere suspended hostility',[19] a 'regulated competition'[20] which remains simply a restrained violence. In the *civitas Dei*, the reverse is the case: the only 'mastery' in that city is the mastery of peace itself. Theology narrates 'the continuous and sometimes decisive interruption of [history] by instances of the reflecting of perfect infinite

---

14. David Burrell, 'An Introduction to *Theology and Social Theory: Beyond Secular Reason*', *Modern Theology* 8, no. 4 (1992): 319–29, 329.

15. Burrell, 'Introduction', 329, quoting *TST*, 423. The biblical text quoted by Burrell appropriately treats Mosaic law concerning divorce, which legislates for division and conflict. It reads (according to the New English Bible, whose different translation captures the point well): 'It was because you were so unteachable that Moses gave you permission to divorce your wives; but *it was not like that when all began*.' The New English Bible (Cambridge: Cambridge University Press, 1961), italics added.

16. Nietzsche is the ultimate exemplar for Milbank: 'The most radical thinker of difference never pretended anything other than that it was grounded in an "ontology of violence"' (Milbank, *TST*, xvi).

17. Milbank, *TST*, 440.

18. '[A] true Christian metanarrative realism must attempt to retrieve and elaborate the account of history given by Augustine in the *Civitas Dei*' (Milbank, *TST*, 391). For Fergus Kerr, it is as an appropriation of Augustine's story of the two cities that *TST* is best read ('Rescuing Girard's Argument?' *Modern Theology* 8, no. 4 (1992): 385–99, 387). For Kerr, Milbank is also in debt to Girard for his conception of ontological peace.

19. Milbank, *TST*, xi.

20. Milbank, *TST*, 336.

peaceful power which is the Good in finite acts of goodness and their necessary compossibility'.[21]

Peace 'is the final end, the *principium* that is being itself'.[22] It is peace which is the real substance of Christianity's story. It is peace which is Christianity's 'unique difference', which sets it apart from all other stories, which makes it indeed the story of stories.[23] 'Only Christianity' sees peace 'as coterminous with Being',[24] for the Triune God is 'transcendental peace through differential relation'.[25] Milbank's doctrine of God is crucial in justifying his agenda for theology as sustainer of peaceful difference, without loss and without violence. For 'God *is* the infinite series of differences, and what he knows is the infinity of differences'; God is 'the reality which includes and encompasses in his *comprehensio* every difference'; 'God is also the God who differentiates'.[26] God is in his very being a harmony of realized difference, discerned not in a reified idea but in the ongoing happening of creation: 'the God who is, who includes a difference, and yet is unified, is not a God sifted out as abstract "truth", but a God who speaks in the harmonious happening of being'.[27] Here '[n]arrative and ontology reinforce each other', because 'God must be known both as the "speaking" of created difference, and as an inexhaustible plenitude of otherness'.[28]

21. Milbank, *TST*, xvi.

22. Milbank, *TST*, 367, citing Aquinas; but note Nicholas Lash, who questions Milbank's reading of Aquinas here ('Politics or Power', 360–2).

23. 'Christianity is not . . . merely one more perspective. It is also *uniquely* different. . . . Nietzsche directed his historical critique particularly against Christianity. This turns out to be not just an aspect of an outmoded metanarrative; on the contrary, Nietzsche was objectively right to the extent that Christianity is unique in refusing ultimate reality to all conflictual phenomena. For this reason, I shall argue, it is the true "opposite" of Nietzschean postmodernism, and also able to deny it in a more than merely despairing, Manichean fashion. By comparison, all other myths, or narrative traditions, affirm or barely conceal an original primordial violence, which a sacral order merely restrains' (*TST*, 262).

24. Milbank, *TST*, 262; he grants to Judaism and Islam a 'lesser' degree of participation in this story. But 'Christianity's universalist claim that incorporation into the Church is indispensable for salvation assumes that other religions and social groupings, however virtuous-seeming, were, in their own terms alone, finally on the path of damnation.' Although his comment here is in historical tone, there is a normativity to it on the logic of his overall account. Needless to say, some are likely to find this concerning; Chapter 3 considers the question of the 'exclusivism' of Milbank's thought.

25. Milbank, *TST*, 6.

26. *TST*, 429–30. This may or may not be convincing theologically; the issue here is to see its function in Milbank's discourse concerning theology's status and purpose; the underlying theology may call for further questioning, such as in relation to its conception of analogical difference/similarity between human and divine difference.

27. Milbank, *TST*, 438, drawing on Eriugena.

28. Milbank, *TST*, 438.

The meaning of peace is apparent only in light of the story of God's city in this world, for peace is not a generic virtue, nor an abstract ideal, but appears in the concrete shape of the life of a particular historical community, the church. As we shall see, this makes Milbank a pragmatist: truth belongs more to action than abstraction. The church's practice tells what reality itself is like: non-rivalrous gift without contrast. The church's peaceful practices bring about a peace unlike that '"achieved" through the abandonment of the losers, the subordination of potential rivals and resistance to enemies'.[29] Rather, the city of God 'provides a genuine peace by its memory of its victims, its equal concern for all its citizens and its self-exposed offering of reconciliation to enemies'.[30] This 'peaceful mode of existence . . . has historically arisen as "something else", an *altera civitas*, having no logical or causal connection with the city of violence'.[31] The 'interruption of history' by the peaceful practice of Christ and the church is '*most especially* a social event', which yet becomes 'the whole story of human history which is still being enacted and interpreted in light of those events',[32] events which are 'inexhaustible', 'the setting of past and future lives'.[33]

Describing *TST*'s achievement, Burrell observes that 'while the route may be roundabout indeed', what Milbank has shown is 'that [Christians'] faith in a free creator of the universe dare not be left entirely implicit',[34] for it is knowable only in life and practice.[35] The dismal failure of the historical church fully to enact such peaceful practices is too staringly obvious to be ignored. One naturally worries that Milbank conflates ontological and historically realized harmony.[36] But for

29. Milbank, *TST*, 394.

30. Milbank, *TST*, 394.

31. Milbank, *TST*, 392.

32. Milbank, *TST*, 390, italics original. Peace is already given but not yet realized: 'In Christ peace has not, indeed, been totally achieved (a building remains to be built) yet it is proleptically given, because only the perfect saving of one man from the absolute destruction of death, this refusal of the loss of any difference, can initially spell out to us perfect peace' (John Milbank, 'Enclaves, or Where is the Church?' *New Blackfriars* 73 (1992): 341–52, 348).

33. Milbank, *TST*, 438.

34. Burrell, 'Introduction', 329.

35. Burrell explains: 'What distinguishes the faith-assertion of a free creation is that it includes a crucial *caveat* lest anyone attempt to describe what it was *like*, so one is pressed to follow the contours of the development of that assertion in the life and thought of those communities which profess so startling a faith.' Burrell, 'Introduction', 329.

36. Milbank is indignant at the suggestion that he is naïve about the appearance of this peace in history. The idea that he espouses 'a kind of blithe wilful Maytime optimism entirely ignores my Pauline insistence on the utter fallenness and demonic captivity of the current world. Only with strenuous difficulty, only indeed as a form of Christian *gnosis* – which Paul yet dared to proclaim in the public forum – are we able to discern the hidden realm of real peaceful being that cosmic evil obscures from our view.' Milbank, *TST*, xv.

Milbank peace is primarily protological and eschatological, a narrative ontology which as narrative is ever unfinished, only partially and falteringly manifest in the historical church;[37] of the church's betrayals of that peace, Milbank has only the harshest condemnation.[38] This does not exonerate him of charges of idealism, and pressing questions remain about the 'difference' of which 'peace' is the infinite harmonization and reconciliation, not least concerning his identification of this story of peace with the Christian metanarrative, which seems prima facie imperialist and exclusivist.[39] Chapter 3 elaborates and assesses these charges in a more detailed examination of the main worries of his critics.

Turning back to our treatment of reason: Milbank has fully inflected the content of reason with this pragmatically defined narrative of peace. True reason has the shape of *one* narrative in particular: the story of God's city in this world, which is a story of peace.

> The non-antagonistic, peaceful mode of life of the city of God is grounded in a particular, historical and 'mythical' narrative, and in an ontology which explicates the beliefs implicit in this narrative . . . [T]he ontological priority of peace over conflict . . . is firmly anchored in a narrative, a practice, and a dogmatic faith, not in an abstracted universal reason.[40]

What this means for reason is our concern in the following sections.

The place of philosophy

The critique of 'philosophical' reason is one of the most well-known aspects of Milbank's project.[41] Modernity invents 'philosophy' as that discourse which, 'beyond doctrinal theology, can tell us the final truth . . . from an alleged superior vantage-point.[42] Escaping the particularity of theology in its reliance on specific

---

37. In 'Enclaves', Milbank pursues an *apologia* regarding this issue, explaining that he has not intended to 'discover in [the Church's] ramified and fissiparous history some single ideal exemplar' (341).

38. 'And either the Church enacts the vision of paradisal community which [God's] judgement opens out, or else it promotes a hellish society beyond any terrors known to antiquity: *corruptio optimi pessima*. For the Christian interruption of history "decoded" antique virtue, yet thereby helped to unleash first liberalism, then positivism and dialectics and finally nihilism. Insofar as the Church has failed, and has even become a hellish anti-Church, it has confined Christianity, like everything else, within the cycle of the ceaseless exhaustion and return of violence' (*TST*, 442).

39. He acknowledges such charges; *TST*, xxii.

40. Milbank, *TST*, 392.

41. See especially 'The Theological Critique of Philosophy'.

42. Milbank, 'Faith, Reason and Imagination', 5–6.

data of revelation, it is considered to possess a unique capacity to conduct a meta-level critical role, the true 'generalism'. But for Milbank theology possesses the only true 'generalism'; its generalism is, paradoxically, a particularism, a narratively grounded claim that its story embraces and saves all things.[43] 'Philosophy' as pure reason is incapable of achieving the catholicity of theology because it founders on the absence of any self-evidence, any absolute beginning for thought. This reveals its claimed purity of vantage point is implicitly a bid for a finally coercive power of arbitration. Theology alone is able to narrate the given as gift and therefore as unlimitedly peaceful. This narration leaves no autonomous zone behind, for 'the invocation of a Creator God must transform one's understanding of the entire natural order', and 'acknowledgment of a historical revelation must revise even that understanding'.[44] For Milbank, theology speaks 'about everything in relation to God, which is to say being as such and all of the fundamental modes of being, besides those decisive historical events of divine revelation which are held to re-construe our very interpretation of the ontological'.[45] Philosophy he defines as 'first of all the name of the discourse which reflects upon being and the ways in which things can be'.[46] In this way he erodes any firm dividing line between the two: 'the philosophy/theology disciplinary boundary in its modern academic form [is] both the offspring of bad theology and . . . the entrenchment of secular reason.'[47]

Blondel is central in Milbank's articulation of a theological reason. He approves Blondel's account of philosophy's subordination to theology but finds his critique of philosophical reason insufficiently radical. In Milbank's reading, Blondel holds that philosophy as a 'science' is limited to demonstrating the incompleteness of an account of reality apart from the supernatural. Because of the textuality of knowing, our being situated already in the middle of the story and our inability to return to a primordial beginning of thought to establish a stable reference point for meaning, in Blondel's account philosophy cannot establish a starting point for thought, not even to demonstrate its own inadequacy. It simply 'points, impotently, to where thought is already begun, already has necessary premises which are beyond the reach of any critique'.[48] The only work of philosophy, for Blondel, is to establish the exigency of grace. Blondel therefore abandons epistemology for

---

43. This is above all an ecclesial particularism, for Milbank, insofar as the actual practice and person of Christ is known, interpreted and exemplified only in the church. This worries some commentators both on grounds of Christology (see, for example, Frederick Christian Bauerschmidt, 'The Word Made Speculative? John Milbank's Christological Poetics', *Modern Theology* 15 (1999): 417–32) and ecclesial idealism.

44. Milbank, 'Faith, Reason and Imagination', 5–6.

45. Milbank, 'Faith, Reason and Imagination', 8–9.

46. Milbank, 'Faith, Reason and Imagination', 8.

47. Milbank, 'Afterword: The Grandeur of Reason and the Perversity of Rationalism: Radical Orthodoxy's First Decade', in *The Radical Orthodoxy Reader*, ed. Simon Oliver and John Milbank (London: Routledge, 2009), 390.

48. Milbank, *TST*, 212.

phenomenology, giving a phenomenological account of action and refusing the invitation to develop an ontology, for 'philosophy is radically incompetent with relation to reality'.[49]

Milbank's view of a 'pure' philosophy's incompetence with respect to ontology is in accord with Blondel up to this point.[50] But Blondel's account of philosophical reason still accords it too great a sphere of competence. For Blondel (as Milbank reads him) thinks that philosophy points towards the necessity of Christianity in particular: the Trinity, the Incarnation, the need for atonement. For Milbank, even the mere *need* of these things can be known only from within the story.[51] Blondel's understanding of action as intrinsically open-ended, emanative *poesis*, which both demands and receives supernatural supplement, fails to exclude the real possibility of nihilism, the non-appearance of meaning altogether. Apart from allegiance to a particular narrative in which action is revealed as love, the open-endedness of action appears only as negative surrender to risk, not as reception of gift. '[T]he logic of action alone "cannot . . . decipher action as love".'[52] Emanative *poesis* is only good news in the context of a prior narrative which appears in practice. As an abstractly deduced necessity of philosophy it remains tragic. Only theology can decipher action as love.

This criticism of Blondel parallels Milbank's attack on postmodern philosophies of difference such as those of Derrida or Deleuze. It is not enough just to undermine the naïve modernist account of transparent autonomous reason. Having done this, the philosophers of difference are unable to found thought in any alternative, surrendering it simply to the play of difference which entails violence and conflict

---

49. Milbank, *TST*, 212.

50. And also with Milbank's hero De Lubac, who explicitly situates himself within theology in explicit opposition to a philosophical bottom-up approach: 'I want to remain firmly within theology. I am not trying to establish a philosophical thesis, but to study a dogmatic statement and all that it implies. I do not say that the knowledge gained by reason of a natural desire, outside any context of faith, "proves strictly that we are called to the beatific vision", and that therefore we can naturally attain "the certainty that we have been created for that end"; on the contrary, I say that the knowledge that is revealed to us of that calling, which makes us certain of that end, leads us to recognise within ourselves the existence and nature of that desire' (Henri de Lubac, *The Mystery of the Supernatural*, trans. Rosemary Sheed (New York: Crossroad, 1998), 209). However, as we see below, this emphasis is somewhat transformed by Milbank who wants to challenge the residual dualism of 'from above' and 'from below'.

51. 'One ought to say that *only* because one first experiences the "shape" of incarnation, of atonement, is one led to formulate the abstract notions of their occurrence; and only then does one construe reality in terms of the need for the perfect offering of love' (Milbank, *TST*, 218).

52. Milbank, *TST*, 218.

as the only perennial condition of thought.[53] Able to invoke nothing beyond appearances, such philosophies cannot even save the appearances themselves; everything vanishes in a nihilistic flux. Theological reason 'suspends' the world, both in the sense of interrupting it and in the sense of anchoring its enduring value and reality over against the void.[54]

Chief in what distinguishes theological reason is its reading of the story of love which is the knowledge of God as intrinsic in rationality itself. Nevertheless, Blondel is the major intellectual star of *TST*,[55] providing the philosophical sponsorship for Milbank's opposition to a 'pure' philosophical reason, or a reason which attempts to be self-founding by providing its own explanations, its own form of secure knowledge. 'Philosophy cannot mark out the site for a necessarily Christian ontology. It is theology, rather, and not philosophy, which explains things . . . which is alone certainty, alone science.'[56]

The value of Blondel's thought lies, in Milbank's analysis, in his insight that the fullest embrace of historicism and perspectivism has an entirely traditional outcome: the universality and all-sufficiency of grace. Blondel rejects the Aristotelian distinction between *poesis* on the one hand and *praxis* and *theoria* on the other.[57] No finite act of knowledge can be circumscribed as merely finite, and the transcendent cannot be policed by a notion of the ineffable sublime, since it enters into every action as a matter of (paradoxically) gratuitous necessity. This amounts to a rejection of both realism and 'reverse realism' (which would locate reality exclusively in an inward Cartesian subject), in favour of theological 'objectivism' which sees the divine as really mediated in every human action,

53. Postmodernism 'raises the spectre of a human world inevitably dominated by violence'; it 'ground[s] violence in a new transcendental philosophy, or fundamental ontology' (Milbank, *TST*, 278).

54. '[T]he theological perspective of participation actually saves the appearances by exceeding them. It recognises that materialism and spiritualism are false alternatives, since if there is only finite matter there is not even that, and that for phenomena really to be there they must be more than there. . . . [B]y appealing to an eternal source for bodies one is not ethereally taking leave of their density. On the contrary, one is insisting that behind this density resides an even greater density – beyond all contrasts of density and lightness (as beyond all contrasts of definition and limitlessness). This is to say that all there is only is because it is more than it is' (John Milbank, Graham Ward and Catherine Pickstock, 'Suspending the Material: The Turn of Radical Orthodoxy', in *Radical Orthodoy*, ed. Milbank, Ward and Pickstock, (London: Routledge, 1998), 3–4).

55. Blondel's philosophy 'is, perhaps, the boldest exercise in Christian thought of modern times . . . Blondel, more than anyone else, points us beyond secular reason' (Milbank, *TST*, 219, 220).

56. Milbank, *TST*, 218.

57. Milbank, *TST*, 216.

including the act of interpreting and reinterpreting the world.[58] No 'science' which insists on operating within rigid boundaries of discerned finitude can offer an account of the way things 'really' are; metaphysics and ontology cannot be possessed by philosophy apart from theology, apart from a reason which is open to transcendence. Theology 'must entirely *evacuate*' an autonomous philosophy 'leaving it nothing . . . to either do or see'.[59] Indeed, faith and reason are 'phases within a single gnoseological extension',[60] an extension wholly characterized by illumination; the illumination of the mind by divine light.[61] There is no 'pure' nature, and so there is no concrete case in which reason operates apart from grace, from its own finite resources; only this narrative, which denies autonomy even at the level of the basic capacities of reason, can prevent the slide into nihilism.

Against dialectics

Milbank's theological reason embraces a radical relativity and defies dialectical adjudication. A *mythos* cannot be refuted, because a notion of refutation supposes some kind of 'objective' rationality which transcends the terms of any one discourse and which is the independent ground for adjudication between discourses. Traditions cannot meet each other except on some pre-existing ground which is always itself traditioned. Milbank defines himself in opposition to Alasdair MacIntyre, a key protagonist, who he finds to be insufficiently relativist: '[He] is still interested in a mode of dialectical validation for narrative preference', so his historicism suffers 'a confinement which actually denies its radical character, along with the affirmation of the priority of *mythos*'.[62]

---

58. Blondel 'succeeds in separating theological objectivism from philosophical realism, and thereby inaugurates a "supernatural pragmatism", for which the reference to an infinite, divine reality occurs through the effort "outwards" from the subject and "forwards" to the future, more perfect repetition of what is already given' (Milbank, *TST*, 219).

59. Milbank, *WMS*, 50, italics added.

60. John Milbank and Catherine Pickstock, *Truth in Aquinas* (London: Routledge, 2000) 21.

61. Reason and faith are 'only different degrees of intensity of participation in the divine light of illumination' (*Truth in Aquinas*, xiii).

62. Milbank, *TST*, 341. MacIntyre's analysis of the rationality of traditions might seem to make him a natural ally of Milbank. But in Milbank's reading, MacIntyre holds to a dialectical conception of the relation between traditions, in which it is supposed that the reason of one tradition can expose another as inadequate, and that through this ongoing process of inter-traditional dialogue and conversation, reason itself can be purified over time. But for Milbank, in contrast to many responders to MacIntyre who charge him with relativism, this conception is *insufficiently* relativistic and historicist; he is 'unwilling to push cultural situatedness to the limit', allowing dialectics to remain ascendant over narrative (Milbank, *TST*, 341).

An astute reader will observe that *TST* is itself dialectical and query whether there is a profound contradiction here. It is therefore crucial to clarify that Milbank does not deny a role to dialectics. He allows it an important role in, for example, testing positions for consistency and coherence.[63] But it is part of a higher logic of persuasion: the employment of dialectics already presumes that self-consistency is attractive, which cannot itself be dialectically established. Further, Milbank does not think that dialectics can grasp the actual process of historical intellectual change and development.

> Positions alter and modify, not just in response to criticism, but quite gratuitously ... The 'poetic' ability to innovate ... is responsible for many decisive shifts in sensibility when an older outlook suddenly appears 'worn out', though it has certainly never been refuted.[64]

There is a fundamental *questionableness* about historical change which cannot be rationalistically analysed or explained; it 'escapes dialectical adjudication'.[65] What triumphs in such change is not a rationally superior position but simply 'the persuasive power of a new narrative'.[66] Rational superiority, or 'the capacity to explain more', can only be adjudicated on the basis of criteria that are entirely tradition-specific. There are no neutral criteria by which more and less adequate narratives can be judged. 'No independent scale of measurement exists.'[67] How can

---

63. Commenting on the anti-dialectical nature of *TST*, Milbank acknowledges the positive significance dialectics has for his enterprise: 'In the case of "dialectics" I acknowledge in Hegel a correct post-Renaissance attempt to integrate theology and philosophy around an account of history and the creative development of the human spirit: indeed, *Theology and Social Theory* is a kind of initial attempt to re-do Hegel in a non-gnostic fashion that refuses a Hegelian transparency of reason ... And although I argue that the ultimate logic of history is not dialectical and that dialectical processes are never entirely necessitated, I acknowledge that certain historical developments can be understood in dialectical terms – such that aspects of my own metanarrative are, indeed, as Rowan Williams pointed out, transparently dialectical' (Milbank, *TST*, xv). Exactly what role Milbank gives to dialectics, in theology and in other discourses such as natural science, is a question to which we return below.

64. Milbank, *TST*, 347–8.

65. Milbank, *TST*, 348.

66. Milbank, *TST*, 348. Jean Porter describes MacIntyre's criterion for the superiority of traditions in terms of 'liveability' or 'practical workability' and describes him as a 'pragmatist realist'. Liveability may be a useful gloss on Milbank's conception of what counts as compelling or attractive in a particular world view. Describing MacIntyre as a pragmatist also highlights how much closer Milbank may be to MacIntyre than he evinces in the pages of *TST*. Jean Porter, 'Openness and Constraint: Moral Reflection as Tradition-guided Inquiry in Alasdair MacIntyre's Recent Works', *Journal of Religion* 73 (1993): 514–36.

67. Milbank, *TST*, 348.

we determine what there is that needs explaining, what constitutes an important question, what constitutes a good explanation, outside pre-existing criteria for identifying what matters? Milbank argues in his critique of MacIntyre that the latter's favouring of scientific development as a paradigm for the emergence of a '"manifestly" more comprehensive theory' is bogus, insofar as in science, 'greater comprehensiveness always means just greater operational success' and thus changes are always in principle reversible, especially where control and predictability are not the key criteria for pragmatic value.[68]

MacIntyre's conception of virtue suffers, in Milbank's view, from the same dialectical isolation from a narrative ground. Virtue 'in general' is of no more value than narrative 'in general'. Form and content cannot be separated; that way lies transcendentalism.

> Nor do I find it possible to defend the notion of 'traditioned reason' in general, outside my attachment to a tradition which grounds this idea in the belief in the historical guidance of the Holy Spirit.[69]

Instead of the fantasy of an untraditioned reason, Milbank defends opinion, testimony and persuasion, from within the Christian *mythos* itself. In his rejection of rhetoric in favour of dialectics, Milbank holds that MacIntyre has failed to escape foundationalism, a fact which is apparent in his opposing postmodern nihilism with a dialectically justified ethics of virtue rather than with another, competing *mythos*. A *mythos* can only be 'out-narrated'; a person abandons a tradition because of the superior persuasiveness of another tradition. If we do, to an extent, manage to enter into more than one tradition of rationality in such a way that they appear dialectically commensurable, then this is because, far from being united subjects of a single consciousness, we are able to hold many different subjectivities 'inside our heads' simultaneously.[70] 'Objective reasoning' can only mean 'the inner consistency of a discourse/practice'; but this '*in no sense* necessarily suggests a new adequacy of discourse to reality'.[71] The comparison of discourse with reality implies a dualism of language/human construction and world, which an understanding of *poesis* as participation in reality disallows.

At its limits, whether inter- or intra-traditional, disagreement must take the form not of exchanges of critical points and counterpoints but of 'a clash of rhetorics', and in this clash narrative is not an appendage, for the story 'really *is* the argument for the tradition'.[72] MacIntyre wants to *argue against* secular reason. Against this, Milbank claims not to attempt to refute secular reason; that would grant too much. '[*M*]*y* case is rather that it is only a *mythos*, and therefore cannot

---

68. Milbank, *TST*, 348–9.
69. Milbank, *TST*, 328–9.
70. Milbank, *TST*, 343.
71. Milbank, *TST*, 331, italics original.
72. Milbank, *TST*, 349.

be refuted but only out-narrated, if we can *persuade* people . . . that Christianity offers a much better story.'[73]

In what way(s) is Christianity a better story? Milbank argues that postmodernity cannot offer as compelling a reading of its own concerns, such as the centrality of human mediation and the inescapability of language, as the terms of Christian orthodoxy. The nihilistic reading of these realities is ultimately arbitrary and shows an underlying preference for violence and conflict. Christianity's peaceable reading of difference is more compelling. This peaceable reading is sustained by a Christianized Platonism which, Milbank argues, escapes the postmodern critique of metaphysics.

Peace and poesis

The Renaissance discovery of human beings as the makers of meaning is, in Milbank's view, already inherent in 'the Christian conception of a creative God' which calls for 'a new combining of notions of ultimate truth with ones of ultimate subjectivity'.[74] It is modernity's refusal of such a combination which Milbank's genealogy identifies.[75] The secular enclosure of reason within immanence occurs at the point at which Baroque *poesis* becomes modern *techne*, or instrumental control.[76] Establishing the *factum* as the only really knowable reality rendered the possibility of technical control coextensive with understanding.[77] The discourse about religion as a social *fact*, that which is constructed by human beings and remains wholly within their control, was simply one aspect of Hobbes's and Spinoza's new science of politics, the science of pure power. Violence and conflict are 'coterminous with the discovery of the human construction of the cultural world',[78] because the humanly made is an autonomous space, constituted by a multitude of individual agents defined in terms of their private wills, who are

73. Milbank, *TST*, 331.

74. Milbank, *TST*, 165.

75. Milbank is emphatic that this insight is in a certain sense 'new'; he is not seeking a naïve retrieval of premodernity but a creative appropriation of postmodernity as expressing a truth latent in the Christian *mythos* from the start ('The Grandeur of Reason', 388ff).

76. 'Secular autonomy, the "enclosure" of reason, establishes itself at the point where *poesis* is publicly defined as *techne*: where the late-medieval/Renaissance discovery of human creative mediation (which could not be gone back upon) takes the direction of locating the essence of the human product as the measurable and quantifiable "wrapping of the world in Cellophane"' (Milbank, *TST*, 246).

77. Milbank, *TST*, 11; this defined the bounds of 'scientific' knowing: '[I]n both [social and natural science], the specificity of modern "scientific" knowledge is to do with an "artificial" method and an infallible knowledge of artifice.'

78. Milbank, *TST*, 4.

continuously and inevitably in competition with one another.[79] But Milbank argues that the Renaissance discovery of the inescapability of human creative mediation did not have to result in a hegemony of the instrumental and the conflictual. Human making is open to another reading which interprets it as 'an opening to transcendence'.[80] It could equally be assimilated into a Platonic participative framework. In Vico and other Christian humanists, Milbank claims to find thinkers for whom the identity of the made and the knowable does not stake out an area of self-evident autonomy but is rather 'the gateway to transcendence'.[81]

> I have always tried to suggest that participation can be extended also to language, history and culture: the whole realm of human *making*. Not only do being and knowledge participate in a God who is and who comprehends; also human making participates in a God who is infinite poetic utterance: the second person of the Trinity. Thus when we contingently but authentically make things and reshape ourselves through time, we are not estranged from the eternal, but enter further into its recesses by what for us is the only possible route.[82]

In *TST*, Milbank considers the neglect of this framework to be due to the influence of Kant's claim to a totalizing knowledge of the finite, which caused later thinkers to exclude transcendence; in containing human beings within finitude, Kant rendered their doings and makings knowably immanent. In Milbank's treatment, Hegel's attempt to transform the philosophical *logos* through an encounter with Christian reason is still beholden to Kant's understanding of pure reason as apart from the understanding, and so fails to question the secular profoundly enough. Milbank's assault on pure reason therefore draws heavily on the German thinkers who embarked on a 'metacritique' of the Kantian critique, Hamann and Jacobi, as well as the other radical pietist, Herder. It is in connection with these thinkers that he develops his analysis of the inseparability of nature and culture, which follows from his identification of the antinomy noted above, that it is impossible to discover a most fundamental category (such as nature) in terms of which another category (such as culture) might appear secondary or derived. We cannot distinguish the 'artificial' from the 'natural', because in language, human beings *make* not just aspects of the world but the world itself:

> because we only think in language, and only grasp the world through language, it is impossible even to disentangle the knowledge we have of ourselves from our knowledge of the world (or 'nature'), [and] vice versa. . . . [B]oth nature and the human subject are 'expressed' in language, although this use of the term should

---

79. Milbank, *TST*, 13–4.

80. Milbank, *TST*, 4.

81. Milbank, *TST*, 12.

82. Milbank, *Being Reconciled*, ix. He contends that *methexis* is more biblical than Hellenic (114–15).

not be taken to mean that language can be decoded in terms of some content, natural or subjective, which is properly pre-linguistic.[83]

Language does not reflect meaning inertly given in the world; it creates it. The Derridean *il n'y a pas de hors-texte* and the post-structuralist legacy are subsumed into a theological perspective which affirms reality as linguistic but without enclosing that reality in immanence: rather, the making of the world in language participate[s] in the Paternal fictioning of the filial *ars*', the utterance of God's *Verbum*.[84] This is 'a participation of the poetic in an infinite *poesis*'.[85]

Without language as a specific making of the world to be world for us, human beings are 'simply contentless'.[86] In Kant's treatment, 'pure' reason is associated with an apperceiving subject which stands above the finite world viewing it from a height. But we are enmeshed in language and finitude from the first. Representationalism and other views, which see language as primarily referential by trading on a separation of words and things, are excluded by this view; language is not a 'third medium between the subject and the world',[87] which makes it meaningless to compare a proposition to the reality to which it is supposed to refer.[88] Milbank is able to concede serenely that this perspective is 'constructivist' without discarding the notion of truth because he rejects the view, which he traces to Cartesian understandings of will and subjectivity and, further back, to a failure of the doctrine of analogy through the influence of Scotism, that the constructed human interpretation of the world is therefore 'manipulative or instrumentalist'.[89] Instead of such an instrumentalism, he draws on the radical pietists' conception of language as a participation in the divine creative expression and on the notion of an 'aesthetic necessity' in which our creative expressions fulfil a goal or *telos*

83. Milbank, *TST*, 149.

84. In the wake of nominalism, it becomes apparent that universals are indeed constructed but are nevertheless real: human and divine utterance converge, as clarified by Cusa (Milbank, *TST*, xxix; 'The two human modes of linguistic fashioning – history and literature, in their complex inter-entanglement both as enacted and as recited history . . . [are] essential to the disclosing of truth'). Catherine Pickstock's use of Derrida to support a broadly Platonic agenda is an important development of this theme; *After Writing: On the Liturgical Consummation of Philosophy* (Oxford: Wiley-Blackwell, 1997).

85. Milbank, *WMS*, x.

86. Milbank, *TST*, 149.

87. Milbank, *TST*, 344.

88. Milbank is critical of Ricoeur's attempt to distinguish formally between 'sense' and 'reference' (*TST*, 264–8). But John Daniels, in 'Not the Whole Story: Another Response to John Milbank's *Theology and Social Theory*, Part I', *New Blackfriars* 82 (2001): 188–96, and 'Not the Whole Story: Another Response to John Milbank's *Theology and Social Theory*, Part II', *New Blackfriars* 82 (2001): 224–40, questions whether Milbank's has really succeeded in avoiding Ricoeur's methodology.

89. Milbank, *TST*, 150.

which is not determined by us but is somehow a fulfilment of nature itself, and therefore underlines humanity as the true end of nature.[90] There is no *a priori* reason to think that our interpretations are arbitrary or purely instrumental. That assumption is an import from a secular conception of power as autonomy, itself a corruption of medieval speculation about the *potentia Dei absoluta*, and of human understanding as imprisoned within subjectivity which resulted from the separation of ontology and epistemology. Understanding cannot be confined by *a priori* categories arising from subjective experience; if thinking is not prior to language, we cannot investigate our thinking instrument 'in advance of its deployment', so any *a priori* knowledge of the categories is bogus.[91] There are therefore no grounds for distinguishing between 'legitimate' knowledge of finitude and 'illegitimate pretensions' to knowledge of the infinite.[92] The finite cannot be rounded upon; the immanent cannot be concretely isolated from the transcendent. This liberates us to pursue eminent or analogical interpretations of our categories of understanding. In this way Milbank's seemingly relativist analysis of human knowing leads paradoxically to a more definite case for the ineradicable openness of language and understanding to the mediation of a transcendent infinite.

The unavailability of a prelinguistic moment means that there is no way of going back to the beginning of our sign-making. We are always situated in the middle, and language is constantly carrying out syntheses which go beyond both the *a priori* and the empirically given, but which are nevertheless necessary for understanding, such as 'the need to know boundaries, against the lack of unquestionable criteria for doing so'.[93] These conditions mean that 'one can never see any meaning as once for all fixed and complete', but rather, within the system of signs, as subject to endless revision; there is 'always a "background" of merely "implicit" meaning which can never be totally clarified and from which it is impossible to exclude "the pressure upon us of a transcendent and infinite reality", presupposing a "transcendent meaningfulness" which is the condition of truth'.[94] In Milbank's treatment, three historical moments contain their own insight into this: postmodern constructivism is paralleled in the Baroque idea of a 'revelation in language', according to which God's revelation is inseparable from our power to make signs and meanings, which itself is the modern counterpart to premodern divine *illuminatio* of the intellect by God's light.[95] Marx's notion that human meanings were originally natural, practical and unambiguous is entirely

90. Milbank, *TST*, 150; he develops the theme of the congruence of nature with language when he explores the notion of 'sympathy' in 'Hume Versus Kant'.

91. Milbank, *TST*, 151.

92. Milbank, *TST*, 151.

93. Milbank, *TST*, 153.

94. Milbank, *TST*, 153.

95. Milbank, *TST*, 161.

questionable, for 'to be human, or to be a cultural being, is *necessarily* to inhabit a fiction'.[96] Humans are *fictioning* beings.[97]

Milbank's emphasis on the transcendent possibilities of human making of *poesis* is supported by his conception of nature and grace. He is at odds with an extrinsicist model of the divine self-gift in which the coming of God is, with respect to our own making of history and culture, unprecedented and discontinuous, breaking into our merely human constructs from the outside. He supports the 'integralist revolution' in Catholic theology, which holds that 'in concrete, historical humanity there is no such thing as a state of "pure nature"'.[98] However, Milbank charges its defenders, including De Lubac and von Balthasar, with failing to face up to its consequences, which include an understanding of the constructed character of cultural reality and the historical condition of human knowing. Blondel's philosophy is crucial to Milbank's attempt to remedy this deficiency. Blondel's phenomenology of action reveals the paradox of the human will which demands a completion that it cannot, of its own resources, supply. *Poesis* is given a supernatural content through the acknowledgement that the product of the will is never equal to the original act of the will; our makings always exceed and escape us, and it is this excessive character of action, the inability of human agents to contain or predict the meaning that we ourselves make, that gives all our makings a transcendent orientation. The excess of the human product means that we are never in control of the significance of our actions. 'Nothing is inviolably "internal", or "our own"'.[99]

For Milbank's Blondel, it is in this excess that a plenitude of the supernatural becomes inescapably apparent to philosophy. Supernatural grace is not so much always required, as always present, in the logic of action as self-transcending in both time and space. Our receptivity to the supernatural coincides not with passivity but with our point of greatest creative initiative; making and receiving are here united.[100] In this way the *factum* becomes not the guardpost of autonomy but the opening to transcendence: 'it is precisely this historicist confinement of our thought which renders it *irreducible* to any immanent process.'[101] Action, not contemplation, is 'the mode of ingress for the concrete, supernatural life' which raises human historical knowing and making to a supernatural dignity.

---

96. Milbank, *TST*, 186, italics original.

97. This leads Milbank to take a particularly appreciative view of fantasy, magic and the imagination as intrinsic to the Christian account of reality. 'Fictioning Things: Gift and Narrative', *Religion and Literature* 37 (2005): 1–35.

98. Milbank distinguishes between French and German versions of integralism, the former being preferred for its refusal to entertain even a *formal* distinction between nature and grace (Milbank, *TST*, 207).

99. Milbank, *TST*, 237.

100. '[I]n Blondel's postmodern regaining of the supernatural, pure receptivity does not reside primarily in the possibility of contemplation: instead, we are receptive at the point of our greatest activity, our own initiative' (Milbank, *TST*, 219).

101. Milbank, *TST*, 219.

Milbank is unafraid to regard this as a pragmatism,[102] in its emphasis on truth as fundamentally a property of action.[103] This 'supernaturalization of the natural' is historicist in emphasis because it does not hypostasize human nature, nor identify the supernatural with any permanent aspect or experience of human existence. For Milbank, Blondel's concept of action calls for a more historicist interpretation of human existence and understanding that underlines, rather than excludes, divine action. Only in this way can one avoid the identification of *poesis* with the sphere of the secular.[104]

The reversal of epistemic priority, attributing primacy to action rather than contemplation, *poesis* rather than *theoria*, is a driving force in Milbank's thought. It is decisive for conceiving the dignity of the disciplines, their purchase on the real; it is as active, not contemplative, that science receives its high valuation. Part II delineates this in more depth.

Metaphysics

A metaphysics of participated transcendence underlies Milbank's critique of the autonomy of the disciplines and makes any 'independence', cognitive or ontological, from God, entirely impossible. God and creation are not to be spoken of as contrastive realities, different poles on a univocal spectrum.

> Participation . . . refuses any reserve of created territory, while allowing finite things their own integrity. . . . [E]very discipline must be framed by a theological perspective; otherwise these disciplines will define a zone apart from God, grounded literally in nothing.[105]

102. Rejecting 'a merely philosophic realism', he defends a pragmatism with 'a realist cast', in which it is action that discloses truth (Milbank, *TST*, 5). Mary Doak describes Milbank's pragmatism as Rortian (123), while noting Milbank's 'evident lack of the sense of contingency and irony that accompany Rorty's pragmatic stance' (note 13) ('A Pragmatism Without Plurality? John Milbank's 'Pragmatic' New Christendom', *Contemporary Pragmatism* 1, no. 2 (2004): 123–35). Doak fails to reckon with the element of teleological constraint Milbank insists upon when she criticizes him for allowing a person to sit comfortably inside their narrative as long as it is 'working' for them. She also finds him inadequately pluralist but does not give weight to the way in which Milbank's simultaneous suspicion of extra-Christian discourses is in tension with his poetic elevation of all action as intrinsically mediative.

103. He sees Cusa as a pragmatist in this sense: for Cusa '"makeability" is the criterion for truth' (Stanton Lecture 5, 'Participated Transcendence Reconceived', http://theologyphi losophycentre.co.uk/papers/Milbank_StantonLecture 5.pdf, accessed 8 June 2015, 27–8).

104. Milbank, *TST*, 209.

105. Milbank, 'Suspending the Material', 3.

There are vertical and horizontal dimensions to participation, because creatures mediate God to one another; on Milbank's understanding of the hierarchy of creation, God is equally intimate to every creature, every level of being;[106] every creature is, so to speak, theologically saturated. He celebrates a 'pan-sacramental hyper-mediation – a theophany of God in everything.'[107] Avoiding both monism and dualism, mediation specifies a way between transcendence and immanence which shows them not as contraries, nor as collapsible into one another, but as distinctive and irreducible categories that actually *relate* to one another – for both identity and difference exclude real relation. Real relation involves 'an irreducible "between", a *metaxu*' – a suspended middle. Relationality, if it is to be real and therefore irreducible, can never dissolve into one or other term of the relations but is 'suspended' between them.[108] Against modernity's immanent, flattened and univocal notion of being, the notion of mediation enables a sense of the non-competitive mutual transparency of God and world, showing the *transcendens* not to be reducible to the merely *transcendental;* rather it is a transcendent height of being which is an utterly intimate, constitutive and infinitely diverse presence in the immanent, and so requires us to attend to the contingent as disclosing the non-contingent. The finite mediates the infinite; the particular mediates the universal; and space, time and materiality mediate the eternal.

So theology cannot be indifferent either to creation or to the disciplines, their subject matters and findings and methodologies, because creatures and the knowledge of creatures mediate God to a degree that is unspecifiable *a priori.* Knowledge is not 'outside' reality looking in; rather, there is a mutual participation here too. 'In knowing, we share in the material universe and this universe shares in our knowledge, in which it comes to a certain fruition.'[109]

Theology's own distinctive account of the world drives it to make all disciplinary zones, all aspects of reality, its own. The questions thrown up by this are the concern of subsequent chapters; what is notable here is that Milbank does think that metaphysics is part of the answer and not only part of the problem. But the term remains ambiguous, and he stresses that it must be correctly understood to be legitimate, that is, it must not refer to a 'science' that is independent of theology, which is the sense of his 'only theology overcomes metaphysics'.[110]

---

106. 'Participated Transcendence Reconceived', 3.

107. Which he credits especially to Cusa; 'Participated Transcendence Reconceived', 30.

108. 'Stanton Lecture 2, Immanence and Life', http://theologyphilosophycentre.co.uk /papers/Milbank_StantonLecture 6.pdf, accessed 4 March 2019, 23. For Milbank this is '[p]recisely a Platonic, neo-Platonic and Catholic "analogical ontology", as [*TST*] contended' (*TST*, xxi).

109. Milbank, 'Stanton Lecture 6: The Habit of Reason', http://theologyphilosophycentre .co.uk/papers/Milbank_Stanton Lecture6.pdf, accessed 4 March 2019, 1.

110. Milbank, *WMS*, 36–55. See also Milbank, 'The Grandeur of Reason', 388–92.

The 'metaphysics' that is overcome . . . is the onto-theological science of transcendental ontology that has prevailed at least since Suarez. The 'metaphysics' that is saved . . . is the perennial 'realism' that lasted from Plato to Aquinas and then was reworked by Eckhart and Cusanus. Here . . . being is not a transcendental framework that includes even the divine; rather being and God are identified as the transcendent source in which all else participates.[111]

In Milbank's work, metaphysics expresses the sense that we cannot cease to speculate about the world or attempt to make statements about what is; but he consistently seeks to radicalize the significance of this inevitability with an emphasis on temporality and embodiment. A fundamental tension results, which pervades his work: metaphysics is implicit in every statement about the world, and yet we cannot undertake that engagement from outside of time, materiality and language, with all the relativity and historicity that implies. Milbank's claim is that Christianity's narrative makes sense of this: it reconciles relativity and ultimacy. Theology is the true metaphysics.

Theology has frequently sought to borrow from elsewhere a fundamental account of society or history, and then to see what theological insights will cohere with it. But it has been shown that no such fundamental account, in the sense of something neutral, rational and universal, is really available. It is theology itself that will have to provide its own account of the final causes at work in human history, on the basis of its own particular, and historically specific faith.[112]

This account must at least partially consist, given Milbank's embrace of narrative, in a re-narration of history, a 'counter-history', from the point of view of the church, and it appears in retrospect that this is what *TST* is.[113] It necessitates telling a different story about reason, a story which does not pretend to be self-evident or rationally transparent; instead it bears 'the marks of the incarnation and pentecost'.[114] The story which is Christianity is not simply *another* story but is in some sense *the other* story: it is 'not just different, but . . . *the* difference from all other cultural systems'.[115] It is at the level of ontology, Milbank suggests, that

---

111. 'Only Theology Saves Metaphysics: On the Modalities of Terror', http://www.theologyphilosophycentre.co.uk /papers/Milbank_OnlyTheologySavesMetaphysics.pdf, accessed 4 March 2019), 1. He comments, '[t]his title deliberately inverts that of my earlier essay "Only theology overcomes metaphysics" . . . However, this denotes no change of heart.'

112. Milbank, *TST*, 382.

113. The unmasking of secular reason in *TST* is a preliminary to the elaboration of a constructive proposal for a Christian countermodernity, which is undertaken partially in *TST*, but major constructive elements, particularly regarding the role of linguistic mediation, are undertaken in *WMS* and subsequent essays.

114. Milbank, *TST*, 383.

115. Milbank, *TST*, 383.

this 'total' difference of the Christian story is clarified and articulated, an ontology which will be a 'counter-ontology' and will not mask its 'ineradicable' reliance on unprovable belief.[116] We first embrace a *mythos*, not a proposition.[117]

The identification of the 'final causes' Milbank refers to is the business of metaphysics, and here the Christian countermodernity rejects the options represented by the postmodern critique of metaphysics and modern theology's response to it. This ranges from complete capitulation resulting in an evacuation of actual theological content (John D. Caputo, in his example) to a resistance which assumes that Christianity requires a defence of traditional epistemological realism and its attachment to the modern subject, and which continues, notwithstanding Nietzsche's attack on metaphysics, to seek 'a positive "once for all" representation of finitude'.[118] Both alternatives represent a surrender to the terms of secular reason which sees the made as necessarily the realm of autonomous power. Theology needs rather to offer a selective response to the anti-metaphysical project of postmodernity. What, then, is the positive vision of reality which theology must propose?

On the one hand theology must abandon unnecessary and, in Milbank's view, ultimately non-traditional intrusions into the Christian *mythos* of philosophical notions of 'presence, of substance, the priority of idea over copy and cause over effect, of a subject with a rational essence'.[119] These notions are, albeit sporadically, rejected by a whole string of Christian thinkers; he cites Augustine, Eriugena, Aquinas, Cusanus, Leibniz, Berkeley, Vico, Hamann, Kierkegaard and Blondel.[120] Christianity has, he argues, gradually but surely rejected substance ontologies in favour of ontologies of relation.[121] On the other, it defends as defeating the postmodern critique those 'metaphysical' notions which are not only indispensable to the Christian narrative but also represent a non-foundationalist 'overcoming' of metaphysics more complete than that of postmodernity; 'transcendence, participation, analogy, hierarchy, teleology (these last two in modified forms) and the absolute reality of "the Good" in roughly the Platonic

---

116. Milbank, *TST*, 383. Milbank works hard to justify his turn to ontology to explicate Christian narrative. He is, he argues, not setting up a dualism between story and metaphysics, for the metaphysics is the story, considered from one point of view; and since the story is entirely about one particular community, the *ecclesia*, it is in that sense a social ontology which is not separable from practices. He explores the positive status of Christian metaphysics at length in a rebuttal of Marion's 'beyond Being' (*WMS*, 36–83).

117. Milbank, *TST*, 340.

118. Milbank, *TST*, 296.

119. Milbank, *TST*, 297.

120. Milbank, *TST*, 297. He recognizes that earlier Christian thinkers reached this insight only partially; the 'Renaissance-Romantic rethinking of authentic Christian tradition' needs to be recuperated by contemporary theology to meet the challenges of postmodernity ('The Grandeur of Reason', 388ff).

121. Milbank, *WMS*, 110–11.

sense'.[122] Platonism's enthronement of the good is saved, but its elevation of pristine original (with its associated conception of truth) over corrupted copy is rejected. Postmodernism's denial of substance in favour of transition is retained, but the interpretation of difference as conflict is resisted.[123] This response represents a discerning reception of postmodernity, where a retrieved Platonism allows itself to be questioned by postmodernism's attribution of primacy to history and change, while simultaneously functioning to critique postmodernism's differential ontology as question-beggingly conflictual. It is the 'critical non-necessity' of such an ontology which shows, in Milbank's view, how postmodernity remains trapped within metaphysics despite declaring that it has ended.[124] Milbank describes this project as 'a "countermodern" articulation of a specifically Christian onto-logic';[125] countermodern because both modern and postmodern buy into the same heretical conception of reason as self-standing (though they draw different conclusions from this), and theology cannot accept these terms.

Crucial to Milbank's advance of this Christian countermodernity is his demonstration of the origins of postmodern nihilism, as in Heidegger, Derrida and Deleuze, in the philosophical conception of being as univocal which was developed principally in the thought of Duns Scotus.[126] In Milbank's treatment, Scotus's claim is that 'being' means the same thing whether predicated of created or uncreated being, so sponsoring the sense that being is a genus (despite Scotus's explicit denial of this). Because all things 'are' in the same way, 'the divergences of genera . . . become sheer, absolute differences', and so along with Deleuze, Milbank argues that 'the reverse side of the univocity of Being is the philosophy of pure heterogeneity'.[127] Univocity is simultaneous with equivocity. Absolute sameness and absolute difference nihilistically coincide. And yet this reading of univocal difference is no more rationally fundamental than the 'Catholic philosophy of analogical difference'.[128] 'Nothing grounds a preference' for this reading of difference.[129] Difference can equally viably read analogically, and therefore non-conflictually.[130]

122. Milbank, *TST*, 297.

123. Milbank, *TST*, 298.

124. Milbank, *TST*, 297.

125. Milbank, *TST*, 298.

126. Milbank critiques Heidegger's reading of difference in light of Augustine's, attempting to show that neither embodies an obviously 'a more basic, a more rational ontology' (*TST*, 300–4).

127. Milbank, *TST*, 306.

128. Milbank, *TST*, 306.

129. Milbank, *TST*, 306; also 'The Grandeur of Reason', 374: 'There are no purely philosophical arguments which can refute the secular decision to refute Being as such to nullity.'

130. See Milbank, 'The Grandeur of Reason', 391.

It is as resistance to the postmodern metaphysic of ontological violence, based on the univocity of being, that Milbank defends an analogical reading of reality and expounds his own metaphysics of participation. This brings his attack on the Kantian circumscription of finitude into full perspective. Metaphysics in Kant's sense is impossible, and yet metaphysics in the sense of speculative reaching towards transcendence is not idle but an indispensable and unavoidable necessity. Although, as Heidegger explained, infinity does not appear, it nevertheless 'has to be presupposed', for we simply cannot do without it, and for Milbank this presupposing can only take the form of 'conjecture': a speculative extension towards the infinite from finitude. An analogical 'exchange of predicates' between finitude and infinitude cannot be ruled out.[131]

> if we are to have norms and values – to say what ultimately counts 'for always' – then [infinity] has to be 'conjectured about' . . . This necessary conjecture must, however, remain always ungrounded, or otherwise one lapses into the 'critical' illusion of transcendentalism.[132]

This echoes Milbank's insistence that '[A] constitutive and not merely regulative metaphysics [is] . . . inescapable. We *have* to say "how things are in general", to be able to say anything at all.'[133] There is no relief from the burden of speculating about reality, notwithstanding that such speculations are ungrounded in the foundationalist sense.[134] Even Derrida's *différance* remains covertly associated with such metaphysical 'real presences' as the fact-value distinction, because in saying that the sense-bearing sign is always treacherous in its arbitrary relation to Being, he upholds a dualism of Being and meaning. Deconstructionism remains helplessly committed to a language-independent *a priori* which is the 'one true universal', namely 'conflictual *différance*'.[135] For Milbank, however, the unavoidability of a *constitutive* (rather than a merely regulative) metaphysics is not troublesome, for the reaching towards a picture of the real and the whole which metaphysics embodies is secured non-foundationally in the uncircumscribability of the finite and of language itself. The analogical sense is for Milbank strictly unlimited; our language 'applies' in ways we could never measure, predict or specify in advance. On the contrary, in Blondelian fashion, we are always catching up with the way our language expresses the world in a manner that exceeds subjective 'intentionality'.

The concrete metaphysical proposals of *TST* are made unsystematically, almost as a coda to the central polemical project of the book, and concern a few central themes which are only partially developed: an alternative to substantialist metaphysics; a defence of a metaphysics of participation; a rejection of 'philosophical realism' in

---

131. Milbank, *WMS*, 11.
132. Milbank, *TST*, 308.
133. Milbank, *TST*, 300, italics original.
134. Milbank, 'The Grandeur of Reason', 388ff.
135. Milbank, *TST*, 311.

favour of 'theological objectivism'; and a retrieval of the doctrine of analogy. Fuller development of these constructive proposals occurs in *WMS*, where Milbank develops analogy as an aspect of an alternative substantialist metaphysics, arguing that the *via eminentiae* properly understood overcomes the Kantian critique of metaphysics. This requires reconceiving analogy in a thoroughly postmodern key, understanding that language 'does not stand for ideas, but constitutes ideas and "expresses" things in their disclosure of truth for us'.[136] *Poesis* is therefore the key to reconceiving analogy.

Against Deleuze, the doctrine of analogy is not of necessity complicit with identity, presence and substance, because it implies simultaneous identity and difference. This 'radical sense [is] liberated' if one discards the metaphysics of fixed, bounded entities and discrete substances in favour of 'mixtures, *continua*, overlaps and disjunctions, all subject in principle to limitless transformation'.[137] Analogy can then be understood as 'all-pervasive, as governing every unity and diversity of the organised world'.[138] It is significant for Milbank that, for Plato, the Good *is* the harmonic blending of differences. In the *Parmenides* Milbank finds the form of the Good described as 'essentially the *source* of diverse goodness, not simply "like" the many goods in the sense of being their totality or the fullness of the common stuff from which they are composed'.[139] For Milbank's Plato, all differences are grounded in the realm of the forms and are non-competitive with one another. If there is a problematic element to the *Parmenides'* understanding, it is in the absolute incomparability of the Good with finite goods, to which Plato responds with an emphasis on horizontal participation between finite goods and between the eternal forms so that in the finite realm the discernment of the good involves the determination of proper combinations and mixtures. In later works Milbank explores the notion of horizontal participation in a way which complements, rather than competes, with vertical participation.[140]

In this transformed sense of analogy, God is not the point of literal sameness at the metaphorical 'top' where analogies converge into identity; God is not any more the subject of the literal application of analogical qualities but the 'infinite realization of this quality in all the diversity and unity of its actual/possible instances'.[141] Analogy among finite beings no longer consists in discrete groups of likeness, but in unfixed contingent unities. This then opens analogical relationships

---

136. Milbank, *WMS*, 29.

137. Milbank, *TST*, 307.

138. Milbank, *TST*, 307.

139. Milbank, *TST*, 336.

140. Graham Ward questions whether Milbank successfully unites analogy and difference, or whether his analogizing has somehow denied difference (Graham Ward, 'John Milbank's Divina Commedia', *New Blackfriars* 73 (861): 311–18, 317). It seems likely that Milbank's opening essay in *WMS*, 'A Critique of the Theology of Right' (7–35), is some kind of response to this charge. The next chapter turns to this.

141. Milbank, *TST*, 307.

to being contingently and passingly constructed, naturally or culturally. This is the sense in which 'philosophical realism', or a picture of language as referring to or describing, correctly or incorrectly, an external world, is unsustainable. Analogy captures the sense that 'God is not something in any way seen, that we could "refer" to';[142] his being is not separable from the being of creatures.[143] Hence theology does not study God, since God is not an object of knowledge, but studies the mediation of God by creatures.[144] It is just this understanding of our knowledge of God that the Scotist notion of being as univocal threatens.

> And as for the finite world, creation *ex nihilo* radically rules out all realism in its regard . . . Knowledge itself is not 'something else' in relation to Being, a 'reflection' of Being, but only a particularly complex form of relation, another happening, a pragmatic intervention amongst finite happenings.[145]

Milbank's use of the classical doctrine of analogy is radicalized by his adoption of the 'Renaissance/Romantic' rethinking of the tradition in the direction of language and embodiment, which always takes the participated transcendence of creatures' *action* absolutely seriously. Milbank's use of Platonism is emphatically non-dualist. He works rather in the Neoplatonic tradition of emanations: hierarchies of being through which the mind ascends to God and through which, in the theurgic tradition, the divine descends into the material, but with the crucial addition that these hierarchies are construed as *gift*, non-necessary donations of divine being. As mediated by Neoplatonism, the eternal is not opposed to the temporal but is its transcendent sustaining source. In the radical pietists' 'expressivist ontology', expression is 'ontologically irreducible', to the extent that nature itself is expressive, is cultural, for God speaks 'through the creature, by the creature' in the words of Hamann – a formulation that is important for Milbank's stress on creation itself as a linguistic mediation of the divine.[146] And yet the nature-culture antinomy opens up again here, for it is human beings who give 'to all creatures their content and character': God 'addresses the creature (from the beginning and always) *as the*

142. Milbank, *TST*, 433.

143. Such a radical account of being as participation of course violates the principle of non-contradiction; but for Milbank, 'relations between the finite and the infinite simply require such a violation' (Wolter Huttinga, *Participation and Communicability: Herman Bavinck and John Milbank on the Relation Between God and the World* (Amsterdam: Buijten et Schipperheijn Motief, 2014), 155). 'If we ask in what we do actually participate when we speak of "participation in God's being", the answer should be "the imparticipable"' (159). But for Milbank this precisely does not issue in an agonistic and irresolvable struggle; it is not 'an impossible contradiction that must be endlessly and conflictually overcome', but 'a paradoxical "coincidence of opposites" that can be persisted with' (158).

144. Milbank, *TST*, 433.

145. Milbank, *TST*, 433.

146. Milbank, *WMS*, 106.

expressive self of this and other creatures', and so in a certain sense "'revelation" *adds nothing* to "creation".[147]

> in language there can be no such independence [of word from world]: there is rather an original confusion. . . . If words arise originally as a hermeneutic response to the world 'speaking' to us (as for Hamann), then we cannot dogmatically say that words are not obscurely disclosive of the infinite.[148]

This underlines the constructive significance of language: language makes the real. Analogy is therefore simultaneously cognitive and ontological. 'Knowledge is not a representation of things, but a relation to events, and an action upon events.'[149]

Milbank's metaphysical option for Plato is robust, and he is not shy to dampen the usual celebration of Aristotle's stature as a metaphysician. He readily declares Aristotle complicit with the heresy of modernity. In referring the ethical to a non-moral standard, '[Aristotle] *already* begins to think secular reason';[150] intellectuality for him is not by its very nature illuminated by the good, as it is for Plato. For Plato, all virtuous practice is mimesis, imitation of the Good; the goodness of our good actions is participative and derives from our seeing the Good, and not primarily from prudential discernment. Further, Aristotle divides *praxis* from *poesis* and renders the latter a non-contemplative activity oriented to what is useful and aesthetically pleasing. Plato does not separate ethical from artistic activity, nor desire from knowledge; all are equally participations in the eternal. True *praxis*, like *poesis*, is a mediation of the Forms; all doing and making is to do with the realization of the good. The Aristotelian alternative led ultimately to the autonomous realm of 'technology', in which making is purely immanent and signifies only our own control by means of a 'cold theoretical gaze' on nature.[151] In fact, in an argument reminiscent of his appropriation of Blondel's account of *poesis*, Milbank rejects altogether the distinction between *praxis* and *poesis*, or rather, *praxis* is simply a dimension of *poesis*: 'only by *convention* are some makings thought to be "doings": only by a particular [cultural] coding.'[152] He laments the 'Aristotelian' tendency in contemporary culture to regard external actions, such as aesthetic or stylistic behaviours and preferences, as non-moral, while the ethical is confined to an imagined 'internal' private sphere. A dichotomy of ethics and aesthetics is pernicious, for both equally pertain to 'the condition of truly desirable beauty';[153] and here Milbank's subordination of dialectics to rhetoric is once again apparent. 'The moral' in this sense 'intrude[s] everywhere' – wherever, in fact,

---

147. Milbank, *WMS*, 74.
148. Milbank, 'The Grandeur of Reason', 388.
149. Milbank, *TST*, 434.
150. Milbank, *TST*, 355.
151. Milbank, *TST*, 357.
152. Milbank, *TST*, 360.
153. Milbank, *TST*, 361.

there is desire.[154] One can see here the sense in which for Milbank any project, any attempt at realization of anything, is moral in the sense of activating our motion towards what is pleasing; science operates in just this way, and what is pleasing is the approximation to 'nature'.

Despite his enthusiasm for Plato, Milbank's critique of antique metaphysics and ethics, which he pursues extensively in the context of a critical examination of MacIntyre's recommendation of antique virtue, strongly emphasizes its radical discontinuity with the Christian. The Platonic version of participation still subordinates time, materiality and making to timeless immaterial permanence; the flux of temporal existence is regarded as fundamentally unreal, and the original trumps the copy. It is Milbank's claim that Christianity redeemed Platonism for time and change through a Trinitarian reworking in the direction of Neoplatonism 'which makes emanation integral to infinite perfection', where the Good which is God does not automatically and accidentally give forth the rays of being which are its emanations, but through free donation – which is paradoxically integral to its being – graciously gives the gift of being.[155] This transformation of Platonism occurred first through Augustine and pseudo-Dionysius and then more recently through Nicholas of Cusa and finally Blondel, though this redemption has been obscured by Aristotle's metaphysics. The trajectory opened up here, only fully realized in Christian countermodernity, is towards a reversal of the Platonic order – to 'ground theory in making, the original in the copy, the cause in the effect, and stable beauty in the midst of the music of transition'.[156] The *logos* of the Greeks remains with a problematic derogation of the materiality, change and embodiment: 'its duality of the "merely" organic and the psychic individual . . . foreshadows secular reason', in contrast to the use of the figure of 'body' in Pauline theology to signify 'that which primarily mediates the divine to us'.[157] In these ways the terms of antique philosophy – virtue, truth, soul, *polis* – are not replicated but transformed in the Christian *mythos*.

Above all, however, it is the 'good' which is narratively dense, which contains a world-picture that can never be unstoried, and which has no self-evident meaning taken by itself.

> It is, ironically, the complacent Catholic moral philosopher who imagines that the term 'good' is somehow more finitely secure, less mythological than the term 'God'. Whereas, in reality, the term 'good' condenses a narrative of absolute finality.[158]

154. Milbank, *TST*, 361.

155. Milbank, *TST*, 357.

156. Milbank, *TST*, 357, although this goes beyond the 'mere' reversal accomplished by Deleuze; 380–1.

157. Milbank, *TST*, 376.

158. Milbank, *TST*, 233.

The return of the Good to the centre of the metaphysical project is one of the ways in which Milbank is most obviously Platonist, but his reception of postmodernity means that there is no good apart from the story of it. Milbank's Good can only be narrated as the peace of God's city.

Concluding Part I: Peace is the truth

It was noted in opening that Milbank pursues a project at once epistemological and ontological. Reviewing this first part of the study, Milbank's account comes across as a kind of theological sleight of hand: he is having his cake and eating it, pushing a comprehensive postmodern relativism with regard to language, culture and tradition, but a robust realism with regard to God, and even claiming that these two positions are mutually reinforcing.[159]

What then, in this account of theological reason, is 'truth'? Although the term does not feature prominently in *TST*'s treatment, asking how Milbank uses and defines it helps to put a finger on the heart of his enterprise.

> Our judgement of the 'truth' of events . . . is essentially an aesthetic matter. We recognize beauty or not, and the measure of truth is likeness to the form of divine beauty of which our soul has some recollection. Augustine is basically right: truth, for Christianity, is not correspondence, but rather *participation* of the beautiful in the beauty of God.[160]

Giving the Platonic picture a constructivist emphasis, Milbank regards the mind's affinity for beauty as the ability of the mind 'to shape events in an "honest" and "decorous" fashion' so that in some sense beauty is a product of the mind's arrangement of things and events into stories in which the world makes compelling

---

159. A fact not missed by commentators, who find his combination of traditionalist realism and postmodernist historicism striking. 'How does Milbank suppose that he can be genuinely postmodern and yet a traditional Christian? How can one be historicist without being nihilist? Milbank's proposal is ingenious. It is true, he says, that all we have is a range of different traditions, and decisions between traditions cannot be made on some "tradition-transcendent grounds." Yet it is possible that one of these traditions might in fact be the truth. This is what the Christian narrative claims to be: it is a meta-discourse that can and should embrace all human life and activity. So in a brilliant ironic move, Milbank turns out to be anti-realist about everything except God. But can this work?' (Ian Markham 'Postmodern Christian Traditionalism?', review of *Theology and Social Theory: Beyond Secular Reason*, by John Milbank, *First Things*, January 1992, https://www.firstthings.com /article/1992/01/002-postmodern-christian-traditionalism, accessed 4 March 2019). This crucial question is addressed briefly here and substantially in the next chapter.

160. Milbank, *TST*, 434.

sense.[161] Indeed, 'to "choose" the Augustinian metanarrative and an Augustinian ontology of peace is also to "elect reason", to fulfil the ineradicable bias of the human mind towards meaning'.[162] In this way Milbank openly indicates that in the Christian *mythos* truth is an aspect of the aesthetic harmony of peace, which is charity. Rather than a straightforward reciprocity between the good and the true, where the transcendentals are as it were equally convertible with one another, for Milbank the Good, translated as the peace of divine charity, is the true form of all the others. (Which is not to say that, for Plato, the transcendentals are 'equally' convertible either, since the Good retains primacy, but for Milbank Plato's Good possesses a unity which makes it problematically opposed to difference, and so it cannot be really peaceful.) This is why there is no secular reason; insofar as truth is love, reason has the shape of desire. True reason just is rightly directed desire, which cannot be cultivated apart from the narrative of the Good which is peaceful difference, and which convinces through attraction and not through dialectics.

> There *is* no evident truth, and truth itself (for *Theology and Social Theory*) can be nothing other than a peaceful communication which is not a consensual reception of the same, but a becoming different of what is received, yet without aggressive rupture. 'Harmonious' transition is peace, is truth.[163]

There is no 'evident' truth in the sense that truth does not simply present itself inertly and externally for intellectual acceptance from an empirically given, uncontestable and universally apparent 'nature' or 'way things are'. Rather truth is constructed (received, and then communicated, as difference not sameness) in the project of imagining and enacting peaceful difference which, Milbank explains prior to the remarks just quoted, *is* the church, the continuous retelling and reperformance of the narrative of God's making and redeeming of the world in the historical form of Christian lives and communities.[164] Truth, as the peace

---

161. Milbank, *TST*, 434.

162. Milbank, *TST*, xvii.

163. Milbank, 'Enclaves', 348.

164. Milbank's conception of the church has been one of the 'Achilles heels' of his theology, drawing much criticism for being 'idealized' and unconnected to any actual historical institution. Aidan Nichols made this point sharply in response to *TST* ('Non Tali Auxilio: Not By Such Help', *New Blackfriars* 73 (1992): 326–32). Since this is not the central concern here, I leave the issue aside, except to note that Milbank is at pains to emphasize what he regards as the *actual* historical failure of the church to write the story of peaceful difference in its own history. '[T]he difference that Christianity has made includes a tragic dimension, because its failure to sustain a "peace beyond the law" enabled a transition from the antique containing of a given violence by reason, to the modern regulation of violence through greater violence' (*TST*, 6). In 'Enclaves' he responds to the potential *aporia* opened up by this admission by insisting that the church is forgiveness, in the sense of the inexhaustible divine gift of renewal and reconciliation.

of mutual charity, is available only in the concrete form of the community of reconciled difference which is the church, and so Milbank regards his position as a form of pragmatism: truth is cashed out in action.

In *WMS*, this is developed to emphasize the creature as a mediation of God, a mediation which is always linguistic and never separable therefore from human processes of understanding and expressing. (This is not to say that expressions are not teleologically constrained, nor that there is no space for a conception of 'sin' as a failure to respond to this teleological constraint, as we shall see in the next chapter.)

> But if there is no bedrock, no absolute *presence*, either of ideas or of empirical objects, then how can there be any objective truth? Hamann is only a step away from Hume, from Derrida. However, that further step . . . completes the distance which the philosophical sceptics have half-travelled.[165]

This distance is the capacity to see the difference of the creature as a mediation which cannot be rightly perceived or appealed to 'outside of a specific faith, reason or desire', and thus is never invoked over against a 'real' which constrains language from without.[166] The creature itself is a 'speaking', and as such, 'nature always manifests itself in the conventionality and bewilderment of cultural sign-systems'.[167] 'Nature' therefore is not the transcendental constraint of culture. Any such transcendental constraint emerges not *a priori* but, somehow, 'from the cultural objects themselves'.[168] In this way culture is 'promoted to the status of a divine transcendental', the *Verbum*, which Milbank takes to be the meaning of Vico's *verum et factum convertuntur*: truth and making are interchangeable. *Verbum* as a transcendental names an intra-Trinitarian act: 'God in his creation *ad intra* in the Logos "incorporates" within himself the creation *ad extra*, including human history', and this way *Verbum* names a primordial difference within the Godhead itself which sustains and peacefully reconciles Unity and Being.[169]

This constitutes a repudiation of any firm distinction between metaphysics, ethics and aesthetics, insofar as all three have their terminus (not a closure but an 'end' in the Augustinian sense) in the overcoming of violence in the beautiful peace which is the city of God. The Good, which is the truly real, cannot be translated into non-value terms, and so ontology cannot start from or point towards a realm of being which is prior to the Good or in some way grounds the Good; rather the Good itself is the source of the real and the true.[170] It is from this position that Milbank refuses the dialectical justification for narrative preference, since it still

---

165. Milbank, *WMS*, 75.
166. Milbank, *WMS*, 77.
167. Milbank, *WMS*, 77.
168. Milbank, *WMS*, 80.
169. Milbank, *WMS*, 80.
170. Milbank, *TST*, 336, 356.

supposes that it is something other than the sheer attraction of the Good that can persuade us to tell one story rather than another. But there is, for Milbank, no 'before' the desirability of the Good. Hence the inseparability of nature and culture and the impossibility of a fact-value distinction: so-called 'facts' are always mediated by our cultural codings in which alone we discern the valuable and desirable.[171] Since there is no real distinction between fact and value, there is no possible reason for finding our evaluative codings more 'subjective' than our other sorts of codings: and there is no sense in thinking of the given world as something *behind* these perceptions, as though the cultural coding came 'between' us and the world.[172] We cannot separate the aesthetic and the erotic from the ontological, culture from nature, or the subjective from the objective.

Milbank's rejection of postmodern philosophy is less to do with its formal ontology than the moral or spiritual freight carried by it – though this way of putting it trades on the distinction which, as we have seen, he rejects. For the univocal coding of reality, insofar as it propagates a pure heterogeneity, is indifferent to its own difference. In contrast, the analogical coding involves 'a constant discrimination of preferences' and an associated erection of hierarchies;[173] difference cannot be celebrated univocally, but only where the differences are different from one another not only in their form of difference but also in their content as differences. Dualism of scheme and content is, in Milbank's treatment, always a flattening which denies the reciprocity between these terms, as in MacIntyre's formal defence of virtue which is not separable from the content of antique virtue, the violent *mythos* of heroism and victory.[174] Analogy overcomes this dualism by recognizing the differences of differences from one another, which involves judgements of preference. Milbank suggests, without offering a full justification in *TST*, that this is only possible if one posits 'a plenitudinous supratemporal infinite which has "already realized" in eminent fashion every desirable effect'.[175] The impossibility of a true valuation of difference in immanent terms is a point to which Milbank often returns in different contexts, including, as we see below, in relation to vitalism. The *nouveaux philosophes* are promoters of a nihilistic indifferent difference. Only in a framework of transcendent peace can difference be truly different.

Milbank's rejection of dualisms is a radicalization of *nouvelle théologie*'s exegesis of grace and nature, world and God.[176] Blondel offers a structure for showing that human construction is the mode of ingress for the divine, and that

171. Milbank, *TST*, 340.

172. Milbank, *TST*, 340.

173. Milbank, *TST*, 308.

174. Milbank, *TST*, 332–3.

175. Milbank, *TST*, 309.

176. It is worth noting, though, that de Lubac did not wish to do away completely with a distinction between nature and grace (David Grumett, *De Lubac: A Guide for the Perplexed* (London: Bloomsbury, 2007), 19f). Milbank may agree with this in principle, but it is not always possible to discern this in his writings.

the philosophical analysis of the world 'on its own terms', so to speak, cannot either replace or operate without a *mythos* within which alone its reasonings have purchase and which cannot ground itself in a 'pure' reason, but can only see reason as an instance of the desire for the Good. Blondel's account of human action as always already graced gives Milbank the philosophical wherewithal to deny that postmodern anti-realism is a threat to theological objectivism, enabling him to accept a fundamentally mythic structure for knowing and being while avoiding the nihilistic price paid by the philosophers of *différance*. All narratives are equally theological but not equal in theological legitimacy or 'truth'. This is simply because truth *is* peace, and the Christian narrative alone is finally peaceful. Peace names all that is good, all that is true; violence and conflict name untruth, unreason. This then is the most fundamental claim of *TST* and that on which its project rides. Truth as peace is affective, aesthetic and erotic. It is sensed not by the exercise of a disembodied dialectics but by a feeling enquiry into what we most deeply desire which is always narratively expressed and fundamentally groundless, but *not* arbitrary or directionless, for the erotic and aesthetic is drawn by a genuine real, which is God.[177]

So there no 'outside' theology for Milbank. The only question is *which* theology we inhabit. Christian theology alone is able to narrate the character of knowing and making, and the uncircumscribable excess of reality itself, in a non-nihilistic fashion. This chapter has offered some consideration of how this might affect the truth and meaning of those discourses which consider reality within diverse intellectual paradigms, particularly the sciences. In what follows, we explore this more deeply and offer a thoroughgoing critical assessment, with particular attention to Milbank's repudiation of dialectical adjudication in favour of narrative reasoning. Thinking along with this method, we explore the implications of his views and raise sequential objections, scoping possible responses to them in turn (Chapter 3) and finally sharpening the critique by a comparison with another interlocutor, Michael Hanby, who exhibits not only a similar approach but also important critical differences (Chapter 4).

---

177. Against indifferent difference, 'one can try to put forward an alternative *mythos*, equally unfounded, but nonetheless embodying an "ontology of peace", which conceives differences as analogically related, rather than equivocally at variance. This strategy . . . sees in history not just arbitrary transitions, but constant contingent shifts either towards or away from what is projected as the true human *telos*, a true concrete representation of the analogical blending of difference.' Milbank, *TST*, 279.

Part II

SCIENCE

In Milbank's work, theology speaks in the tones of history, politics, philosophy and economics. This is one of its most distinctive characteristics, expressing the confidence of a theology which has shrugged off its modern confinement. Indeed, it is defining of his theological agenda. Chapters 1 and 2 attempted to show what prerogative theologians possess to undertake such a speaking, what theology is such that this speaking is mandated. Part III will turn towards an attempt to speak 'also' in the tones of scientific discourses about life. Part II attempts to prepare the way for this speaking by means of a careful assessment of Milbank's position. Specific questions which will have arisen in previous chapters will be identified and sharpened. In what sense does theology 'disrupt'? And how does such disruption affect the discipline in question? Part II thus prepares the way for the more risky venture of Part III, which attempts a theological 'disruption' and 'making strange' of biology via the term 'life'.

Chapter 3

THEOLOGY ALONE IS SCIENCE

ASSESSING MILBANK

Disruption and making strange

In *The Word Made Strange*, Milbank's first major work subsequent to *TST*, he says that discourses are 'overlaid' by theology; the kind of difference that theology makes is 'ambiguous', and the result is not the eradication of another discourse but a 'making strange'.[1] 'Disruption' and 'overlaying' retain some quality of *TST*'s 'mastery', while 'making strange' is more benign, and the admission of an 'ambiguity' acknowledges the justice of a certain caution or hesitancy. The combination of these images for theology's approach to the disciplines shows something of the internal tension in Milbank's conception of theology's agenda.

The two chapters of this part argue that the Milbankian model is able to negotiate these tensions and does have the resources both to raise criticisms against itself and to respond to them. It thus demonstrates the fruitfulness of its own narrative – and also obliquely confirms Milbank's argument that dialectics occurs meaningfully only within a particular narrative – while making clear that the pugnacity of his style and approach is inappropriate to what is fundamentally, beneath and behind his voice, an eirenic project.[2]

This chapter revisits some important methodological issues in order to define the question more exactly, before turning to critical objections and responses. Chapter 4 engages an alternative view from Michael Hanby which acts as a

---

1. 'A "theological" word only overlays these discourses – or can be judged to do so, since the overlay is never unambiguous – in a certain disruptive *difference* that is made to them. Here, also, there is a "making strange"' (Milbank, *WMS*, 3).

2. Oliver, 'Radical Orthodoxy: A Conversation', 47. Milbank has recognized the importance of moving away from a purely polemical style and into a broader and more sympathetic mode of engagement. He implies that the aggressive mode of *TST* was a reaction to theology's ghettoization in modernity, and is not an absolute standard for theology's ongoing engagement, which needs to avoid party polemics. He also acknowledges the need for a more explicit humility, without abandoning the original commitment to a theological ambition appropriate to its task.

helpful foil to Milbank. While having a great deal in common with Milbank, Hanby's understanding of the nature of theology nevertheless diverges in key ways. The present chapter refines and critiques aspects of Milbank's own position in the context of an approach to biology. The outcome of Part II is to propose that theological speaking constitutes a disruption of sorts because it remains interrogative, it remains a judgement, but the disruption is also a 'making strange' which ultimately constitutes that discipline more deeply in its distinctiveness, and in which theology performs its proper work of speaking about God through speaking about the world.

How to argue with Milbank: Methodology revisited

Before embarking on this chapter, it is important briefly to reconsider some methodological issues which concern the criteria that are to be employed for assessment, and to clarify the purpose of this examination. As a thinker whose authorial voice can be opaque, clarifying Milbank's claims is a worthwhile task, one I attempted in the last chapter. In light of that clarification, it is apparent that a critical treatment of his model of should, among other methods of critique, measure it by the standards it sets, namely its option for rhetorical over dialectical reasoning and its pragmatic criteria for truth. The goal is not to pronounce a sentence on Milbank's position *tout court*. As I argue below in accord with some of Milbank's interpreters, he has deliberately put his position beyond 'refutation' as such. Instead I seek to understand his agenda and explore what it does and does not entail, to suggest some possible developments and qualifications, and using these to pursue the question at hand regarding the relationship between theology and the disciplines, and theology and biology in particular. This approach respects his own criteria for theoretical 'success', where truth is measured by peace.

The sense of the 'pragmatism' which Milbank calls for, and the care with which he specifies the role of dialectics, indicates that for him argument always occurs within a prior framework of narrative, reason and desire – and particularly, in the emphasis of Milbank's own more recent work, imagination.[3] An argument 'works', or doesn't, only against that background.[4] My exploration

---

3. 'Faith, Reason and Imagination' indicates some of the landscape: '[T]he theological necessarily links rational reflection with the contemplative regard of historical events and visualised pictures or symbols. Its elusive blend of idea and image belongs precisely to the realm of the imaginative "between"' (24).

4. 'Argument will take you only so far. As soon as we get on to issues that really matter to anybody existentially, we're into an area where argument serves an incredibly important purpose in trying to get everything consistent and in persuading people by saying: If you think this then that would mean you thought that, and you don't really think that. . . . But it goes only so far' (Oliver, 'Radical Orthodoxy: A Conversation', 42).

in this chapter attempts to put this kind of dialectic into practice: for example, if you think *x* (theology is the master discourse), do you inevitably end up saying *y* (the disciplines are theocratically evacuated)? This is important as a response to those who argue that Milbank's wholesale rejection of dialectics is inconsistent because he himself uses it. The point is that dialectics is pragmatically valid but not exclusively sufficient.

The potential of Milbank's approach can therefore best be made apparent in the context of a sympathetic thinking-through undertaken in a critical spirit, rather than exclusively through dialectical adjudication. One must try to put it into practice and see if it 'works': does it live up to its self-understanding? How would we know? What is the criterion for 'working'? It must be a criterion drawn from its own narrative, and the criterion this narrative supplies by which to measure itself is its peaceableness: is it as peaceful as it wants to be, as it says it is? Specifically, does it really support 'difference', of which 'peace' is the harmony? This is the bar against which I measure it below, and in light of which I discern a partial failure, manifest in Milbank's engagement with sociology. I follow this with a few tentative proposals for how it might, with some developments, succeed in peacefully enabling difference. In this process, it appears that Milbank's account of theology can be successfully self-critical, that is, it can raise against itself the questions needed to refine its operation towards that goal which it sets for itself, which is peace.[5] This not only demonstrates its resourcefulness and consistency but also exemplifies its own contention that dialectics properly functions internally to narratives. I also hope that both the advantages and the difficulties raised by Milbank's approach will be usefully illuminated. Milbank invites such a mode of criticism insofar as to adopt an 'outside' perspective is to beg the question he is continually trying to frame.

By this discussion I hope to show what it looks like to think through the logic of Milbank's position: how does it play out for the disciplines, for theology? I therefore do *not* attempt an 'external' or total assessment in which Milbank's claims are critiqued from every angle. By adopting this approach I do not mean to deny the serious questions which can be raised against Milbank's framework in many crucial areas, some of which are flagged up in the notes. Rather, it is to say that this is one illuminating mode of critical assessment: let us see what it is like to think like this, to find out whether it 'works' as it says it does; in so doing we may perhaps improve the performance. Because my intention is to undertake an 'internal' thinking-through, I have deliberately allowed the enquiry to generate questions in the process of its own discussion, attempting responses as part of an unfolding exploration, rather than schematically pursuing a bird's-eye view. For this reason the reader will hopefully find that the questions she finds herself asking of the argument are in due course raised within the discussion.

---

5. A mode of understanding narrative 'success' drawn from MacIntyre (*Whose Justice? Which Rationality?* (Notre Dame, IN: Notre Dame University Press, 1988), Chapter 8).

Theology and the disciplines: Sharpening the question

The last chapter considered Milbank's argument that showing the inescapability of narrative is part of the claim that there is no 'outside' theology; theology intrudes everywhere. What has not been established is exactly what kind of primacy a specifically theological narration retains. The relation such theological reasoning should have to the processes of so-called 'scientific' knowledge remains unspecified. 'John Milbank's turn . . . may be described as a bombshell meant to shatter all modern disciplines.'[6] Does theology's narration have as its goal the supplanting of biology's own language, because the virtue and truth of the earthly city is not the virtue and truth of the city of God? Simon Oliver offers a somewhat tempered version of Milbank's more aggressive account of the theological agenda towards the disciplines, by combining the insistence on the impossibility of their autonomy with the requirement that their difference from theology be carefully guarded.[7] How can one can maintain the difference and distinctive role of the

---

6. Meyer, *Metaphysics*, 407.

7. '[N]o discourse which seeks truth can count itself as wholly autonomous from issues of transcendent origin and purpose – that is, issues of theology. However, this is most certainly not to suggest that other discourses are thereby collapsed into theology any more than it is to suggest that, within the framework of participation, creation collapses into God. . . . [T]he peculiar character of non-theological discourses must be maintained while denying that those discourses are self-standing and autonomous from, or indifferent to, theological considerations' (Oliver, 'Introducing', 19).

With his stipulation that the 'peculiar' character of each discipline be maintained, Oliver typically expresses a more nuanced view of the matter than Milbank. Referring to his own study of motion, the final volume in the original *Radical Orthodoxy* series (*Philosophy, God and Motion* (London: Routledge, 2005), he says that theology 'can't and shouldn't necessarily supplant the accounts given in other discourses, but it can certainly complement or challenge them. For example, the understanding of motion might properly belong to physics, and yet there could be other kinds of motion analogically related to the local variety which properly belong within the purview of theology, like the motion of learning or thinking' (Oliver, 'Radical Orthodoxy: A Conversation', 37). From this one might gather that Oliver remains at least partially committed to the thought that the disciplines do have a *kind* of autonomy (since they can 'complement' theology), and theology does have a *kind* of specialism (a 'purview'). He also speaks of 'an account of motion in physics and an account of motion in theology' as being genuinely different, in the sense of not 'univocal' (Oliver, 'Radical Orthodoxy: A Conversation', 38).

With due caution, since I offer no sustained analysis of Oliver's own account, I would cautiously suggest that the view proposed in this chapter departs from Oliver's in rejecting the idea that theology could in any sense 'complement' the disciplines or be alongside them as an account of the world, since it is neither external to them nor generically comparable with them, while agreeing that the disciplines do remain distinctive and are not univocally replaceable by theology, since this would be a category mistake. Oliver's comment, quoted

disciplines, while not attributing to them a false autonomy from theology? Oliver notes that '[t]he nature of that relation ... require[s] very careful and sophisticated articulation'.[8]

The key issues can be framed in terms of two critical questions.[9] Firstly, will theological specifications about life theocratically eradicate other accounts of 'life', such as the biological? What, on Milbank's view, would be the problem with such theocratic eradication? In the view of one commentator, this is exactly what he intends: '[the] attempt to *collapse* modern social theory back into theological terrain is the gist of Milbank's negative apologetic'.[10] Social science is installed by Milbank as a subdiscipline of theology; 'society' is translated into 'the church'.[11] How is it possible that biology, or any other science, can survive as a discipline with its own methodology and its own integrity, under the aegis of such a theology? Should theology be trying to preserve the integrity of the disciplines at all? Milbank's treatment of sociology in *TST* evinces no concern that it should.

The second question, inseparable from the first, is whether Milbank's conception of knowledge and reason undermine the notion of a 'natural' science in the first place, insofar as the idea of a given 'nature', and an autonomous knowledge based on such a nature, itself is comprehensively critiqued. How, in this scenario, could natural science 'know' anything of its own, by itself? As our considerations in Part I indicated, it is the meaning of 'science' and 'nature' that is at stake in these questions: what constitutes true knowledge and its object.[12] We will find ourselves returning more than once to charges made by critics against Milbank's conception of knowledge, both the legitimacy of his interpretation of narratives

later in this chapter, that the disciplines *participate* in theology, aptly expresses the kind of view I will try to defend.

8. Oliver, 'Introducing', 19.

9. The importance of asking both these questions together – about theology and the disciplines, and about science and nature – will become apparent at the end of this chapter, where I argue that it is precisely a poetic account of knowledge and a participatory ontology, both of which are universal only through their narrative specification, which can fully satisfy the tension between the two claims we would like to make: the 'scientific' knowledge of life is poetic and disclosive of the ultimate and is constitutively metaphysical and theological; but the Christian *mythos* alone remains the true knowledge of life, revealing the transcendent signification of life itself.

10. Meyer, *Metaphysics*, 409; italics added.

11. '[T]here can only be a distinguishable Christian social theory because there is also a distinguishable Christian mode of action, a definite practice ... The theory, therefore, is first and foremost an *ecclesiology*' (*TST*, 380).

12. Milbank is not the only one who argues that 'science' and 'nature' are co-constituting. See Neil Evernden, *The Social Creation of Nature* (Baltimore: John Hopkins University Press, 1992); Noel Castree, *Making Sense of Nature* (Oxford: Routledge, 2013); and Louis Dupré, *Passage to Modernity: An Essay in the Hermeneutics of Nature and Culture* (New Haven: Yale University Press, 1993).

(e.g. Graham Ward) and his rejection of knowledge as referential (e.g. Paul Janz), and reiterating the rationale behind his position in answer to them. Milbank's claim is that theology has a prerogative on science; or rather, it 'is alone certainty, alone science';[13] and that there is no self-contained 'nature' demarcatable from supernature. How can this claim not be a theocratic one? And how can it leave science, in the modern sense, intact? These questions are intimately connected to Milbank's denial of epistemic priority to contemplation in favour of action: truth as fundamentally something we make, not something we receive. The significance of an active conception of knowledge for conceiving 'science' will be decisive in this and the following chapter.

I hope to offer a suitably cautious response to these questions in this part of the book, one which is consequently somewhat lengthy. It will have the following structure: firstly, via a critical enquiry into Milbank's claims about the status of theology in relation to the disciplines, I will qualify his position, arguing that it is not in fact theocratic; secondly, I argue that Milbank's assessment of the status of scientific knowledges is, somewhat unexpectedly, a very high estimation of their value; thirdly, I argue that the pre-eminence of theology actually establishes the difference of the disciplines from theology.

A theocratic agenda?

This issue is a chief worry of many of Milbank's critics, as a survey of the early responses to *Theology and Social Theory* makes clear. His denial that there is autonomy for anything outside theology cannot help coming across as 'epistemological imperialism',[14] just as *TST*'s fearless confidence in what is an inevitably challenging cross-disciplinary exercise in analysis and judgement of sociology inevitably appears to some inside the target discipline as the predictable caricature resulting from theological arrogance.[15]

---

13. Milbank, *TST*, 218.

14. Kieran Flanagan quoting John Orme Mills in his critical response to *TST*: Kieran Flanagan, 'Sublime Policing: Sociology and Milbank's City of God', *New Blackfriars* 73 (1992): 333–40, 335. Flanagan is admiring of Milbank's competence in his handling of the titans of sociology Weber, Luhmann and Durkheim, while noting certain oversights and simplifications of these and other key figures.

15. It is argued, for example, that Milbank mistakenly construes sociology as always and everywhere opposed to theology, rather than accepting that some of sociology's analyses of the human assist theology in its exposure of the limited and theory-laden nature of culture, and do not need to be 'mastered' as enemies. Flanagan argues that Milbank has failed to be sensitive to internal differences in emphasis between traditional and contemporary sociology of religion. Furthermore, he 'needlessly' undermines sociology's capacity to generate helpful and penetrating analyses of the human and the cultural (Flanagan, 'Sublime Policing', 337). Peter Berger is Flanagan's example of a sociologist whose work militates against just the sort

In a critique which captures the spirit of this concern, Romand Coles mounts a passionate assault on the 'compulsive singularity' of Milbank's account of Christianity as an imperialist exclusivism which condemns all other stories to 'the waste bin of nihilism and subjugation'.[16] While Coles's worry is primarily sociopolitical in nature, its intellectual purchase is evident. Reading Milbank's work, Coles is 'haunted' by the memory of those who found themselves in the hands of Christians certain of the superiority of their story, confident that they had nothing to learn from stories other than their own.[17] In 'insisting upon the . . . dissipation of those narrative practices which do not refer desire to God, what of the other's difference does Milbank actually claim to love?'[18] For Coles, Milbank's metanarrative imperialism justifies the silencing of others and their stories. 'These "others" call us to wonder whether [Milbank's] type of story does not create soils rich for diverse imperialist proliferations whose textures, insistences, and epistemological and ontological underpinnings are ripe with danger.'[19]

Milbank denies that the disciplines have any legitimate autonomy from theology. This seems like a ruthless assimilation of the disciplines into theology's

of reductionist treatments of the social Milbank himself is challenging. Flanagan argues that Milbank misses the opportunity positively presented by sociological analysis to point up the emptiness inherent in modern disbelief. In a later work, Flanagan presents Bourdieu as an expositor par excellence of this understanding of sociology, in profound continuity with Milbank's project and resembling in certain important ways Milbank's reading of Blondel with respect to philosophy. See Kieran Flanagan, *The Enchantment of Sociology: A Study of Theology and Culture* (London: Macmillan, 1996), especially 59ff; also Kieran Flanagan and Peter Jupp, eds., *Postmodernity, Sociology and Religion* (London: Macmillan, 1996).

Richard Roberts argues that Milbank has generated an unnecessary opposition between theology and social theory, misconstruing both in the process and failing to note the element of moral normativity in social theory properly understood; 'Transcendental Sociology? A Critique of John Milbank's 'Theology and Social Theory Beyond Secular Reason', *Scottish Journal of Theology* 46, no. 4 (1993): 527–36). He explores a more synergistic relationship between the two in *Religion, Theology and the Human Sciences* (Cambridge: Cambridge University Press, 2002).

16. He asks: 'Does any human have but the most infinitesimal portion of the unfathomably vast and complicated knowledges that would be required to make such proclamations?' Romand Coles, 'Storied Others and Possibilities of *Caritas*: Milbank and Neo-Nietzschean Ethics', *Modern Theology* 8, no. 4 (1992): 331–51, 332.

17. Coles, 'Storied Others and Possibilities of *Caritas*', 333. Coles takes as exemplary the suffering of the native peoples of South America at the hands of Catholic colonists, who, though they did not all bear the sword (and some, such as Las Casas, did recognize the intrinsic humanity of the natives), all equally disregarded the narratives owned and practiced by those they went to 'convert'; they assimilated them as 'others' into their own narrative without remainder.

18. Coles, 'Storied Others and Possibilities of *Caritas*', 339.

19. Coles, 'Storied Others and Possibilities of *Caritas*', 333.

metanarrative, as though there were nothing to learn from them. Many see in Milbank's project an ideological violence, a forcing of others' stories (whether cultural or disciplinary) into the terms of his own. Graham Ward and Rowan Williams both expressed versions of this concern shortly after the publication of *TST*.[20] Ward observes that Milbank inevitably distorts and simplifies history for the sake of his own grand narrative; Williams that there is a desire in Milbank for a 'last word', a lack of patience and a failure to be aware of the way in which history and narrative themselves require that one live creatively with the impossibility of closure.[21] These authors worry that Milbank's narrative is totalizing and ahistorical. Graham Ward adverts to this when he recognizes that Milbank's version of intellectual history in *TST* only makes sense if the treatments of individual thinkers are read in terms of their place in the entire story, with the goal of the story clearly in view.[22]

Hyman argues that Milbank's narrative has a totalitarian desire to assert its 'mastery' by rhetorical force,[23] concerns that are echoed by Williams who worries that despite his emphasis on historicism, Milbank assumes a rather 'ahistorical framework' which implicitly raises his narrative to the level of a suprahistorical true story which dominates all other stories, violently foreclosing conversation.[24]

20. Graham Ward, 'Commedia'. Rowan Williams, 'Saving Time: Thoughts on Practice, Patience and Vision', *New Blackfriars* 73 (1992): 319–26. Milbank acknowledged the concern, though without directly admitting its purchase on him, recommending 'a vulnerable exposure to risk, failure and the tragic misinterpretation by others of our own ventures (as Rowan Williams has repeatedly stressed in his theology)' (xvii–xviii).

21. Both critics express the concern summarized by Shortt in conversation with Milbank: '[T]he engagement with difficult and uncooperative detail can be absent from your canvases, notwithstanding the qualifications you've given' (Oliver, 'Radical Orthodoxy: A Conversation', 39). This is surely one aspect of Williams's concern over Milbank's lack of 'patience'. Ward and Williams are both qualified admirers of Milbank's project, and I try in the following discussion to recognize the force of this worry while holding, as they seem to, that this is not a terminal charge but simply an invitation to perform the project more faithfully; in Milbank's own response to Williams, 'I'm not sure that Rowan is saying anything that really goes against our basic argument' (Oliver, 'Radical Orthodoxy: A Conversation', 39).

22. 'Analyses of individual secular thinkers and schools of thought only become meaningful within the context of the whole book. They need to be read within the context of Milbank's overall design. Each analysis has its place in the grand narrative he is composing. Each analysis is subservient to this grand narrative.' Ward, 'Commedia', 311.

23. Hyman, *Predicament*, 74.

24. Williams, 'Saving Time', 321. Shortt quotes Williams from an unpublished interview: 'Another perception is that you don't allow enough for what Rowan Williams terms "the sinfulness, the provisionality and muddle of the Church: all subjects on which an Anglican may be expected to have eloquent views"' (Oliver, 'Radical Orthodoxy: A Conversation', 30). Shortt points out that this kind of worry crops up widely in critical

These concerns would seem to be corroborated by Milbank's rejection of 'dialogue'.[25] Ward argues that Milbank's 'distorting' use of his sources, his retelling of others' stories in the framework of his own, itself displays a certain violence,[26] a point Hyman elaborates, saying that Milbank inevitably does violence to those his theological narrative 'positions' since it forcefully alters the meaning of their stories.[27] Hyman also thinks that Milbank's violent insistence on Christian truth in opposition to nihilism actually generates further violent dualisms and denigration of subsidiary narratives.[28]

Milbank's agenda for peaceful difference

How are these charges to be answered? Flanagan's charge regarding Milbank's poor use and interpretation of sociology can be willingly accepted without destroying

responses to Radical Orthodoxy. In fact Milbank insists, in the final part of *TST*, that the Christian church has mostly been a failure, an admission that few critics seem to note: 'However, if this [the *altera civitas*] is salvation, then we are forced to admit that it can only have been present intermittently during the Christian centuries. . . . [W]hile it is possible to recover the narrative and ontological shape of the Christian "interruption" of history . . . one should also recognise that this interruption appears to have tragically failed, and that it is the course of this failure itself which has generated secular reason.' He even acknowledges that 'Christianity has helped to unleash a more "naked" violence' (*TST*, 440–1). So it is not the case that Milbank explicitly denies the sinfulness, provisionality and muddle of the church, even if this knowledge is not always clearly foregrounded in his re-narration of the Christian interruption.

25. See 'The End of Dialogue', 174–91 (though Milbank is concerned here specifically with religious difference, and is not denying the value of talking per se, but rather the idea that there is an 'unknown' all parties are aiming at). One of the purposes of *TST* is 'to "end" the dialogue between theology and sociology' (*TST*, 4; cf. 236). As Smith notes, the rejection of dialogue is not a 'suicidal sectarianism' as Douglas Hedley proposes (Hedley, 'Should Divinity Overcome Metaphysics? Reflections on John Milbank's Theology and Social Theory and Confessions of a Cambridge Platonist', *Journal of Religion* 80, no. 2 (2000): 276). It does not entail a refusal to 'talk to' secular disciplines: 'Even a cursory view of [Radical Orthodox texts] would show that this is a mistaken conclusion'; rather, it is mandating 'a distinctly theological engagement with the world – and the academy that investigates this world' (Smith, *Introducing Radical Orthodoxy*, 69).

26. Ward, 'Commedia', 312.

27. Hyman, *Predicament*, 74.

28. '[T]he initial dualism [between Christianity and nihilism] gives rise to a violent warfare between theology and nihilism as well as to violent treatments of all other, subsidiary narratives.' Hyman rightly observes that '[t]hese characteristics are particularly problematic because much of Milbank's rhetoric depends on his contention that (his) theology is the only metanarrative that can resist dualism, violence and mastery' (*Predicament*, 6).

his project as a whole. That the different disciplines have valid perspectives and voices does not mean that they have to be 'outside' theology, although Flanagan's vision of social science does suggest that it can function to assist theology in something like the traditional role of handmaiden, which on Milbank's view would remain a problematically extrinsicist mode of thinking. We return to this problem in more detail later in this chapter. The charges from Ward, Williams and Hyman are more fundamentally challenging, since they concern the very shape of Milbank's conception of 'mastery'.

Ward says that Milbank's reading of other figures introduces an element of 'distortion',[29] but this begs the question: distortion in comparison to what? The true, unbiased story?[30] The point of Milbank's genealogy is that there is no 'undistorted' story, because there is no external place from which we could judge what constitutes distortion and what does not: only the illumination of God discerned in multiple modes, only one of which is 'reason', can make truthful discernment possible. Ward recognizes this in acknowledging that *TST* cannot be refuted, 'for there is no position available from which to claim that this story is right or wrong'.[31] This does indeed make Milbank difficult to argue with, and the frustration of his critics reasonable, since it is not clear what one could appeal to if one wants to resist, object or demur. It is this difficulty which has informed my approach here: Milbank must be measured against his own measure, judged by his own standard, which is peace.

As Smith argues, the genealogy of modernity offered by Radical Orthodoxy is self-consciously narratival, since it conceives all reason as narrative.[32] Telling its own story of origins is central to its overall agenda, and the actors in this narrative are given their roles accordingly. Milbank's genealogy should not be read as another attempt at a neutral, rational account of 'how we got here' but a faith-based, prophetic, situated reading of history.[33] It is a theologically weighted

---

29. Ward, 'Commedia', 311.

30. Wayne Hankey raises the concern rather elegantly: 'There is a deep conflict with historical objectivity at the origins of postmodernity, a conflict belonging to its subordination of *theoria* to desire. In their opposition to modernity and their yearning to get beyond its struggles, postmoderns cannot love the necessity in which we have become what we are. The consequence is an incapacity for the loving contemplation of difference which a non-manipulative relation to history requires.' Wayne Hankey, 'The Postmodern Retrieval of Neoplatonism in Jean-Luc Marion and John Milbank and the Origins of Western Subjectivity in Augustine and Eriugena', *Hermathena* 165 (1998): 9–70, 10.

31. Ward, 'Commedia', 315.

32. Smith, *Introducing*, 89.

33. Indeed, Milbank's very point is that the way one tells the story of the tradition just is that tradition – and represents the only real 'argument' for it. '[T]he story of the development of a tradition – for example, in the case of Christianity, a story of preachings, reflections, visions, speculations, journeyings, miracles, martyrdoms, vocations, marriages, icons painted and liturgies sung, as well as of intrigues, sins and warfare – really *is* the

retelling of a Christian heresy, 'modernity', and its orthodox antidote.[34] Of course this raises serious problems concerning the possibility of 'truth' at all, or of responsibility, accountability and intellectual virtue in general, issues which we return to below in light of Janz's critique. Nor does it answer the pressing worry which hovers behind Ward's question: the fact that there is no neutral ground for interpretation does not mean that there is no ground for critical discrimination in the way an interpretation is made.[35] But this in itself is Milbank's point: he is

argument for the tradition (a perilous argument indeed, which may not prove persuasive at all), and not just the story of arguments concerning a certain X (for example the nature of human virtue) lying outside the story' (*TST*, 349, italics added).

34. The recent Milbank recognizes the problematic consequences of trying to hang history on a few ideologically conceived turning points which function as a sort of theological 'fall'. 'I'm not trying to say that the kind of meta-history that we're talking about captures everything that matters. Far from it' (Oliver, 'Radical Orthodoxy: A Conversation', 39–40). He also says that the historical judgement offered in his historical genealogy is not meant to supplant the scholarly work of historians, but rather draws from it, attempting 'to do our amateur best to make sense of the finest research done by philosophers and historians of mediaeval thought', specifically those who are working to show that the Kantian turn is fundamentally a response to Scotism and so is mediaeval in its origins (he names Ludwig Honnefelder, Jean-Francois Courtine, Olivier Boulnois and Jean-Luc Marion as key examples). However, he does emphasize that *insofar* as the changes are fundamentally theological in nature, the pre-eminent competence of theology to interpret these changes is clearly borne out: 'Modern philosophy then has no autonomous ability to assess the conditions of its own genesis. This is the most radical and fundamental of all the claims made by Radical Orthodoxy' (Oliver, 'Radical Orthodoxy: A Conversation', 35–6). In this way, despite perhaps seeming more moderate in tone in comparison to *TST*, he is really reiterating the right of the theologian to be a historian, as well as a scientist, a philosopher, a sociologist and so on.

35. This is the substance of Paul Janz's spirited critique, to which we turn again below. Janz objects to the conception of the intellectual project which underlies Milbank's approach, rather than simply the poor practice of it. He laments the '*formal* (i.e., logical) loss – and thus the utter loss – of the ability to engage in [any] kind of *attentiveness to original intent* or concern, around which I want to focus my critique of what I will call "the new culture of obscurantism" arising from post-subject kinds of thinking, specifically as this is borne out in Milbank's Radical Orthodoxy project. I do not of course mean to suggest that there is one "correct" way of understanding Kant (or any other writer), only that there *are* wrong ways of understanding him' ('Obscurantism', 368). But Janz begs the question to which Milbank is attempting a comprehensive response: if there is no 'right' way, what would it mean for there to be a 'wrong' way? This issue is covered in depth when we turn to the status of natural science in Milbank's thought but is directly raised throughout this whole discussion. Who can authoritatively say what counts as rightness? What standards do they call upon to do so?

attempting to specify just such a criterion. Thus Ward's worry calls for the kind of process undertaken in this book.

Milbank's debt to Augustine's history of the 'two cities' is crucial in understanding the deliberate generation of the antinomial style of his narration. The relation to Augustine, and its faithfulness to that original vision of history, is arguable.[36] Hans Boersma suggests that Milbank's move to do away with boundaries, to welcome all stories, is in irreconcilable tension with the Augustinian presentation of two narratives.[37] But regardless of the historical question, it is this tension which we are bumping up against in trying to respond to Ward, Hyman, Williams and the others who have asked how Milbank's rhetoric of peace can possibly be believed given the violence of his enactment of theology's mastery. Answering Hyman, Milbank explains that the rhetorical persuasiveness of the Christian narrative is not a violent forcing but a peaceful attraction of the good.[38] This disappointing response, cursory to the point of dismissiveness, indicates that there is an *ad hominem* justice to Hyman's worry. But what is at issue here is what Milbank's narrative makes possible. From that ground one can say that Christianity just is that story which is capable of avoiding the violent suppression or denial of difference, because difference is construed as peace. This is the meaning of the claim that the 'mastery' of the Christian narrative is non-mastery.[39] The very force of this claim exposes Milbank's manner of expounding his narrative as unduly supremacist, dualistically generating conflictual antinomies between narratives and thus failing to reflect the

36. See Hans Boersma, 'Radical Orthodoxy and the Rejection of Boundaries', *Pro Ecclesia* 15, no. 4 (2006): 418–47, who argues that Radical Orthodoxy is not Augustinian in the full sense.

37. Boersma, 'Radical Orthodoxy and the Rejection of Boundaries'. Boersma's concern is to defend the need for boundaries and thus discern necessary limits to theology's peaceableness. He sees a troubling failure to defend absolute moral norms in Milbank's rejection of exclusionary logic, taking Milbank's 'liberal' sexual ethics as a case in point. Surely, though, Milbank's contention is that the rejection of exclusionary logic just is the absolute moral norm which is to stand as the guide for all other moral discernment. This moral norm must be located somewhere, and if one is not to locate it in the divine will voluntaristically (and so arbitrarily) conceived, one must locate it in some indelible character of the divine nature which is not simply nominalistically indeterminate. In Milbank's treatment, this is peace.

There is also the simple fact that Milbank (presumably) simply disagrees with Boersma about where non-negotiable moral norms may be; for Milbank, the norms are discerned pragmatically, in a community's life of peaceful embrace of difference through its constantly renewed practices of forgiveness and reconciliation. This is not to say that Milbank's sexual ethics may not be deficient; simply that what Boersma sees as a failure to draw boundaries may simply be a substantive disagreement on the location of non-negotiable moral practice.

38. Milbank, *TST*, xvi.

39. Milbank, *TST*, 6.

Christian story's claimed content of peaceful construal of difference.[40] His style, especially in his earlier work, is frequently confrontational, even 'ruthless'.[41]

We might allow Milbank the rationale offered by another author who, in apology for his own style, explains that irritating minds is the best way to open them, and in Milbank's case it has certainly had the worthy outcome of invigorating discussion and response.[42] But it remains a troubling feature of his work, as it appears prima facie incompatible with his proclamation of 'the path of peaceful flight' as the true way of theology.[43] It witnesses against, and so undermines, the fundamental direction of the narrative, which is to show theology as master discourse precisely in its unique capacity to generously and unlimitedly embrace difference. But if and when he fails to peaceably construe certain differences, or too hastily positions certain narratives as 'over against' the Christian story, this is a disappointing but corrigible failure (as some critics recognize). The content of his proposal does genuinely seek to construe theology in such a way as to bring about reconciled difference: divergent stories do not have to be 'chosen between' but coexist harmoniously as participations in the Good, which as Trinitarian is itself infinite peaceful difference.

A necessary overcoming

Crucially, however – and I offer this qualification as direct response to Coles, and a partial response to Williams and Boersma, who occupy opposite poles of criticism here: Williams wanting a fuller inclusion, Boersma a more definite exclusion –

---

40. Hyman, *Predicament*, 76–8. I am not foreclosing here the question of whether Milbank's approach to knowledge per se actually makes sense or is desirable. That is another question which is touched on repeatedly as this and the following chapters unfold. My point is simply that a total concession be made on the point of Milbank's poor performance (though locating the areas of worse and better performance in relation to his sources is beyond my brief). John Hoffmeyer pursues just the sort of sympathetic approach I am attempting to enact here, taking Milbank at his word when he says he wants an ontology of charity and examining what this would look like if it was consistently applied to the endeavour of interpretation (John Hoffmeyer, 'Charitable Interpretation', in *Interpreting the Postmodern: Responses to 'Radical Orthodoxy'*, ed. Rosemary Ruether and Marion Grau (London: Bloomsbury T&T Clark, 2006), 3–17). Notably, Hoffmeyer suggests that one of the marks of charitable interpretation would be *questionability*, and he invokes Rowan Williams on this point. This is the virtue of allowing oneself to be questioned as well as questioner; and it would not be unfair to charge Milbank with having failed to exhibit precisely this mark.

41. Flanagan, 'Sublime Policing', 334.

42. J. Scott Turner, *The Tinkerer's Accomplice: How Design Emerges from Life Itself* (Cambridge, MA: Harvard University Press, 2007), 2.

43. Milbank, *TST*, 442.

Milbank *is* involved in claiming that certain narratives must be 'overcome' by the Christian story, and these are the narratives which deny peace by construing difference as violence, or which ascribe necessity or ultimacy to conflict.[44] The ontological finality and ultimacy of peace are for Milbank definingly characteristic of the Christian narrative. To dispense with this is to dispense with Christianity altogether. This dispensation may indeed be something Coles is happy to countenance in the name of listening to others' stories – or Hyman in the name of the infinite deferral of any final priority.[45] But since Milbank grants a final priority to the Good as the ultimately peaceful construal of difference, there is an inevitable sense in which non-peaceful construals of difference or attributions of ultimacy to conflict and violence will be countered as incompatible with the Christian metanarrative.[46] Milbank's story is unavoidably committed to competing, for persuasiveness and attractiveness, with stories which narrate an ineradicability of evil and conflict, for Christianity *refuses* the loss of any difference.[47]

Coles finds Milbank's project to out-narrate other stories offensively imperialist. But the insistence on protecting and elevating the difference of others *depends* on taking something to be ultimately and non-negotiably the case. Milbank has taken the only step available if one desires finally to save every story: he has attributed ultimacy only to that which is definitionally incompatible with violence, domination and exclusion, namely harmonious peace. There is only one alternative to this, an alternative which must follow on Coles's and Hyman's accounts in which Christianity really is just another story: to make no uncompromising assertion about reality, and in doing so to give away all they have attempted to save with their talk of difference. To make no final claim about reality is ipso facto to hold to an ultimate undecidability between peace and violence, which is itself the attribution of ontological ultimacy to conflict.[48] Coles attributes no permanent, indispensable value and role to the Christian story: '*if* aspects of the Christian story still have some allure'.[49] Using words of de Certeau, he calls for 'the death of [Christianity's] ideological reassurance of its missionary totalism'.[50] But if this

---

44. See, for example, *Being Reconciled*, 12ff, where Milbank rejects Kant's defence of a freedom *prior to* good and evil.

45. Hyman, *Predicament*, 96.

46. Perhaps this highlights Milbank's fundamental Augustinianism: in the *civitas terrena*, coercion cannot be entirely avoided (*TST*, 423).

47. '[T]he perfect saving of one man from the absolute destruction of death' signifies the '*refusal* of the loss of any difference'; this is what 'spell[s] out to us perfect peace' (Enclaves, 348, italics added).

48. As Milbank comments, on Hyman's view '[t]here would, indeed, have to be a "playful" (but the game is played with money and guns) wandering between these grand stories, implying once more that there is really one single nihilist metanarrative and ontology of violence' (*TST*, xx).

49. Coles, 'Storied Others and Possibilities of *Caritas*', 349.

50. Coles, 'Storied Others and Possibilities of *Caritas*', 350.

death were to occur, if there were after all no story that underwrites the value of every difference beyond all effacement, then anything goes, and for the price of an extinguished metanarrative one has sold off everything else as well. Neither Coles nor Hyman shows evidence of having grasped this: that lacking though Milbank may be in the performance, he is attempting the only conceptual balancing act that will *uncompromisingly* protect and elevate all stories, all others, which will draw a line of total refusal at any loss of difference. That is to claim that a metanarrative of peaceful difference in love is the true story of stories in which all others participate.

Strenuously to refuse ultimate reality to conflict, violence and loss will contingently appear as a denial more often than not. But denying other stories *in their character as enthronements of conflict as ultimate* does not constitute denial in the usual sense; competing with them is not competition in the usual sense.[51] It is more that by articulating a positive one casts the negative in clear relief. In the same way we might say that denying evil is an affirmation. This sort of paradox is intrinsic to belief in the final and exclusive reality of the good; its appearance as exclusive is just its inclusivity seen from a certain point of view. One could construe the decisive option for such finality as the dogmatic insistence that one have the last word. But one could equally argue that it is only by holding 'dogmatically' to the ultimacy of the good that one can defend an *absolute*, and not merely contingent and conditional, space for the other to continue speaking, and for oneself to continue learning.[52] It is surely apparent that Milbank has not successfully enacted this, but his agenda for theology is for the sake of that space, even if he himself closes it down in what we could (generously) see as an overcompensation for theology's historic confinement.[53] This is indeed a lack of patience in the performance but not a fault in the vision itself.

51. Although it would bear extended elaboration, this is the sort of defence that would need to be made against Hyman's claim that Milbank erects a violent dualism between Christianity and nihilism which spawns multiple other dualisms. For insofar as – in Milbank's account – difference and the Good really coincide, stories that deny other stories are deficient precisely as stories; they are, so to speak, suffering privation as narratives. A denial of dualism is not inconsistent with the 'necessary overcoming' defended here. Cf. Milbank, *Being Reconciled*, Chapters 1–2, which outline his account of evil as privation.

52. This sort of defence is surely adumbrated in Milbank's daring, if partial, apologia for the Nietzschean affirmation of power: 'For if, as for Catholic truth, the Good is entirely positive, then power as power is indeed the Good itself in its original inexhaustible plenitude: insofar as it is evil, it is weakness in a final, ontological sense of false unnecessary limitation.' *TST*, xviii. '[O]ne narrates not simply the military tale of the devices and victories of arbitrary power, but also the continuous and sometimes decisive interruption of this story by instances of the reflecting of perfect infinite peaceful power which is the Good.' *TST*, xvi.

53. Milbank's impatient treatment of those to whom he owes most, such as Alasdair MacIntyre and René Girard, has not escaped notice by critics. See, for example, Kerr, 'Rescuing Girard's Argument?', who argues that what Milbank has in common with Girard

In the case of disciplines whose narratives ascribe ultimacy to conflict and/or deny their own necessarily theological character, which for Milbank are mutually reinforcing positions, theology's stance towards those disciplines will necessarily be critical. This is of considerable relevance in an approach to biology. Hanby, Cunningham and others show that biology does often deny its metaphysical status and also perpetuates a nihilistic narrative,[54] and as we shall see, the philosophical biology offered by Jonas evinces ontologically conflictual elements.

Milbank's failure to carry through the peaceableness of the Christian narrative in his own practicing of that narrative calls not for the abandonment of the claim for the ultimacy of peace but for a more faithful enactment (intellectual and material) of that ultimacy in peaceful practices, which will always involve resistance to stories of a final reality of violence.[55] (This is not to foreclose the question of whether we are able always, or usually, correctly to identify such stories.) The rhetorical force in Milbank's prose which has drawn such criticism is to be read in this sense; the emphasis is directed to persuasively showing that peace *is* more compelling than violence. If in its emphasis it fails to be peaceful, then it falls by its own standard, but the standard remains. Further, if Milbank has used violent language of overcoming and conquest in relation to disciplines which do *not* make the sort of claims he is objecting to, then this not an error of principle but rather a sort of empirical error, a failure of attention to the content of those stories of the kind that Flanagan and others have observed in relation to sociology, and an error which is rooted in a basically innocent concern: to liberate theology's gift to every discourse, which is peace.

Thus the basic impetus is non-violent: theology's story is the story which has room for all stories. Theology's own 'difference', which is its 'mastery', is the difference of peace, which it effortfully narrates here below, always with varied consistency and success. Discussing the character of the church, Milbank clarifies the nature of the paradox involved here: the church must deny only that which denies. His view on this acts as a crucial exegesis of his claims to theological

far exceeds what separates him, and that many of Milbank's judgements of Girard in *TST* are tendentious at best.

54. As, for example, in Conor Cunningham, 'Trying My Very Best to Believe Darwin, or, The Supernaturalistic Fallacy: From Is to Nought', in *Belief and Metaphysics*, ed. Conor Cunningham and Peter Candler (London: SCM, 2007), 100–40. Hanby is treated below in Chapter 4.

55. Patience has been mentioned by Williams; more careful attention to sources by Janz; Milbank himself acknowledges the need for humility (Oliver, 'Radical Orthodoxy: A Conversation', 47). It strikes me that the word missing from critics' lexicon as they discuss what is lacking in Milbank is *respect*: a respect grounded in the awareness that to those living them, other narratives possess a total compellingness. To access this totally compelling quality of other narratives as much from 'the inside' as possible must surely be foremost in the mind of the Christian interlocutor.

mastery. There is a 'No' that is required in theology's 'Yes' to difference, but this is emphatically not a 'real exclusion'.

> One way to try to secure peace is to draw boundaries around 'the same', and exclude 'the other'; to promote some practices and disallow alternatives. Most polities, and most religions, characteristically do this. But the Church has misunderstood itself when it does likewise. For the point of the supersession of the law is that *nothing really positive is excluded – no difference whatsoever –* but *only the negative, that which denies and takes away from Being: in other words, the violent.* It is true, however, that Christians perceive a violence that might not normally be recognized, namely any stunting of a person's capacity to love and conceive of the divine beauty; this inhibition is seen as having its soul in arbitrariness. But *there is no real exclusion here*; Christianity should not draw boundaries, and the Church is that paradox: a nomad city.[56]

For Milbank all theology is, in a certain sense, ecclesiology, in that there is no theology outside the church and all theology is done as the church's own reflection on the church's story.[57] The manner in which the church excludes, namely that it excludes only the exclusive, is thus reflective of the right practice of theology, which pursues the church's own goal: 'If [the church] has an abstractly specifiable goal, this is now consensus itself, meaning a society without violence and unjust domination.'[58] It is for and by and on behalf of this *altera civitas*, the peaceful city, that theology is 'queen of the sciences'.[59] That this is a broadly correct understanding is borne out by Milbank's proposal that the church seeks never to foreclose on

56. John Milbank, 'Postmodern Critical Augustinianism: A Short Summa in Forty Two Responses to Unasked Questions', in *The Radical Orthodoxy Reader*, ed. Oliver and Milbank (London: Routledge, 2009), 49–61, 53; italics added. Establishing as normative a principle 'excluding only the exclusive' does not short-circuit the pragmatic discernment that would be required to see how this principle is to be concretely applied in diverse ethical and other fields. Homosexual practice, for example, could be construed as a refusal of difference or not; the question would be to establish the criteria for such refusal.

(Boersma is exercised about Milbank's failure to defend a 'traditional' sexual ethic ('Boundaries', 441ff). Milbank accepts the morality of homosexual unions (*Being Reconciled*, 208), though he rejects same-sex marriage ('Gay Marriage and the Future of Human Sexuality', *ABC Religion and Ethics*, 13 March 2012, http://www.abc.net.au/religion/articles/2012/03/13/3452229.htm, accessed 12 January 2017)). Chapter 7 represents an interpretation of what it might mean to 'exclude only the exclusive' in the context of an approach to biology.

57. '[T]o think a Christian theology, and at the same time to think theology as a social science, one must . . . sketch out a "counter-history" of ecclesial origination, which tells the story of all history from the point of view of this emergence.' Milbank, *TST*, 383.

58. Milbank, *WMS*, 155.

59. Milbank, *TST*, 382.

material and social realities but rather seeks always to gain 'the widest possible "perspective" upon things, a ceaselessly renewed vision of nature and history'.[60] Nothing and no one is to be left out. The goal, which 'is not really beyond the way', is yet eschatological, recapitulatory; it neglects no history, no event, no person; it is 'a perfect reconciliation that implies an absolute consensus'.[61] For Milbank, this just is the truth; as perfect peace, it embraces all non-conflictually and so cannot be a threat to anyone or anything, since it persuades by inclusive invitation.[62] In this sense 'truth is self-authenticating'.[63]

Laying aside the ecclesiological questions that arise from Milbank's comments regarding the nature and constitution of the church,[64] a comment made by Karl Rahner in criticism of Balthasar, a key influence on Milbank, raises the question of whether this non-violence *theologically conceived* is still totalitarian in spirit,

---

60. Milbank, *WMS*, 155.

61. Milbank, *WMS*, 155.

62. Milbank, *WMS*, 250.

63. Oliver, 'Radical Orthodoxy: A Conversation', 43.

64. For a critical discussion of that question, see Boersma, 'Radical Orthodoxy and the Rejection of Boundaries'. While there is no remit here to take up this important issue or to engage with Boersma's critique, particularly as regards Milbank's seeming vacillation regarding actual ecclesiastical (denominational) alignment, it is worth noting once again what many critics seem not to acknowledge: Milbank's own very definite assertion of the failure of the historical church and its sponsorship of extremely non-ideal habits and practices. The accusation that Milbank's ecclesiology is 'idealized' needs to be balanced by a recognition of this admission of the historic entanglement of the institution of the church in violence and exclusion. This 'tragic failure' expresses the divine judgement: 'In the midst of history, the judgement of God has already happened. . . . [E]ither the Church enacts the vision of paradisal community which this judgement opens out, or else it promotes a hellish society beyond any terrors known to antiquity: *corruptio optimi pessima*', and he freely admits that this latter has been historically preponderant (*TST*, 432–3).

Gregory Baum describes Milbank as 'an Anabaptist or Mennonite Barth' who defends 'an Anabaptist, Mennonite ecclesial project, expressed today in the work of John Yoder and Stanley Hauerwas' (Gregory Baum, *Essays in Critical Theology* (Kansas City, MO: Sheed and Ward, 1994), 52, 54. But this is a typical example of an oversimple assumption that Milbank is an idealist about the church. Milbank thinks that the entanglement of the church in sin and brokenness is not only contingently inevitable but almost obligatory, and that a pacifist ecclesiology is idealist. He does, for example, believe in a legitimate coercive power of the church, in the style of Augustine, despite this tugging forcefully in the opposite direction from divine peace (*TST*, 423ff.). This is not meant to exonerate Milbank's theology from charges of ecclesiological ambiguity or lack of concrete engagement; but it is meant to balance the widespread perception that, when it comes to the church, he inhabits cloud-cuckoo land.

insofar as it prematurely manufactures harmony.[65] The denial of denial is all very well, but isn't the forcing of differences into reconciliation, via theological (or ecclesial) mastery, just another form of violent control of others' stories? Given that Milbank is at pains to emphasize the non-excludability of anyone's perspective (acknowledging that he fails in enacting this), this worry is at least in principle answerable: the church just is (albeit only, in its fullness, eschatologically) that body in which no one's point of view is forced into anything. Nevertheless, the concern raised here touches on an important and perhaps salutary divergence between Milbank and his only acknowledged teacher of theology, Rowan Williams.[66] A long-standing difference of view between these two concerns the status of conflict, tragedy and suffering in the pre-eschatological era. Williams is more persuaded by a broadly Hegelian account of the historical inevitability of tragedy and incommensurability of goods in a contingent world; Milbank insists vigorously on the non-inevitability of evil and conflict notwithstanding contingency. This leads them to quite different relationships to the conflicts and incompatibilities of goods suffered in the present:[67] Williams counsels patient refusal to anticipate resolution, to avoid domesticating others by premature ownership of their meanings.[68] This

---

65. 'If we were to behave as if our being Christian gave us a "world-view" in which everything fits together harmonically, we would, in the end, be setting ourselves up to be God. This is because the whole of reality is a symphony only for him. To make pluralism into a symphony – as good old Balthasar does – a symphony that we can hear as such: this is fundamentally impossible' (Philip Endean, *Karl Rahner and Ignatian Spirituality* (Oxford: Oxford University Press, 2001), 259, quoting Rahner).

66. Milbank, *TST*, i.

67. Milbank holds that one must recognize 'a universal tragic condition' but must absolutely avoid ontologizing it (*Being Reconciled*, 149). This would render it intrinsic to being as such and therefore normative, inaugurating an agonistic metaphysics, an error he attributes to Hegel. It is the Good as original plenitude which prevents this error, since it alone can represent a wholly non-reactive moral ontology, which thinks the good as always before and prior to evil. Williams's emphasis on the *agon* intrinsic to the project of truth tugs in the opposite direction from Milbank, who sees agonism as the essence of conflictual ontology. Myers summarizes Rowan's approach: 'There is no final harmony of shared truth, no synthesis, but only a slow limping history of dispossession and negotiation. . . . Above all else it demands patience, the refusal of any anaesthetic against the "agon" of truth. Patience is never a sedate acceptance of things as they are but a costly commitment to endure unresolved difficulty, vulnerability and loss. . . . [W]e must resist the desire to mend the tragic quality of human relationships' (Benjamin Myers, *Christ the Stranger: The Theology of Rowan Williams* (London: T&T Clark, 2012), 55).

68. Myers discussion obliquely illuminates Williams's profound effect on Milbank's theology (though Milbank is never mentioned) by highlighting the presence in Williams of Hegelian themes which strongly resemble Milbank's own fundamental concerns, specifically the social mediation of truth and the non-opposition of identity and difference. It also throws into sharper relief the deep divergence between the two: for Williams, difference

divergence could be framed in terms of different relationships to the *eschaton*: Milbank could be accused of immanentizing the eschaton, which he holds we always (albeit remotely) anticipate, a problem which is particularly acute if there is vacillation over the exact character and location of the church in history;[69] Williams, on the other hand, might be held to overemphasize the *eschaton*'s remoteness and discontinuity from the present.[70]

This prompts a theological reader of Milbank to want to make a further step explicit in order to secure the agenda as non-theocratic: a fully peaceful form of this account would stipulate that theology cannot prematurely shut down, deny or silence the divergences and immanent-historical incompatibilities between stories, notwithstanding that these may result in a kind of violent competition at the human and conceptual level, including within the church. Milbank anticipates this sort of account when he says that the sought-for consensus of the church occurs only 'unpredictably, through the blending of differences, and by means of these differences, not despite them'.[71] To forcibly shut these kinds of conflicts down would be an act of violent foreclosure of the sort Williams warns against. Living patiently with such conflicts, aware of their necessarily irresolvable character before the *eschaton*, theology narrates only the non-ultimacy of such conflict and not the detailed manner of its resolution. This is not to say that Milbank's emphasis on the non-inevitability of such conflict needs to be abandoned – only that its practice needs to fit its principle. The real continuity between the approaches of Milbank and Williams is the refusal to sponsor conflict, even though Williams is more likely to say that we cannot avoid wounding others given the structure of the pre-eschatological world.

Having accepted this important stipulation, two qualifications against Rahner and Williams should be voiced. First, to enact such peaceful practice does involve

---

is to be 'endured'; the encounter across difference results not in peace and harmony but in dispossession; and the exchange that occurs is characterized by arduous negotiation rather than gratuity: 'the distance between myself and another is never overcome but only reasserted and sustained' (*Stranger*, 54–5).

69. John Milbank, 'The Programme of Radical Orthodoxy', in *Radical Orthodoxy? A Catholic Enquiry*, ed. Laurence Paul Hemming (Aldershot: Ashgate, 2000), 33–45, 34; also *Being Reconciled*, 9.

70. For Milbank the anticipation of eschatological peace and plenitude is the essential quality of truly moral action. '[H]ope . . . that it may be given to me in the next moment to act well, is inseparable from hope that there may be a universal acting-well, and at last a non-futile mourning; to be ethical therefore is to believe in the Resurrection, and somehow to participate in it. And outside this belief and participation there is, quite simply, no "ethical" whatsoever' (*Being Reconciled*, 148). How these different views translate into the life of the church is a question beyond this study, although one cannot help noting that Williams's ecclesiology seems on the whole the more concrete of the two, no doubt for good vocational reasons.

71. Milbank, *WMS*, 155.

theology in interrogating and resisting narrations in which conflict is determined as what is finally real. Second, if reality is indeed a symphony only for God, then it is for theology constantly to attempt a narration of this symphony from the midst of history. '[T]he gospel instruction to love all, is an instruction to narrate all, attain to the highest possible perspective' which is nevertheless 'an impossible act of perfect remembrance'.[72] This always-renewed re-narration just is Christian practice: it is telling the story of the world's history as salvation history. This telling is a reading of all things in light of their beginning, which is God's uncoerced and unrivalrous gift of being, and their end, which is the divine peace of the city of God. Such a narration is a necessary enactment of the faith that God's purposes and historical time do truly converge, not just chronologically 'at the end', so to speak, but ontologically now, as a result of the gift-character of creation itself. On this view, theology has the humanly impossible task of making the space for differences to be themselves peacefully, while recognizing the paradoxical outcome of this – that theology must deny denials of difference. This requires of theologians a peculiar asceticism: to deny only by affirmation; to reject only by the limitless welcome of charity.[73]

This paradox is pervasive in Milbank's thought, even if its presentation is often inconsistent and partial, and the mortification necessary to practice it is not always evinced. It is congruent with another paradox which is equally ubiquitous in his work: the paradox of needing to say something ultimate, not being able to avoid saying something ultimate, while recognizing that one is constitutively incapable of saying anything that is not relative and mediated. Milbank deals with this paradox by refusing the presentation of these options as alternatives: ultimacy and relativity are reconciled (but not reduced to one another) by participation, by the impossibility of securing self-referring immanence on its own terms.[74] Thus he is able to say, without embarrassment, that 'every human difference is itself elevated to universality': every difference is to be paradoxically universalized.[75]

---

72. Milbank, *WMS*, 156.

73. One doubts that this defence would satisfy Williams, who, one can guess, would still be concerned about the danger of totalitarian foreclosure even on this carefully qualified reading of 'mastery'. Williams is surely Milbank's most astute critic, and the former's theological style, in its patience, care, and continual qualification of its own claims, a serious reproach to Milbank's theological voice. But as Graeme Richardson observes, 'Williams the cautious ecclesiastic is likely to be bound in ways that Milbank the speculative theologian is not' ('Integrity and Realism', 268).

74. 'The Double Glory, or Paradox Versus Dialectics: On Not Quite Agreeing with Slavoj Žižek', in *The Monstrosity of Christ: Paradox or Dialectic*, ed. Creston Davis (Cambridge, MA: MIT Press), 110–234, particularly 163–4.

75. Milbank, *WMS*, 156. Contrasting Christianity's combination of universalism and particularism with the other Semitic faiths, he explains the uniqueness of Christianity in terms of Christ as the convergence of these two movements: 'the universalist thrust of Christianity is more extreme than that of Judaism and Islam, besides being more complex.

Milbank attempts to concretize this in his Christological poetics, which is dedicated to showing that this paradox is fully visible only in Christ.[76] No doubt this formulation is too abstract, circumventing actual human differences in their angularity: the difference of being a Hitler versus a Mother Teresa, for example. An insistence on the privative quality of evil would be crucial for him in negotiating this sort of question: Hitler's 'difference' is limited and impoverished by the evils he commits. Whether or not Milbank is successful in this sort of account, it is the underlying direction of his narrative, notwithstanding contraindications of style; it remains the lens through which to see the function and intention of the narrative as a whole.

In this narrative, it is only the nihilistic myth of autonomy that makes us think ultimacy and relativity are mutually incompatible opposites. The Cusan model of conjecture is central in Milbank's negotiation of this drive towards ultimacy from immanence, which we explore further below. These paradoxes are parallel to the further and most fundamental paradox of grace and nature which, interpreting Milbank as a member of the *nouvelle théologie* project, drives his whole enterprise: nature is nature only through its constitutive orientation to grace; it has its being only as, in fact, not 'having' it at all, but constantly receiving it from above as an inexhaustibly new and unexpected gift.

Returning to our principal question regarding the relationship of theology to the disciplines: how can we apply these reflections to that specific aspect of theology's intellectual practice? Are we still required to deny 'autonomy' to the disciplines? Theology's making-space for differences must include welcoming the differences of the disciplines. And yet for Milbank this role of enabling difference is exactly what makes an 'outside' of theology impossible: the dignity of discourses cannot depend on, or be constituted by, their independence of a theological account of the world. Such an independence would be both impossible and nihilistic. Exactly how theology's denial of autonomy can constitute a positive enablement remains to be fully explicated, and it is this which we explore in more depth in the next chapter. But we can stipulate on the basis of what we have said that theological 'mastery' would be, in principle, *not* a dominating mastery but the establishment of the conditions for the flourishing of the other disciplines. Theology is committed to challenging disciplinary narratives which court nihilism by ascribing ultimacy to conflict, and so there is an element of critique in this 'mastery' of other disciplines which contingently appears as an 'overcoming'. But what is overcome is violence, denial of difference, not any specific disciplinary difference in its positive reality.

For on the one hand, the final revelation of God as Man suggests that the traces of truth are found everywhere within the *humanum*. On the other hand, it suggests that humanity can only be re-united through the common recognition of this one man, Christ, as the concrete event, beyond all laws and prescriptions, of the arrival of fully restored human truth' ('Faith, Reason and the Imagination', 4).

76. Milbank, *WMS*, 121–68.

To anticipate the next step of this argument developed below, what calls for challenge is the conception that an authentic science is one which is non-theological, as this amounts to scientific self-destruction. In this sense it is indeed the case that science's autonomy is being radically denied, but this denial amounts only to the claim that science too is a metaphysics which is theological in its constitution. If it denies transcendence it becomes nihilistic, for no science can secure itself from below. The denial of autonomy for the disciplines is therefore an affirmation which *contingently* appears as a denial. So this agenda for theology does not theocratically eradicate difference, including disciplinary diversity. Rather, it insists that there is no 'outside' theology, no 'outside' God, and this grounds the meaningfulness of the disciplines.

Hans Boersma, discussing the traditional title of theology as 'Queen of the Sciences', proposes a new one which should regulate it: theology as 'Queen of Hospitality'. Theology welcomes the difference of the disciplines without relinquishing its claim to definitive authority. Boersma is clear that this view of theology as queen of hospitality is not only compatible with but actually follows from a denial of autonomy to the disciplines.[77] It is because there is no outside to *God's* hospitality that theology conducts its role as host.[78] Boersma argues that this theological authority operates in relation to the disciplines as an internal voice and not an extrinsic de jure force. This specification of theology as queen of sciences is an approach we shall find space for in Chapter 4's discussion.

The status of 'scientific' knowledge

Allowing that Milbank's position is not *in principle* destructive of difference, even if it ends up being so in practice, the question remains regarding how this applies to the disciplines in particular. This will be the concern in Chapter 4, where an extended comparison with Michael Hanby helps to expose the specific shape of Milbank's account of theology in relation to the disciplines. In advance of this treatment, we turn to the second concern mentioned in our introductory comments to this chapter: does this conception of knowledge itself undermine natural science? This section explores the effect of Milbank's conception of knowledge and reason on the nature and possibility of 'scientific' knowledge. It is argued that, despite its seeming lack of promise, such a conception of knowledge secures the integrity of science as a discourse which seeks the real.

77. Though his account of this denial is less than comprehensive. Hans Boermsa, 'Theology as Queen of Hospitality', *EQ* 79, no. 4 (2007): 291–310, 303.

78. 'If theologians are to fulfill their role well, they need to remember that theology's authority is an authority of servitude. The queen of hospitality serves to draw people into the divine future of truth, goodness, and beauty.' Boersma, 'Theology as Queen of Hospitality', 306.

To engage this question we need to revisit the kinds of concerns raised by Janz, who focuses on the status of reference and accountability in Milbank's work.[79] He proposes that by 'overcoming the subject', Milbank's approach involves abandoning values intrinsic to intellectual virtue,[80] such as accuracy and clarity: what he calls 'obscurantism'. If there is no subject, how can there be an object to which the subject is accountable? While Ward remains fundamentally sympathetic to the narrative project, Janz represents a more recognizably Enlightenment account of critical reason. If 'about-language', intentionality, referentiality and the aspiration to true description are rendered nonsensical by the dissolution of the epistemological subject, how can the project of 'natural science' survive?

That Milbank's work in *TST* is 'obscurantist' in the sense of evincing a certain recklessness with regard to sources or history has been admitted. And it has already been said that an Enlightenment conception of neutrality, 'accuracy' to a subject-independent reality, representation of world by mind, dialectics over rhetoric and narrative, embodies a loaded and contestable standard of what constitutes intellectual virtue which, in Milbank's picture, buys into a deracinated conception of reason. But more than this, in terms of the substance of Milbank's conception of knowledge, Janz's comprehensive assault on Milbank's 'obscurantism' fails to identify the critical dimension of Milbank's account of reason. Although Milbank is committed to rejecting representationalism and other kinds of reasoning based on a subject-object dualism, he does not frame reason in a way that absolves it of any constraining or governing end. Indeed, for him the secular space is defined precisely as 'the sphere of the arbitrary', sheer power or *dominium* ungoverned by any *telos* outside the will.[81] True reason is convergent with harmony and the good. Regardless of how and whether this is successfully cashed out in his work, the point is that for Milbank reason and, therefore, truth are not simply what we want them to be but are shaped and governed by a *telos*. The overcoming of the subject does not signify that there is no normativity, simply that normativity is not to be framed as a spurious objectivity; it exceeds anything that a self-contained reason could 'independently' accomplish or demonstrate.

Milbank's idea of 'teleological constraint' is elucidated below. For now, this approach allows us to see the normative force of an emphasis on one particular narrative as defining the shape of true reason. The fact that, on the sort of view of truth Milbank is defending, there is no such thing as 'intellectual virtue' outside

---

79. Janz takes the fundamental text here to be Milbank's 'The Theological Critique of Philosophy', but he regards subsequent works as continuing and reinforcing the same trajectory. He sees an anti-rational, anti-epistemological attitude as the defining characteristic of Radical Orthodoxy itself. 'Obscurantism', 365.

80. Janz lists these as the 'virtues of clarity, logical consistency, argumentative integrity (e.g., avoidance of gratuitous circularity), modesty, economy, circumspect self-critique, avoidance of grandiloquence, and a commitment to certain basic principles of intellectual charity' ('Obscurantism', 366).

81. Milbank, *TST*, 18.

a particular tradition of what constitutes rationality and responsibility does not signify an 'anything goes' mentality, as the charge of anti-rationalism would have it. It is simply that the notion of responsibility to history, or of intellectual probity, emerges from the Christian evaluation of time and change and the conception of a divine truth in which human minds participate. The values which Western philosophy and natural science take as axiomatic are far from 'axiomatic' in the sense of self-evident and obvious to all; rather, they derive historically from a particular narrative of the creation, redemption and sanctification of *this* singular, unrepeatable world through its linear unfolding in time, which imparts the highest dignity to matter and history, gives them a definite purpose and an intrinsic intelligibility, and so makes them worthy objects of knowledge. To isolate them from this narrative brings about a loss of coherence. It is in this sense that for Milbank *mythos* has a priority to *Logos*: it is through the *story* of the Word, the attraction it exercises over us, that we have come to believe in this truth, which is not a truth like other truths.[82] 'Science' is subsequent to story; but the mode of distinction between stories is not random.

This claim for the priority of story does not, therefore, have the effect of undermining science, but rather gives it a purchase, since it is only in the light of a particular version of what reality is and how it can be known that the notions of 'truth' or 'rationality' are meaningful at all. The effect of Milbank's claims on the status of science is not undermining of its legitimacy as a realist discourse, although 'realism' must necessarily have its own meaning in the Christian *mythos*, where the real is measured as peace, and so is in a certain sense 'pragmatic'.[83] To understand what this means concretely, the following sections look more closely at exactly how Milbank conceives 'reality'. The means by which he does this is through his theological valorization of *poesis*, which occupies the next section. Since knowing is an instance of making, 'science' is fully included in this valorization. This use of *poesis* thus avoids dualist correspondence-style realisms which undermine the reciprocity of 'mind' and 'world', while remaining committed to the real significance of human thoughts and actions through attributing to them some participation in the divine making. This position is what Milbank calls, via Blondel, 'theological objectivism'.[84] He employs the Christian narrative to give the very highest estimation of our knowledges: all knowledge is theological.

82. This is not at all to deny that the truth is uncompelling in the absence of the virtues it implies, such as charity to opponents, humility which is expressed in a willingness to listen and a sense of not being in sole personal possession of the whole narrative. In Milbank's terms, one can simply say that the absence of these virtues renders truth impossible: not 'true' because not peaceful.

83. 'I reject . . . [a] merely philosophic realism in favour of "linguistic idealism" and a variant of pragmatism – even though this assumes a realist cast within my final theological perspective' (*TST*, 5). The meaning of this pragmatism is considered below.

84. Milbank, *TST*, 219.

Milbank continues and extends the *nouvelle théologie*'s account of nature as always already graced by taking more seriously the ubiquity of cultural and linguistic mediation, historicizing both grace and nature in the process. This involves placing theology on the side of postmodern constructivism and relativism with respect to the status of nature and knowledge, by claiming that the postmodern primacy of temporal and historical mediation was latent in the Christian *mythos* from the start. The distinctive addition is that, because making, of which knowing is an instance, is construed as a participation in God, this constructivism does not lead to nihilistic anti-realism. The claim that there exists a 'real world' to which our language must 'correspond' is denied without denying the real itself; instead the real is defended by re-envisioning the relationship of mind and world, soul and body, God and creation in an analogical, participatory manner. The self-excessive character of human action that Milbank finds articulated in Blondel, for whom our doings exceed not only our own intentions or conceptions but also the opposition between subject and object on which modernity trades, allows him to elevate human fabrication in a way that allows for a fuller theological appropriation of postmodernity. Whether one thinks this is coherent or not, it is clear that Milbank is not seeking an 'anti-realism' but is aiming to transcend modernity's dichotomy of realism versus anti-realism by challenging the divorce of epistemology from ontology which leads first to Descartes and finally to the captivity of theology by philosophical modernity.[85]

This does, of course, constitute a critique of 'natural science' as commonly conceived. At the very least it involves contesting modern constructions of 'nature'. Where 'nature' refers to a self-contained sphere of pure immanence, in which wholly external and controllable objects are perceived by a wholly internal mind, the truth of whose conceptualizing consists in its mirror-like correspondence with nature, then '*natural* science' is indeed targeted. In the mode of participatory metaphysics supported by Milbank, where it is married to a historicizing programme, the revision of the meaning of 'nature' extends to the relativization of scientific narratives of it. Every scientific narrative is constructing nature in a particular way – usually, in the modern period, by internalizing a theological construction of nature as autonomous and self-contained. To grant to any science an 'autonomy' would be to say that there could be non-theological, non-narrative sciences and that there is an inert nature/life/society which can be empirically known as a purely external object. But since nature is not given in a positivistic manner, it can only be known through construction, and my contention in this

---

85. Hyman argues that a penetrating critique of Milbank is possible only once one has grasped that Milbank has precisely not opted for a mere anti-realism but has decisively rejected the realist/anti-realist alternative as remaining trapped within the schema of modernity. Thus 'if a critique of Radical Orthodoxy is to be effective, it must move beyond and leave behind the realist/anti-realist framework altogether' (*Predicament*, 6). Cf. Olivier Tromans, 'Analogy, Synergy, Revelation: Divine-Humanity in John Milbank's Poetic Theology', *New Blackfriars* 102 (2021): 189–204.

section is that given Milbank's theological appropriation of *verum quia factum est*, science's relativization is not an impugnment. The opening sections of *TST* explore the point that such an insight is not as foreign to the history of the natural sciences as might now be assumed.[86] It fits comfortably with the self-understanding of the early scientists who sought a technical manipulation of nature, a turning of nature to our use, rather than a merely contemplative *theoria*. Knowledge of nature was correlated with human artifice. The value or disvalue of this move is a point we shall find Milbank and Hanby differing on, an important divergence which can be framed as a disagreement over the relative priority of action and contemplation. For Milbank the problem was not modernity's emphasis on the *factum* per se, which he celebrates as proper to orthodoxy, but the identification of this with the sphere of the secular, the autonomous; the objectionable element was the equation of the artificial with the instrumental.[87]

Poesis *revisited*

Where then, in this relativizing programme, does 'the real' appear? This is the key question for understanding how 'science' can survive as a discourse defined by its aspiration to knowledge of the real. Milbank's answer to this in *TST* is the 'theological objectivism' he finds Blondel supporting through his interpretation of *poesis* as inherently transcendent in orientation. In his philosophy of action, according to Milbank, Blondel 'succeeds in separating philosophical realism from theological objectivism', by inaugurating

> a 'supernatural pragmatism', for which the reference to an infinite, divine reality occurs through the effort 'outwards' from the subject and 'forwards' to the future, more perfect repetition of what is already given. . . . . [He] shows that if theology embraces a more thorough-going perspectivism, pragmatism and historicism, it can escape from the 'modern' illusions which claim that a purely finite, immanent science (including social science) can offer an ontology, or account of 'the way things really are'.[88]

Our knowledges are not self-referential but strain beyond themselves. The key here is the uncircumscribability of the finite and the analogous exchange of predicates between finite and infinite, which renders immanence so entirely pervaded by transcendence that theology need no longer fear perspectivism, pragmatism and

---

86. The agenda of Mary Hesse and the instrumentalist philosophers of science resembles Milbank's own to a degree; Hesse targeted the 'hypothetico-deductive method', which Milbank mentions with disdain (*TST*, 271). See, for example, Michael Arbib and Mary Hesse, eds., *The Construction of Reality* (Cambridge: Cambridge University Press, 1986).

87. Milbank, *TST*, 11–12.

88. Milbank, 220.

historicism, since perspectives, actions and history really mediate the divine. Materiality, time, language and human intellectual acts mediate God to an extent that we cannot measure or define. This removes nature and therefore metaphysics from the exclusive competence of an autonomous reason, 'philosophy'. It is this recognition of the entire permeation of immanence by transcendence, the non-definability of immanence 'by itself', so to speak, which leads Milbank to give to Blondel his highest praise: 'Thus Blondel, more than anyone else, points us beyond secular reason.'[89]

Blondel pursued a phenomenological account of the subjective appropriation of God's revelation, to a degree that led him to be accused of modernism.[90] He vigorously accused his contemporary opposition, a movement both theological and political which called for a return to neo-scholastic Thomism, as '*monophorisme*', or a 'single-afference' conception of the operation of grace which held grace to be exclusively objective, given from without, resulting in nature-grace extrinsicism.[91] It is in Blondel's account of 'science' that the burden of the current discussion and of Milbank's elevation of *poesis* becomes clearer.[92] Blondel's conception of 'science' is presented in explicit criticism of a Cartesian model, being a defence of a broader account of the nature of scientific understanding than was then reigning under the positivist conditions of the day. It is anti-representationalist in arguing that it is action itself which overcomes the modern subject-object dichotomy. Action surpasses the subject-object poles and unites them; it is more concrete, more immediate, than 'knowledge' externally conceived. Action is the true science:

---

89. Milbank, 220. It is worth noting that, notwithstanding this high praise, Blondel sought to maintain a securer distinction between philosophy and theology than Milbank would support, and indeed Milbank makes his departure from Blondel clear on this point (*TST*, 218). Milbank's account of nature and grace is more radically eliding of any delimitable boundary between the two, following de Lubac (on his interpretation, at least), attributing to human action a higher and more supernatural value. This is related to Milbank's denial of a purely philosophical account of human action, which Blondel explicitly seeks, notwithstanding that he argues that such an account brings philosophy to acknowledgement of its own incompleteness. For Milbank, Blondel's philosophy is still too autonomous. Oliva Blanchette clarifies Blondel's conception of the status of philosophy, with reference to his works on this subject after *L'Action* of 1893, in 'Rationale for a Catholic Philosophy', *Revista Portuguesa di Filosofia* 60, no. 2 (2004): 329–48.

90. The historical context of Blondel's work is ably summarized by William Portier, 'Twentieth Century Catholic Theology and the Triumph of Maurice Blondel', *Communio* 38 (2011): 103–37; see especially 107–10, where he discusses the place of Blondel's thought in the modernist crisis.

91. For my account of Blondel here I am indebted to Oliva Blanchette's 1984 translation of *L'Action*, and his later biography of Blondel, *Maurice Blondel: A Philosophical Life* (Grand Rapids, MI: Eerdmans, 2010), as well as his 'Blondel's Original Philosophy of the Supernatural', *Revista Portuguesa di Filosofia* 49, no. 3 (1993): 413–44.

92. Milbank, *TST*, 215–16.

'it is the fiction itself which enables us to reach reality',[93] in the sense that action is fiction, doing is making. It is in this light that Blondel's project to elaborate 'a *science* of practice' should be understood: the science of practice is the knowledge of action, the knowledge that action *is*: making, or fictioning. 'The final certitude remains grounded on the initial fiction.'[94]

> [Blondel's] appeal to 'the science of action' was not to establish a new foundationalism but to undercut late nineteenth-century scientific foundationalism by acknowledging that all sciences presuppose certain fictions, or what postmodernists might call narratives. As Jean-François Lyotard has observed 'Scientific knowledge cannot know and make known that it is the true knowledge without resorting to the other, narrative, kind of knowledge, which from its point of view is no knowledge at all.' How else can scientific 'discoveries' be understood and explained except by means of a story with actors, a setting, a context of activity, a beginning and an end?[95]

While for Blondel, action is the true science, the true knowing, for Milbank, the only science is theology. But this is simply because it is theology alone which establishes action – the whole panoply of human doings and makings – as true science, which, due to his divergence from Blondel regarding the competence of philosophy, Milbank thinks philosophy cannot accomplish by itself.

Blondel needs, Milbank claims, to be read as theology, not philosophy. As theology, he reads Blondel's account of action in terms of grace, through which alone action can be deciphered as love.[96] In Blondel's treatment, according to Milbank, every act of knowing demands supernatural supplement. This is because, for Blondel, 'the willing will' (*la volonté coulante* – the condition or underlying root of all willing) can never be equalled by 'the willed will' (*la volonté coulue* – determinate acts of the will). This is simply to say that the human will finds no adequate object for its willing; by the very nature of the will, such an adequation cannot be finitely available.[97] The aspiration of willing itself exceeds the bounds of finitude. The exigency of the supernatural is established by the unavoidable presupposition or willing itself: for Blondel, the ground of every action in the subject is an implicit faith, inherent in the very character of the willing will, that 'a new and correct "synthesis" will be discovered, and that this self-grounded norm is more than arbitrary'; and since we experience the inadequacy of our own will

---

93. Maurice Blondel, *L'Action, Essay on a Critique of Life and a Science of Practice*, trans. Oliva Blanchette (Notre Dame: University of Notre Dame Press, 1984), 68.

94. Blondel, *L'Action*, 70–1.

95. Adam English, '"Science Cannot Stop with Science": Maurice Blondel and the Sciences', *Journal of the History of Ideas* 69, no. 2 (2008): 269–92, 289–90, quoting Lyotard.

96. Milbank, *TST*, 218.

97. Blanchette gives a fuller account of this inadequation in 'Blondel's Original Philosophy of the Supernatural', 414ff.

to establish this norm, we implicitly presuppose an infinite power beyond the finite series of actions which is alone able to bring our actions to such synthesis, in which alone the satisfaction of our will can be established.[98] This is the exigency of the supernatural appearing in action, and it expresses the mysterious *concursus* of divine grace with human freedom: 'Every action is entirely our own, and entirely transcends us.'[99] But for Blondel, although philosophy can establish this exigency, it cannot ascertain the actual presence of this gift. By more definitely overcoming an *a priori* difference of philosophy from theology, Milbank moves decisively towards a concrete assertion of the real historical presence of grace in human action on the grounds of the logic of action itself. This is beyond Blondel, and Blondel would not recognize it as 'philosophy'; but Milbank's intention is always to blur the distinction.

Milbank pushes this in the direction of the linguistic turn by interpreting it in terms of signification: our actions cannot avoid transcending themselves in an excess of signification over which we are never in control. Read as theology, the escape of signs is not the vicious Derridean *différance* of endless deferral but the virtuous excess of transcendence freely giving itself, appearing unmeasurably within immanence. Again, this alternative cannot be 'rationally' discriminated; the theological option must convict through rhetorical performance, which will be primarily in the acted-out story of the city of God in history. Blondel's philosophy read as theology becomes theological objectivism: the divine is the real in every human action. The objectivism is theological because it is God who is inescapably implied in the fiction which makes reality, not simply an unknown surd which escapes untraceably into a dark future. This is the 'location' of the real in our thoughts, imaginings, speech acts and physical interventions in the world. Language about the real is, then, properly configured in terms of the presence of God in our makings as grace or gift, which specifies the connection Milbank always seeks to make between 'truth' and 'peace': the divine is present in our makings as gratuitous donation without contrast and thus is wholly non-conflictual. But this is only what we should expect, since the true and the real of the Christian narrative are not the 'truth' and the 'reality' of the earthly city.

It is only such a treatment which saves science from postmodern flux negatively conceived, insofar as no act of knowing of anything is just a knowing of that thing. The centrality of this theme for Milbank is clear in his favouring of the Meno problematic, received via Augustine. Knowledge is always more than we know it to be in each act of knowing: you can't know anything *by itself*, you always know more than you know, and this is the 'faith' dimension of knowledge.[100] On a modern

98. Milbank, *TST*, 215.

99. Milbank, *TST*, 215.

100. See Milbank, *TST*, xxiii; also John Milbank, 'The Programme of Radical Orthodoxy', in *Radical Orthodoxy? A Catholic Enquiry*, ed. Laurence Hemming (London: Routledge, 2017), 33–45, 35, where he explains at more length: 'And just as both reason and faith are framed by the participation of our being and knowing in the divine being and intellection,

conception of reason as pure and autonomous, this is inevitably construed as making knowledge impossible: you can't know anything without knowing everything, and since you can't know everything, you can't know anything. This is the spirit of nihilism, of an infinite deferral with inscrutable origins. But there is no *a priori* reason against the alternative: to construe this state of affairs as a participation in the excess of transcendence. The sheer 'rational' undecidability between these two options is precisely Milbank's point about the arbitrariness of the nihilistic option; it is no more grounded in 'fact' than is the reading of participated transcendence. A metaphysics of participation means that we know God implicitly in everything we know and so accounts for how we do, mysteriously, know more than we know in every act of knowing. There is therefore an eschatological dimension to every act of knowing; it anticipates a fullness beyond its horizon.[101]

Coupled with a poetic construal of knowledge, signification as infinite regress, *différance*, is saved by transcendence pervading the uncircumscribable finite; nothing is knowable merely as finite, as circumscribed. What causes us to see negative regress or intrinsic orientation of finitude to transcendence is, ultimately, only a matter of desire and attraction. The role of rhetoric is based on the beauty of God as the infinite harmony of reconciled difference, and so it is not (in principle, at least) the rhetoric of the earthly city, which is a rhetoric of coercive power. This point could be expanded on to pacify critics of Milbank on this issue: 'reason' alone cannot establish whether the unboundedness of signification, the faith-begging character of knowledge, is gift or curse. Only the attractiveness of one story rather than another, something like Aquinas' aesthetic category of *convenientia*, 'fittingness', can give us a 'reason' for thinking one or the other.[102] For Milbank the final form of truth is peace: it is the truly desirable, the most compelling, precisely because it is that which leaves nothing and no one out, it excludes only that which excludes, and as peace it coerces no one. But this priority of peace is for the sake of grounding reason, not for the sake of undermining it. Only if reason and language do not have to be self-justifying will their instability, their lack of closure, not be their dissolution.

So for Milbank, just as there is 'virtue', 'truth', 'soul' and 'polis' in the earthly city, and there are those things differently in the city of God, there are equally two constructivisms – a theological and a (putatively) secular. The latter is a Plotinian-style idealism which emphasizes the interior construction of appearance by

so also they are both – reason as much as faith – framed by eschatology. For reason to think at all, it must somehow already know what it seeks to know; reason, to be reason, must therefore also be faith, and in articulating this view in different ways Augustine, Anselm and Aquinas are all conscious that at the heart of their Christian articulation of grace and revelation they are nonetheless radicalising and resolving the specifically Platonic view that reason, to be reason, in some fashion knows before it knows.'

101. Milbank, 'Programme', 35.

102. Discussed in Milbank and Pickstock, *Truth in Aquinas* (52ff.); we turn to this theme again below.

thought, which he finds in modernity paradigmatically represented by Fichtean constructivism. The former is to be found in the 'alternative modernity' he celebrates, which counters univocity and representationalism with a symbolic, analogical participatory model, transforming the Platonic conception of participation into a symbolic realism which attends better to the mediation of the infinite eternal by time, language and bodies. Beginning with the Proclean theurgic tradition and represented in modernity by Vico, Hamann, Jacobi and Coleridge, the alternative modernity conceived of human making in a different way. Milbank has pursued a

> consistent distinguishing of a modern-yet-conservative 'internal' and 'idealist' constructivism – of appearances by thought – from a 'shadow-modern' yet more radical external and *more 'realist' constructivism* – of culture and to a degree nature by the human psychic-corporeal unity.[103]

The idealist, interiorized constructivism obscures the real mediative significance of human action. Our construction does not occur within us in a pristine self-contained realm of pure thought but is radically external; as 'outside' us, our action makes the world as mysteriously more than ourselves.

'Science' is a fiction. How this is construed, as nihilistic regress, or as mediative *poesis* which participates in the real, depends on whether modernity or Christian countermodernity determines the content of our fictions.[104] For Christian theology is the true science of action, in which every act of human knowing is regarded as uncircumscribable participation in God.

Conjecture and theurgy

'Conjecture' and 'theurgy' are crucial markers in the 'alternative modernity' Milbank sponsors, marking the 'upward' and 'downward' dimensions of human action: both express the presence of the real *in* action and not simply as its object. The 'downward' movement is expressed for Milbank by the Neoplatonic theurgic tradition.[105] As

103. Milbank, *TST*, xx; italics added.

104. Johannes Hoff, *The Analogical Turn* (Grand Rapids: Eerdmans, 2013), represents perhaps the most incisive attempt to trace the real, though forgotten, possibility of a Christian countermodernity and the 'knowledge' that it makes possible. Hoff proposes that Cusa represents a the true 'analogical' alternative to the univocity of modernity and the equivocity of postmodernity. Hoff's critique of representationalist epistemology echoes many of this chapter's key concerns.

105. Iamblichus' materialization of Platonism is central for Milbank: there is 'a basic convertibility of Christianity and the Iamblichian paradox of participation' (John Milbank and Aaron Riches, 'Foreword', in *Theurgy and the Soul: The Neoplatonism of Iamblichus*, ed. Gregory Shaw (Kettering, OH: Angelico Press/Sophia Perennis, 2014), v–xviii, xi). For Iamblichus the human soul, as fully and not partially (unlike for Plotinus) descended,

liturgical beings we summon the divine into our performances; God is demanded by our action and yet his presence in it, though necessary to the integrity of our action, is paradoxically entirely free. The free descent of God in the Incarnation, who plays both the man who summons and the God who is summoned, remains the true type and fulfilment of this.[106] The second direction is 'upward', the spontaneous reach of human action towards the transcendent. This 'upward' movement is expressed by Milbank principally in the Cusan style of 'conjecture' which emphasizes human action as creative expression reaching towards infinitude.[107] The necessity of this conjecture, for Milbank, is the necessity of a constitutive metaphysics in the absence of a rationalist 'guarantee' of its contents: 'infinity does not appear, yet has to be presupposed, if we are to have norms and values.'[108] This conjectural character of thought is not

accessed the divine precisely by the mediation of material realities: '[T]he highest good was not realised by escaping from materiality but by embracing matter and multiplicity in a demiurgic way'; 'matter and images . . . truly communicate the transcendent' (vii, xiii). Particularly important for Milbank is Iamblichus' conception of theurgy, the divinizing activity in which human action both summons and mediates the divine, which via Proclus, Dionysius, Augustine and Maximus is continuous with the Christian conception of sacrament and incarnation (*TST*, xx). This embraces upward and downward movements: '[Christianity] finally understands the ascent of the human soul to God, not so much as a mere ascent of the soul, but rather as a paradoxical ascent of the soul rooted in the Incarnate descent of God from heaven relived and participated in Christian liturgy' (viii).

The hierarchies which result are, through this reciprocal movement, dynamic, reversible and mutually implying. '[T]here are only differences because there are multiple hierarchies, often reversible – just as angels are above as pure spirit, yet we are above angels as microcosmic mediators of spirit with matter. Nor are any of these hierarchies fixed: rather they are always a matter of reaching down in order to elevate upwards – and matter itself . . . is immediately by rebound on a journey of reversal to the One, travelling backwards and upwards through all the intermediate degrees' (John Milbank, 'The Surprise of the Imagined', Stanton Lecture 8, theologyphilosophycentre.co.uk/papers/ Milbank_StantonLecture8.pdf, 27–8).

For some of the complications arising when Neoplatonism is appropriated in a postmodern key, see Hankey, 'The Postmodern Retrieval of Neoplatonism in Jean-Luc Marion and John Milbank and the Origins of Western Subjectivity in Augustine and Eriugena', 9–70.

106. Both Christianity and Neoplatonism 'discern the common paradox that is the heart of being, whom Christians profess in Jesus Christ, the Paradox Incarnate', expressing 'the double and co-belonging ideas of "descent all the way down" and "participation all the way up"' (Milbank and Riches, 'Foreword', xv). Catherine Pickstock's '"liturgical consummation of philosophy" offers exactly the same innovative theurgic emphasis' (Milbank, *TST*, xx).

107. For Cusa, thought is 'speculation . . . which participates in God . . . For all participation is a kind of approximation, and therefore a conjecturing . . . The conscious human attempt to know is therefore, inversely, an intensified participation. Moreover, we must conjecture not only about God but about each and every creature' ('Participated Transcendence Reconceived', 26); also Milbank, *TST*, 308–9, 12.

108. Milbank, *TST*, 308.

restricted simply to statements which appear explicitly to be 'about' the transcendent, since every action is implicitly an attempt to grasp or respond to what is (even if only by saying what is not), and so conjecture is characteristic of human action as such; and conjecture is always ontological.[109] Milbank's stress on the validity of this reach towards ultimacy in the absence of secure grounds for speculative assertion is important in the validation of (modern) scientific language and thought. The unwarrantedness of science's narratives is not a fault, unless it refuses the conclusion of this unwarrantedness; neither does it undermine science's constitutive desire for the real but rather supports it by relaxing the modern stranglehold on what counts as proof and reference, and so liberating science from the impossible task of supplying its own grounds by giving an account of a mind-world relation that is securely immanent.

When brought together with the Blondelian explication of action, 'conjecture' expresses the speculative extension of knowledge beyond the (perceived) boundaries of its 'original' or 'intended' scope. Against Kant, whose transcendental categories were indicted by Hamann as no less question-begging than any of our immanent categories, we cannot

> list once and for all the general a priori categories, both conceptual and sensory, into which the finite is organized. Yet if this cannot be done, if local and particular experiences always enter into our general conception of epistemological categories, making them endlessly revisable, and justifiable neither de facto and a posteriori, nor de jure and a priori, then these culturally particular categories can only justify themselves as a kind of 'conjecture' about the transcendent, and the relation of this transcendence to finitude.[110]

This ineliminably conjectural character of every act of knowledge means simply that when we speak of the world we are never speaking *only* about the world. Language is unrestrictedly analogical across all human discourses. The mediation of infinite reality by finite realities entails that sciences, all knowledges about anything whatsoever, are never limited to only those objects but extend beyond them in ways that cannot be defined or determined in advance. This is why all constructions are necessarily metaphysical in supposing something ultimate about the world and cannot abandon this constitutive orientation. Metaphysics can never be merely regulative but is always constitutive because no *a priori* boundary can be drawn around our constructions. Thus the denial of a 'pure' nature and a 'pure' reason does not entail a denial of the abiding significance of our acts of knowing but actually underwrites it.

For Milbank, Cusa shows that our creativity is a genuine 'arriving at "new things"' in what remains paradoxically a 'solely divine act of absolute creative

---

109. '[W]ithout a Cusan "conjecture" as to the invisible dimension of what appears (the "ontological"), nothing does ever really appear to us' ('The Grandeur of Reason', 389).

110. Milbank, *TST*, 66.

positing of being'.[111] Our conjecture is not for Cusa primarily abstract and interior; rather, he emphasizes the *externality* of expression, which exceeds in significance what we planned or imagined. In this expressing we are both original and yet analogically participating in God's prior creative gift. The Incarnation remains the paradigm of this gift and, by being paradigmatic, once and for all locates truth for us within the temporal unfolding of human action. 'For Cusa . . . there can only be for us truth *tout court* because the Truth has redemptively become incarnate in time'.[112] This theological ground of our conjecturing is a real participation of our temporal conjectures in the eternity of the intra-Trinitarian life:

> *factibilitas* is the condition of possibility for human knowing and belongs to a human conjectural *explicatio* or the divine intellectual 'comprehension' of the second person of the Trinity.[113]

Nominalism's reduction of universals to names represented a partial recognition of the role of linguistic mediation. The theological problems motivating this recognition were real, and so nominalism, as found in the works of Scotus or Ockham, makes a simple return to Aquinas out of the question.[114] Rather the force of the nominalist critique needs to be recognized, and this can only be by a radicalization of the principle of analogy and a recognition of the human power of naming.

> [I]f universals are constructed, but are not thereby to be regarded as mere human fictions, then fictioning as such must participate in the Paternal fictioning of the filial *ars*. The two human modes of linguistic fashioning – history and literature, in their complex inter-entanglement both as enacted and as recited history . . . are now seen as essential to the disclosing of truth.[115]

The nominalist argument that universals are constructively named by human beings correctly identifies the role of linguistic invention in determining what counts as 'real' for us. This is to be countered not by denial but by a radicalization of this very point: 'our grasp of particulars is always [also] a matter of constructive naming'.[116]

The next chapter considers the import of conjecture and theurgy for the necessity of a specifically theological attention to organic life. The point for our current question has been to show that Milbank is not intending to undermine the purchase of human knowing, 'scientific' or otherwise, on the real itself, but quite the opposite; and further, that he extends this purchase to all human activity

---

111. Milbank, *TST*, xxviii.
112. Milbank, *TST*, xxx.
113. Milbank, *TST*, 12.
114. Milbank, *TST*, xxvi.
115. Milbank, *TST*, xxix.
116. Milbank, *TST*, xxvi.

such that the experimentation of the scientist too is conjectural in an entirely valid way and is in profound continuity with the rest of human activity. There is no comprehensive undermining of knowledge, simply a radical reconfiguring of it, stemming from the recognition of action's entire permeability to infinitude, and the impossibility of evading our role as mediators, not simply spectators, of the real. This appears as a threat to science simply because such a knowing cannot be autonomous and cannot specify in what ways its own describing, experimenting and hypothesizing exceeds its own grasp of things and signifies in ways that cannot be theoretically or practically controlled.

The saving of human making by theology is necessary precisely because this exceeding of control otherwise becomes a marker of the secular. It is this secularization of knowledge which has happened in the reign of modern natural science, in which technological control has become coextensive with knowledge, in such a way as to make scientific knowing identical with the autonomy not just of knowing but of nature itself as a self-contained realm of the manipulable. As we shall see below this is a concern for Hanby as well.

Reference and accountability

At this point, a critical question presents itself as urgent, relating once again to the worries raised by Janz about the disappearance of referentiality from Milbank's discourse. We can frame this worry in terms of 'accountability'. How is it, if all human action participates in divine reality just by being action, that we can discover some way of distinguishing faithful from unfaithful action or accountable from unaccountable speech? How could there be anything 'to which' language is accountable if there is no reference? If we have done away with a notion of external world to which internal expression or conceptualization seeks to conform, the grounds for discerning action as more than arbitrary are difficult to identify, and so the possibility of critical distinctions within scientific (or moral) enterprise becomes impossible to make. Insofar as modern science trades on the discrimination of accountable from unaccountable theoretical and practical conjectures, this issue demands a full response.

Milbank recognizes this challenge and does seek to give an account of what constitutes our making as more than arbitrary, what 'true' or 'false' could mean for action (of which language is an instance). He emphatically denies any arbitrariness in his account.

> [F]rom the point of view of my ontology, the 'choice' for peaceful analogy and the Augustinian metanarrative is not really an ungrounded decision, but a 'seeing' by a truly-desiring reason of the truly desirable.[117]

---

117. Milbank, *TST*, xvi, where he is responding to criticism from Hyman.

How does this 'seeing' discriminate? There are two key criteria: the aesthetic and the ethical. What governs our choice to act in one way rather than another is the intuited harmony we perceive, and the sense of appropriateness or fittingness we look for here presupposes a quest to grasp the meanings of the other acts in the series. This is the sense of the 'synthesis' Blondel sees as intrinsic to our judgement about how to act. Action thus has an aesthetic dimension, which embodies our search for what is fitting, appropriate, given the series. This search is inherently conjectural and speculative; it is insecure, in that it always goes beyond the absolutely warranted, but is also necessary as we must sense how to act fittingly in a series which can never be completely knowable because it is not exclusively our own, even if we are the author of it; our actions 'mean' and 'effect' in ways that escape our 'original' intentions. This final point indicates how the quest for authentic action also has an ethical dimension, as for (Milbank's) Blondel action is always sacrificial if undertaken truly. This is because to assent to the true nature of our action, our willing will, we have to surrender control of it and its adequation, and this is a kind of self-immolation.[118] This is why the necessity of reading Blondel as theology is pressing, for without the divine assurance of comprehensive meaningfulness this risk, allowing our action to escape our control and make its way into meaning without our command of it, appears to the actor only as negation. Action can be deciphered as love only in light of its revelation *as* love, which comes, so to speak, from above. To beg supernatural supplement is not enough; the supernatural must be truly present.

In light of this account of action, untruth is (ethically) to fail to give such assent, to refuse to take that risk, which inhibits action and denies its true character; and it is (aesthetically) not to attend to or effortfully intuit the fitting place of one's action in the series. Thus the epistemological criterion of untruth is 'sin' or 'ugliness', and true action is necessarily 'love' and 'beauty', releasing one's own being in action towards others and towards the world in search of both harmony and reconciliation, which are aesthetic and ethical aspects of the same peace. In these ways, action is governed – if we choose to act in obedience – by a *telos* which is both ethical and aesthetic, and which does function as a criterion for distinguishing between 'true' and 'false' action. This is underlined by the fully theological consideration indicated above, that our action is a participation in the intra-Trinitarian generation of the *Logos*. In this way our making is teleologically constrained, not arbitrary: it is not the case that we can just say or do anything at all and it will be equally good, equally valid.[119]

---

118. Milbank, *TST*, 214–5.

119. Hyman's trenchant criticism of Milbank touches directly on this point: if there is no 'objective' ground for preferring one narrative to another, isn't there, behind all narratives, a bad infinity of ungoverned and undirected possibility so that the true metanarrative is simply anarchy? Milbank's response (also quoted above) indicates how important for him is the element of teleological constraint in answering just this worry: '[F]rom the point of view of my ontology, the "choice" for peaceful analogy and the Augustinian metanarrative

This Blondelian theme links to Milbank's appreciation for the Thomist notion of *convenientia* or 'fittingness', which is taken to apply above all to the divine economy of creation and redemption. As so often in Milbank's selection of key concepts, the term has a mediating connotation for him, indicating a middle between the arbitrary and the necessary (like his construal of the notion of habit, discussed later). But as his use of Blondel indicates, *convenientia*' also signifies how we discern and discriminate in human action: something's rightness is judged above all in an aesthetic manner by its place in a series which remains ineradicably temporal. Milbank regards it as functioning for Thomas in the same way as notions of proportion, harmony, suitability, appropriateness or ordinateness.[120] Right or true action is that which is determined simply by our sense, which may be inchoate, of what *seems best*, where 'best' is determined in light of an unmeasurable diversity of inner and outer senses, including our perception of what has come before and what is anticipated to come. Indeed, Milbank says that for Thomas the notion of fittingness is actually convertible both with beauty and with being itself, and he himself even uses the term interchangeably with 'truth'.[121]

To explicate this in terms of action as conjecture, or action conceived as an attempt to say something 'true': the point is that although all sayings and doings are equally conjectural, because of the unavailability of a purely external standard of reference by which some actions could be regarded as successfully referring and others as failures, this does not render conjectures equal with regard to the ultimacy they intrinsically aspire to.

> [Our] necessary conjecture must, however, remain always ungrounded, otherwise one lapses into the 'critical' illusion of transcendentalism. To speak of a univocal Being indifferent to the differences of being is a conjecture, and to speak of an analogical Being which shows hierarchical preference amidst the differences of being is also a conjecture. As to what we should conjecture, nothing helps us decide apart from the subjectively recognized lure of analogical participation itself.[122]

Only if 'difference' is not univocal is such hierarchical preference between differences possible. Analogical difference alone can ensure this. Difference alone is not what is sought, but the difference which is different, that is, is analogy rather than univocity. Only difference analogically conceived can imagine harmonious reconciliation rather than univocal sameness: there is a right discrimination between conjectures, but this cannot be adduced externally or foundationally.

---

is not really an ungrounded decision, but a "seeing" by a truly-desiring reason of the truly desirable' (*TST*, xvi). See also Milbank's recent *Beyond Secular Order: The Representation of Being and the Representation of the People* (Oxford: Wiley-Blackwell, 2014), 104–5.

120. Milbank and Pickstock, *Truth in Aquinas*, 52.

121. Milbank and Pickstock, *Truth in Aquinas*, 55.

122. Milbank, *TST*, 308–9.

This brings Milbank surprisingly close to other accounts of truthfulness in language and human action which seem at first sight quite distant from his own and shows that his rejection of 'referentiality' is offered in aid of a richer account of the weight of human action. He does deny that truthfulness can be comprehensively described in terms of reference, a form of accountability in which subject and object are externally related. Rather he embraces a pragmatic measure of truthfulness as peace which is yet realist in its regard of human making as mediation. 'Aboutness' in the sense of Janz's critique is too troublingly dualist in presupposing a kind of determinable distance between speech and world across which reference can obtain, and also in bypassing the ethical and aesthetic character of truthfulness which are, for Milbank, not dispensable in favour of a 'fact-based' account of what is true. The relation which is truth exceeds aboutness, because the real is not present exclusively as the object of action but in the action itself. A recent account by Rowan Williams which attempts to preserve the purchase of language on reality without such a referential dualism is more similar to what Milbank is aspiring to. Although Williams more strongly emphasizes an ongoing accountability to something beyond the speakers, careful consideration reveals a convergence.[123] For Williams, we need 'a repertoire of styles and idioms that undercut the possibility of understanding our speech as straightforward description'; language is 'always "in the wake" of meaning, rather than owning and controlling it'.[124] Notwithstanding a disappointing obscurity on this point, Milbank is implicitly supporting such an accountability when he proposes that the story in which our actions seek synthesis never belongs only to us, and the synthesis we seek is not in our own control. Lest this seem still empty of definite content, that to which we are accountable is no more and no less than peace. Truthful uses of language are those in which language is not 'for its own sake', circularly self-referring, but is for the sake of peace.

'Pure' difference, difference immanently conceived, is indifferent to its own difference and so collapses into nihilating heterogeneity. Such a notion is countered with a pragmatic conception of truth as peace, whose theological key makes it stubbornly un-utilitarian.[125] Williams is therefore speaking in terms recognizably similar to Milbank's terms of the fittingness or otherwise of actions in a series which is more than just our own:

> But that 'next thing' [to say] cannot be just anything. . . . Mere difference . . . is not enough. . . . [A]nd once we have moved beyond the idea that difference is all that matters, the question of truth comes back . . . our speech is 'engaged' . . . it is not without relation to what is given . . . a point between or beyond speakers,

123. Rowan Williams, *The Edge of Words: God and the Habits of Language* (London: Bloomsbury, 2014).

124. Williams, *The Edge of Words*, 173.

125. Though Milbank is not afraid to embrace an Augustinian utilitarianism in which *usus* is properly the role of all creatures as each one ascends to God who is alone the true object of *frui* (*TST*, 439).

a point to which both are gesturing. . . . [W]hat we recognize in each other as speakers is a shared agenda of wrestling with what belongs to neither of us . . . as if we were always catching up with a reality never seen as standing still enough to be absorbed or fully embraced or mastered.[126]

Milbank would agree: 'mere difference' is not enough, for difference per se is not salvation; it is difference-in-peace which is the goal. This is given concrete shape through its emphatic ecclesiological grounding. The subjectively recognized 'lure' is nevertheless 'objectivist' in spirit, because it is governed by the social practice of the church, and this underlines the Blondelian perspective that truth is a property of actions, and supremely the action of the church in history, which reconciles differences and imagines harmonies.[127] Milbank's preference for conjecturing action teleologically constrained is a search for a way of conceiving 'truth' that does not result in a demotion of fictioning – something more expansive than 'aboutness' as the criterion of truth. Love, rather, is the criterion, which retains the presence of the real *in* human action and retains the vital constitution of the real as peace. In this way one can avoid looking for the appearance of the real in a quasi-scientific criterion of accurate identification of that which is talked about: we simply do not know *a priori* in what ways our actions disclose reality – in some sense we really do not know, ever, what we are talking about – and yet that is not to say that all actions are equally faithful or accountable. In this connection Milbank mentions Blondel's quasi-eschatological picture of a domain where 'the great peace of science reigns':[128] knowing and peace are not extrinsically related.[129] This goes some way towards providing a kind of criterion for theology's approach to the disciplines: how their difference is to be protected and enhanced, but also judged and discriminated. Chapter 4 develops this notion to form a specific agenda for theology towards the disciplines. Part III applies it to life science.

126. Williams, *The Edge of Words*, 92.

127. This is a position at once 'historicist and pragmatist, yet theologically realist – as suggested in particular by Maurice Blondel. In such a position, no claim is made simplistically to "represent" an objective social reality; instead, the social knowledge advocated is but the continuation of ecclesial practice, the imagination in action of a peaceful, reconciled social order. . . . It is this lived narrative which itself both projects and "represents" the triune God, who is transcendental peace through differential relation. And the same narrative is also a continuous reading and positioning of other social realities. If truth is social, it can only be through a claim to offer the ultimate "social science" that theology can establish itself and give any content to the notion of "God". And in practice, providing such a content means making an historical difference in the world' (Milbank, *TST*, 6).

128. Milbank, *TST*, 215.

129. This discussion of accountability is necessarily partial insofar as it does not refer to ecclesiology which, for Milbank, is the locus of all accountability: 'Theology . . . is answerable to reason precisely in so far as it is answerable to the Church' (*Being Reconciled*, 133).

An elevation of science

To return to the principal question of this chapter: on Milbank's approach, the separation of mind and world which is used to justify accounts of truth as a mirror-like accuracy to extra-linguistic phenomena would be not an overestimation of science but an underestimation of it. Such separation trades on nature-supernature dualisms which are used to secure an arena of pure immanence so that cognitive projects can be safely defended in a citadel of pure reason, for the sake of the apparent security of truly autonomous knowledge. But reason is not 'pure' in this sense; the immanent and transcendent cannot be externally demarcated from one another. This impossibility of drawing an immanent-transcendent boundary elevates 'science' as a discourse which is about 'the real' in a more expansive way than pure immanence could have dreamt. The instability of signification is then virtue not vice; although it puts science beyond the grip of 'professional' scientists, and so makes for an unstable conception of scientific knowledge, it is only the refusal to draw a definite boundary around what one thinks one means and intends that actually allows thought and language to be 'about' the real in the first place. This lack of control may be disturbing to the average scientific practitioner, but it is abundantly evident in scientific history in many phenomena now familiar to philosophers of science. A key example would be the way in which metaphors scientifically employed tend to run away with themselves and end up saying more than they were 'originally intended' to say.[130] This is a sign of scientific language reaching its full stature, exemplifying the way language functions: in constantly exceeding itself, it expresses its metaphysical constitution, always straining for a more comprehensive reach.

Milbank notes that in linking science with peace, incorporating notions of sacrifice, refusing negation and celebrating contingency, Blondel is taking up and putting to orthodox use many traditional positivist themes. This is an instance of the kind of overcoming which is a saving; positivism, as an attempt to elevate 'science' as true knowing, calls not for wholesale refusal but for redeeming through transformation, containing as it does many elements of latent Christianity.[131] Inevitably, Milbank's treatment of knowledge appears threatening to science conceived according to the canons of modernity. But, whether one finds it convincing in principle, it at least demonstrates that Milbank does not seek for natural science to abandon its aspiration to knowledge of the real. He does not

---

130. 'It is just because metaphors play roles in explanations that one is not entitled simply to say, "Oh, that's just my way of putting it". Even when they perform little or no explanatory work, moreover, metaphors carry a good deal of metaphysical and epistemological freight. Indeed, wherever there is a deficit between theoretical reach and empirical support the difference is usually made up by invoking ontology to do the missing work' (David Depew and Bruce Weber, *Darwinism Evolving: Systems Dynamics and the Genealogy of Natural Selection* (Cambridge, MA: MIT Press, 1997), 374).

131. Milbank, *TST*, xv.

eviscerate science of its constitutive ambition to speak of what is. Indeed, he expands the scope of its language beyond, no doubt, what most scientists would be comfortable with. Natural science never speaks only or reductively about its objects but is always gesturing beyond itself, even where it does not intend to. Part III argues that it is this, at least partially, that a notion of vitalism theologically conceived captures.

Returning, on the basis of these considerations, to our question about scientific knowledge: the sciences are theological in the fully positive sense of being about the infinite in and through being about the finite. There is no such thing as speaking only about the finite, only about the material; so the seeming specialism of science in finitude, in materiality, does not constitute a 'specialism' in the restricted sense on which scientists themselves usually insist, excusing themselves of any competence in what exceeds 'the natural'. Just as theology cannot be compartmentalized as speaking only of transcendence, neither can science be confined as speaking only of immanence. This account of knowledge raises science to a higher dignity than it could have had in a picture of science as securely cordoned off from discourses about transcendence. Indeed, Christian theology can in a very specific sense 'learn from' the sciences, for 'the traces of truth are found everywhere within the *humanum*';[132] Christianity is 'a universalism' which is 'open to difference – to a series of infinitely new additions, insights, progressions towards God'; it claims that these 'differential additions' can be 'a harmony "in the body of Christ"'.[133] It becomes apparent, then, that although Milbank appears to undermine 'science' as conceived in modernity, the logic of his conception of *poesis* provides grounds for an extremely high estimation of scientific knowledge, one in which science's knowing of the world is itself disclosive of an ultimacy: science's physics is always also a metaphysics, its nature is not isolable from supernature, and its 'discoveries' are therefore less restricted and parochial in significance than some, both scientists and philosophers, would like.[134] Rather it has an ultimate import, and an aspiration

---

132. Milbank, 'Faith, Reason and the Imagination', 4; but in Christ alone is 'the arrival of the fully restored human truth'.

133. Milbank, 'Postmodern Critical Augustinianism', 51.

134. As he acknowledges, 'secular reason' cannot be wholly 'bad', wholly to be opposed, but always contains elements that theology must 'recoup': '[My] attitude towards 'secular reason' is never as negative as it appears to be on the surface. For it is viewed not as what it primarily proclaims itself to be, namely the secular, but rather as disguised heterodoxy of various stripes, as a revived paganism and as a religious nihilism. In each case my attitude cannot be simply oppositional, since I regard Catholic Christianity as fulfilling the best pagan impulses, heresy as exaggeration or thinning-down of the truth, and nihilism as a parody both of the Christian view that we are created from nothing and that therefore all that is finite is indeterminate, and equally of the likewise Christian view that ordered beauty is paradoxically in-finite. It follows that there remains truth in all these distortions and even that, just as Irenaeus learned much from Valentinus, the distortions develop better certain aspects of orthodoxy which orthodoxy must then later recoup' (Milbank, *TST*, xiv).

to ultimacy, which cannot be erased even by the most thoroughgoing sociological critique. On this view, to say that metaphysics is integral to the sciences does not impugn their dignity as truth-seeking disciplines, but actually constitutes this dignity, in affirming that they cannot but pursue what is 'really' the case, while affirming that this 'really' is dependent on a narrative that does not emerge from science but informs it.

Chapter 4

LEGITIMA AUTONOMIA? DEFINING THEOLOGY'S MASTERY

This chapter pursues a concrete agenda for theology in relation to the sciences through an engagement with Michael Hanby, who defends a universal objectivity of reason which grounds a genuine autonomy of the disciplines. The chapter establishes the contours of a divergence between Milbank and Hanby, identifying a tension in the latter's account that points towards a resolution on Milbank's logic. It is suggested that Milbank's narrative hermeneutic, enabling peaceful difference, governs the constructive normative ontology which Hanby offers; it is from the point of view of the Christian *mythos* that the universalism of this ontology is supportable. The interaction with Hanby allows us to access the possibilities of Milbank's hermeneutic more fully. The chapter arrives at a practical specification of theological reason in its approach to the sciences.

Enabling the difference of the sciences

The apologia for theology's 'mastery' aimed to show that Milbank's mastery is not intrinsically a hostile one, though it needs careful qualification, and that the appearance of domination is in fact the rejection of that which excludes. It sought to demonstrate how a conception of knowledge as *poesis* attributes to the act of scientific knowing a uniquely high dignity.

The conception of mastery I have been defending is supposed not only to protect but actually to enable differences in their particularity. As a project to sustain difference peacefully, Milbank's thought should be judged to stand or fall by its success in this. His focus on the role and status of theology as the sole adequate 'manager' of this peace suggests that disciplinary difference should be a prime test case, and yet it is exactly in this respect that we might judge his approach to fall short. In his dedication to rescuing theology from its perceived Babylonian captivity, Milbank's account of difference has neglected the difference of the disciplines: he focuses on the 'disruptive difference' that theology makes, but at the cost of that which is made a difference to. If this mastery does truly nourish and sustain difference, if it successfully avoids theocracy and the homogeneity which would result from it, we should be able to see this at work in one of the most sorely contested flashpoints between theology and science, namely biology and its account of the living. In this sense the question of natural sciences, and the life sciences specifically, offers an avenue by which to press the account of 'theology' above by applying it concretely. The specification of life that theology expresses would have to be shown *not* to trump or violently displace biology's discourse about life, while at the same time making the 'disruptive difference' to it that Milbank looks for as a mark of theological authenticity.

To be successful, this account would not focus on valorizing difference 'in general' but would actually valorize *each particular* difference, the difference of, for example, biology as a distinct discourse. To valorize difference generically would be to erect it into a genus with multiple instantiations, a strategy which leads to that indifference to difference which Milbank identifies in the postmodern philosophers of *différance*. Difference valued only in general leads to the homogenizing neglect of the particular. The difference of each difference must have its own unique significance, its own difference from other differences. Part III tries to frame the distinctive difference of biology through an enquiry into its subject, 'life', explicating this in terms of vitalism. Before proceeding to that issue specifically, however, the question is how the difference of the sciences can be articulated in a way which does not separate them from theology or create a domain outside the theological in which their difference becomes a vacuous autonomy generative of conflictual and so nihilistic multiplicity. At the very least, the 'disruptive difference' theology makes involves discerning metaphysical commitments in scientific thinking which might embody ontologically conflictual narratives. This disruption challenges any essentialist notion of 'science' as a self-contained and self-standing enterprise. But this interrogation, if it is to meet its own standard of witnessing to reconciled peaceful difference and challenging denials of that peace, should show that its critique actually illuminates and supports a difference of the sciences. If Milbank's account of theology is broadly correct, namely that theology's narrative constitutes the possibility of peacefully sustained difference, we should be able to see the fruits of this in an increased integrity of discourses which enquire into different aspects of the world without contradicting the fundamental vision he is outlining. It needs to be shown how and why the claim that there is no space outside theology, no reserve of created territory independent of God, can actually establish the conditions for the flourishing of disciplinary difference *in principle*.

Michael Hanby, a Catholic contributor to the *Radical Orthodoxy* series,[1] attempts an extensive response to this problematic in his *No God, No Science?: Theology, Cosmology, Biology*.[2] Hanby's position shares a great deal with Milbank's view of the nature and status of theology with respect to philosophy and the disciplines, and he lists *TST* as the decisive influence in his intellectual evolution; in fact he regards *No God, No Science* as an explicit extension of that project towards biology.[3] But his account has a crucially different emphasis. It is in many

---

1. Michael Hanby, *Augustine and Modernity* (Oxford: Routledge, 2003).
2. *No God, No Science?: Theology, Cosmology, Biology* (Oxford: Wiley-Blackwell, 2013).
3. Commenting on the origins of the book, Hanby explains the evolution of ideas and interests that led him to the writing of it. Reading *TST* at the beginning of his theological career was, he says, 'like a bomb going off . . . reading that book changed my life'. He

ways exemplary of the sort of interrogation of the disciplines by theology that Milbank calls for, disinterring the hidden (unorthodox) theologies that dominate modern biology. But Hanby acts as a foil to Milbank in that, while holding a similar position on the nature of theology, he defends the Catholic claim that the sciences have a *legitima autonomia*.[4] To do so, he emphasizes the primacy of a doctrine of creation as underpinning the intrinsic intelligibility of the created order, and being rationally apparent from within that order as a *theologia naturalis*; and he takes reason to be a *theoria*, not a *poesis*. An examination of Hanby's position can therefore illuminate both in complementarity and contrast what Milbank has to say about the disciplines and their status, being a strong account of theology's regnant position while protecting the 'difference' of the sciences.

This chapter treats Hanby in three stages: firstly, by exploring his own conception of the theological character of reason itself, and therefore of scientific knowing; secondly, by looking at his argument that a theological metaphysics, specifically a metaphysics of form and *esse*, 'saves' science by restoring the intrinsic intelligibility of the world as created; and thirdly, off the back of these two claims, to explore exactly what kind of 'autonomy' he grants to the sciences. Following this, it attempts an account of a profound divergence between Milbank and Hanby and then tries to bring their approaches into a unified perspective in which the difference of the disciplines can be protected but without granting them extra-theological status. The goal is to show how Hanby's theologically grounded valorization of the dignity of the disciplines as conducting novel and coherent enquiries 'in their own right' can be consistent with Milbank's denial of autonomy to the disciplines.

Theology within *science*

Given that Hanby is working explicitly in the Catholic tradition of *legitima autonomia*,[5] the first point of interest in his approach is that it accords with

---

found the prospect of theology's recovery of confidence and return from its modern exile 'exhilarating' and went to Cambridge 'inspired by Milbank' and 'intoxicated with the elixir of what would become Radical Orthodoxy', 'determined to write the next *Theology and Social Theory* of evolutionary biology' (qualifying, 'though that was and is a pretentious comparison' and that the conception of the project evolved considerably – an evolution we will be implicitly illuminating in this discussion). He also felt an early attraction to Aquinas and, in particular, to the doctrine of creation as a theological key (https:// vimeo .com/118888426, accessed 24 June 2016).

4. Hanby references *Gaudium et Spes*, 36 (Michael Hanby, *No God, No Science: Theology, Cosmology, Biology* (Oxford: Wiley-Blackwell, 2013), 12).

5. What is meant by this bears some clarification, and its extent and character is not by any means established in Catholic scholarship. John Paul II's *Fides et Ratio* is an authoritative starting point, though it is itself subject to somewhat diverse interpretation; see, for example, David Foster and Joseph Koterski, eds., *Two Wings of Catholic Thought:*

Milbank's analysis of the presence of theology and theological agendas within scientific discourses in a way which exposes the fantasy of a self-grounding reason. The following description intends to highlight both the convergence between Hanby and Milbank on this point and the distinct emphases they give to it. Hanby's account is oriented towards a discernment of a universal structure of rational enquiry, apparent to any rational agent without the *explicit* influence of theology, even though theology arises in its very heart. This is in contrast to the persistent emphasis on the ubiquity of narrative frameworks in the structure of knowledge within which Milbank situates his critique of autonomous reason. We return to an exploration of this divergence below, after a closer examination of Hanby's approach.

Hanby argues that science is constitutively and inseparably related to metaphysics and theology on three grounds: theological, philosophical and historical. The first refers to the fact that no study of being in any of its aspects can be indifferent to God, since creation is properly constituted *as a relation.* 'There can be no "outside" of relation to God in either the cognitive or the ontological order.'[6] (This view is obviously persuasive only to those who already recognize the constitutive character of this relation.) But Hanby holds that this relation necessarily (because of the character of creation itself) appears within a 'purely' philosophical approach, if one pays attention to the 'intrinsic necessities' of reason itself. We discuss his account of this in more detail below, but briefly: every act of knowing, and every account of knowledge, must presuppose something about that which is to be known, 'nature'. Specifically, one cannot identify the object of knowledge, 'nature', without 'simultaneously distinguishing it from that which is not nature – namely God – and without giving tacit specification to this "not"'.[7] Conceptions of nature therefore always imply some conception of God and so are never neutral with respect to theology. In this way the distinction between God and the world is inherent in the very idea of 'world' itself; it is 'the most primitive of distinctions' and so an implicit conception of the God-world relation inheres in every subsequent distinction and, in fact, in the very idea of 'distinction' itself, which appears in philosophy.[8] Thirdly, the inseparability of science and theology is historically evident in the actual development of modern science, which, outstandingly in the case of biology, is 'parasitic' on theological and metaphysical developments, just as the modern conception of 'nature' is parasitic on a particular

Essays on Fides et Ratio (Washington, DC: Catholic University of America Press, 2003). For a critical discussion of the interaction of theology and the disciplines in the modern university which takes *Fides et Ratio*'s model as authoritative, see Gavin D'Costa, *Theology in the Public Square: Church, Academy and Nation* (Oxford: Blackwell, 2005). Michael Hanby considers himself an expositor of an authentically Catholic view of *legitima autonomia* specifically in relation to biology.

6. Hanby, *Science*, 18.

7. Hanby, *Science*, 19.

8. Hanby, *Science*, 19.

(unorthodox) conception of God.[9] For these three sorts of reasons, an 'extrinsicist' view of the science/theology relation, in which the two are regarded as different domains which never come into contact, is unsustainable.

Focusing at length on the second of these points, Hanby argues that the act of knowledge is 'irreducibly metaphysical and theological' in its very structure.[10] He insists on the insecurity of reason considered in itself, its lack of its own ground and its vulnerability to collapse when it seeks a completeness or self-authentication in isolation from theology. The argument is philosophical in form but proceeds in such a way as to show the ineluctable implication of theology in philosophy's project. Via Erich Przywara's account of 'the suspended middle', he gives an account of reason which echoes Milbank's rejection of *a priori* limits to reason. Reason can be neither purely *a priori* nor a posteriori; both starting points are elusive considered in themselves, because each implies the other. The former presupposes that one could see from the vantage point of the first principle, which is impossible, and the latter cannot avoid a theoretical point of departure for experimentation, which is not wholly derivable a posteriori. At the same time a particular transcending universal is the implicit goal of a posteriori inductive reasoning, and the deductive *a priori* approach will always be finally faced with the 'irreducible historical remainder' which is continually in excess of any idea.[11] And yet both approaches constitute the very form of thought: they are necessary and impossible, and each seeks the other in its end.

This scenario is also expressed by Hanby in Przywara's language of 'metanoetic' and 'metaontic', terms which refer to different aspects of metaphysics; the former, metaphysics about thought, the latter about being. Przywara shows that these two aspects of metaphysics cannot be successfully disentangled; we find the one in the heart of the other, indicating the mutual implication of being and thought. The metanoetic and the metaontic, the *a priori*/deductive/timeless and the a posteriori/inductive/historical cannot be clearly separated by an external limit. They are intrinsically reciprocal and pervade one another. But they are also necessarily distinct, being irreducible to one another: and it is this sense of not being able to settle in one or the other, not being able to do without either of them and not being able to proceed from either point without implying the other that leads Przywara to see reason as situated in 'a suspended middle'. This 'middle' obtains not only between metanoetic and metaontic, *a priori* and *a posteriori*, deductive and inductive; it also refers to the middle between the historical/temporal and the eternal, the relative and the absolute. Thought oscillates continually between these poles, knowing obscurely their unity but without being able to account fully for this unity.[12] Both movements press towards comprehension of the whole, from

9. Hanby, *Science*, 20.

10. Hanby, *Science*, 9.

11. Hanby, *Science*, 24.

12. Resulting in a relationship of 'polarity' as described by Balthasar. Hanby, *Science*, 24–5.

each direction, but this whole is not self-explanatory, 'the less so the more that each pole of approach reveals its dependence upon the other'.[13]

Metaphysics is therefore an 'impossible possibility': it must start from somewhere, but each somewhere presupposes its goal in the pole towards which it seeks: the particular in the general, the general in the particular; the world in the idea and the idea in the world.[14] There is no Archimedean point outside being, from which its totality is apparent; there is no 'rounding upon the finite', and attempts to secure reason as once-for-all *a priori* or *a posteriori* always represent such a rounding.[15] Thus, the prior metaphysical commitments that inform scientific work are not per se regrettable but rather constitute the form of thought as such. 'As obvious as it may seem, we need to be (continually) reminded that all science is undertaken *by* human beings from *within* the world.'[16] Although this situation is inevitable, it does constitute 'an aporetic dilemma' for reason as it leaves philosophical/scientific thought with no exclusively adequate starting point which it can establish for itself. But this dilemma is turned into a virtuous and not a vicious paradox by theology. The move to theorize about being from within being, to try to say what is true in general on the basis of the particular and what is true in particular on the basis of the general, is symptomatic of creaturehood, as location *within* the order of being. Attempts to collapse the suspended middle in order to round upon being inevitably result in a denial of creaturehood as situatedness within the order of being. In this way Hanby embraces the endemic incompleteness of reason which results from the impossibility of *a priori* limits to reason and its possibilities.

Every attempt to know, then, is formally metaphysical, and so science never falls outside of theology. But the ontology latent in modernity's 'science' is in denial of the inexorably metaphysical-theological form of reason, and so is divided against itself, because it must take as axiomatic things it cannot establish from within its empirical, positivistically conceived remit. 'Irreducibly metaphysical judgements as to the nature of being, form, time, space, matter, cause, truth, knowledge, explanation, wholes, parts and the like are the starting point of science, not its conclusions.'[17] Hanby elaborates this specifically through a discussion of the nature of distinction and abstraction in scientific methodology.[18] Abstraction always

13. Hanby, *Science*, 26.

14. Hanby, *Science*, 21ff.

15. Hanby borrows the phrase 'rounding upon the finite' approvingly from Milbank, quoting the latter's critique of the possibility of a once-for-all distinction between 'necessary finite knowledge and a superfluous and pretended transcendent knowledge'. *Science*, 43 (see note 63), quoting *TST*, 63.

16. Hanby, *Science*, 14.

17. Hanby, *Science*, 17.

18. David Schindler is an evident influence on Hanby here; see particularly 'The Given as Gift', where Schindler emphasizes the God-world distinction as the primitive form of distinguishing as such.

occurs to whole from part as well to part from whole, and so there can be no 'regional' limit on science; it cannot be that science focuses 'only' on particulars and so is indifferent to matters concerning the whole. The more basic notion of 'distinction', being able to identify one thing over against another, involves notions of limit in which a tacit notion of what is beyond the limit, as well as the relation obtaining across that limit, is always implied. Extrinsicism, being an attempt to eradicate metaphysics from the conception of the nature and of the objects of knowledge, fails to see that the very attempt to be preontological in abstraction and distinction involves a questionable notion of limit, whether in knowledge or in being. Specifically, it is a Cartesian conception of limit as geometrically conceived line, a pure externality across which no *relata* are imagined to obtain.

There is no question for Hanby that scientific abstraction is legitimate in principle as a tool of analysis, since such abstraction occurs in every act of attention.[19] But the extrinsicist conception of abstraction and distinction dominant in modern science, by becoming ontological, produces atomized entities in the style of nominalism, whose relations with one another are completely external. This makes parts ontologically indifferent to the wholes in which they belong, resulting in a mechanist model of relations as push-pull applications of force: causality is reduced to efficient causality, with a consequent notion of being or nature as 'brute facticity'.[20] An intra-worldly extrinsicism mirrors the God-world extrinsicism, for the notion of distinction and relation has been colonized by mechanism and externality at every level. There is a failure to see that the supposition of 'no relation' is itself the positing of a kind of relation, and so notions of limit can never form an absolute boundary; and that the modern notion of 'world' implies a particular notion of 'God', even though this is in the form of denial. Specifically, the 'God' implied in the externality of these notions of abstraction and distinction is a finite object alongside created things, sharing with them the same ontological plane. Manufacture and artifice, which are fundamentally external conceptions of making, become in modernity dominant metaphors for comprehending nature. 'Creation' as an internal and constitutive relation is replaced by an external shaping force.

The central substantive claim of Hanby's critique of a science 'outside' theology is that the hermeneutic of manipulation instead of contemplation, and of external shaping instead of creation, makes form epiphenomenal with respect to matter (i.e. a merely secondary effect, with the implication of possessing an illusory or unreal quality) and so destroys the very intelligibility on which the sciences' quest is predicated. Regarding its objects of study as composites of externally related parts, it denies them as subjects of their own acts of being, reducing act to brute facticity. Biology, specifically, loses the capacity to justify or explain natural species, or to give a metaphysical account of the whole organism, in light of which alone analysis of it in terms of parts or behaviours is pointful. A terminally inconsistent

19. Hanby, *Science*, 33.
20. Hanby, *Science*, 14.

and contradictory situation results in which 'science' vitiates itself, denying the distinct existence of its own objects of study as intelligible entities. We return to this point in more depth below, which is relevant here insofar as it relates to the inescapably theological constitution of the sciences, but is also relevant to the subsequent argument regarding the non-reductive understanding of organismic life with which we concern ourselves in Part III: a theological vitalism answers the problematic set by Hanby by illuminating exactly how an organism is the subject of its own life.

Is it philosophy or theology that is being done here? Although Hanby recognizes a distinction between philosophy and theology, he sees philosophy as incapable of specifying its own limits; the distinction, rather, is theologically granted;[21] we only know what reason is in light of theology. Thus the 'autonomy' of philosophy is radically relative to philosophy's specification by theology. This is simply because, in the paradoxical situatedness of reason in a 'suspended middle', there is an orientation towards the transcendent: '[b]ecause [reason's] aspiration to ultimacy commences from within this "suspended middle" . . . I would be reluctant to place any *a priori philosophical* restrictions on philosophy's capacity for God'.[22] This is simply because the notion of limit always implies some tacit notion of what is beyond that limit, and so it is only from the point of view of theology that reason's 'limits' could ever be discerned. The task, therefore, is not to expunge theology from science, or from philosophy, but to discern the true theology which will enable scientific discourse. It is this true theology, uniquely supportive of science, which Hanby elaborates in terms of a doctrine of creation *ex nihilo* which overcomes the bad theology of the Enlightenment and restores coherence and credibility to the scientific enterprise.[23]

To summarize so far: on Hanby's view, 'science' is necessarily integrally related to theology, since reason operates in a creaturely manner without an absolute beginning or end; modern science contains its own theology, but it is a bad theology producing atomism and mechanism. When he turns finally to Darwin,

---

21. Hanby, *Science*, 27.

22. Hanby, *Science*, 26; italics original. '[T]he philosopher's self-transcending location in the order of being to which there is no "outside" renders philosophy's definition of its own boundaries impossible' (*Science*, 25). Hanby objects to philosophies which operate as theologies in a covert manner, while insisting that a *theologia naturalis* 'is implicit in every science' (*Science*, 29): natural theology 'begins with metaphysics and does not end' (*Science*, 30).

23. It appears that for Hanby this was the original critical insight in his approach to biology and to science in general as he formulated the ideas presented in *No God, No Science*: it concerned the omnipresence of metaphysical and indeed theological judgements in natural science, and therefore its susceptibility to theological analysis and critique (https://vimeo.com/118888426, accessed 24 June 2016).

Hanby therefore deals with him as 'Darwin the Theologian':[24] via Darwin, biology as bad theology accelerates, propagating its own conception of God and world.

Hanby and Milbank compared: Theology saving science

Milbank and Hanby agree that the task of articulating the general relationship between philosophy, theology and the disciplines is necessarily a *theological* task, to be undertaken by theology and not by science, theology being the most 'holistic' framework because it sees creatures in the widest possible perspective. They see reason as intrinsically oriented to transcendence and suggest that it cannot be confined to immanence from within immanence; it cannot be *a priori* limited. Both agree that thought cannot be systematically total or comprehensive, nor can an absolute beginning for thought be discovered in which nothing is presupposed, and yet thought nevertheless legitimately aspires to ultimacy. Only theology can accept the paradox of the equal necessity and impossibility of metaphysics without constituting that as a defeat for thought. Both agree that a metaphysics of participated transcendence is the only way of securing immanence as immanent, insofar as only God's complete transcendence can ground his utter immanence to every existing thing.

In contrast to Milbank's articulation of theology's mastery of the disciplines, however, which takes as its goal the liberation of theology from its modern captivity, Hanby's account takes as its chief concern the *conflation* of science and theology which results in science posing as theology, as in the work of the New Atheists, or theology posing as science, as in creationism, both of which are among Hanby's targets. For Hanby, this conflation arises when the distinction between God and the world is misunderstood in an extrinsicist fashion: God as an object outside the world (which may take both theist and atheist forms). Other than in his valuing of difference, we would not easily learn from Milbank what would be wrong with theology displacing biology. Hanby, however, is at pains to protect a distinct domain of science, vigilantly guarding against attempts by theology to assume biology's proper function. The outcome of such an intrusion, in his account, would be difficult to distinguish from a fundamentalism in which God and world are terminally conflated.

How can we explain the difference between them here, with Milbank defending theology's mastery, theology as the *only* true science, and Hanby the correct *distinguishing* of theology from the disciplines? For Hanby, there is a universal structure of reason which is apparent to the observer who is paying attention, a reason which reveals its creaturely character in its own inability to find an absolute point of departure. This universal structure of rational enquiry grounds a definite distinctness of the sciences vis-à-vis theology: reason reveals certain intrinsic necessities of thought and being, such as the priority of form, which science itself

---

24. Hanby, *Science*, 186ff.

will discover as internal to its own operation, if it is not hobbled by bad theology. Milbank, in contrast, emphasizes reason as alone sustained by and discoverable within the Christian *mythos*; outside of theology's narrative, there is no given structure of being which 'reason' will discern. For Milbank *logos* is subordinate to *mythos* in that sense: Christianity's reason (which may look entirely like the reason defended by Hanby) is a distinct product of its narrative. This leads to a more thoroughgoing evacuation of the sciences and subordination of them to theology's reign, theology's 'reign' simply being the exclusive sufficiency of the narrative of orthodoxy for establishing the shape of reason. It is this narrative which must come first, for Milbank, rather than being discerned as the objectively right one on the basis of observing the world. This is in strong distinction to Hanby, for whom the theological arises within the objects of scientific study, spontaneously, as a result of their objective character as creatures, and equally within the act of scientific knowledge which reveals itself as creaturely. The doctrine of *creatio ex nihilo* makes sense of this as it were 'after' the fact, noetically (not ontologically). For Milbank, it may be the case that theology can 'apologetically' demonstrate the truth of creation within scientific acts and objects, but there is emphatically nothing 'objectively' compelling to this demonstration outside of a broader rhetorical project.

In light of this brief comparison, which anticipates a further treatment below, we return to asking Hanby our guiding question: how does theology establish the difference of the sciences in a way which preserves their difference rather than simply assimilating their differences to itself? For Hanby it is the doctrine of creation itself which establishes the distinction between theology and science: the distinct difference of the sciences follows from the distinction between God and world properly understood. This is how the ubiquity of theology in every form of knowledge paradoxically allows for a meaningful distinction between theology and other kinds of knowing: through the God-world distinction, the fundamental 'form' of distinctions as such. Once a real difference between God and the world is allowed to obtain,

> the sciences are permitted *to be* and to be science, not least by being 'other than theology'. But their being 'other than theology' is not *external* to theology any more than science is external to itself.[25]

Science lacks autonomy precisely in the sense that it cannot establish or secure its own first principles, and so it cannot be its own law – *auto-nomos* – its own 'queen'.[26] But the God-world distinction, theologically grounded, does not require that creatures be outside of or apart from God to be themselves. Rather it is God's intimacy to them that establishes their distinction from God. Distinction is not separation; it is only the impossibility of a God-world separation that establishes

25. Hanby, *Science*, 30.
26. Hanby, *Science*, 30.

the distinction which secures the creature's integrity, and correlatively the integrity of the sciences. Hanby argues this at length in his chapter on the meaning of *creatio ex nihilo*.[27] Created being cannot be reducible to God's being and so the creature does constitute a legitimate object of enquiry in itself, not simply as an aspect of God. But neither can it be separated from God as its interior source. It is God's constitution of the world non-competitively from within, as its utterly intimate source of being, which secures the world as world, and so secures science's integrity as a discipline of enquiry into the world as world. 'Without God there is no science, because ultimately without God there is no world.'[28]

The rather in-depth discussion which occupies the remainder of this chapter is meant to suggest four fundamental divergences between Milbank and Hanby, in a context of particular relevance for an approach to biology. Firstly, it shows how Hanby's critique of modern science is not primarily narrative but dialectical; secondly, that for Hanby a profound distinction between being and history is required for science's activity to make sense; thirdly, and relatedly, that for Hanby reason remains *primarily* contemplative and receptive. Finally, it indicates that Hanby's main mode of objection to modern science's operative metaphysics is primarily 'rational' in the sense of coherence, comprehensiveness and ability to account for its own operations and objects, in contrast to Milbank who typically translates all claims about rationality and sense-making into a primarily moral language; unreason is violence, is conflict; reason is peace and harmony. The overall intention is to show that, for Hanby, a doctrine of creation is *rationally* vindicated. This sets the stage for the critical interaction with Milbank.

Hanby: The rational superiority of a metaphysics of form

Hanby argues that the disabling metaphysical outcome of denying creation is the loss of a metaphysics of form and *esse*. His critique of modern science is focused above all on its incoherence without an ontological primacy of form, and his principle charge against Darwinism in its various versions is that by denying the primacy of form it cuts off the branch on which it sits, making causality unintelligible, erasing the very organisms which biology studies and misconceiving the nature of explanation to the extent that in the end nothing at all is explained.[29] Rather than critiquing the inherent conflictuality, premised upon an original violence, of non-theological narratives, Hanby argues negatively through critical analysis that the ontology (admitted or not) of modern science is incoherent. Positively, he argues that theology establishes the distinct difference of the sciences by grounding them in a more expansive ontology within which alone their operation can make sense and which is already, in practice, presupposed in every scientific

---

27. Hanby, *Science*, 297ff.
28. Hanby, *Science*, 36.
29. See particularly Hanby, *Science*, 336–64.

act. It is the presence of theology within and not outside of scientific theorizing which establishes the 'autonomy' of science, securing the legitimate operation of scientific methodologies within their own spheres by establishing the distinction-without-separation which is the ontological structure of creation. As projects which pursue an ever-greater intelligibility in their objects of study, the sciences are saved from contradiction only if this intelligibility is saved from the illusoriness of epiphenomenality. Theology accomplishes this saving by showing intelligibility as original through its doctrine of creation. Thus for Hanby the emphasis is not on the rhetorical superiority of theology, the greater power of its story or on its moral critique of narratives but on the rational superiority of its metaphysics, which is judged by its more comprehensive accounting for the possibility of coherent intellectual acts at all.

This accounting is only possible through a distinction between the order of history and the order of being, which a metaphysics of form expresses: reality is never just historical, never just story.[30] By grounding the transcendence by the order of being of the order of history, but without separating the two orders, theology provides the rationale for the intelligibility and reality of form, that is, the reality of entities as ontological wholes and only heuristically as aggregates of parts, which is only possible if the being of an entity is regarded as act, or in other words, if form transcends temporal flux. Without these metaphysical axioms scientific analysis becomes self-defeating.

As 'self-communicating meaning', the primacy of form explicates the intrinsically rational structure of creation. 'The claim that form is ontologically basic is essentially the claim that reason – *eidos*, *logos*, or intelligibility – is internal to the heart of being as such.'[31] Insofar as every act of thought is an attempt to discover meaning, this is not only apparent from the side of theology, so to speak; it is inherent in the very act of thinking itself, which cannot help presupposing the prior reality of form. The analysis of an entity in terms of its parts can be coherent only so long as the abstraction from the whole is seen as theoretical contrivance rather than ontological assertion. For Hanby the fragmentation and atomization entailed by the ontologization of the scientific method is its own worst enemy. Unless thought retains that priority of whole over parts, analysis of parts is always reductive: it reduces form to an aggregate of externally related 'pieces' whose apparent coherence in time and space is accidental and therefore, ontologically speaking, illusory. A metaphysics of form restores the primacy of act over fact, by making each entity the subject of its own existence, of its own act of being: only through a primacy of form can an entity be a *per se unum*. This unity is 'ontologically anterior to a unity of either aggregation or organization'.[32] This point is central to Hanby's critique of Darwinism, since denying this in the case of organisms results in a particular incoherence of biological reasoning, for it is only

---

30. Hanby, *Science*, 397ff.
31. Hanby, *Science*, 337.
32. Hanby, *Science*, 276.

qua subjects of their own being that the behaviour of organisms Darwinistically conceived can make sense at all. Hanby's point here will be important in connection with a vitalistic conception of an organism's life.

> It is not finally possible to describe the organism's contingent development from one historical moment to the next as the development *of the organism* unless the organism has an indivisible actuality, and thus an abiding unity, that transcends this sequence. Even less is it possible to describe an organism's activity without this transcendent unity, since actions are distinguished from mere events by this very transcendence . . . in virtue of which [transcendent unity] we are able to say that one instance in the series occurs 'for the sake of the next'.[33]

Hanby grounds this assertion in a strong defence of a metaphysical distinction between the order of being and the order of history; being always exceeds history, just as truth always exceeds appearance, and it is only this exceeding which makes truth possible at all. The distinction between the orders of being and of history is not an *a priori* opposition; rather,

> it is precisely this 'supratemporal' unity [of form] indivisible by duration and extension that makes the organism not just the *product* but the *subject* of its own development, thus making it possible to predicate a developmental history as the history *of* the organism in question, a history that is fully implicated . . . in its every action.[34]

It is only an acceptance of an order of being distinct from an order of history that can make sense of Darwinism's continual weddedness to a fixity of species as the constant against which the temporal flux of evolutionary change is measured. Apart from this fixity a notion of 'transmutation of species', of inheritance and descent or of natural selection collapses. A metaphysical nominalism results. Without permanence, without organisms as real things with an abiding identity rather than formless aggregates, a notion of 'change' – on which Darwinism depends – loses all content. The only coherent challenge to this nominalism is a participation of form in being which saves it from epiphenomenality without at the same time extracting it insensibly from history. No science can avoid recourse to such an order of being, distinct from the order of history, because it is unable to expunge the indicative mood: the spontaneous pressing for normativity which expresses a faith in a 'way things are' which exceeds any accidental, particular or temporal arrangement: 'reality's superiority to all our theories about it'.[35] '[W]ithout this excess of being to truth, the very notion of truth disintegrates into mere logical

33. Hanby, *Science*, 276.
34. Hanby, *Science*, 277.
35. Hanby, *Science*, 20.

coherence.'[36] Being *precedes* knowledge,[37] just as 'truth' depends on a distinction between reality and appearance.[38] The 'more than appearance' which the notion of truth presupposes is the inner depth, what Hanby calls the 'intensive infinity of finite *entia*', which is explicated by the orthodox doctrine of being as love, implied by *creatio ex nihilo*: 'a gratuitous surplus of infinite depth' which saves the 'more than appearance on which the truth of appearance itself depends'.[39] Against this, the assimilation of truth to function, pragmatic success or logical coherence always tends towards an elevation of history at the expense of being, undermining science's intrinsic drive towards normativity.

The restoration of the metaphysics of form includes, in Hanby's treatment, a more subtle conception of the relations between entities in the world, negotiated with the concepts of *esse commune* and *essentia*. This distinction, which is not a separation, founds the mutual irreducibility of the different sciences to one another and to metaphysics. Although the truth of being manifests in every part of the whole, what is true of a part is not always true of the whole. 'Form' has its own intelligibility as form, and being has an intelligibility as being, which are mutually irreducible epistemically: in Hanby's example, being a rhinoceros is not a property of being as such, even though a rhinoceros *is*. The particular sciences are not simply branches or subsets of metaphysics: they could not be deduced from or reduced to it, and they 'do represent a genuine novelty "over and above" metaphysics'.[40] This novelty is not 'outside' metaphysics but rather arises from the very shape of the metaphysics of creation in which the particular act of being of each thing, *essentia*, is in proportion to, and not in competition with, the being it shares with all other beings, *esse commune*. The parts on which science legitimately focuses in analysis cannot be exempted absolutely from their near-infinite relations to the whole except by an abstraction which always remains artificial. And yet as a distinct intelligible form the creature can be considered *qua essentia*, and not only *qua esse commune*. The analysis of entities trades not only on the prior intelligibility of form which itself depends on the unity of the creature's own act of being but equally on the being which all entities share in common and which alone constitutes the possibility of real relations between them (thus saving causality). These two aspects are fundamentally linked, since the loss of a conception of unity of act, with its mechanized atomization, effects an externalization of all the object's relations. This inevitably falsifies the entity, which is substantially and not merely accidentally in constitutive relationship to other entities, sharing their being while at the same time instantiating that being uniquely.

36. Hanby, *Science*, 20.
37. Hanby, *Science*, 16.
38. Hanby, *Science*, 386.
39. Hanby, *Science*, 386.
40. Hanby, *Science*, 31.

Additionally, the primacy of form considered via a doctrine of creation posits God as the ground of every entity and so introduces an infinite outward intelligibility and an infinite interior mystery as directly proportionate to one another, both supporting and tempering science's constitutive ambition to comprehend ever more fully. Each entity as created has an 'intensive infinity', which is the presence of God in it as its depthless source, and this intensive infinity renders it irreducibly novel and inexhaustibly intelligible so that one can, in principle, analyse it ad infinitum, rendering the scientific project intrinsically unfinishable and ordered towards mystery in its very constitution. Science's legitimacy as an analytical project requires its acceptance of this intensive infinity, which is the acceptance of its own programme of discovery as unfinishable in principle. So, while the goal of exhaustive intelligibility which results from a totalization of the analytic method is both idolatrous and incoherent, the project of unlimited analysis and the ambition to grasp the whole as such actually follows from and is legitimated by the intensive infinity of created beings whose interior source is God.

Hanby calls this metaphysical project 'saving the appearances', because the alternative always renders appearances epiphenomenal on (what is taken to be) a more basic reality which is not what appears; forms are regarded as parasitic on conglomerates of parts which are ontologically anterior. In this way the world of objects and organisms becomes fantastical and, ultimately, inexplicable. The appearances are saved only if created entities are seen in terms of the act of being which makes them their own subject, possessors of their own identity, and therefore as really being what they seem to be: objects with an identity which persists through time; of which predications can really be made; to whom, in the case of living entities, actions can really be attributed; which are seen as really and internally related to all other entities and so can be brought into meaningful causal relationships; which spontaneously communicate their intrinsic intelligibility to the created intellect.

His confidence in the self-revealing character of creation's rational structure makes Hanby able to say that, insofar as the explicitly theological appears *within* the methods and objects of any discipline and not simply through the application or addition of theological data, the detailed specifics of the relation of any one scientific discipline to theology are to be determined *from within that discipline*. This is a critical qualification to what might appear otherwise to be a denial of autonomy to the disciplines. It remains true that only theology generates the 'space' for the sciences to coherently and legitimately operate according to their own methods. For Hanby the distinction of the sciences from theology is

> *theologically* granted, not, of course, in a juridical sense by theologians and ecclesiastics but by the metaphysical and theological truth of science's own creaturely constitution.[41]

41. Hanby, *Science*, 30; italics original.

But the sense in which each science encounters the difference of theology must, according to Hanby, be articulated from within that science by its own practitioners, because each discipline seeks to comprehend its objects in a distinctive way, and so the created character of its objects manifests differently. Theology's competence to rule over all is thus qualified by the exclusive competence of each discipline to specify the way in which it manifests that rule in its own manner of proceeding. So although theology 'rules', it rules from inside of the discipline in question, from within its objects and within its noetic acts, and thus in no sense is it the rule of 'theologians'.

Insofar as the order of being exceeds and is never reducible to the order of history, Hanby regards reason as structurally contemplative and locates action as subordinate to contemplation in the noetic order. Being manifests itself to the intellect, making the intellect's primordial position receptive; the active appropriation occurs within the receptive *theoria*, for being is not manufactured by our activity, and does not have laboriously to be disinterred from deceiving appearances, but radiates its own truth of its own nature. Hanby does recognize Vico's formula, *verum quia factum*, as legitimate insofar as knowledge 'must always be "made" and "made anew", in order to "catch up" with what the object gives out of its inexhaustible depth', which means that there is *within* the priority of contemplation a unity of action with contemplation, a 'creative, "poetic" dimension inherent in contemplative receptivity'.[42] In contrast to this, modernity has assimilated contemplation to action in continuity with the modern conflation of nature and artefact, the reduction of act to brute facticity or inert givenness, with the inevitable result being an 'unprecedented coincidence of knowing and making' which undermines truth itself.[43] Science and technology become a single project, the measure of scientific success being the Baconian view of nature as that which is manipulable: nature as a made thing. For Hanby, only a primacy of contemplation preserves the transcendence by the order of being of the order of thought, which is the condition of truth. We receive before we make, and what we receive is the order of being itself, which comes to us from outside ourselves.[44]

Reason: Universal and objective, or narratively specified?

At this point, a critical divergence between Milbank and Hanby is apparent. Hanby adheres to a universal objectivity of reason and a fundamentally contemplative

---

42. Hanby, *Science*, 390.

43. Hanby, *Science*, 391.

44. Hanby's language about the givenness of truth, the equation of truth and being and its priority to the made resembles Joseph Ratzinger, *Introduction to Christianity* (San Francisco: Ignatius, 2004), 61, although Benedict has only critical words for Vico's *verum quia factum est*, as Peter Kucer stresses (*Truth and Politics: A Theological Comparison of John Milbank and Benedict XVI* (Minneapolis: Fortress Press, 2014), Chapter 1).

structure of knowledge. There is an intelligibility inherent in the objective order of things which necessarily, of its own nature, manifests itself to the knower regardless of that knower's presuppositions. In *contemplating* that order, the mind *receives* the truth, even if there is always an active process of appropriation 'within' that receptive *theoria*. 'The truth of being imposes itself on the act of thought in spite of the quality of our thought about it.'[45] 'The world' spontaneously discloses its created character to the knowing mind, even if that mind's prior frameworks darken or obscure the light of intelligibility emanating from being itself.

Hanby therefore acknowledges a certain qualified self-evidence to the structure of being, which is determinate: it is truthfully explicated in terms of form and *esse*. It is not only that science inevitably presupposes a metaphysics which attributes primacy to formal intelligibility, even if it denies this, but also that this intelligibility spontaneously makes itself evident to the mind by virtue of the intrinsic structure of created being. '[F]orm and *esse* hold ontological and epistemic primacy and are thus tacitly operative in *any* conceptual scheme', rendering differences of paradigm and conceptual scheme radically secondary.[46] Paradigms can be rationally adjudicated in the sense that they compete on the level-playing field which is accounting for what is real. Christian metaphysics is 'rationally superior' because it most comprehensively accounts for our universal 'elementary experience' of the world as being structured in a certain way. This elementary experience actually reveals the primacy of intelligibility, which is only explicable through giving ontological priority to form as 'self-communicating meaning'.[47] Hanby does acknowledge that there is an aesthetic dimension to rational superiority but emphatically does not subordinate the true to the beautiful; rather, it is the particular strength of the doctrine of creation that it allows for an integration of the objectivity of truth with its beauty, creation's 'depth of incommunicable being'.[48]

So there is, for Hanby, a universal structure of reason which transcends cultural difference: 'The act of theorizing *as such requires* a metaphysics of *esse* and an ontological conception of truth.'[49] There is no theorizing anywhere which avoids this requirement, no matter how forcefully it is denied. Although Hanby marries this to a principled acceptance of the absence of a neutral or uncommitted epistemic starting point, as we saw in his adoption of Przywara's 'suspended middle', he nevertheless links this with a definite assertion of universal self-evidence of a given structure of created being to the created intellect. I suggest below that the tension between these two claims represents a certain ambiguity in Hanby's account, but it is not an ambiguity which diminishes in Hanby the clear claim for a universal normativity of rational structure. This universality appears within the sciences' drive for normativity, even where its possibility is implicitly denied by the

---

45. Hanby, *Science*, 398.
46. Hanby, *Science*, 398.
47. Hanby, *Science*, 384.
48. Hanby, *Science*, 402.
49. Hanby, *Science*, 400, italics added.

reductionist method in question, as for example in Darwinism read as ontology, Hanby's major target. 'The truth of being will continually reassert itself even if our theories obscure it and our action will confirm this truth in some measure in spite of itself.'[50] Hanby thus explicitly repudiates a primacy of conceptual scheme which would suggest that there is no self-evidence of a rational structure of creation at all. This rational structure, both noetic and ontological, appears equally in all conceptual schemes.[51] The truth of being is guaranteed by its distinction from the order of history, which it always transcends. Apart from this transcendence of being by history, a notion of truth as a relationship between appearance and reality no longer has any purchase.

For Milbank, however, there is no universal self-evidence of reason, or being, or the norms of thought – no 'elementary experience' unformed by narrative. There is no appearance to every created intellect of an inescapably objective meaning in the order of things; no 'self-evidence' of the true and the good. 'Truth' does not consist in a correspondence of appearance to reality, nor are being and history demarcatable orders. Where, for Hanby, the distinction between God and world established by the doctrine of *creatio ex nihilo* grounds the difference between theology and the sciences, Milbank's metaphysics of participation questions a too-definite distinction of God from world: the world is the mediation of God for us, and God is not for us 'an other' to the world.[52] Milbank undercuts an autonomy of being or thought at every turn.[53] This means that theology is precisely *not* indifferent to the content of scientific thought but is intimately concerned with its every detail. Hanby, in contrast, stresses that the claims of evolutionary biology are neither here nor there from the theological point of view, so long as they do not trespass into covertly theological constructions.

Milbank is clear that his claims cannot be established on the basis of a universal reason. The peace of the narrative itself must convince. 'If my Christian perspective is persuasive, then this should be a persuasion intrinsic to the Christian *logos* itself, not [to] the apologetic mediation of a universal human reason.'[54] Consequently for Milbank there cannot be a dialectical superiority of Christianity's narrative; this would imply a sense in which it is more 'adequate to reality', but our perceptions of what is real, what there is to be adequate to, are not narrative-independent. We can only measure adequacy to reality from within the story we are in, which supplies us with the criteria for adequacy.[55] Certainly, for Milbank, one's view of the world

---

50. Hanby, *Science*, 400, italics added.

51. Hanby, *Science*, 398.

52. Eckhart and Cusa are crucial in Milbank's defence of this; TST, xxvi.

53. Meyer parses this in terms of a denial by Milbank of both substantive (metaphysical) and formal (noetic) autonomy (*Metaphysics*, 415).

54. Milbank, *TST*, 1.

55. In his discussion of Kuhn and MacIntyre Hanby seems to acknowledge this but does not draw the same conclusions. Hanby's invocation of MacIntyre here is interesting in that for MacIntyre it is perhaps not entirely clear exactly where standards of assessment and

cannot be rationally vindicated on the basis of a universal reason. Metaphysics is retained, but 'rational' vindication is rejected: he 'seeks to assert and foreground the ontological while, at the same time, resisting any attempt to positively or rationally vindicate such claims'.[56] Milbank could not, therefore, agree with the sense of Hanby's claim when he says that creation can be 'rationally vindicated'.[57] Hanby's reason, on Milbank's view, would be still too autonomous, and therefore his 'disciplines' are too autonomous as well, notwithstanding that this autonomy is theologically granted.

We have also seen that Milbank overturns the traditional priority of contemplation over action, of nature over culture. He would therefore be uncomfortable with the distinction Hanby makes between the ontological and noetic orders. For Milbank the distinctive quality of the Christian narrative is in its overcoming of the modernist dualisms of thought and world, making and being, acting and contemplating, culture and nature, time and eternity. In contrast, Hanby is invested in discerning a limit to human mediation in a discovery of an objective order of being which is independent of our making, despite his welcome of Blondel's account of 'mediating action'. In Milbank's use of him, Blondel's philosophy of action is seen as granting to the human power of making, our fabrication of the world, a positive theological value: we do 'make the world up' – precisely *not* in the Baconian sense of ever-greater control of nature but rather in the Blondelian sense of our lack of control of our own actions: they exceed and escape us. The problem in modernity is not its discovery of the unlimitedness of human mediation, its inescapability, but its interpretation of that mediation as signifying autonomy and self-referentiality. The regard of nature as manipulable, both made and makeable, which the arrival of modern science as technology rides on, is problematic only in its regard of this makeability as a marker of the 'secular'. When in modernity 'science' and 'technology', knowing and making, become a single project, the problem is precisely not this in itself but the interpretation of it as delimiting a sphere of the secular, when it does not have to be read that way. Whether or not it is read that way is dependent on how it is narrated, and *TST* argues that there is no prior rationale, apparent to all, for reading it one way or the other. It is simply a matter of persuasion, aesthetic attraction, fittingness (not in a correspondentist sense but rather an intuitive aesthetic-moral appropriateness which is judged by its place in a series); and Milbank's point is that the ubiquity of mediation can, with greater compellingness, be narrated in line with the

---

justification are supposed to obtain: within or beyond particular traditions. For a discussion of MacIntyre's critics on this point, and a constructive proposal, see Jennifer A. Herdt, 'Alasdair MacIntyre's "Rationality of Traditions" and Tradition-Transcendental Standards of Justification', *Journal of Religion* 78, no. 4 (1998): 524–46; of course the 'transcendental' solution offered here would not please Milbank. Herdt's treatment offers some support for Milbank's charge that MacIntyre is not fully historicist in the sense that Milbank is pursuing.

56. Meyer, *Metaphysics*, 411.

57. Hanby, *Science*, 402.

alternative modernity he discerns in Vico, Hamann, Jacobi and so on, who see in it an uncircumscribable participation in divine creativity.

How suspended is reason? Putting mythos before logos

There appears to be a profound impasse which undermines any complementarity between the two projects and seems to render the differences between their conceptions of theology and the disciplines irreconcilable. Hanby thinks the disciplines have a legitimate autonomy on the basis of their capacity to respond to the self-manifesting nature of being; Milbank thinks that they have no autonomy because 'reason' is not universal and truth is narratival. A nuanced response to this problematic presents itself here.

Firstly, a profound congruence of agenda underlies the divergence. For Milbank the Christian narrative of creation and redemption uniquely enables created difference as intrinsically irreducible and ontologically non-conflictual, and beyond this, as more than merely compatible without loss, but rather as actively harmonious. For Hanby 'autonomy' refers properly to the integrity of creation as 'different' from God and thus as constituting a worthy object of investigation 'in its own right', manifesting its createdness in its very structure and so revealing its distinction-without-separation from God which the orthodox doctrine of creation specifies. There is a congruence here between Hanby's 'autonomy' and Milbank's 'difference', which can be simply stated: theology never takes away from the dignity of created things but is rather the unique and pre-eminent way of establishing that dignity more deeply. Milbank's name for this dignity is 'difference'; Hanby's is 'autonomy'.

However, this congruence casts the disagreement in sharper relief, for the two are choosing to name the value of created being with quite different terms. An underlying tension in Hanby's account highlights this. Insofar as (Hanby's) reason originates in a suspended middle, whether Christian or not, it has no *absolute* starting point; and yet the universal objectivity of reason seems to function as an absolute starting point insofar as it trustworthily grounds the truth of thought in being. One could read Hanby as saying that the account of the world (story) which makes best sense of this is the Christian account of *creatio ex nihilo* and might argue for allowing him a legitimate *aporia* here. But he is equally committed to a real *externality* of truth to the mind; to an inherence in the order of being of a really determinate rational structure, in faithfulness to which alone the mind receives the truth; to the priority of *theoria* in the structure of knowledge; to the transcendence of the order of being over the temporal order. By simultaneously affirming the 'suspended middle' that reasoning is, he generates a more problematic *aporia*, and doubly so, than does Milbank; for not only do these theses pull more impatiently against a 'suspended' ungroundedness of reason, but they also limit his space to affirm an inherent, all-pervasive irresolvability in principle. Hanby admits a positioned reason with one hand, while endowing it with a capacity universally and reliably to know being with the other, and one must ask whether he has not smuggled back in an *un*suspended reason in so doing, or at the least allowed its suspension only partially to penetrate into the character of reasoning itself. For Milbank, in contrast, reason's positioning goes 'all the way down' (or perhaps 'all the way up'). Embracing a radical historicism and relativism, and a poetic account of knowledge, he carries through the 'suspension' of reason to the very end. He maintains a 'theological objectivism', which vindicates the aspiration to ultimacy in every narrative by invoking a teleological constraint on our makings, ethical and aesthetic, without conceding an inch on the matter of self-evidence; there is no given world that manifests itself to all. And yet, yoking thought to a constant seeking for a synthesis that is fitting beyond the present moment of making, Milbank is able to deny an intellectual 'anything-goes'. Refusing reason an absolute starting point, Hanby nevertheless seeks to secure a universally accessible knowledge. But this seems prima facie less consistent, less ready without embarrassment to embrace the *aporia* which 'knowing' is, than Milbank's 'complete *concession*' to cultural and historical relativity:[58] the suspension of reason must relinquish completely any attempt to anchor that suspension in some 'way the world is'.

But this section will argue that Hanby's chief concerns are readily saveable within Milbank's overall logic. An account of the 'self-evidence' of the rational structure of creation is licit, but *only* from within the utterly particular outlook of Christian orthodoxy. Hanby's understanding of the way in which the doctrine of creation enables the sciences to operate coherently would then be read from within a Milbankian model as the way in which the Christian *mythos* underwrites creaturely difference – as a working out of the meaning of the Christian narrative for the sciences. On this view, Milbank's fundamentally moral language – conflict and violence versus peace and harmony – is prior to, and informing of, a language of rationality, a commitment which will inform the appreciation and critique of Hans Jonas's philosophical biology pursued in Part III.

Considering Milbank's claim that 'only theology overcomes metaphysics', Hauerwas explains:

> Milbank does not mean to deny that theological speech is inherently metaphysical; rather, like Barth, he insists that a theological metaphysics cannot pretend to be more determinative than God.[59]

For Barth, Christian metaphysical claims are accessible only from the particularity of revelation. Milbank would agree with this, but by affirming 'the infusion of grace and the supernatural down into all forms of reasoning', he changes the content of the claim that reason is subordinate to revelation.[60] Rejecting revelatory positivism

---

58. Milbank, *TST*, 1–2.
59. Quoted in Meyer, *Metaphysics*, 315.
60. Meyer, *Metaphysics*, 424.

for a metaphysics of mediation, he deliberately blurs reason and revelation.[61] Every creature is revelatory to a degree that cannot be determined in advance and cannot be circumscribed, and so metaphysics *from the creature* which yet aspires to ultimacy is legitimate; and every act of reason is supernatural in orientation and scope. 'Conjecture' can validly begin anywhere – and does begin, inescapably, in every human action. This gives Milbank the wherewithal to have and eat the theological cake: reason is only itself as subject to revelation; but creatures and human acts are revelatory in themselves as participants in divine being. In this way there is space within a hermeneutic of narrative particularity for a legitimate universality of reason; it is not simply the presence of recognizably Christian cognitive content which legitimates knowledge (even if this is interpreted loosely in terms of a metaphysics of form), for reason and being are intrinsically disclosive and by virtue of their conjectural character they break the bounds of immanence. But reason is universal always and only on the basis of the irreducibly specific story about the mediative constitution of each creature and each act which Christian orthodoxy is.

The force of this particularist universality is expressed in Milbank's ecclesiology: the task of the church is to tell its story as universal in scope and significance but utterly particular in origin and validation.

> [A] gigantic claim to be able to read, criticize, [and] say what is going on in other human societies, is absolutely integral to the Christian Church, which itself claims to exhibit the exemplary form of human community.... [T]he logic of Christianity involves the claim that the 'interruption' of history by Christ and his bride, the Church, is the most fundamental of events, interpreting all other events.[62]

Appeals to 'reason', then, are and should be indistinguishable from appeals to the church. 'Theology, therefore, is answerable to reason precisely in so far as it is answerable to the Church.'[63] On this kind of view, the claim that a rational structure of creation is 'self-evident' would be regarded as an expression of the Christian narrative and would be guarded carefully lest it appear to be invoking a spurious 'objectivity'. Normative claims about what the whole of reality is like for everyone everywhere are narratively based on this 'most fundamental of events' which is

---

61. Douglas Hedley argues at length that Milbank is essentially a Barthian ('Should Divinity Overcome Metaphysics? Reflections on John Milbank's Theology and Social Theory and Confessions of a Cambridge Platonist', 271–98, 274). But Milbank works hard to distinguish himself clearly from Barth, and the rejection of revelatory positivism is the key step; for him, Barth is too Kantian and accepts the circumscription of reason, which is the heresy of modernity. Milbank's relationship with Barth is discussed helpfully in Meyer, *Metaphysics*, 421ff.

62. Milbank, *TST*, 390.

63. Milbank, *Being Reconciled*, 133.

universal in scope only as it remains non-negotiably particular and rhetorical. *Logos* is subsequent to *mythos*. 'Overall, it is clear that for Milbank "the universal mythos" of the Christian ontological vision is and must remain "an alternative *logos* to the *logos* of reason".'[64]

In this vein, if Milbank's hermeneutic is allowed to govern, Milbank's emphasis on peace and Hanby's emphasis on reason can be fully congruent.[65] Milbank's repudiation of the creeping ontologies of conflict characteristic of modern thought clearly comprehends the epistemic aspect of modern nihilism which elevates irrationality over rationality, meaninglessness over meaning. Hanby's tracing of the self-referential incoherence of Darwinism as undermining the ground of the world's intelligibility is, on this view, an exposure of its ontologically conflictual narrative and one whose moral-ethical consequences he recognizes.

Two examples from Milbank's oeuvre can be adduced to support this approach. Firstly, his response to other Catholic authors who propound the sort of 'objective' rational structure of creation that Hanby is defending is instructive. His treatment of the thought of Ratzinger/Benedict evinces a respect for a Catholic sense of the universality of reason.[66] His approving description of Benedict as 'a theologian in the lineage of the *nouvelle théologie*, which tends to stress the implicit yearning of reason towards faith and the completion of reason by faith, even within its own proper sphere of human understanding' could equally well apply to Hanby.[67]

---

64. Meyer, *Metaphysics*, 472, quoting Milbank, *Being Reconciled*, 170.

65. For Milbank unreason is conflict, an Augustinian theme comparable to Ratzinger/Benedict's persistent marriage of truth and love. Arguably Milbank can hold to this more forcefully than either Hanby or Ratzinger/Benedict, since he has wholly retracted *any* ground for the discernment of the truth other than the good: 'I do not, however, need "criteria" for persuasion, else it would not be truth that persuades. Since truth is also the good and good is also peace and harmony, it is the latter which persuade.' 'So the historical lure of love . . . is also the permanent witness of the understanding.' John Milbank, 'Invocation of Clio', *Journal of Religious Ethics* 33 (2005): 3–44, 41, 42.

66. 'With Pope Benedict, therefore, we proclaim the "Grandeur of Reason" in its unlimited reach' ('The Grandeur of Reason', 392).

67. Ratzinger says that '[e]ssentially [belief] is entrusting oneself to that which has not been made by oneself and never could be made' (Ratzinger, *Introduction to Christianity*, 70). This seems diametrically opposed to Milbank's emphasis on the poetic constitution of our knowledge of God. And yet Ratzinger is mentioned several times with the highest approval in 'The Grandeur of Reason', where Milbank explicitly identifies Ratzinger's defence of 'the Grandeur of Reason' with his own (392; see also John Milbank, 'The Future of Love: A Reading of Benedict XVI's Encyclical *Deus Caritas Est*', in *The Future of Love: Essays in Political Theology* (Eugene, OR: Cascade Books, 2009), 364–70), which expresses a sense of a common project). For Milbank a traditional emphasis on the 'objectivity' of faith, its resting on that which we did not invent, is an aspect of the *logos* for which the Christian *mythos* alone provides a framework. The difference between the two is treated in Kucer, *Truth and Politics*, where the contrast is correctly framed in terms of truth as created (Milbank)

Milbank treats Benedict's marriage of truth and love as a project continuous with his own, despite Benedict's appeal to a *shared* reason which we genuinely hold in common. Milbank's reading of Benedict suggests that his articulation of the narrative-specific character of *all* knowledge, the inescapability of conceptual schemes and the relativity and historicity of reason are meant to obtain at what we might call a meta-level. We return to Milbank's warmth towards Ratzinger/Benedict in a moment, but to offer a preliminary interpretation: for Milbank, there is an intrinsic and evident intelligibility of the natural order from the point of view of the Christian narrative. From within this narrative any number of claims might be made about the character of the natural order with a perfectly normative force. This vindicates Hanby's dialectical critique of Darwinist ontology as a rationally incoherent account of natural history, as well as Milbank's own employment of dialectical methods in *TST*, which he defends as legitimate exactly insofar as it takes place within the bounds of a rhetorical conception of the selection of the best stories.

To bear this out, a second example, of particular pertinence to our concerns here, is that Milbank seems to defend the normativity of a notion of formal essence teleologically conceived in negotiating biological reality, and he is welcoming of a realist account of form in the attraction of nature to universal forms, linking this to the notion of evolutionary convergence.[68] He marries this loyalty to form with his customary insistence on a foundational inexplicability in all functionally explanatory notions, and his approach to this theme takes place within a broader rhetorical project to elaborate the attraction of a framework of participated transcendence. Exploring the puzzling appearance of coherent 'species' in the context of evolutionary change, he develops a characteristic 'both-and' account of the endurance of form in the all-encompassing '*glissando*' of unceasing variation.[69] Indeterminacy and determinacy are reconciled, not opposed.

Thus Milbank willingly uses and defends a normativity of certain theological and philosophical concepts and often appears to do so in a dialectical manner, as when arguing that biological thought is compelled to acknowledgement of certain features of organisms. Although reading such comments in isolation might lead one to regard Milbank as closer to Hanby than I have presented him here, to construe them properly in Milbank's usage one must pay close attention to the grander narrative in which they are situated. In this narrative, capacity to 'fit' and explain the observed reality of the world is not denied as a 'valid' criterion of preference, but as we saw in our discussion of fittingness earlier, it is regarded ultimately as an aesthetic-rhetorical criterion, since the notion of 'reason' only obtains within the narrative of orthodoxy, which itself can only persuade by awakening desire. 'Fittingness' does not name a 'universal' reason, since the

versus truth as uncreated (Ratzinger/Benedict). Kucer narrates the debate in terms of their different responses to Vico's essentially historical conception of truth.

68. Milbank, 'Immanence and Life', 13.

69. Milbank, 'Life, or Gift and Glissando', 126.

capacity to identify something as fitting arises as a result of seeing the world in a certain way, having a certain conception of what there is to 'fit', and how one determines criteria of fittingness (e.g. what there is to be explained, what counts as good explanation) cannot be done on the basis of a universally apparent structure of being: one cannot say that a metaphysics of form and *esse*, for example, is compelled upon one by the universally observable nature of things. If one adopts a model like this, a narrative hermeneutic governing a universal reason, one does not have to surrender the universality of rational claims to allow that they are only apparent and defensible from the point of view of the narrative of orthodoxy. This interpretation is in accord with Milbank's move to overcome the oppositionality of relativity and truth sponsored by secular reason.[70]

Most importantly, such an interpretation underlines the specification of truth as peace. This is illuminated by Milbank's rejection of the violent and coercive character of a rationalist ethics, a view shared by Hauerwas who represents the problem as follows:

> An ethic claiming to be 'rational' and universally valid for all thinking people everywhere is incipiently demonic because it has no means of explaining why there are still people who disagree with its prescriptions of behaviour, except that these people must be 'irrational' and, therefore (since 'rationality' is said to be our most important human characteristic), subhuman.[71]

This critique throws light on Milbank's rejection of rationalism in favour of a reason which has a universal reach only from within its situatedness. On the model of a universal self-manifesting rational structure of being, failing to observe and consent to this self-manifestation is failing to see: implicitly if not explicitly, one must claim that such persons are blind, whether culpably or not. If the universality of reason is apparent only from the vantage point of a particular narrative, it is no longer a necessary (if unacknowledged) condemnation of others if its claims, founded on that reason, are not apparent to them. They simply could not be.

70. [There is a] need for at least some modicum of universal attachment, universal *mythos*. But there . . . transcendence offers a thought of the universal not as something clearly grasped, spatially fixed and operable, but rather as something eternally present yet not fully accessible. This universal is instead only available as diversely mediated by local pathways, as Augustine already divined. . . . But inversely, it is only by virtue of a local ecstatic opening to this universal that one has giving, or community, or sacred locality at all' (Milbank, *Being Reconciled*, 173).

71. Stanley Hauerwas, *Resident Aliens: Life in the Christian Colony* (Nashville: Abingdon, 2014), 101. For Milbank this too necessitates a priority of rhetoric over reason. 'Only [rhetorical] persuasion of the truth can be nonviolent, but truth is only available through persuasion. Therefore truth, and non-violence, have to be recognised *simultaneously* in that by which we are persuaded.' *TST*, 398, italics added.

With this in mind, we can make better sense of Milbank's approbatory attitude towards Ratzinger/Benedict, for whom a commonly held reason is a means of dialogue between peoples. The capacity to be rational unites us and can be the ground of political, religious and civic harmony. Reason in this sense is 'public'.[72] Were Milbank a straightforward relativist on the model of other modern deniers of 'truth', we would not expect a participation in the defence of a public reason; but his 'relativism' denies only the claimed obviousness of secular noetic autonomy, in favour of truth as peaceful illumination by the divine mind, to which there is no 'outside' and which can therefore never be externally assessed by comparison or contrast. He is therefore happy to background relativism and historicism in order to foreground a claim to universality and objectivity appropriate to the narrative's own logic: standing on the platform of the *logos* which itself is only the working out of the Christian *mythos*. Here it should be stressed that any 'meta-level' metaphor is limited by its spatial purchase: it implicitly imagines that the Christian narrative occupies a position 'above' the actual operation of rationality, whereas it is intrinsic to it: the emphasis on the relativity and historicity of reason is a pragmatic engagement with postmodernity from within the terms of the Christian *mythos*. If all is indeed myth, and one necessarily operates within the terms of a myth, there can be no objection to this: objectivity and universality are legitimate modes if based on the Christian *mythos*, and anyway (as Hanby's own genealogy suggests) these notions are emergent from a Christian conception of 'world' as 'creation' and thus are already mythically specific.

This short discussion highlights the radical nature of Milbank's claims about reason and its entire subordination to *mythos*, as well as showing how this view may be reconciled to a more recognizable account of critical reason, as long as the narrative hermeneutic remains prior. The difficulty of enunciating this position is characteristic of Milbank's project with its persistent favouring of paradox: to reunite the objective and the relative, the true and the constructed, as complementary rather than oppositional. The priority of narrative is retained even as that narrative is used to foreground a conception of the universal manifestation in creation of the *logos* which is Christ.

At this stage, it is appropriate to attempt a presentation of some conclusions from our investigation of theology's relationship with the disciplines. This is offered in light of the stipulations just elaborated: reason is 'relative' and incapable of dialectical vindication with respect to competing narratives but legitimately universal from the point of view of the Christian *logos* which is always wholly specified by the Christian *mythos*; it is not any the less 'true' because it is incapable of dialectical adjudication but rather alone tells the truth which exceeds any possible measurement on a fantastical level-playing field of narrative comparison.

---

72. Obviously the relationship between the rationality of faith and 'public reason' is complex in the thought of Ratzinger/Benedict. See Aidan Nichols, *Conversation of Faith and Reason: Modern Catholic Thought from Hermes to Benedict XVI* (Gracewing: Leominster, 2009), 190–206.

Theology is not a discipline: Theology and the disciplines revisited

The contrast between Hanby and Milbank generates a sense of two ways forward. On the one hand there is the view that every noetic act cannot help but encounter the truth about being. Scientific thinking is therefore legitimately autonomous with respect to theology. On this picture, the findings of the sciences have legitimacy regardless of the religious narrative in which they are situated. Theology makes no internal difference to the science in question, since the science itself can discover the truth about being 'from below'. On the other hand is the view that a science is only trustworthy insofar as it is narratively informed in the correct manner, that is, by the Christian *mythos*. Theology makes a total difference to the science in question, and outside of that narrative the science is untrustworthy. Milbank's problematization of a universal self-manifesting rational structure of creation suggests that the first of these options cannot be legitimate, and Hanby's trust in the universal self-manifestation of reason excludes the second. Is it the case that biology can discover 'the truth' about life only if it is operating from within the Christian *mythos*? Or does it have a legitimate 'independence' from theology?

On Milbank's logic, these are not genuine alternatives. The previous section defended a reason which claims universality only from its utterly particular *mythos*. Through this reason, universal only through its narratival particularity, the structure of creation is discerned to be an ontological mediation. An earlier section examined Milbank's estimation of science as *poesis*, arguing that every noetic act is intrinsically disclosive of ultimacy. Between these two points, the dichotomy presented here is transcended. The metaphysics of mediation specified by the Christian *mythos* protects science from a fideistic subordination to revealed doctrine, without cutting it loose into secular autonomy, because the story told by the Christian *mythos* is the story of participated transcendence and entire permeation of every aspect of immanence, noetic and ontological, by the divine. Every action mediates the supernatural; every existence is a participation in God. It was argued above that this has a radically liberating effect on the status of science, which is shown to be constitutively metaphysical in every act of knowledge; as inherently conjectural, it is disclosive and revelatory in its very constitution. If this approach is pursued, Milbank's aggressive rejection of the false theology which is modern sociology needs to be completed by an appropriate counterpoint. There must be a *legitimately* theological mode for social science or any other science, which would not be a trespassing but simply an expression of its own metaphysical constitution. Every discipline is inescapably theological and for it to be theological is, in fact, its only and exclusively honest mode. From within this context, the point can be safely stated in (Hanby's) terms of 'universal' reason: each discipline is an expression of the form of knowledge and being as created, in a mode appropriate to its disciplinary characteristics. Simon Oliver expresses both ideas when he suggests that 'all human discourses "participate" in theology by attending to the fundamentally *created* nature of their subject matters'.[73] We might add that since

---

73. Oliver, 'Introducing', 19.

for Milbank nature is all graced, the subject matters are theological not only as created but equally as redeemed and sanctified.[74] The subject matter carries as it were an entire theological load and not a partial one. Each discipline's participation in theology thus paradoxically gives it its own dignity as a discourse while at the same time underlining its comprehensive *lack* of independence from theology. In this way we can see a realization of what was sought in the opening sections of this chapter: theology actually constitutes the difference of the disciplines.

Milbank expresses this in his conception of the dispersal of faith in all the discourses of human reason. There is no human reason that is not already an illumination by the *Logos*. '[I]f reason is already Christological, then inversely, faith, until the *eschaton*, remains dispersed in all the different discourses of human reason.'[75] Insofar as every discipline is internally theological, not simply in an external relation to posited ultimates, one would expect theology's 'making strange' of the disciplines to be apparent, to characteristically occur, from within that discipline's own operation: one should look within the discipline for its own revelatory character, both in the (noetic) activity of its subjects and the (ontological) activity of its objects – activities which are not demarcatable but 'horizontally' participate in each other.[76] This then would be the legitimate burden of Hanby's point about the power of each discipline to discern its own specific opening to transcendence. It is no impugnment of biology to describe it as a theology. When Hanby describes Darwin as 'a theologian', this cannot be, by itself, a criticism. It is the type of theology which Darwinism is that begs question. It is therefore *not* the case that only a biology which is located consciously and explicitly within a Christian narrative, cognitively acknowledged, can 'know the truth' about life. Rather biological knowing is all *poesis* and biological objects are entirely a mediation of the divine. One can support the universality of reason – knowing and being do spontaneously reveal themselves – while holding that one narrative alone reveals the true character of knowing and being, naming them as peace.

The brief remark from Oliver which was quoted in the introduction to this chapter suggested what an account of theology's relationship to the disciplines should aim for: '[T]he peculiar character of non-theological discourses must be maintained while denying that those discourses are self-standing and autonomous from, or indifferent to, theological considerations.'[77] Part III of this study attempts to give some content to this: what would it actually look like to do this with, for example, biology's account of life? The 'making strange' Milbank calls for should make the 'peculiarity' of a discourse even more pronounced, because it is Christian theology which secures differences *as different*, saving them from sameness or conflictual

---

74. Milbank indicates the importance of this in his approach to Blondel, who 'does not merely wish to appeal to the God of creation: his philosophy marks out the place of the supernatural tout court – also as redemptive, and sanctifying' (Milbank, *TST*, 216).

75. Milbank, 'Programme', 35.

76. Milbank, 'Participated Transcendence Reconceived', 2.

77. Oliver, 'Introducing', 19.

jostling. The unique nature of each disciplinary difference is to be distinguished from theology's difference from the sciences, which is not a univocal difference but a different difference. It is this different difference which constitutes the 'disruptive' character of Christian theology: it disrupts because it comes, on this metaphor, from above, not from the same level; its interaction with the disciplines are not conversations between equivalents. When they become so, a bad extrinsicism is governing the exchange. For this difference between differences to be a difference of true peace, it simply must be narrated theologically. Such a narration renders less containable a discipline's objects and its noetic processes and so heightens and does not flatten the depth and distinctness of a discipline's own language about its objects, such as biology's language about life. Instead of dull homogeneity resulting from a fundamentalism which absorbs every knowledge into a single discourse of revelatory positivity, the result of such disruption would be a 'making strange'. The prerogative of discerning and where necessary critiquing that discourse by exposing ontologically conflictual elements – which may include, drawing from Hanby, the attribution of inherent irrationality to nature, or the granting of ontological priority to parts rather than wholes – is important in this, since these elements limit and homogenize a discipline and its objects. Most importantly, the critique will be most fundamentally a moral discernment: insofar as a discipline erects a foundational conflictuality at the heart of reality itself, it begs theological judgement and disruption.

To attempt a programmatic statement, the underlying methodological point is this: only if the discipline is regarded as a *kind* of theology in its own right, a *kind* of discourse about ultimacy, a conjecture which is intrinsically metaphysical in scope and reach, will its distinctness and irreducibility be apparent. The discipline must be allowed to be a 'theology' in its own way, for speaking about creatures is always a kind of speaking about God. This kind of view is distinct from the now widely acknowledged point that sciences often depend on (acknowledged or unacknowledged) historical theological assertions in their forms of reasoning.[78]

---

78. See for example the analysis of Dobzhansky's evolutionary biology in Stephen Dilley, 'Nothing in Biology Makes Sense Except in Light of Theology?', *Studies in History and Philosophy of Biological and Biomedical Sciences* 44 (2013): 774–86, which is an instance of the sort of analysis we are seeking to challenge, since Dilley sees theology as only *limitedly* operative in scientific thinking, and therefore as in principle excludable. Acknowledging that theologies of one sort or another are pervasive in the thought of many eminent biologists such as Ernst Mayr, Richard Dawkins, Charles Darwin, Francis Collins, Stephen Jay Gould and others, Dilley admits that 'for a paradigm that putatively outgrew God-talk a long time ago, the presence of so much theology remains a striking curiosity' (774). Dilley observes the explicit operation of theological data in Dobzhansky's thought, which he rightly questions at the level of theology but still thinks that there could be an evolutionary biology without theology: 'Of course, I do not claim that evolutionary theory, or the polemic for it, requires theology per se' (774). Contrast the approach of historian John Hedley Brooke, who resists a science-religion 'essentialism' which seeks to store the

Observing the way in which particular theologies function in scientific discourses is informative, but trivial in comparison to the comprehensive claim that science itself is always, inescapably and altogether, a 'theology'; the theology is not 'drawn on' by the science in an external sense but actually is the doing of the science.

In light of this reading of the disciplines as legitimately theological, one must ask what has happened to theology and to theologians. Does Christian theology as a distinct discipline exist at all on this view? The elevation of all discourses as theological in danger of making the activity of the 'theologian' unintelligible. Where is the boundary between 'theology proper' and the theology which is biology, or any other discipline? If theology is a constant speaking 'in the voice' of other disciplines, does it have its own voice at all? This persistent ambiguity highlights the fundamental paradox at the heart of Milbank's approach, which this chapter has attempted to clarify but which presses our treatment the more severely as we have extended the term's purchase. What actually is 'theology' in the sense in which a Christian 'theologian' does it? The next chapter opens with a consideration of the theological task in light of this question, but a tentative attempt to resolve it is called for to conclude the treatment of this chapter.

Milbank makes three specifications which confirm that he does not support the loss of a distinct role for Christian theology. Firstly, when he says that theology speaks always 'also' in the tones of history, economics, etc., the force of this 'also' is that theology is not reducible to the disciplines, even if the boundary with the disciplines is not easily specified and notwithstanding that he himself does not attempt an exact specification. Second, only an irreducibility of theology to the disciplines can secure as 'disruptive' the prophetic difference which Milbank claims theology makes.[79] Thirdly, if theology *alone* is science, it is not the case that it can simply be replaced by the other discourses.

The appearance of contradiction persists because of the ever-present temptation to picture 'theology' and 'the disciplines' as occupying the same genus, the genus of 'disciplines' with delimited subject matters. The fitting response to the question 'Where is theology?' is to deny that theology is '*a discipline*' at all. This safely keeps it from beginning, by oversight or habit, to share a genus with other knowledges and thus begin to compete with them, which brings in all the dangers of extrinsicism, as identified by Hanby, and suggests that 'God' is the object of theology in the same

two categories in safe isolation from one another. John Hedley Brooke and Geoffrey Cantor, *Reconstructing Nature* (Oxford: Oxford University Press, 1998).

79. '[W]hile insisting that no human discourse has any "secular" or "scientific" autonomy in relation to theology, I seek to recognise equally that theology has no "proper" subject matter, since God is not an object of our knowledge, and is not immediately accessible. Instead, theology must always speak "also" about the creation, and therefore always "also" in the tones of human discourses about being, nature, society, language and so forth. A "theological" word only overlays these discourses – or can be judged to do so, since the overlay is never unambiguous – in a certain disruptive *difference* that is made to them. Here, also, there is a "making strange"' (Milbank, *WMS*, 3).

way that, say, animals are the object of zoology.[80] This would illuminate Milbank's rejection of 'dialogue' between theology and the disciplines.[81] Such a 'dialogue' is not possible where there is no equivalence whatsoever between the interlocutors.

Addressing the question of theology's credibility in a secular era, Hauerwas says that theology's worth depends on it being able to say what cannot adequately be said otherwise, or in other language. If all theological terms can be translated into other terms without loss, it lacks credibility as a necessary voice:

> [J]ust to the extent this [translation] strategy has been successful, the more theologians have underwritten the assumption that anything said in a theological framework cannot be of much interest. For if what is said theologically is but a confirmation of what we can know on other grounds or can be said more clearly in nontheological language, then why bother saying it theologically at all?[82]

What is it that theology has to say about life that cannot be said apart from theology? Which could not be said except in a theological voice?

Although this way of framing the question is attractive, on the view we have been considering it needs to be qualified to avoid smuggling in a problematic conception of theology's role. Milbank's view is that theology does not speak in one voice only; it is not a voice which supplements or adds to other accounts. It speaks in the tones of other discourses and has no subject matter of its own, because transcendence is not a compartment of being. Milbank would premise theology's credibility not on theology's specific competence to say something 'of its own' but rather on theology's competence to show that nothing at all is said 'non-theologically', because every creature mediates God. It is not that some kinds of talk are theological, and some not, and our task is to explain the rationale for the specifically theological kind. Rather, all kinds of talk are theological, and the credibility of theology is to show that, and then to narrate it peacefully. Theology therefore exceeds 'relevance', just as God is not 'relevant' to the world.[83]

---

80. The invention of the modern university, with departments which sit alongside one another each with their own fields of study, inevitably contributes to this impression. The present study makes no attempt to consider the implications of the thesis for the institutional place of theology in contemporary higher education. Gavin D'Costa, *Theology in the Public Square*, and Paul MacDonald, *Christian Theology and the Secular University* (Oxford: Routledge, 2017), offer usefully divergent accounts of the various options.

81. Cf. Smith, *Introducing Radical Orthodoxy*, 69–70.

82. Stanley Hauerwas, 'On Keeping Theological Ethics Theological', in *Against the Nations: War and Survival in a Liberal Society*, ed. Hauerwas (Notre Dame, IN: University of Notre Dame Press, 1992): Chapter 2, 25.

83. 'Any attempt to evaluate Milbank's [theology] in terms of its "relevance" would represent a betrayal of the vision he is trying to share. Its truth is not judged by its relevance. . . . The whole point is that it beckons as a radical alternative.' Pat Logan, *Policing the Sublime: Tradition and Transformation. Report of a Seminar with John Milbank, 5–7 July*

What does it mean then to say that theology '*alone*' is science? Theology remains the true 'science' because it is the form of knowledge itself. The form of knowledge as itself theological is what means there can be 'other' sciences, which are only sciences as participations in the science which is theology, the knowing of God. In other words, we could reverse the metaphor we are using here and say that there is only one discipline, theology, and the other 'subjects' are not disciplines at all. This formulation foregrounds the fact that there is only one true *scientia*, and that is the *scientia* of God. But Milbank's relentless stressing of the mediative character of all human knowing is perhaps better captured by the refusal to specify theology as 'a' discipline. The alternative inescapably suggests that theology is a delimitable field with discernible boundaries, a specifiable object and a single method, whereas Milbank's point is that it is not delimited and has no boundaries, because it is a participation in God's knowledge. In any case, the force of the point is the same: theology is not comparable to the others and does not occupy the same plane. Only in this way can the both-and approach that is so characteristic of Milbank be maintained.

One precaution which would indicate the true character of theology's task, while resisting the impression of theology as *a* discipline, would be to use the term 'mastery' only in the most circumspect manner, when its paradoxically peaceful character has been fully specified. 'Mastery' by itself sounds inherently combative, generating just the impression we are trying to avoid: a picture of theology alongside the disciplines, competing with them for the same space. Boersma's title for theology, 'Queen of Hospitality', might be preferable, not only because it better encapsulates the non-violent nature of theology's 'mastery' but also because there is a dissimilarity of genre between 'host' and 'guest': they are fundamentally not the same sort of thing. Insofar as theology is framed as 'host' and the other disciplines as 'guests', the discontinuity between them is clearly framed. A 'host' is at home, but 'guests' are not in a space they own. Milbank's emphasis in appropriating this metaphor would be that it is only if theology is allowed to *preside* as host that the disciplines can be welcomed into a peace which enables their distinctive operations and does not play them off against one another. The peaceable role of 'host' does not preclude recognizing that some disciplines have become so pseudo-theological that within this picture they are not welcomed by theology as presider.

Where 'mastery' implied a continual subjugation of the disciplines in a relationship which was disturbingly framed in terms of domination, the metaphor of 'host' emphasizes that theology is constitutively averse to competing with them, except where one of them arrogates the role of host to itself, and so undermines not only itself but everything else too. It is just this usurpation of role as presider which biology and other disciplines have arguably attempted in the modern era, in trying to become the *most* basic account of reality to which all others can be reduced.

1995, Anglican Association for Social Responsibility, 1995, 30, quoted in Malcolm Brown, *After the Market: Economics, Moral Agreement and the Churches' Mission* (Oxford: Peter Lang, 2004), 163.

But as false presiders, they can only be pseudo-hosts, wolves among sheep, since to them guests are ultimately competitors to be assimilated to themselves in an act of power.[84] It is for the sake of peace and difference that theology narrates all; to it belongs the presiding role of host, because it alone narrates harmonious difference, and so heightens and does not flatten the distinctive and mutually irreducible character of the disciplines, creating space for 'guests' in the first place. Startling as this may seem in light of Milbank's decidedly inhospitable treatment of sociology, the argument of this chapter has attempted to show that this is the true logic of his position: theology makes real difference possible, including disciplinary difference; but it can only do this as both unique and pervasive in the intellectual enterprise. The critical side of this role, where theology's narration appears as a No rather than a Yes, is that as presider it retains the prerogative of interrogating and disrupting any disciplinary endeavour which attempts to assume that role itself. This interrogation is undertaken for the sake of the disciplines which can have integrity only so long as theology is host, securing peace (or in Hanby's terms 'reason'). Theology is the Queen of Hospitality because it constitutively cannot seek to eradicate difference by reducing or assimilating all others to itself, since its discourse just is the celebration of created difference; but, paradoxically, this queenship can only be exercised through its possessing the prerogative to narrate all differences within its peace.

What then, to repeat, *is* Christian theology? It is simply the reasoning internal to the narrative of peace. What is its *specific* task? Its task is to narrate that peace for all, again and again, in all the different voices of human knowledge.

The eschatological hospitality of Jesus could provide a concrete model for this task: 'I go to prepare a place for you.' How could Christian theology 'prepare a place' for each of the disciplines, in such a way as to enable that specific created difference each one concerns itself with?[85] This puts to bed the fear of theocracy, while at the same time establishing that the true 'location' or identity of the disciplines is always narrated theologically. While this is not without judgement, nevertheless the intention is to support and to nourish, not to deny or undermine. Expressing the matter in this way illuminates the specificity of each discipline and the particular difference it expresses, and equally recognizes that the true identity of each discipline is as a member of the knowledge of God that is theology, and so constitutes an elevation of the disciplines to a theological dignity. It also functions as a reminder that the realization of that welcome in its fullness is necessarily eschatological and calls for a practice marked by hope, trust and humility.

---

84. Biology is particularly egregious in this respect; for a recent example, see E. O. Wilson, *The Meaning of Human Existence* (New York: Liveright, 2014). The aspiration to ultimacy is a legitimate expression of biology's theological constitution as we have discerned it here, but the conflictual and exclusive character of the explanatory project, not to mention its fantasized autonomy, shows it as a confused exercise of that constitution.

85. Jn 14.2 (NRSV). The Conclusion tentatively suggests what specific practice this might entail for theologians.

The question which has been our concern so far is now asked more precisely, and answered more directly, in such a manner as to justify the concerns of the second half of this book which turn to specific questions in 'another' discipline, life science. Simply put, it is only by such an attending to the disciplines that Christian theology expresses a genuine faithfulness to its own logic, which is the refusal of an 'outside' to its domain. It finds its voice in and through the theological character of all knowing. 'To speak about God [theology] must speak about something else; indeed its speaking about God really is only the difference it makes to speaking about something else.'[86] Indeed, we cannot speak about God directly at all: 'to speak about God [one] *must* speak about something else.'[87] In fact 'the whole point of speaking of God at all is found in the difference it makes for speaking about other subjects'.[88] It is only in such a speaking that Christian theology finds its voice.

Concluding Part II: Hospitality and prophecy

Those who remain unconvinced at this stage will not unfairly point out that Hanby's attempt at a specification of the relationship between theology and the disciplines is superior in precision, coherence and consistency to the thoroughly ambiguous and paradoxical nature of the picture generated by Milbank's position. Hanby has sought to give a detailed and careful analysis of the theology-science relation, delimiting responsibilities and tasks. Milbank achieves no such clarity, and exactly what and where 'theology' is for him remains remarkably difficult to pin down. Some may consider him the loser simply on these grounds.

At the close of this chapter, one needs frankly to acknowledge this – but also, in response, to advert to the fact that (for Milbank) to expect or require such exactitude is wrong-footed in principle. Parts I and II of this book have attempted the awkward task of working with this decidedly uncooperative stance, attempting to introduce what clarity is possible while refusing to iron out its un-systematizable character. All that can be said in defence at this stage, *pace* Janz, is that the nature of knowledge itself seems to call for an approach that is permissive in just this way; and that if we are sympathetic to a vision in which reality and knowledge just are participations in God, we are going to be led continually in this direction.[89] This

---

86. Milbank, 'Programme', 35.

87. Milbank, 'Programme', 35, italics added.

88. Meyer, *Metaphysics*, 424.

89. This results from acknowledging 'the sheer impossibility of isolating cognitive or logical borders both discrete enough and of wide enough scope to be of any use in the business of searching for truth' ("Immanence and Life", 3). Transcendence conceived participatively is the only way forward, 'a kind of natural, even common-sensical oscillation between the finite and the infinite, which one can dub "participation in the infinite"', for '[w]ithout this sense of participation whereby one mysteriously claims somewhat to know the unknown, one is left with the yet more exorbitant complexities of trying either to absolutise

in no way precludes the speculative adoption of principles and expectations, since on this picture intellectual virtue is a continual seeking of the fitting next act in the series, fraught with risk but mandatory nevertheless. The concluding paragraphs of this chapter, and the opening sections of Part III, are just such a seeking.

Looking again at a summary statement of the assertive and unapologetic nature of theology's agenda in light of the approach defended here, it is apparent that far from diminishing the force of Milbank's account of theology's mastery, the present critique has rather increased it, simultaneously with illuminating the peaceable nature of the project.

> Unlike correlationist strategies that defer the 'truth' of the natural sphere to secular sciences . . . [Radical Orthodoxy] claims that there is not a single aspect of human existence or creation that can be properly understood or described apart from the insights of revelation. . . . 'Radical Orthodoxy defers to no experts and engages in no dialogues because it does not recognise other valid points of view outside the theological'.[90]

The elevation of the disciplines as intrinsically and legitimately 'theological' is not a 'deferring to experts', a 'dialogue' or an apology. It is a confident declaration of the status of all knowing and being in line with Christianity's own logic: the participation of all things in God.

In light of these reflections, and in preparation for the next chapter, how should theology engage the modern sciences of life? Two moments can be observed. The first moment can be called 'prophetic' in the sense that it comes at a critical angle to a discipline immanently conceived. It expresses the basic proposition that 'nature', 'society', 'life' and so on simply are not the same when narrated by the Christian *mythos* as when narrated by a *mythos* of pure immanence. This is the sense of theology's 'making strange': at home in the story of the world created and redeemed, 'life' is not the same thing as in a world defined in terms of the autonomy of the secular. We must not underestimate the discontinuity that obtains between a science conceived in terms of pure immanence and that science 'at home' in the house of theology: the former is two dimensional, depthless; the latter infinite and unfathomable. It is precisely that striking continuity-in-discontinuity which the language of 'making strange' encapsulates: similar enough to be recognizable; different enough to be new, unexpected, unfamiliar. The 'prophetic' moment prevents the language of theology as 'host' from attenuating this sense of the difference of a discipline narrated in theological voice versus the

---

the finite or of claiming fully to know the infinite' ('Immanence and Life', 4). It is just this that constitutes, he says, what Benedict XVI calls 'The Grandeur of Reason' ('Immanence and Life', 3).

90. Smith, *Introducing*, 69–70, quoting John Milbank, 'Radical Orthodoxy: Twenty-Four Theses', in *Radical Orthodoxy? – A Catholic Enquiry*, ed. Laurence Hemming (Aldershot: Ashgate, 2000), 33–45, thesis 5.

same one narrated in a voice of fantasized autonomy. Narratives of life which are ontologically conflictual, or in which life is defined principally in reference to death, or in which life is explained exclusively in terms of matter reductively conceived, rather than 'from above' in reference to God's own life, beg prophetic disruption.

The second moment is 'hospitable', because it elevates the knowing of the disciplines by illuminating them as participations in theological knowing. It expresses the way in which the narration of knowledge and being in the Christian *mythos* results in the highest estimation of biological knowledge and its objects. In this moment, biology is recognized as always already a kind of theology. The knowledge of the sciences of life is recognized to be poetic and to have transcendent and not merely immanent purchase, and the world of organic life is regarded as a theological object, which is just what a metaphysics of mediation specified in the Christian narrative mandates and requires. This is the moment in which Christian theology might be said – with suitable caveats – to 'learn from' biology, because life itself is revelatory as a participation in transcendence. This is what we shall see occurring in Chapter 6 in Jonas's philosophical biology: the organism testifies to its own irreducibility. But this 'hospitable' learning and speaking by theology remains critical in manner, since it is fully discriminating with regard to narratives of pure immanence and always looks for the aesthetic-ethical teleological constraint in the discernment of noetic acts. It is also a project of engagement which is in principle unfinishable, since the analogical mediation of transcendence by immanence has no *a priori* limit.

However, theology's 'speaking in the tones of' the discourses and disciplines of human reason is a performance that crosses the bounds of these two moments and unites them. Theology's logic is to speak of God by speaking of the world. If there is no unmediated knowledge of God, theology concerns itself with immanence as its privileged means of attending to transcendence: Christianity 'requires, as a full exercise of reason . . . infinite exact study of the natural world'[91] – for 'our knowledge of God, since it is analogically mediated, is *always* and *only* given through a shift in our understanding of the things of this world'.[92] Jonas's philosophical biology partially represents such a 'shift' in which our knowledge of the world of life shows itself as a true analogical mediation of our knowledge of God.

To summarize: theology makes a disruptive difference to biological discourse by illuminating it through a higher estimation of it, both 'subjectively' (the knowing of its practitioners) and 'objectively' (the status of its object, life) than it could 'autonomously' support; but at the same time life itself and the knowing of that life is prophetic for ontology, breaking the bounds of immanence and so performing this theological work for the sciences of life themselves. In this way our knowing of life comes to be a knowing of God, and vice versa. Part III undertakes the risky endeavour of carrying out both elements of this project to imagine a theological

---

91. Milbank, 'The New Divide', 30.
92. Milbank, 'Foreword', 13.

speaking in the voice(s) of the sciences of life. The discussion attempts to preserve a sense of the inevitable ambiguity that Christian theological 'overlay' brings to its engagements with the disciplines. In its combination of interrogative judgement of conflictual ontologies, and its narration of the poetic and disclosive character of life and the life sciences' own knowing, theology reveals life; but the life it reveals is always already a speaking of God.

Part III

LIFE

In *TST*, theology interrogated the use of 'society' by social science. What would it look like for theology to undertake such an interrogation of 'life'? This third part of the book is an exercise in attention to the particularities of a certain set of creatures, namely the living, to discern in what sense they cannot be contained by immanence, which is to say, by themselves considered as circumscribable controllable 'facts' (in the modern sense), and equally to the biological language in which understandings of creatures are expressed. This is meant as a speculative playing out of the narrative we are working with: namely that immanence is never analysable as purely immanent; transcendence is not brought in from outside as an extrinsic addition based on a positivity of revelation but manifests itself in the excess by the creature of itself.

Part III thus attempts an examination of biological phenomena in such a way as to show the intrinsically theological character of life itself and of the knowledge of that life: life breaks the bounds of finitude and is prophetic for ontology. In critical exchange with Hans Jonas, the book explores what it might look like to narrate this prophetic character according to the Christian *mythos*. The hope is that this will constitute a creative challenge to theology and to the sciences to take more seriously the significance of life per se: not simply human life but life as such.

Chapter 5

THEOLOGY AND BIOLOGY

THE MEANING OF 'LIFE'

Defining a vitalist agenda

This part of the book attempts to put the work of the previous parts to use in a specific and applied manner, so a brief recap is appropriate.

The first two chapters examined the view that Christian theology is characterized by a unique generality: it is interested in 'the way in which the epiphany of God makes a difference to everything'.[1] Two expressions of theology's interest in everything have been discerned, which correspond to an ontology and epistemology. Firstly, theology is obliged through its very constitution to concern itself with the mediation of God by the world in every respect. Revelation is not in this sense an extra to creation but is the deeper visibility to the eyes of faithful reason of what creation has always been, namely an uncircumscribable mediation of the infinite by the finite. Theology therefore concerns itself with transcendence by and through concerning itself with immanence. In this sense it is bound to attend unlimitedly to every kind of enquiry into creatures. This is why organic life as such is a theological object. Secondly, in both exposing the narrative form of knowledge and embracing it without loss of difference, Christian theology interrogates the narratives of all knowledges, with the particular mission of narrating them in the ontological framework of peace which is its own story, and in the process exposing and redeeming violent or conflictual elements in those narratives. Theology questions the disciplines by bringing to bear on them a regard of each creature as a mediation of God. It was also suggested that metaphor of hospitality is suitable for expressing the complementary nature of these two dimensions of theological work, since the host must prepare a place for each guest, which involves attending to each one in its specificity; and at the same time, for the sake of all, it must resist attempts by guests to usurp the role of host as the one exclusively competent to narrate the peace of the Father's house. This is not a passive peace of mere cohabitation but a plenitudinous peace of infinitely diverse harmony.

In considering the shape of theology's engagement with the modern scientific knowledges of life, it has been suggested that there are two moments. One expresses

1. Oliver, 'Radical Orthodoxy: A Conversation', 30.

the discontinuity between the modern scientific knowing of life and knowledge of life which is the Christian *mythos*, which results in a 'making strange' of life when it is narrated by theology. The second expresses that narrative's estimation of noetic acts as intrinsically conjectural, aspiring to ultimacy and in some mysterious sense actually constituting the world as world by participating in God's creative act. In this way the modern knowledges of life are regarded as being intrinsically theological. Both elements stand for that 'shift' in our knowledge of this world by which alone our knowledge of God is given.

The remainder of the book defines a vitalist agenda for theology as the best expression of these interests and concerns with respect to life. 'Theological vitalism' would be a theological speaking in the tones of biology which attends to the concrete reality of the embodied organism and attests to the ultimacy and peacefulness of life. Jonas's view of the organism, which manifests life as irreducible to non-life, irreducible to death, is narrated as the claim that life is what is finally real. A theological vitalism constitutes a claim for what life most fundamentally is and is like, namely, that it derives its being from the non-rivalrous life of God, which, as gift without contrast or contest, is peace. In relation to Jonas, this represents both hospitable reception and prophetic disruption.

Theological vitalism embraces the paradox of knowledge which Milbank's account has unashamedly courted: knowing life is knowing God, and knowing God is knowing life. This is the always-puzzling character of theology, which speaks of God by speaking of everything, and speaks of everything by speaking of God. The notions of 'conjecture' and 'theurgy', which have already been touched on, explicate this. As mediations of the infinite, the objects of any discipline cannot be securely finitized, just as the cognition which grasps them cannot do so in terms of pure immanence. Speaking about creatures is intrinsically speculative: it represents a kind of informed, always-evolving 'guess' or 'conjecture' as to what is really the case. 'Theurgy', on the other hand, describes the presence of the highest in the lowest; attention to the lower is itself an attention to the higher. Whatever is true of creatures is not true only or limitedly of the creature but always manifests the real in excess of itself. Thus, divine life can be understood from below, 'conjecturally', while creaturely life is understood from above, 'theurgically'. This paradox is defining of orthodoxy itself, since in the Incarnation flesh becomes our privileged means of seeing God, yet God alone remains the adequate condition for seeing flesh. Conjecture and theurgy are images of one another: God's descent to us and our ascent to God are inseparable in the Logos who is both divine and mortal flesh: a living organism whose fleshly life was itself the life of the one God. This is the coincidence of organismic with divine life. In light of this, the project of a participative metaphysics applied to the biological realm is simply the logic of incarnational orthodoxy extrapolating itself to the whole created order.[2]

---

2. Celia Deane-Drummond pursues a doctrinally focused treatment of the significance of the Incarnation for nature and ecology in 'Who on Earth Is Jesus Christ? Plumbing the Depths of Deep Incarnation', in *Christian Faith and the Earth: Current Paths and Emerging*

The complexity of the following enterprise now becomes apparent, since there are two readings going on: the organism reveals God; God reveals the organism. The role played by Jonas in this book reflects this complexity, for it proves impossible to say once and for all what Jonas's philosophical biology 'does' for Christian theology, how the theologian 'uses' him.[3] For it is not just the case that 'theology' reads 'biology' and brings to it its unique narrative, within which alone biological 'facts' are saved for transcendence; this remains too extrinsic a conception. It is that the characteristics of organismic life, and the knowledge of that life, are seen to be theological, show themselves as theological. The organism is a theological fact, and biological language about organisms is mediative. This reflects the two moments of theology's engagement with the disciplines. But in light of the vision of reason considered above, the theologian should be undaunted by the seeming impossibility of 'beginning' this reciprocal reading from somewhere, because the lack of a given starting point has been peacefully narrated: it is the character of knowledge as such, not a negative *aporia* but 'suspension' in which reason's nature is revealed as faith and nature's nature is revealed as grace.

Considering life

The form of knowledge means that concepts foundational to moral and intellectual discourse are narrative-dependent. For *TST* the key cases of such terms are 'virtue', 'truth', 'soul', '*polis*'.[4] In his analysis of social science Milbank subjects the notion of 'society' to critique: in the very fact of being 'empirical', it embodies some claim about what is most basic to human being and so carries a narrative freight. Outside of a theological narrative the concepts of virtue, truth, soul, etc. will necessarily

---

Horizons in Ecotheology, ed. Celia Deane-Drummond, Denis Edwards, Sigurd Bergmann and Ernst Conradie (London: Bloomsbury, 2014), 31–50.

3. In other words, one cannot say exactly what the 'meta' in 'meta-narrative' specifies. In a critique of Lindbeck's 'meta-narrative realism', Milbank says of Christianity as 'meta-narrative' that 'one simply cannot exhibit in what its "meta" character consists, without already carrying out this interpretation, this regulation, to the widest possible extent'; 'the metanarrative ceases . . . to be only a privileged set of events, but rather becomes the whole story of human history which is still being enacted and interpreted in the light of those events' (Milbank, *TST*, 390).

4. Commenting on Radical Orthodoxy more generally, Oliver describes the task of engagement with the concepts central to other disciplines as follows: 'It's not an interdisciplinary outlook which claims that theology must in some sense fit itself into other discourses by finding banal similarities, nor one that seeks accommodation with the rationalities, priorities and conceptualities of other discourses, as was true of much liberal theology in the 1960s and 1970s. Rather, this approach allows us to question fundamentally the very histories of the concepts that many forms of discourse so often take for granted and deploy unreflectively' (Oliver, 'Radical Orthodoxy: A Conversation', 38).

embody other narratives of meaning, of what is given;[5] if adopted without criticism, they will be like covert enemy agents causing sabotage behind the lines.[6] As 'society' is for social science, so 'nature' is for the natural sciences and 'life' for biological sciences. In this sense there is a congruence between society, nature and life; these terms might be seen to function similarly in the discourses of their respective sciences, playing the role of the positive given which is yet the thing to be explained. And, in the same way, none of these sciences can narrate the antinomy which appears at their foundation: is their operative term – 'society', 'nature', 'life' – that which does the explaining, or that which is the explained? For Milbank only a *theological* reason can narrate this lack of an absolute beginning for thought. And so one 'prophetic' task for theology would be to look closely at the notion of 'life' in biology and bring to bear on this the way in which Christianity narrates 'life'.[7] The centrality of 'life' to so many modern and postmodern discourses, and its lack of substantive analyses in either philosophy or theology, makes such an enterprise timely and important.

> The 'biosphere', 'the right to life', 'life-support', 'neurobiology', 'biotechnology' . . . 'life coach', 'life, liberty and the pursuit of happiness', 'the good life'. These words and other phrases are blithely spoken and understood in popular discourse, but what *life* means – understood contextually, historically, intentionally, unintentionally, implicitly – is rarely addressed in any substantive way. In the most fundamental way, the question of life is at the root of the scientific,

5. Milbank does nevertheless think that theology's language about these things can be minimally accessible to outsiders ('I do not apologise for residual apologetics'); but this is precisely not translation, accommodation or correlation; rather, it is allowing the faith's own 'discursive developments that are to a degree [intelligible and] convincing even to those outside faith's circle'. Milbank, 'Programme of Radical Orthodoxy', 37.

6. Commenting on the uncritical adoption of Newton's conception of motion, Milbank comments, '[T]heology can be wrong-footed if it simply assents to what the secular world takes for granted, especially as Newton's ideas were very much informed by theological assumptions' (Oliver, 'Radical Orthodoxy: A Conversation', 37). Conor Cunningham, *Darwin's Pious Idea: Why the Ultra-Darwinists and Creationists Both Get It Wrong* (Grand Rapids, MI: Eerdmans, 2005), and Hanby, *Science*, are particularly interested in the theological assumptions of key concepts in Darwinism and neo-Darwinism and cover this ground well.

7. Oliver recognizes that the mandate to confidently interrogate 'concepts that have traditionally been held solely within the purview of other subjects' has made Radical Orthodoxy attractive to many younger scholars; he mentions motion, space and time as concepts which have received theological treatment within Radical Orthodoxy ('Radical Orthodoxy: A Conversation', 36–7). 'Life' is an equally fundamental concept in the physical sciences which study the natural world, though part of the point of the present section is to suggest that it is actually rather insecure as a concept even within those sciences themselves. This will be borne out in Part III.

the political, the ontological. . . . [It gets] at the root of *what is* biologically, anthropologically, sociologically.[8]

The role of a concept of 'life' in biology is traced by Michel Foucault, who argues that it was a certain (new) conceptualization of life which brought about the rise of life science as such. '[T]he new science of life, biology, was made possible . . . only on the basis of its object, life, and crucially . . . this object is, properly speaking, a transcendental one.'[9] In taking that central place in the foundation of the new science, 'life' also, paradoxically, made 'life science' in the closed and naturalistic sense impossible, because it eludes conceptual containment.

> Life, a transcendental required for the establishment of its science, occupies 'that never objectifiable depth from which objects rise up towards our superficial knowledge'. Life is nowhere to be found in the positive objects of the science of life itself; it is strictly speaking unknowable and occupies 'the unknowable depths' of this new nineteenth century *episteme*.[10]

This illusoriness of a stable positivity of 'life' as a starting point for life science is captured by its antinomial character within biology's discourse, as with nature and society. However, in Jonas's philosophical biology we shall see the way in which biological life specifically, not merely in its conceptual role in the discourse of life science but via organic existence phenomenologically considered, exhibits this elusiveness. We shall shortly consider that 'vitalism' is a way of responding to life's conceptual unknowability, offering an interpretation of this in terms of transcendent plenitude of being, rather than in terms of the merely 'transcendental', which would lead to a problematic flux.

The centrality of the term 'life' to biology, considered historically or systematically, makes it the starting point for a theological interrogation of life science. This kind of examination would reveal the way in which, in the biosciences, the term 'life' is already loaded in theological ways.[11] Concretely, the claim of positivist natural science, that its putative 'facts' are 'merely empirical'

---

8. Scott Campbell and Paul Bruno, eds., *The Science, Politics and Ontology of Life-Philosophy* (London: Bloomsbury, 2013), xiii. The authors lament contemporary philosophy's abandonment of life philosophy (xv).

9. Mary-Beth Mader, 'Modern Living and Vital Race: Foucault and the Science of Life', *Foucault Studies* 12 (2011): 97–112, 100.

10. Mader, 'Modern Living and Vital Race', 100, quoting Foucault.

11. Given Milbank's concern with function as a key concept in modern science, it is interesting that Foucault conceives 'the new, modern notion of function, which is central to the emergent science of life, to be conceptually integrally related to that new object of knowledge, life. Function in biology will be bound by definition to the concept of life.' Mader, 'Modern Living and Vital Race', 100.

with no ontological or ethical content, would be analysed as theological.[12] This positivist claim is already problematically implied in the notion of 'nature' which the term *natural* in 'natural science' indicates, since it implies something inertly given, external, autonomous, perpetually in stasis: nature as normativity, a given prior standard. 'Life' too, co-opted by this conception of nature, is not a neutral biological datum but a constructed and storied concept. Christian theology considers these stories in light of its own conception of what 'nature' and 'life' are, proposing these as the most profitable and comprehensive framework for the meaning of both science and life.

Milbank on life

Milbank thinks that 'life' is equally as basic and irreducible as 'nature' and 'society' and generates the same fundamental antinomies; and, relatedly, that life is ontologically ultimate, and in being so, must be identified as peace. Rather than offering a lengthy exposition and enquiry into Milbank's development of vitalism, however, the business of this third part of the book is to conduct an exchange with a different figure, Hans Jonas, whose kinship to these concerns is considerable and whose contribution is important, but largely overlooked. Why give priority to this over a more detailed engagement with Milbank? Firstly, Milbank's engagement

12. We have seen how Hanby pursues an interrogation of the theologically loaded character of modern biology's account of life, and the *aporias* that plague it. Another theologian associated with Radical Orthodoxy, Conor Cunningham, pursues a similar project in *Darwin's Pious Idea*. The genealogical emphasis of these approaches is significant in a confrontation with the postmodern, insofar as it is a genealogical mode of suspicion that exemplified the first comprehensive destabilizations of the Christian narrative. Darwin's 'evolution' as a form of historical explanation is an exemplary case of genealogical suspicion (discussed extensively in Cunningham, *Darwin's*; see, for example, 183–5), but one which is naïve to its own narrative form. By a genealogical exposé of genealogical suspicion, in biological or any other form, the 'masters of suspicion', Nietzsche along with Darwin, are played at their own game. Milbank's emphasis on the logical ungroundedness of narrative, and the singular rhetorical superiority of Christianity's narration of the impossibility of a secure fixity of origin which can stabilize meaning, can be appreciated in this light: Christianity overcomes the postmodern mode of genealogical unmasking by out-narrating modes of suspicion that still trade on covertly modern givens. The Christian story is the genealogical mode par excellence because it shows genealogy as the basic form of knowing without allowing this to defeat knowledge itself.

For an approach which resists a primacy of theological narration but which is still fully genealogical, see Michael Ruse on the relationship between culture and evolutionary theory: *Darwin and Design: Does Evolution Have A Purpose?* (Cambridge, MA: Harvard University Press, 2003).

remains, by and large, a historical-cultural one,[13] paying more attention to cultural theory and philosophy than to 'biology' conventionally conceived.[14] This book has attempted to indicate how and why theology should seek to speak about life in the tones of biology, promoting an engagement with the 'facts' of biology as mediative. Accordingly, the hope is to define for theology a vitalist agenda which would be grounded in the reality of the embodied organism, which would speak in the tones of biology while expressing the Christian narration of life. This is what Jonas accomplishes. Secondly, Milbank's account cannot be taken forward in engaging the life sciences without addressing the key task which emerges from any treatment of life that proceeds from his fundamental suppositions, namely what it could mean to identify life as ultimate and as peaceful in the context of a biological knowledge of organisms.[15] The prophetic character of the organism and the

13. Milbank calls for vitalism in the context of exchanges with several different thinkers, employing theological appropriations of the categories of habit, feeling, imagination and reciprocity, and calling for a re-enchantment of nature in terms of sympathy and gift exchange. Hume is particularly important; Milbank argues that, for Hume, 'feeling' is a more fundamental category than 'reason' or 'faith', which are both species of feeling. For Hume, Milbank suggests, nature itself is characterized by feeling. His elevation of will over causality – causality is not perspicuous to the senses but must be deciphered in terms of our experience of willing – indicates for Milbank that Hume is a vitalist, in the sense that he views nature as somehow possessed of a 'will'. Milbank's Hume gives the fundamental place in epistemology to sympathy, an occult sense in which an obscure and connatural knowing, which characterizes nature itself as well as human understanding, is primary over deduction and abstraction ('Hume versus Kant', especially 282). Milbank regards Bergson as continuing this lineage, insofar as he does not distinguish between thinking and feeling.

Kucer points out that Vico rejected hylomorphism in favour of hylozoism, in which 'the truth humanity encounters is defined not by stable forms but rather by the constantly flowing energy of life present within the fundamental elements of the universe' (Kucer, *Truth*, 14). Milbank's vitalism can be seen to take its place in this lineage. It is consistent with his larger project to overcome a dualism of God and world and so restore the paradoxical depth of the created order which is simultaneously nothing, in itself, and divine, in its participation in God.

14. This study has touched frequently on the issues raised by the notion of 'nature', so I frame this point advisedly, insofar as on Milbank's showing (and in accordance with Vico) we can only know historically and culturally. By taking the approach outlined I do not mean to contest this but rather to draw attention to the fact that biology too is a culture, and its knowing of nature is a legitimate voice of culture and is no less fabricated than the knowing of history.

15. Milbank certainly gestures towards the difficulties that may arise here: commenting on Darwin as Malthusian, he says, 'Perception of natural agonism is not of course wrong, but it can be overstressed by too exclusive a preoccupation with the biological individual, rather than the smaller and the greater drifts within which it is swept up' (Milbank, 'Life, or Gift and Glissando', 127).

irreducibility of life are considered in the course of exploring Jonas's account of the organism (Chapter 6); the question of reading life as peace is raised in the course of the critical discussion (Chapter 7). Thirdly, as I shall try to show, Jonas in many ways carries through the logic of Milbank's position. Milbank favours a 'nuanced version of panpsychic vitalism in which a self-organising power operates with different degrees of intensity at every level of physical reality from the inorganic to the consciously rational'.[16] It is just this project which Jonas assumes in a more specifically biological key, respecting and assuming the biological language about the organism.

It is in a brief consideration of Darwinism that Milbank comes closest to a detailed engagement with biological thinking, arguing that Darwinism itself presupposes something like vitalism, defying the Newtonian physics which Darwinism may appear, at first sight, to be aping (a view we shall find eloquently defended by Jonas). In accord with his customary focus on the impossibility of absolute beginnings, Milbank vigorously critiques ontological uses of Darwin as a failure to explain: to say that life is an epiphenomenon of matter is simply mystifying. 'Natural selection' is no more explanatory than anything else, just as the 'drive for survival' is no less question-begging and anthropocentric than any other kind of biological teleology, a point which we will again see in Jonas. Milbank explores the notion of continuous biological variation as a 'glissando' of change which defies discrete boundaries, a continual variation which 'is essentially vital rather than mechanically physical'.[17] 'Quite simply and briefly,' he says, 'the vitalist view makes more sense than the Darwinian one.'[18]

Seeing life as 'habit', after Ravaisson, Milbank suggests a 'panpsychism', a 'spiritualisation of nature' which 'requires one to extend the natural desire for the supernatural and even the beginning of prevenient grace from angels and humans to the entire cosmos'.[19] Taking 'habit' as the key term for life indicates for Milbank its beginningless and inexplicable character, for 'habit' describes the perfectly suspended middle between the spontaneous and the automatic; it allows one to think the impossible beginning without beginning which is grace, and also life itself. The outstanding feature of Milbank's account is that life's elusion of 'explanation' is expressive of its ontological ultimacy.

[A] 'vitalist' view (for want of a better word) of the evolutionary process makes more sense [than Darwinism]. For it appears that life is not exhaustively subject

16. Milbank, 'Grandeur', 37. The reciprocity between nature and culture, object and subject, the constituting of one by the other, means that the world is always giving itself to itself. The world relates to itself as to another; as culture and as nature, it receives itself from itself, 'as gift which it must then give to itself' ('Immanence and Life', 23). It is 'purely relation', 'purely medium'; and so 'the inner reality of the cosmos is vital, even psychic . . . since only the psychic is reflexively self-giving' (23).

17. Milbank, 'Life, or Gift and Glissando', 126.

18. Milbank, 'Life, or Gift and Glissando', 96.

19. Milbank, 'Immanence and Life', 32.

to mechanical or to even merely physical and chemical laws, but is instead a kind of self-organising force or *habit* grounded in nothing before itself. Life endlessly engenders life and does not as life die – for if death cannot generate life, then the priority of life over death renders it immortal; there is no life without resurrection, as Russian philosophy has often argued. Nor is it born, as Michel Henry today points out, since it is not caused.[20]

Vitalism is here taken to mean that life can be described and accounted for in no terms more basic than itself. Rather, 'life' should be taken to indicate what is fundamental to reality itself. '[L]ife is not built-up from the pre-living'; instead 'something like a "living" impulse, a totally unpredictable auto-creative force underlies all of physical nature'.[21]

Bergson is the principal modern thinker of life, with other postmodern philosophers 'play[ing] variations on [Bergson's] themes'.[22] While he is critical of Bergson's vitalism, Milbank lauds his conception of life as auto-originative, for Christian orthodoxy too must see life as in some mysterious sense self-generating, or rather as divine, ungenerate. Bergson's account of life as *autopoetic* substantiates this regard of life as prior to non-life: if life is not made from non-life, life beginninglessly is, and originates itself.[23] But Milbank regards any immanent vitalism, whether Bergon's own or one of its inheritors such as Deleuze, as problematically dualist: in Bergson's case, notwithstanding the claim

20. Milbank, 'Immanence and Life', 14–15. Scott Lash, 'Life (Vitalism)', *Theory, Culture and Society* 23 (2006): 323–9, regards an auto-originative conception of life as defining of vitalism: 'The primary distinction between mechanism and vitalism may be in terms of vitalism's *self-organisation*. In mechanism, causation is external: the paths or movement or configuration of beings is determined. In vitalism causation is largely *self*-causation. . . . in vitalism, the power of self-organisation is extended from humans to all sorts of matter' (324).

21. Milbank engages extensively with the notion of soul ('The Soul of Reciprocity Part One: Reciprocity Refused', *Modern Theology* 17, no. 3 (2001): 335–91, and 'The Soul of Reciprocity Part Two: Reciprocity Granted', *Modern Theology* 17, no. 4 (2001): 485–507), defending its reappropriation for the language of life and arguing that soul needs to be understood as pervading nature and the non-human world. As narrated by Christianity, both habit and soul show the inextricability of transcendence and immanence, overcoming false dualisms. He celebrates Bulgakov's *Sophia* as capturing this notion: 'She is that power of self-engendering life which logically must be prior to death . . . [O]ne can think of all natural processes and the one process of nature herself as Sophia, as created wisdom, the first of God's works' ('Sophiology and Theurgy: The New Theological Horizon', in *Encounter Between Eastern Orthodoxy and Radical Orthodoxy: Transfiguring the World Through The Word*, ed. Adrian Pabst and Christoph Schneider (Farnham: Ashgate, 2009), 45–85, 63–4).

22. 'Immanence and Life', 16.

23. Florence Caeymaux outlines Bergsonian 'life' in 'The Comprehensive Meaning of Life in Bergson', in *The Science, Politics and Ontology of Life-Philosophy*, ed. Scott Campbell and Paul Bruno (London: Bloomsbury, 2013), 47–64.

for a hierarchical continuum there remains a persistent subordination of space to time, and for Deleuze, the virtual creative factor is only partially and never adequately manifested by the actual, but remains occluded by it.[24] In opposition to these immanentist vitalisms, Milbank claims that life is best read in terms of a transcendent plenitude: biological life is 'an intense manifestation on the surface of a transcendental "life" that undergirds all of finite reality and is even coterminous with being as such'.[25] It is the attribution of ontological ultimacy to life itself which will be the platform for our engagement with Jonas, since it commits him both to an intrinsic inexplicability of life as defeating reduction and to an identification of life with peace. We will find that Jonas answers well to the first but is found wanting by the second.

The following chapters do not attempt fully to elaborate a transcendent vitalism adequate to the demands of orthodoxy.[26] This would require engagement with a vast range of source material. Instead, they attempt to put the notion of a theologically described vitalism to work by seeing how one thinker helps us to engage more deeply with the living organism in a key which is simultaneously biological and theological. Specifically, I consider how Jonas shows the ontologically prophetic character of the world of organic life, while at the same time instantiating the insufficiency of a purely philosophical reason. A theological vitalism can be the expression, in relation to life and the life sciences, of the conception of every discipline as theological, the interruption of all forms of pure immanence. At the same time, a Christian 'vitalism' is disruptive or prophetic in relation to other vitalisms, because it finds life to be ultimate as peace.

Vitalism: Key themes

'Vitalism' is a term with a complex history and a polymorphous use: it has 'a rich and sometimes even overwhelming complex of meanings'.[27] It has been important in the emergence and self-definition of modernity itself, crystallizing many of the most basic divergences in the understanding of knowledge, reality and life in society.[28] While it does not come into explicit use until the eighteenth century, the term is used to refer to a family of views which began in antiquity with Aristotle

---

24. Milbank, 'Immanence and Life', 16ff.

25. Milbank, 'Life, or Gift and Glissando', 129.

26. In a condensed argument drawing on William Desmond's metaxology, Milbank proposes that 'the only perfected metaphysics of vitalism must be a Catholic Christian one, a philosophy that is equally a true exegesis of the Gospel' (Milbank, 'Immanence and Life', 25).

27. Sebastian Normandin and Charles T. Wolfe, eds., *Vitalism and the Scientific Image in Post-Enlightenment Life Science* (London: Springer, 2013), 11.

28. Frederick Burwick and Paul Douglass, eds., *The Crisis in Modernism: Bergson and the Vitalist Controversy* (Cambridge: Cambridge University Press, 1992), gives some idea of the breadth of vitalism's influence on modernity's self-understanding.

and others, continued through early modernity with resistance to the mechanizing trend of modern science and revived in the nineteenth and twentieth centuries both in science and philosophy.

Modern vitalisms emerge both as theories of culture and society, and as formulations which respond to modern life science. One author, describing the historical background to Jonas's brand of vitalism, summarizes its role as a reaction to Darwinism: '[I]n opposition to the mechanistic implications of the doctrine of natural selection, vitalism claimed that life could not be explained in exclusively causal terms.'[29] Inspired by Goethe's philosophy of nature, 'it preferred to view organic life as ensouled'.[30] It is with these kinds of issues, especially as they were discussed among biologists of the eighteenth and nineteenth centuries, that the term 'vitalism' has been most readily and widely associated, where it referred broadly to the claim that 'the explanation of living phenomena is not compatible with, or is not exhausted by, the principles of basic sciences like physics and chemistry'.[31] In this most common understanding, vitalism corresponds to a claim for life's irreducibility to matter and is the counterpoint to mechanism and reductionism in life science. Vitalism, at least in modernity, might therefore be widely characterized as 'an essentially reactive discourse', 'a protest against'.[32] Despite its chequered history in modernity, frequent declarations of its death have turned out to be premature, a fact which is itself suggestive that a progressivist view of science is oversimple.[33] In the twentieth century it has been significant

---

29. Richard Wolin, *Heidegger's Children: Hannah Arendt, Karl Lowith, Hans Jonas, and Herbert Marcuse* (Princeton: Princeton University Press, 2015), 124.

30. Wolin, *Heidegger's Children*, 124.

31. Monica Greco, 'On the Vitality of Vitalism', *Theory, Culture & Society* 22 (2005): 15–27, 16. Normandin and Wolfe see a resurgence of a specifically bio-scientific interest in vitalism in recent decades, in contrast to a preponderant concern with vitalism as a theory of culture and society in the early twentieth century (*Vitalism*, 1).

32. Donna Jones, *The Racial Discourses of Life Philosophy: Négritude, Vitalism, and Modernity* (New York: Columbia University Press, 2010), 6.

33. Hilde Hein identifies the vitalist debate as exemplifying the limits of a purely 'rational' account of scientific understanding and development: '[S]ome historic controversies, notably that between mechanism and vitalism, do not fit the stated pattern of scientific inquiry; that is, as being settled by an appeal to evidence and critical standards acceptable to all sides of the dispute. Some controversies are meta-theoretical in character and involve fundamental commitments on the part of their antagonists which do not depend upon scientific evidence for their retention, and which will not be shaken by evidence to the contrary. I have identified such commitments as based upon primary attitudes or "political" orientations which may have a psychosociological explanation, but which are themselves not subject to rational justification. It is, in fact, one's rootedness in such attitudes and convictions that determines what sort of justification one will regard as "rational" and what sort of evidence one will accept as pertinent to the establishment of scientific conclusions' (Hilde Hein, 'The Endurance of the Mechanism-Vitalism Controversy', *Journal of the*

in cultural theory, being central to the thought of critics and theorists such as Giorgio Agamben, Gilles Deleuze and Antonio Negri: '[M]odern cultural theory has centered on reassertions of Life.'[34] But in biology, although there are some revivals of a naturalistic style of vitalism, by and large it remains an object of opprobrium, as well as in the philosophy of biology which is dominated by analytic and naturalistic approaches. 'Many of those who share an interest in the life sciences today, perhaps most, would agree with the claim that vitalism is obsolete.'[35] In science it continues to be associated with mystifying dualisms which define life as a nonphysical presence in physical organisms: it is seen as a kind of biological supernaturalism which is used to set an arbitrary limit on scientific competence.[36] Vitalism is 'a derogatory label associated with lack of intellectual rigour, anti-scientific attitudes, and superstition.'[37]

Notwithstanding the hostility to vitalism in modern biology, the emergence of the discipline in the nineteenth century was integrally linked to vitalistic thought.[38]

History of Biology 5 (1972): 155–88, 160). This 'non-rational' character of the matter at stake here is explored further in Chapter 7.

34. Jones, *The Racial Discourses of Life Philosophy*, 7.

35. 'Scientists and philosophers have continued to address vitalism – mostly in order to reject it'; Greco, 'On the Vitality of Vitalism', 15.

36. 'Many of those who share an interest in the life sciences today, perhaps most, would agree with the claim that vitalism is obsolete. Some prominent biologists now use "vitalism" as a derogatory label associated with lack of intellectual rigour, anti-scientific attitudes, and superstition. Other scientific commentators treat the term more seriously, but equally arrive at the conclusion that vitalism is an untenable perspective. [Some] have described vitalist concepts as meaningful for biology within the broader scientific context characterized by Newtonian physics, but as having been made redundant by 20th-century developments both in physics and in (molecular) biology' (Greco, 'On the Vitality of Vitalism', 15).

Francis Crick seems to regard 'vitalism' as a synonym for views held by 'cranks' in biology: 'To those of you who may be vitalists, I would make this prophecy: what everyone believed yesterday, and you believe today, only cranks will believe tomorrow' (*Of Molecules and Men* (Seattle: University of Washington Press, 1966), 99). Susan Oyama ('Biologists Behaving Badly: Vitalism and the Language of Language', *History of Philosophy of the Life Sciences* 32 (2010): 401–23) and Scott Gilbert and Sahotra Sarkar ('Embracing Complexity: Organicism for the 21st Century', *Developmental Dynamics* 219 (2000): 1–9), reject contemporary attempts to use the term naturalistically, because of its supernaturalist overtones.

37. Greco, 'On the Vitality of Vitalism', 16.

38. 'The nineteenth century also brings with it the very complex of ideas that is biology, and as classic treatments of the period suggest, vitalism is central to the negotiation of this new terrain' (Normandin and Wolfe, *Vitalism*, 4). Greco quotes Foucault in support of vitalism's essential role in defining biology from physics and chemistry: '[I]f the 'scientificization' process is done by bringing to light physical and chemical mechanisms . . . it has on the other hand, been able to develop only insofar as the problem of the specificity of life and of the threshold it marks among all natural beings was continually thrown back

Indeed, vitalism appears as the foil against which life science has continually defined itself: 'Vitalism remains vital . . . because of its epistemological role within the history of the life sciences'; it is 'the negative term of reference against which biological thought and techniques have progressed', and it represents 'a significant motor force in the history of biology'.[39] It is vitalism's persistence despite its seeming obsolescence that is perhaps its most important feature.

Vitalism's decline is also moral and political. Discussions of 'life' and 'vitalism' disappeared after the Third Reich 'because many associated it and its foremost proponents – Friedrich Nietzsche and Henri Bergson – with Nazism and the extreme right'.[40] In Nietzsche's vitalism, life is viewed as a special case of the will to power which pervades the whole of nature,[41] and vitalism has an enduring association with imperialism.[42] 'Is there something intrinsic to vitalism, to faith in the autonomy of life, that allies itself with violence?'[43] This ambiguous legacy may perhaps be one reason why Jonas himself was reluctant to use the term to describe his own views.[44] Vitalism has recently been shown to be implicated in discourses of race, particularly around Jewish and Black identities: Donna Jones argues that twentieth-century vitalism has been so closely intertwined with 'racialism' that it cannot be properly understood without it.[45] In this third part of the book the ambiguous moral implications of vitalism are brought to the fore, not in historical perspective but through the study of Jonas who, I contend, is not free of these

as a challenge. This does not mean that 'vitalism' . . . is true. . . . It simply means that it has had and undoubtedly still has an essential role as an 'indicator' in the history of biology ('On the Vitality of Vitalism', 17).

39. Greco, 'On the Vitality of Vitalism', 17, quoting Canguilhem.

40. Lash, 'Life (Vitalism)', 324–5.

41. One commentator describes Nietzsche as rejecting the choice between mechanism and vitalism but then oddly goes on to describe him as holding a position that seems thoroughly vitalist except for its rejection of supernaturalism – underlining the extent to which the conversation about vitalism is trapped by the perception that vitalism is a supernaturalism (Christoph Cox, *Nietzsche: Naturalism and Interpretation* (Berkeley: University of California Press, 1999), 238). However, many twentieth-century vitalisms are immanentist, such as that of Gilles Deleuze.

42. George Canguilhem, one of the foremost twentieth-century exponents of vitalism, called for a new 'imperialism' of biology (Greco, 'On the Vitality of Vitalism', 19, in *Inventive Life: Approaches to the New Vitalism*, 15–28). Cf. Lash, 'Life (Vitalism)', 324.

43. Jane Bennett, *Vibrant Matter: A Political Ecology of Things* (Durham, NC: Duke University Press, 2010), 89.

44. '[B]y the mid 1930s issues of nature, life and biology are entwined with Heidegger and National Socialism.' Nelson Eric, 'Biological and Historical Life: Heidegger Between Levinas and Dilthey', in *The Science, Politics and Ontology of Life-Philosophy*, ed. Scott Campbell and Paul Bruno (London: Bloomsbury, 2013), 15–30, 17.

45. Jones, *The Racial Discourses of Life Philosophy*.

problematic associations, and whose philosophical biology can be saved from these only by Christian narration.

Despite the general decline of vitalist thought, it has seen a revival in contemporary cultural criticism, where it has emerged as a response to the changed image of the sciences, as well as the rise of informatics, technological innovation and new forms of media.[46] In one recent collection, this movement describes itself as '*the* new vitalism', claiming the term for postmodernity.[47] For these authors vitalism names the endless flux, uncertainty and void of secure identities which characterize contemporary social consciousness, but it does so without reference to transcendence; this is the only world we have, a world 'which might be different, but is not'.[48] Vitalisms of this kind do not embrace an idea of pure flow but rather a tensioned flux in which there are continually reappearing contraries and unreconciled difference; they recognize emergent form which generates conflict.[49] These vitalisms too, in their necessary agonism, call for disruption by Christian narration of life.

Although all these themes are historically influential, a recent study focusing on meanings and uses of the term emphasizes that 'vitalism' is best understood to be not a fixed philosophical claim with definite content but rather 'meta-theoretical commitment', a view of life as eluding exact definition.[50] 'Vitalism' has had a characteristic role as a mediator between recurring dualisms or polarities, between different descriptive or explanatory accounts of the living: 'between the spiritual and the material, the digital and the analog [*sic*], reductionism and holism . . . the inert and the animated . . . the dead and the living, the closed and the open'.[51] It indicates an apophatic take on organic existence: 'vitalism nominally implies the acceptance of the unknown as a central fact of life.'[52] Mechanism, the traditional counterpart to vitalism, would correspond to a claim for a full (at least in principle)

---

46. A well-known example of vitalism as a response to changes in our understanding of nature is Donna Haraway, *Simians, Cyborgs, and Women: The Reinvention of Nature* (London: Free Association Books, 1991).

47. Mariam Fraser, Sarah Kember and Celia Lury, eds., *Inventive Life: Approaches to the New Vitalism* (London: Sage, 2006), 2; italics added.

48. Fraser et al., eds., *Inventive Life*, 1 (quoting Donna Haraway, *Modest−Witness@Secon d−Millennium.FemaleMan− Meets−OncoMouse: Feminism and Technoscience* (London: Routledge, 1997), 97). In Lash's view, 'Deleuze is the leading contemporary vitalist' ('Life (Vitalism)', 326).

49. Lash, 'Life (Vitalism)', 323.

50. Normandin and Wolfe, 5. According to Jones, '[V]italism may not have an essence but only be the name for the set of multiple doctrines and movements premised on life variously understood' (*Racial*, 7). Cf. Hilde Hein, 'Mechanism and vitalism as meta-theoretical commitments', *Philosophical Forum* 1 (1968): 185–205.

51. Normandin and Wolfe, *Vitalism*, 12.

52. Normandin and Wolfe, *Vitalism*, 2.

knowability and definability.[53] Normandin and Wolfe argue that vitalism typically involves the questioning of boundaries and the production of new disciplinary hybrids. They criticize those who 'too easily dismiss [vitalism] as outdated or merely idle spiritualism and mysticism', missing the opportunity which vitalism represents to gain a deeper understanding of the always-changing concept of science itself.[54] On this view, the importance of vitalism is not its normative plausibility in any given age but its persistent attractiveness. 'The imperative to refute vitalism is superseded by the need to account for its permanent recurrence.'[55]

Theological vitalism

Vitalism is a lens on the heritage of modernity and its unfinished project to determine what counts as knowledge and how the world is constituted. Engaging with vitalism is one way for the Christian theologian to grapple with the complex of certainties and uncertainties characterizing modern self-understanding. This points theology clearly towards organic life as a critical site of enquiry. But strangely, vitalism is a theme largely untouched by theologians. This seems a missed opportunity: if the debates around vitalism somehow give voice to the crisis of knowledge in both modernity and postmodernity, it is begging for theological scrutiny.

Theologians have perhaps kept their distance from vitalism because of its anti-scientific associations; they have had enough of that, and the important thing now is to show science that theology is not the opposition. This is understandable, but on the conception of theology we have defended in this book, wrongheaded. Like 'nature' and 'society', 'life' and 'vitalism' will have a different meaning within the Christian story. Both terms carry portentous loads of meaning that Christian theology will sift, question and prophetically discern, while at the same time recognizing their usage as conjectural and disclosive. The disruption that is necessary can take place while retaining a grasp of the historic and normative content of the term, so as to assure meaningful continuity. My approach to the theme is an attempt to be in keeping with the history of vitalism as a flexible term with constantly adapting denotations, recognizing the importance of some consistency of meaning while disrupting previous meanings. Minimally, I hope to

---

53. Lash expresses this contrast in terms of flux versus form, and this perhaps captures something of the contrast between Hanby and Milbank (though Milbank does not embrace an absolute flux, he does challenge substance ontologies). '[T]he notion of life has always favoured an idea of becoming over one of being, of movement over stasis, of action over structure, of flow and flux. [. . .] One could trace this opposition . . . back to that between Heraclitus' metaphysics of flux and Plato's predominance of form.' 'Life (Vitalism)', 323.

54. Normandin and Wolfe, *Vitalism*, 7.

55. Greco, 'Vitalism', 17.

show as too confident the blithe assertion of one commentator: 'Vitalism today is indeed nothing but history, and that is that.'[56]

The considerations of this book thus far concern both 'science' and 'nature'; a theological vitalism would concern the character of knowledge, of organic life and of reality altogether. I appropriate vitalism as a recurring instrument of disciplinary and especially scientific self-definition, noting that the role vitalism has often played – standing as a denial of a fixity or totality of conceptualization in relation to either science or its object – is not dissimilar to the role I have conceived for theology in this book.[57] But at the same time elements of its history call for an emphatic discontinuity. The conception of vitalism as a belief in a supernaturalistic 'vital force' buys into the very dualism we are intending to challenge, and I use the term specifically in resistance to this notion,[58] as well as its association with power, imperialism and tensioned flux. I embrace vitalism as a challenge to an understanding of 'science' as aiming for exhaustive description and explanation of phenomena, but this needs to be read theologically: life's elusion of categorial containment is more than merely immanent or transcendental, and is not primarily negative but plenitudinous.[59] The failure of projects of totalizing knowledge is saved

---

56. Spas Spassov, 'Metaphysics and Vitalism in Henri Bergson's Biophilosophy: A New Look', *Analecta Husserliana* 52 (1998): 197–206. Spassov attempts to demonstrate that Bergson's vitalism is independent of his metaphysics such that the former could be dropped while the latter could be utilized.

57. 'The oscillation that characterizes biological thought, of which the alternative between vitalism and mechanism is but one expression, is the symptom of a form of knowledge marked by a paradox: the science of life is, itself, a manifestation of the activity of the living, a manifestation of its own subject matter. Once it is understood performatively, as resistance and excess with respect to the remit of positive knowledge, vitalism therefore appears valid' (Greco, 'On the Vitality of Vitalism', 18).

58. For some, vitalism is more strongly associated with philosophical monism (Lash, 'Life (Vitalism)', 324), while for others, it is plainly a dualistic thesis (Hein, 'The Endurance of the Mechanism-Vitalism Controversy', 164). Jonas and Milbank both consider dualism and monism to be fundamentally alike. I am suggesting that 'vitalism' be allowed to stand for the overcoming of the underlying premise of dualism and monism, an overcoming which begs a metaphysics of participation as a framework for its narration.

59. Invoking Canguilhem, Greco says that vitalism is 'not a valid representation of life, but it is "a valid *representative*"' ('On the Vitality of Vitalism', 18, italics original). She points towards Jonas's metaphysical agenda when she says that 'classical vitalism commits a philosophically inexcusable mistake when it takes the "originality" of life to mean that life constitutes an "exception" to the laws of the physical milieu. Classical vitalism, in this sense, is a purely reactive form of thought: it implicitly acknowledges the logical priority, and the normativity, of the world described by the sciences of physics and chemistry' (18–19). 'The originality of life cannot be claimed for a segment of reality, but only for reality as a whole' (19). It is just this that Jonas proposes, which I will suggest a 'theological vitalism' is able fully to narrate.

from nihilism if they are located in a metaphysics of participated transcendence where the always-frustrated ambition fully to know reality appears as superfluity rather than void, and where the immanent change which makes total knowledge impossible is rooted in and expressive of, not opposed to, transcendent eternity. Most importantly, I am defending as vitalism a regard of life as ontologically ultimate and so as coincident with peace, which is a regard of life as graspable only by narration. This is the prophetic interruption generated by the specifically Christian narration of life. For distinction, I am calling such a vitalism a 'theological vitalism'.[60]

Positively speaking, what would such a theological vitalism propose? It would simply be a spelling out of the implication of Christian orthodoxy that the mystery of life must be in some way the mystery of God himself, in the same way that being and goodness are patient of no more fundamental 'explanation' than the being and goodness of God. Life insists on being narrated, like other terms which, in being simultaneously foundational and aporetic, call for theological explication. Creaturely life must be simply the life of God endlessly participated by and differentiated among the diversity of creatures.[61] Christianity narrates life as peace by telling the story of life in creation and *eschaton* as non-rivalrous gift without contest or contrast, in its beginning and its ending. Life is originally innocent, and in redemption and sanctification life is returned to this innocence. The narrative bears elaboration and investigation, but the biblical outline remains normative: life in the beginning does not require death. Sin brings killing into the world and makes living contingent on killing. In the new heavens and the new earth, the wolf lies down with the kid, the lion eats straw like the ox, and they do not hurt or destroy on all God's holy mountain. In this renewed creation, death is conquered, and God is the true life of all. There is thus a threefold shape to the Christian narration of life: in the beginning, it is intrinsically peaceful and innocent; in the present age, death and conflict intrude on that fundamental innocence; its restoration to peace and innocence is promised.

How would the analogical ontology defended in previous chapters explicate this narrative of life in its own terms? Speculatively, it might go as follows. Firstly, 'life', like 'good', 'true', 'real', etc., would properly be predicated of God, and only

---

60. An appellation to distinguish my own proposal seemed necessary for clarity, but it is an unhappy choice, since it suggests that there could be a non-theological vitalism; so the label 'theological vitalism' has a hidden term, '*Christian* theological vitalism', in my usage.

61. For Milbank, the favoured theological context for developing these insights is sophiology, which gives us a way of thinking mediation more fully: *Sophia* allows us to conceive of the real presence of God in the created world, particularly the world of nature, without eliding transcendence or overidentifying the divine with nature's dynamic and conflictual unfolding. It stands as the most promising attempt to overcome conceptual problems in understanding God's relationship to creation, allowing a fuller articulation of the infinite intimacy and distance which characterize the relation that is creation ('Sophiology and Theurgy').

secondarily of creatures. God, who is 'the living God', is alone truly 'alive', and creatures have life only as participating in God's life. God the Holy Spirit is 'the Life-Giver', God's 'imperishable breath (spirit)' animates all that lives,[62] so all life is a free gift of God's own life to creatures, where it remains primarily *God's* life analogically participated in.[63] We therefore speak of the 'life' of creatures only analogically, and we cannot understand or conceptualize that life adequately in isolation from the eminent application of the term 'life' to the undying and exhaustible life of God. Further, because God is simple, 'life' in its full sense cannot be conceived apart from the real and the true. Secondly, for Christian orthodoxy the meaning of 'life' cannot be specified apart from 'resurrection' which spells life as finally indistinguishable from immortality. True life, insofar as it is God's life, is immortal. The source and real meaning of mortal life is immortality, 'eternal' life, which is in Christ; mortal life, life-under-death, is in a certain sense not 'life' at all.[64] Thirdly, as God's life is a life of infinitely harmonious reconciled difference, 'life' is narratively specified as no more and no less than peace, which the resurrection establishes as the only truth and the final good; conflict possesses no ultimate reality. 'Life', then, as specified in the Christian narrative, is intrinsically inimical to death and conflict, and is always to be understood as ontologically ultimate insofar as it is God's gift of God's own life, analogically participated in by creatures.

These themes together can be taken as a gestural outline of a theological vitalism: life is ontologically ultimate and, in being so, is coincident with peace. This is a conception of life and the living which takes the life of God as the pre-eminent life but which expects to find the poetic disclosure of this ultimacy in the embodied and material life of creatures. Narratives of life which are ontologically conflictual,

---

62. *Wisdom of Solomon* 11:27–12:1.

63. Stratford Caldecott argues that life should be considered an 'eschatological transcendental'. This captures the theological insight that life in its fullness has not yet been revealed, which I have expressed slightly differently here in my second point. But life is surely equally a 'protological transcendental', and in being so it qualifies not just life's destiny but somehow brackets it as a whole. The absence of this perspective results in failing to give sufficient credit to the fundamental continuity of biological with spiritual life, in which regard Jonas's philosophical biology is so powerful. Caldecott's interest in ascribing 'life' to all of reality is in tension with his claim specifically about *organic* existence. Stratford Caldecott, 'Is Life a Transcendental?', *Radical Orthodoxy: Theology, Philosophy, Politics* 1 (2012): 188–200 (journal.radicalorthodoxy.org/index.php/ROTPP/article/download/79 /13, accessed 9 June 2017).

64. Michel Henry considers transcendental life the only life (*I Am the Truth: Toward a Philosophy of Christianity*, trans. Susan Emanuel (Stanford: Stanford University Press, 2003), 33–52. Though his use of the term 'transcendental' here slightly muddies the waters given the Kantian baggage of that term, it seems in this chapter, 'The Truth Called Life', Henry is making substantially this point: it is God's life that is real, and it is by this life that the 'life' of biological existence is to be measured, rather than the reverse. This ordering elevates rather than diminishes biological existence.

or in which life is defined principally in reference to death, beg theological interruption. A theological vitalism will exercise this disruptive function in relation to Jonas, contesting the construction of life as conflict which we see in his philosophical biology. It will also question Jonas's adhesion to a dialectical paradigm, for peace bears equally on epistemology: the impossibility of 'fixing' knowledge, of containing finitude, signifies not meaninglessness and conflictual flux but a harmonious plenitude of meaning, as the discussion of Blondel was meant to intimate.[65]

Jonas shows how attention to the embodied reality of the organism manifests life as neither securely material nor exclusively spiritual but as occupying a 'between' which makes metaphysical dualism impossible. A theological vitalism is characterized by the inherence of that claim in a Christian narration, in which context life's mysteriousness signifies not the defeat of reason but its perfection, and its conflictuality appears as an inessential and not defining feature. The resulting vitalism will be 'theological' also in the sense that it indicates life's breaking of established boundaries in knowledge and knowledge production, and so points to its pre-eminent suitability as a heuristic device to aid the kind of work we have been undertaking in this study, which questions the notion of secure disciplinary identities.[66] A theological vitalism recognizes life as prophetic for Christian

65. Though I engage only with Jonas explicitly, the discussion will be relevant to any account of life organized fundamentally in terms of power, conflict or violence (as is arguably the case in 'traditional' Darwinism and neo-Darwinism); in fact, on the Milbankian view taken here, this would include any narration of life other than its narration as peace. *Mutatis mutandis*, the treatment of Jonas stands as an implied critique of other accounts of life which construe its defiance of conceptual capture as a signifier of the emptiness of language and thought.

66. 'Most foundational controversies involve, sooner or later, questions of disciplinary identity' (Gregory Cooper, *The Science of the Struggle for Existence: On the Foundations of Ecology* (Cambridge: Cambridge University Press, 2003), 1). This comment introduces a study of the disciplinary identity of ecology which attempts to 'fix' this identity. The especially intense struggle which ecology has faced in establishing secure disciplinary boundaries is particularly reflective of its origins in the life sciences more generally, which suffer from the prevalence of a conception of 'science' which throws their own methods and procedures into doubt (a problematic engagingly treated in Alex Rosenberg, *Instrumental Biology: Or the Disunity of Science* (Chicago: University of Chicago Press, 1994), which surrenders biology's claim to *be* a science in anything like the same way as the other physical sciences). Cooper invokes the presumption of the universalizable normativeness of that conception of science to highlight by contrast a disciplinary failure in ecology: '[T]he most striking feature of this debate [concerning the existence or not of a "balance of nature"] is the inability of the discipline to let empirical evidence settle what are so obviously empirical questions' (Cooper, *The Science of the Struggle for Existence*, xiii). On the kind of view defended here, the elusiveness of disciplinary boundaries is reflective of the character of knowing as such, and furthermore, in the case of the sciences which study life, testifies

theology, because life, like theology, belongs to no specialism; theology finds in life the impossibility of epistemological closure and the uncontainability of finitude which are its own constitution. Thus theological vitalism expresses not only theology's transgression of the established compartmentalization of knowledge but life's transgression of that compartmentalization, witnessing in some way to the impossibility of secure disciplinary divisions *tout court*.[67] For such a vitalism, organic life plays a unique role in ontology: by defying univocal ontological capture, it testifies to the inextricability of ontological categories. Jonas describes life as 'prophetic for ontology', a trespasser in our divisions of knowing, continuously goading metaphysics to a higher integration. Theological vitalism takes 'life' as an outstanding case of what a metaphysics of participated transcendence is trying to defend.

Notably, these specifications indicate that this theological vitalism is critically discontinuous with another common summary definition: vitalism as the view that 'life' is irreducible to 'matter'.[68] Although on the kind of ontology I have been defending this is true, it is not sufficiently nuanced, because of its implied boundary between 'matter' as finitely describable and 'life' as eluding that capture. If a theological vitalism is a regard of life's transcendence of disciplinary boundaries, as is characteristic of vitalist claims, to it I am adding Jonas's crucial insight that it also overcomes metaphysical boundaries; so, to repeat, while life is not 'merely' material, neither is it 'merely' spiritual, as though the 'vital force' was conceptually isolable. It is therefore important that the irreducibility claim is formulated in terms of life versus non-life.[69] Not only does this avoid the problematic dualism implied by the former version of irreducibility, but it brings us directly to the key characteristic of a theological vitalism: life's ontological ultimacy. This is the theology of life that the Christian narrative brings to the encounter with modern biology and philosophy of biology.

crucially to the character of that life as uncircumscribable: there are no *purely* 'empirical' questions.

67. This is not to say that disciplinary divisions do not have a heuristic value, nor that they may not be pragmatically necessary for the organizing of learning. But it does suggest that the division of labour in knowledge production calls for a kind of critique that will not only be historical (e.g. examining the origins of the modern university) but also normative. (It also suggests the need for a careful examination of the way in which disciplinary divisions may generate the notion of 'knowledge production' per se, and the marketization and commercialization of knowledge which occurs when it is interpreted primarily in the terms of 'production' and 'consumption'.)

68. Bennett, *Vibrant Matter*, 87.

69. In this I am departing from one trend in the history of vitalism, at least according to Lash's account, which is to see death not as an opposite to life but as somehow within or part of it ('In vitalism life is not at all counterposed to death. Instead death is part of life. . . . it does not define itself against death'; Lash, 'Life (Vitalism)', 326). If Lash is correct, this is one respect in which Jonas is exceptional, no doubt due to his Heideggerian background.

Curiously, we are still nevertheless in a position to agree with Canguilhem's proposal that 'biology must affirm its own "imperialism"'.[70] This 'imperialism' of biology is just what Jonas is reaching towards: the 'right' of biology to be the lens through which the other sciences are to be understood. A certain congruence with theology's 'mastery' presents itself here. It is by being an *authentically theological biology* that life science exercises this 'imperialism' rightly, in the sense of showing life as incapable of being translated into the terms of reductive physical sciences without loss; life cannot be 'got behind' but must inflect our understanding of reality as a whole.

Jonas shows biological life as always exceeding its bounded self; as irreducible to non-life; as intrinsically purposeful, subjective, free and self-transcending. But at the same time, his philosophical biology perpetuates a hermeneutic of conflict. It does not hold to an ontological ultimacy of life, though it reaches for it. It remains captive to dialectics and so resistant to narration as the fundamental form of thought itself, whether science or philosophy, which makes peace, in the end, out of reach. One of the most important outcomes in our consideration of Jonas's analysis is that it shows that the thesis of the irreducibility of life to non-life does not by itself establish life's ontological ultimacy, nor does it save life from being mere self-assertion in the face of emptiness, and thus fundamentally aggressive. The vitalistic construal of life as narrated by Jonas thus demonstrates the inadequacy of a purely philosophical reason which remains principally dialectical and so does not tell the story of peace. This is only possible for a reason illuminated by the Christian narration of peace.

Theological vitalism encapsulates in relation to life two insights which we have been considering in this work: that there is no non-speculative knowledge; and no containable finitude. For this reason, a theological vitalism must not, on pain of contradiction, present itself as a finished thesis with a finally delimited content.[71] It functions more as an invitation to continual speculation and conjecture in our approach to life, while foregrounding the embodied, fleshly character of the living organism. This disrupts the association with imperialism and its projects of totalizing knowledge which have dogged modern vitalisms.

In sum, a theological vitalism unites the poles of historicity and materiality on the one hand and participated transcendence on the other. It represents a view of life which is both 'from above' and 'from below': biology-as-theology and theology-as-biology. In this way it demonstrates the inescapability of a governing narrative which will always exceed the world; such a narrative is more than 'under-determined' by the evidence, since the evidence itself is conceived, selected and adduced on the basis of the narrative. Life does not 'have' to be read in the way that I, via Jonas, am going to read it; a theological vitalism is not forced upon one by the 'evidence'. The claim that life is fundamentally peace, which is the overarching burden of the vitalism I am defending, emerges on the logic of the Christian story.

70. Greco, 'On the Vitality of Vitalism', 19, quoting Canguilhem.

71. It thus avoids the charge of 'imperialism' in the sense of external rule; see Lash, 'Life (Vitalism)', 324.

Chapter 6

HANS JONAS AND THE TESTIMONY OF LIFE

This chapter explores Jonas's philosophical biology. The intellectual genealogy with which he sets the stage is outlined, with particular attention to his identification of the living body as the locus of its solution. His vitalistic uses of Darwinism and metabolism are examined.

Biology as theology

The work Jonas will do for this study is both positive and negative in manner: positive in the sense that Jonas shows how biological 'facts' defy a reading in terms of closed immanence; negative in the sense that without a Christian narration this life remains conflictual, defined by death and suffering, and dialectics remains methodologically primary at the expense of a more comprehensive story of life. In the following account, the focus is on Jonas's concerns and priorities in his inquiry into life, but in such a way as to show that his philosophical biology is continuous with a 'theological' biology, a theology which speaks in the tones of life science.

Jonas is a philosopher who undertakes a phenomenological analysis of life, and we therefore face an urgent initial question in making use of him: we have suggested that a philosophical analysis by itself will necessarily be sterile. Does this not vitiate Jonas's usefulness to theology or make him only a negative foil? Anticipating the argument to come, two points can be made. Firstly, unlike other readers of Jonas, I contend that his account of life neither claims to be purely rational nor manifests such an assumption. Rather it remains implicitly theological in the sense considered, insofar as he expresses certain narratives in his philosophical analysis and frankly rejects an Enlightenment model of knowledge as externality, whether cognitive or causal. Although it appears dialectical, his account of life foregrounds desire, temporality and embodiment in ways which are not indicative of supposedly narrative-free reasoning and implicates a participative elevation of history and matter.

Secondly, the following account is meant to show that to the extent that Jonas's philosophy of the organism does remain autonomous with respect to theology, it does not live up to its own expectations. The discussion intends to highlight the continuity of Jonas's philosophical biology with a theological narration of life, while at the same time arguing that by operating (he thinks) independently of a narrative of creation, sanctification and *eschaton* which grounds a metaphysics of the participation of the world in God, Jonas ultimately fails fully to narrate the ontological ultimacy of life, which his philosophy reaches towards, or to ground the narrative character of knowing itself.

A number of resonances between Jonas and the theological programme we have been outlining will be apparent in the following account: most importantly, the critique of philosophical modernity, the assault on dualisms and the overcoming of metaphysical boundaries. Like Milbank, Jonas narrates the rejection of modernity and its boundaries by an intellectual genealogy, exposing the unacknowledged sources and implications of modern philosophy, questioning the distinctions it generates and rejecting its philosophical options as equally buying into one fundamental error: Milbank names this 'univocity', Jonas 'dualism'. Like Milbank also, Jonas undertakes his own investigation of ontology which is characterized by the overcoming of boundaries: between organism and world; between non-human and human life; between mind and matter. Where the projects diverge is in their choice of the key which is taken to unlock the true ontology: for Milbank it is peace; for Jonas it is life.

Crucially, this most important difference is reflected in a further divergence regarding the respective roles of dialectic and narrative. Jonas's method is principally dialectical: positions x and y are contrasted, pros and cons negotiated and a final position z is adopted. It has been acknowledged that, for Milbank, a primacy of narration does not exclude dialectics, though narration remains the determinative framework for the employment of dialectics. Accordingly it is possible to make full use of the way in which Jonas employs a dialectical method to defend life's irreducibility while maintaining that the way in which this irreducibility is put to work must remain narratival. In fact Jonas's own philosophy of the organism itself points towards this narratival structure, insofar as the organism itself is a story of purposes unfolding in time, never containable in any one moment.

The argument for vitalism

The Phenomenon of Life: Toward a Philosophical Biology is Jonas's attempt to respond to 'the testimony of life'.[1] His argument can be broken down into five stages.

1. A genealogy of Western metaphysics, beginning with archaic panvitalism as the primal human ontology, explaining the transition to metaphysical dualism and then in the modern period its two offspring, the partial monisms of materialism and idealism.

---

1. (Evanston, IL: Northwestern University Press, 2001), 2.

2. An examination of the kinship between dualism and nihilism, and of materialism and idealism as buying into dualism's (nihilistic) premises, which include the prohibition of anthropomorphism and the consequent extrusion of teleology from the physical world and its evacuation of positive meaning.

3. The failure of ontologies with dualistic premises to accommodate the reality of the living body, in which mental and physical, inward and outward, cannot be extricated from one another.

4. The use of Darwinism negatively to expose the inadequacy of mechanistic interpretations of life, and positively to rehabilitate teleology and demonstrate the continuity of mental and physical.

5. A constructive philosophical analysis of the living body in terms of metabolism, and the radical metaphysical implications of the distinction between form and matter in living organisms which metabolism brings about, showing that freedom, inwardness, and purpose are coextensive with organic life.

Jonas offers two forms of reasoning: negative/polemical and positive/constructive. The negative reasoning concerns the incapacity of metaphysical dualism, and the partial monisms it gives rise to, to capture the reality of the living body which trespasses into several metaphysical realms simultaneously. Demonstrating the defeat of reductive ontologies by the living organism is the key of Jonas's negative argument. The positive reasoning proceeds by way of three arguments: an argument from Darwinism, an argument from metabolism and a phenomenological argument from felt experience.[2] In this he ably demonstrates the fruitfulness of life's revelation of its own transcendence 'from below', in a conjectural manner.

Recovering nature

Just as the *nouvelle théologie* regarded the nature of nature as theologically critical, and made a retrieval of an authentic conception of nature central to their task, Jonas takes an analysis of modern 'nature' as the first step in the construction of a true metaphysic.[3] The discovery which set Jonas's intellectual trajectory occurred

2. Despite its begging the theological question, Jonas's philosophy of life has the critical advantage that it starts from an analysis of the data of the life sciences, working with the biological facts of evolution and metabolism, and moving on this basis to address metaphysical questions. Jonas's careful attentiveness to the life sciences is celebrated by David Levy, *Hans Jonas: The Integrity of Thinking* (Columbia, MO: University of Missouri Press, 2002), 45–6. His patient attentiveness to scientific data is one of his most outstanding qualities.

3. Nature is 'an essentially contested concept' (Walter Gallie, 'Essentially Contested Concepts', *Proceedings of the Aristotelian Society* 56, no. 2 (1956): 167–98); both 'normative'

through his early studies of the Gnostics, when he observed that Gnosticism was recurring in even more pernicious form in modernity than it did in antiquity: the human being is regarded as an alien in the world, but whereas in Gnosticism, the human being still has a home in another world, in contemporary existentialism that other home is exposed as an illusion, and now the human has no future and no purpose. Leo Strauss, a fellow student of Heidegger, wrote to Jonas that Gnosticism was the most radical rebellion against the Greek notion of *physis* that Western history had yet seen,[4] an assessment which Jonas would have disagreed with insofar as he viewed existentialism as a second coming of nihilism in even more apocalyptic form. Nature is the key, because nihilism always begins with a change in the understanding of nature itself, 'an estrangement between man and the world' which makes it impossible to discern value in the world itself. Gnosticism brought about 'the loss of the idea of a kindred *cosmos*',[5] and modern existentialism is a radicalization of the same sense of bereavement. The main burden of Jonas's intellectual genealogy is simply this: the philosophical root of cosmic nihilism, whether ancient or modern, is a dualism in which humanity and world are irreconcilable – a definition of nature as *opposite* to humanity, meaning, freedom and purpose. In the case of Gnosticism, the world is the creation of a malignant demiurge and is ordered by *heimarmene*, an 'oppressive cosmic fate'[6] which is inimical to human freedom; for existentialism, the human being lives in an absolute solitude of vertiginous freedom, a freedom which can refer to no innate and given sense or orientation in human nature that mirrors the world. The Gnostic world, governed by a power-hungry deity, is a world 'degraded to a power system', and such a world 'can only be overcome through power'.[7] This mirrors the contemporary nihilistic assessment of humanity's possibilities, in which 'the countering of power with power is the sole relation to the totality of nature left for man'.[8]

Jonas' project in *The Phenomenon of Life* could be summarized as the revivification of what he calls a 'cosmic piety' by the restoration of a fundamental kinship between human life and life as a whole. He recovers our human identity as members of the living, of a community which extends to the most primitive forms of metabolic existence. This community is generated not by a reduction to a perceived materialist common denominator, a kind of neo-Darwinist

and 'ambivalent', it is critical for establishing the content and role of 'collateral' concepts (Noel Castree, *Making Sense of Nature*, 26–7ff) such as 'God' and 'man/humanity'. Of course Milbank would argue that 'nature' is as much a collateral of God as the reverse.

4. Benjamin Lazier, 'Overcoming Gnosticism: Hans Jonas, Hans Blumenberg, and the Legitimacy of the Natural World', *Journal of the History of Ideas* 64 (2003): 619–37, 620.

5. *The Phenomenon of Life* (Evanston, IL: Northwestern University Press, 2000).

6. *Phenomenon*, 220.

7. *Phenomenon*, 221.

8. *Phenomenon*, 221.

proclamation of human beings as *merely* material, but through the elevation of the whole community of life to mindedness and inwardness.

Jonas takes Heidegger's rejection of the natural world as meaningful as instantiating the nihilistic alienation of human from non-human. Heidegger repudiated the understanding of humanity as 'animal', claiming that this epithet places man too low, making him subject to a definable nature or predetermined essence.[9] For Heidegger the 'co-presence' of things, the material objects (living and non-living) with which humanity shares the world, is something bare; non-human things are 'merely and indifferently extant'; the world of things is 'being . . . stripped and alienated to the mode of mute thinghood'.[10] Their presence is ontologically weak, for they have no share in human freedom. Freedom for Heidegger is having no constraints, no nature, no given essence. But to be without a nature, says Jonas, is to be without norm, to have no inner connection to the world.

The connection between the status of non-human beings, 'animals', on the one hand, and human meaning and freedom, on the other, is decisive for Jonas. If to be 'animal' is to be something deficient and low, nature has been given away to meaninglessness. Jonas's philosophy of life retrieves meaning precisely by the elevation of animal (and vegetable) life to a true kinship with human beings. Saving meaning requires saving nature. Both the Gnostics and the existentialists desire to free humanity from nature, to define the 'natural' as unfree, to make the animal *merely* fleshly. But the loss of the natural and the animal ensures not freedom, but its opposite, casting us loose from any possibility of an order of meaning and purpose discoverable in the world which would simultaneously provide a compass for human action and restore a sense of belonging, a harmony or resonance between the human person and the world she finds herself in. Instead of resonance, reciprocity and harmony, dualism and its heirs opt for an ontology of 'thrownness', where the 'throwing' of the human spirit into the world is an original

---

9. Turner's discussion of Aquinas' definition of the human as 'rational animal' casts further interesting light on Heidegger's disvaluing of the animal; Denys Turner, *Faith, Reason and the Existence of God* (Cambridge: Cambridge University Press, 2004), 90–1, 189. One might consider that Aquinas' treatment of the human as rational animal 'answers' in advance the modern alienation of human from nature which Heidegger sponsors with his rejection of animality. Jonas would be uncomfortable with the rational/non-rational dualism which Aquinas' definition sets up and would likely regard this as smuggling the dualism back in, with alienation from the non-human inevitably following. He would be more likely to make use of contemporary work in ethology which demonstrates a continuity of 'rationality', in the sense of a range of broadly contiguous types of sense-making, between human and non-human animals. Rather than regarding this as a demotion of human nature, he would see it as a salvific revelation of the pervasive mindedness of the non-human world: salvific because it makes our persistent tendency towards dualism even harder to sustain.

10. *Phenomenon*, 231; but as we shall see, Jonas's account of life does not evade the Heideggerian imputation of violence to life at an ontological level.

act of violence which makes alienation the defining condition of humanity, as in Heidegger's *Geworfenheit*.[11]

Jonas's philosophical analysis of biological facts raises the non-human living to the dignity of mind. He sees this raising in Platonic terms, arguing that to prioritize being over becoming, eternity over time, essence over process, is the only way to secure the value of the world of things. In existentialism, the present is overshadowed by both the future, the ultimate nullity of approaching death, and the past, the 'unalterable datum of its already having become this'.[12] There is no present that is not subsumed by past and future; the co-presence of things with humanity in the world is an irrelevance. Gnosticism too denies a real present, a present that is not simply sucked into the bleak mortal future or the dead fixity of the past; this world is inexorably trapped in a flux of time, a flux in which the 'present' is 'nothing but the moment of crisis between past and future'.[13] For these nihilisms there is no 'repose in the present',[14] no *theoria* which beholds the still reflection of eternity in the changing world of things. This is a theme that Jonas returns to frequently in his analyses of the philosophical assumptions of contemporary science. '[I]t is eternity, not time, that grants a present and gives it a status of its own in the flux of time'; the disappearance of eternity spells 'the absolute victory of nominalism over realism', in which values are not beheld in a vision of being but are 'posited by the will as projects'.[15]

Jonas's comparison of Gnosticism and existentialism shows how nihilisms are underwritten by a picture of nature that strips it of meaning, allowing it no positive significance. This provides Jonas with the negative statement of his project: by rehabilitating nature to rehabilitate meaning, purpose and value, to restore the common root of humanity and the world, the resonance of one with the other that allows the human being to be at home in the world of things and ultimately – though this is beyond the purview of *Phenomenon* – to take responsibility for it.[16] The consequence of nihilism is that both human being and world are given over to the will as the naked exercise of power with no responsibility to a given prior order. Rediscovering a home in nature requires a retrieval of the natural as more than a vacuous play of power which holds only negative meaning for the human – as, rather, the site of the disclosure of the true and the good. In Jonas's analysis, this must come about through a reminding of the living world, a restoration of the psychic to the somatic, a reintegration of spirit and flesh.

11. *Phenomenon*, 229.

12. *Phenomenon*, 231.

13. *Phenomenon*, 232.

14. *Phenomenon*, 232.

15. *Phenomenon*, 232.

16. Which becomes Jonas's concern in his more well-known work *The Imperative of Responsibility: In Search of an Ethics for a Technological Age* (Chicago: University of Chicago Press, 2005).

Life: The therapy for nihilism

The resemblance between Jonas's concerns in his philosophical biology and Milbank's own genealogy (and indeed the agenda of the *nouvelle théologie* altogether) is striking. As Gnosticism evacuates the given world of meaning and truth, secular reason and 'pure nature' posit a natural realm which can be considered apart from transcendence. Both Milbank and Jonas are resistant above all to ontological dualisms, which would concentrate meaning in a divine 'elsewhere' with no inner and intrinsic presence in the 'ordinary' world. Modern metaphysics, whether dualist or monist, pictures a world which can be adequately described in only one voice: the world of matter and mechanical causation. In contrast, our interlocutors seek to show the impossibility of adequately describing the world in only one dimension. In Jonas's hands, the organism becomes the prime testimony to this fact, which is what makes the organism, in my proposal, an exemplary solvent of secular reason. As Jonas analyses it, the organism's very existence is a denial of that absolute metaphysical separation which would provide the security of a total metaphysical closure of the world in which we live. Jonas uses the organism to demonstrate what Milbank, as inheritor of the *nouvelle théologie*, seeks to defend: there can be no compartmentalization in reality which would allow us to say that some key datum – reason, nature, matter, bodies – can be 'pure' in the sense of requiring nothing beyond itself to make sense of what it, by its nature, is in itself. Jonas argues that biological life pre-eminently does this work of the breaking of false metaphysical boundaries, and so points theology towards biological life as the solvent of secular reason. This evokes something of the elusive and antinomial character of 'explanation' which was explored in the previous chapter. It is part of what Milbank means by a primacy of narration, and one reason why, although Jonas employs a dialectical method, the thrust of his analysis pushes in a narrative direction.

Jonas's guiding insight is that mind-world, spirit-matter dualism is the father of nihilism, just as for the opponents of pure nature it is the nature-grace dualism which fathers nihilism; both emerge from a failure of metaphysical integration. In this sense, Jonas's choice of subject in *The Phenomenon of Life* is his most significant contribution: life is the therapy for nihilism. Already at this point an interesting congruence between life (Jonas), grace (*nouvelle théologie*) and peace (Milbank) suggests itself. Aside from the substantive arguments of Jonas's philosophical biology, its lasting importance consists in its contention that the fundamental question for a philosophy of being – and therefore for theology as the true science – is the nature of organic life. It inescapably suggests to the theologian that life will be central in its account of what being is, and therefore in the theological narration of grace and peace as what are finally real. By taking it seriously on its own terms as metaphysically laden, Jonas restores to life a unique depth and promise: life alone holds the key to our predicament, and by this Jonas does not mean life abstractly conceived, but *biological* life, the very life which we share with all the living. In its very materiality and limitedness, it prophetically shows forth the deepest character of being itself, demonstrating that a profounder integration lies beneath seeming difference: if we attend to life we will see that there are no true *opposites* in being, just as a metaphysics of participation affirms that all being is sharing in the one divine reality. Just as Jonas asks how life shows itself as exceeding its own immanent bounds, Milbank asks how nature shows itself as uncircumscribable, how science shows itself as uncontainable by immanence. As 'pure nature' and a self-contained secular are to Milbank, a metaphysically contained organism is to Jonas: for both, these things abundantly demonstrate their own impossibility.

Mounting coherent opposition to dualism requires a rejection of dualism's basic premise: the absolute alternative of same versus different. Jonas's use of the phrase 'the living middle' to describe the phenomenon of life expresses the failure of monistic and dualistic ontologies alike to capture the 'between' quality of the living body.[17] Given that Jonas presumably was not aware of Przywara's 'suspended middle', his use of the vocabulary of 'middle' and 'between' is striking. Rather than focusing on reason as occupying that middle, irresolvable into any one pole, Jonas takes organismic life as that which most comprehensively resists ontological reduction. For a participatory metaphysical scheme, this is a particularly useful move, insofar as it invites us to see the suspension at the level of material and not solely intellectual existence; or rather, to be more faithful to Jonas, it invites the view that in the world of the living there is no non-intellectual reality, no 'mere' body. (Jonas's middle is in a certain sense 'suspended', insofar as it is not tied off, but we shall see that its suspension is not accounted for in the terms of his own analysis.)

Jonas argues that accepting a mutual exclusiveness of same versus different gives only one alternative to dualism: a monism which collapses mental and physical into one another, annihilating one of the two or rendering it unreal or merely

---

17. For Jonas, monism and dualism buy into the same problematic premises. The ontological 'middle' he is seeking plots a course between materialism and idealism, which both presume the opposition he is challenging, even if they attempt to solve it by eliminating one pole. Modern materialism has 'inherited the estate of a defunct dualism' (*Phenomenon*, 14), suffering in consequence from a profound incoherence, which Jonas investigates in more depth in the context of a critique of Cartesianism. The contraction of metaphysical dualism into monistic materialism represents the 'total triumph of the death experience over the life experience' (*Phenomenon*, 15). The other contraction of dualism is an idealistic monism which, accepting the divorce between mental and physical, posits mind as the only reality and matter as a mere epiphenomenon or function of the mind. In Jonas's view, idealism is the secondary contraction because it is parasitic on materialism, which is the real representative of post-dualistic ontology and the true modern counterpart to archaic panvitalism; idealism is but an 'epiphenomenon' of materialism, because idealism arose in response to 'a world objectified to pure extensive outwardness', which 'leaves opposite itself a pure consciousness which has no share in it' (*Phenomenon*, 20). It was the reduction of the physical plane to dead extension that raised consciousness to idealism's precarious estimation of it.

apparent, which is what happens in both materialism and idealism.[18] Where one of the two aspects is undermined and destroyed in this way, the *nihil* remains the governing hermeneutic; rather than intensifying the qualities of life in the non-annihilated pole, in the choice for a monism both sides, matter and mind, lose their integrity and reality, as the history of ontology demonstrates. Only a philosophy of the middle will keep hold of the reality and distinctiveness of both as inextricable dimensions of the one living body; the organic is the conceptual site on which that true ontology can be constructed, since it manifestly resists reduction to either pole.

There is a consequence for the way 'the disciplines' are understood. If life cannot be captured exclusively in terms of the material or the mental, but belongs fully in both, then multiple fields of human enquiry from physical sciences to philosophy will be involved in the elucidation of life. To ask the question 'What is life?' is already to have entered on a field of enquiry that escapes the bounds of any single discipline; life is inherently a trespasser over disciplinary boundaries.[19] Just as life challenges our division of the world into fields of knowledge, so it defeats philosophical solutions that try to explain or account for life univocally.

Life, then, cannot be captured within one field of enquiry, refuses metaphysical compartmentalization and raises the spectre of irresolvability in terms of pure reason. This is why, for Jonas, the phenomenon of life is a stumbling block for ontologies of all kinds, the proof test which exposes the vacuity of oversimplified, totalizing explanations. Only an ontology which does not attempt to contain immanence, nor hive off transcendence to a safe distance, could adequately respond to life; this would be an ontology which celebrates the impossibility of total explanations, absolute starting points or secure boundaries for matter or spirit.[20]

18. In its far-reaching effects, 'the rise and long ascendency of dualism are among the most decisive events in the mental history of the race' (*Phenomenon*, 13). Dualism gathered all aliveness and transcendence into a supermundane realm and left the immanent world in a state of vacuity, 'drain[ing] the spiritual elements off the physical realm' leaving a world 'denuded' and drab (*Phenomenon*, 13). The modern ontologies of materialism and idealism are unhappy children of dualism which do not overcome the fundamental antinomy in being which dualism has set up.

19. It is 'intrinsic in the subject' that 'its discussion should involve me in theories of being from Plato to Heidegger, and in matters stretching from physics and biology to theology and ethics. The phenomenon of life itself negates the boundaries that customarily divide our disciplines and fields' (*Phenomenon*, xxiv; Jonas's attribution of 'a' contribution made by theology here is obviously problematic). In light of his later emphasis on the omnipresence of the living observer, we would be bound to say that there is no discipline which is not implicated in it.

20. It is our response to life that is the test of our openness to reality: 'The nondogmatic thinker will not suppress the testimony of life.' *Phenomenon*, 2.

Jonas employs a close examination of the metabolizing organism and its emergence by evolution from organic history to demonstrate the inadequacy of the modernity's ontologies: Cartesian metaphysical dualism, mechanistic materialism or Enlightenment idealism. Against all these philosophies, which seek containers for what cannot be contained, organic life stands as the accuser.

Primitive panvitalism

Jonas argues that life itself is the originary ontology of humanity, which sets later ontologies in a critical light.

> When man first began to interpret the nature of things – and this he did when he began to be a man – life was to him everywhere, and being the same as being alive. [. . .] Soul flooded the whole of existence. . . . Bare matter, that is, truly inanimate, 'dead' matter, was yet to be discovered – as indeed its concept, so familiar to us, is anything but obvious. That the world is alive is really the most natural view, and largely supported by prima-facie evidence. [. . .] Earth, wind, and water – begetting, teeming, nurturing, destroying – are anything but models of 'mere matter'.[21]

Jonas makes us sharply aware of the novelty of modernity, its non-self-evidence, just as Milbank's genealogy of secular reason echoes Charles Taylor's argument against the subtraction theory: there is nothing 'obvious' about materialism, just as there is nothing 'obvious' about secularism. The self-evident conceptual response to the world, claims Jonas, is to believe that everything is alive; life is the rule, the 'intelligible, self-explaining, "natural" condition'.[22] Panpsychism, hylozoism, animism – these were the instinctive world views of early human beings; Jonas's preferred term is 'panvitalism'.[23]

In such a panvitalism, which accepts life as the primary, given condition of things, the baffling anomaly is death. Death, in Jonas's treatment, is the first phenomenon to deserve the name *problem* in the history of thought: the realization of mortality inflicts a '"logical" outrage' on the panvitalistic world of newly

---

21. *Phenomenon*, 7.

22. *Phenomenon*, 8.

23. To a certain extent there is a tension here with the approach we have been taking in this study, in which nothing is regarded as self-evident outside a particular genealogy. But Jonas's treatment is at some level cognizant of this. His argument reflects the basic understanding that whatever is taken to be the horizon of normality determines the significance of everything else, and that there is a certain inexplicability to this: the place which is chosen to begin the story of what the world is cannot really have a rationale, insofar as it provides the rationale for anything at all.

awakened conceptual awareness.[24] Life, in the archaic world view, is what makes sense; death offends the mind and begs explanation and account in terms of life; life is the narrative into which death must be assimilated. Whatever death is, it 'must still belong to the total context of life';[25] it must be an appearance of cessation, in which the one reality of life simply takes on a different form or temper. It is argued below that a perspective of broadly this kind is native to the specifically Christian narration of the world: it is death which offends, which contradicts; death whose finality and self-evidence is denied.

Jonas discussion taken as a whole reflects an allegiance to this primitive panvitalism: a pre-rational instinct for life as ontologically basic. Whether or not his claim is historically plausible, it shows which narrative, for him, has the most powerful native claim on the human imagination. But Jonas cannot establish this as ontologically normative from a critical metaphysical point of view: panvitalism, for Jonas, cannot survive either the full realization of mortality or the onslaught of modern mechanism, but must be qualified by them. His problematic distance from the panvitalistic world view is evident in his granting the most central role to conflict as the context of organic existence, conflict generated by the ever-renewed threat of mortality. This is, for him, the definitive setting of life's self-perpetuation and therefore of the ontological status of life itself.

Modernity's ontology of death

Jonas contrasts primitive panvitalism with modernity's turn to mechanism and reductionism. Modernity has opted for an ontology of inert lifelessness over dynamic life: panvitalism has been replaced by pan-mechanism. The ontology which succeeded the scientific revolution has as its 'model entity' pure, inert matter, 'stripped of all the features of life'.[26] 'This denuded substratum of all reality could only be arrived at through a progressive expurgation of vital features from the physical record and through strict abstention from projecting into its image our own felt aliveness.'[27] Spatial extension came to be regarded as the criterion of the real; quantitative description, 'measurement', was the only reliable means of knowledge. Living bodies were regarded only in terms of physical extension, in which respect they were treated in just the same way as lifeless bodies; lifelessness was seen to be the knowable and natural state. A changed conception of explanation is central: life is the explained, and death is what does the explaining. When modernity asks, 'What is life?', it answers with a *nihil*: it is a nothing, a deceiving appearance of vital autonomous force that cannot be taken at face value; it cannot be explained in its own terms, in the language of life, but is wholly accounted for only in terms

24. *Phenomenon*, 8.
25. *Phenomenon*, 8.
26. *Phenomenon*, 9.
27. *Phenomenon*, 10.

of what is alone taken to be self-explanatory: lifelessness. No longer in modernity, says Jonas, is the question posed, how did death come into the world? – but rather, how did life come into the world, into the lifeless? In this scheme, an organism is comprehensible only when a corpse; divested of its puzzling qualities of aliveness, it re-enters the predictable and unambiguous world of inert bodies. And so '[o]ur thinking today is under the ontological dominance of death'.[28]

Like Milbank with his concern for the antinomy of explanation in modern sociology, Jonas recognizes conceptions of explanation in biology as pivotal, since they reveal that which is taken to be most basic, what can be taken as read, and which is used to generate explanatory power, and that which does the explaining is the point at which the *aporia* of knowledge itself opens up. A careful reading of Jonas on this points towards the critique undertaken in Chapter 7.

In this mechanical universe, death is not explained in the overarching narrative of life but life in the terms of the lifeless; the apparently purposeful in the terms of the purposeless. The purposeful, sentient organism was the puzzling exception in a world of mere matter in which death is 'the natural and intelligible condition'.[29] 'To take life as a problem is here to acknowledge its strangeness in the mechanical world which is *the* world; to explain it is – in this climate of a universal ontology of death – to negate it by making it one of the possible variants of the lifeless.'[30] Jonas's acknowledgement of this reversal indicates that, even if he does not confess it theoretically, he does acknowledge the fundamentally narrative character of thought as such, in which a story – considered externally – just has to begin somewhere: with death, or with life. However, the dialectical character of his analysis is apparent in that for Jonas there is an evidential reasonableness to modernity's change of horizon. He explains the origin and 'motivational history' of dualism in the universal evidence of mortality which the panvitalist creed 'could appease but not silence'; as death gained force as an opposition to life, not simply as subsumable within it, 'the naive monism broke up into a dualism' whose causative factor, 'the sight of the corpse', eventually 'spread over the face of the physical All' to the point that '[d]eath . . . conquered external reality' altogether, without remainder.[31] The soul or life was now seen to dwell 'like a stranger in the flesh which by its own nature . . . is nothing but a corpse'; death is the 'original truth' of the body in which mind is now alien.[32] There was a 'fateful divorce' between inner dynamic life and outer inanimate nature; the external world was not even demonic, but simply bare and indifferent, for what is extended and physical is lifeless; '[t]he whole world is a tomb'.[33] Reality is now a uniform physical plane of measurable quantities; a living universe is replaced by 'a field of inanimate masses and forces',

28. *Phenomenon*, 12.
29. *Phenomenon*, 10.
30. *Phenomenon*, 11.
31. *Phenomenon*, 13.
32. *Phenomenon*, 13.
33. *Phenomenon*, 14.

a 'denuded substratum' which was arrived at by 'a progressive expurgation of vital features from the physical record'.[34] Everyone now admits life's strangeness in 'the mechanical world which is *the* world'.[35]

What becomes apparent here is the incapability, as 'purely' philosophical, of Jonas's philosophical biology to furnish the kind of account of life he is reaching for. He finds death so omnipresent and unanswerable that its deadening effect on ontology appears inevitable. But although death is, for him, an ubiquitous darkness which makes our instinctive panvitalism untenable, he still moves to maintain life's ontological primacy. His treatment of the living body makes a powerful dialectical case, in the apologetic sense we saw affirmed by Milbank in the previous chapter: if we think x, we must think y. Jonas's achievement in his philosophy of the organism is to show that if we believe in Darwinism; if we correctly understand metabolism; if we attend to our felt experience, then we must think life as irreducible, as ontologically primary. Nevertheless, his capture by the existentialist conception that it is only as over-against-death that life is correctly understood undermines this apologetic dialectics. The impossibility of establishing dialectically an ontological ultimacy of life goes to show the primacy of narration, while at the same time Jonas's use of apologetic dialectic to expose logical relationships within our operative conceptual models exemplifies the heuristic value of dialectical reasoning.[36]

34. *Phenomenon*, 10.

35. *Phenomenon*, 11.

36. One cannot but be struck by the resemblance between Jonas's contentions here and the language adopted to express contemporary applications of the Christian narrative in recent decades, specifically the now almost canonical notion in the Catholic world of a contemporary 'culture of death' versus the 'culture of life'. (The *locus classicus* for this notion is John Paul II, *Evangelium Vitae* (London: Catholic Truth Society, 1995). Donald De Marko and Benjamin Wiker, *Architects of the Culture of Death* (San Francisco: Ignatius, 2004), re-read European philosophy through the lens of this concept. Bennett, *Vibrant Matter*, refers dismissively to the 'culture of life' as a 'soul vitalism' which dogmatically holds to an anthropocentric hierarchy of creation (Chapter 6).)

This highlights the distinctive importance of Jonas to the formation of adequately expansive Christian narratives of life. Jonas's analysis shows that the narrative of life versus death is not exclusively, or perhaps even principally, relevant to intra-human value. Rather it gains its intense significance because of its purchase on the whole world of life: the organic altogether, which turns out to be a lynchpin of the possibility of meaningfulness in the world as a whole. Jonas's philosophical biology illuminates the solidarity of all life: either life is ontologically basic everywhere and for all the living or for none of them. It points to the solidarity involved in embodiedness as such. The notion of a solidarity of being alive, a solidarity among the bodily living, is readily recognizable as an incarnational theme, and yet broader Christian narratives around 'sanctity of life' remain stubbornly intra-human: 'life' is functioning restrictively, we might say univocally. (I deliberately avoid the term 'anthropocentric'. It remains legitimate to place human life at the centre; as we shall see

The living body: Prophetic for ontology

It is the living body which exposes the inadequacy of all post-dualistic ontologies which accept a mind-matter polarity as axiomatic. Jonas does not try to restore meaning to organic life by interpolating a 'spiritual' element but by showing its biological character as exhibiting an inwardness and a freedom all the way down.

The living body cannot be accommodated by materialist or idealist monisms. The 'integral monism of prehistory in which the two sides were still fused undifferentiated' is now lost to us;[37] a new integration must absorb the polarity 'into a higher unity of existence'.[38] Hence modern metaphysical thought is marked by the search for a more comprehensive monism, whether materialist or idealist, that faces the dualistic spectre and rejects its transcendentalism by fitting all the phenomena into its chosen straitjacket, proclaiming one pole the real one and the other a consequential or derivative one. Both materialism and idealism can 'dissemble their monistic . . . character' by a methodological epoché so that we end up with 'a phenomenology of consciousness and a physics of extension, and the method of one discipline would be as necessarily idealistic as that of the other materialistic' – an 'ontic', not an ontological, separation.[39] On this view idealistic and materialistic idioms would be considered complementary rather than alternative. But the two 'elements', mind and matter, cannot be bracketed one from the other, because the living body exhibits a 'psychophysical unity' which 'renders the separation illusory': the 'actual coincidence of inwardness and outwardness in the *body* compels the two ways of knowledge to define their relation otherwise than by separate subjects'.[40]

In this way Jonas moves towards locating in the living body an ineffable mutual participation of matter and spirit. The notion of *methexis*, used by Milbank, seems apt to describe what he is reaching for: the 'mixture' which the living body is testifies

---

Jonas's own emphasis on anthropomorphism points in such a direction.) Jonas draws us to question this usage. Either all of life is sacred or none of it is. Clearly, such a formulation in no way entails that all of life is 'equal', nor that there are no relevant distinctions between different kinds of life. If Jonas is right in his analysis of life, then we are obliged to think solidarity at a deeper level, and this should surely make a profound difference to the way Christianity narrates life altogether, and the way this narrative points us towards certain kinds of values and practices. Solidarity would be an appropriate conceptual tool to begin articulating this theological vitalism in practical terms, being one of the four foundational themes of Catholic Social Teaching. (Russell Hittinger, 'The Coherence of the Four Basic Themes of Catholic Social Doctrine: An Interpretation', *Pursuing the Common Good: How Solidarity and Subsidiarity Can Work Together*, Pontifical Academy of Social Sciences, *Acta* 14, Vatican City, 2008.)

37. *Phenomenon*, 16.
38. *Phenomenon*, 17.
39. *Phenomenon*, 17.
40. *Phenomenon*, 18.

to an inextricability of spirit and matter which yet does not evacuate the distinctive qualities of the things mixed. Jonas freely uses the notion of 'transcendence' to describe the way in which our attempts to isolate the different dimensions of bodily life are defeated, although for Jonas it is a contrastive transcendence in relation to the organism, while for Milbank it is non-contrastive transcendence.[41] This asymmetry militates against any naive transference of Jonas's language about the organism into Christian metaphysical language. Nevertheless, one can discern in it a similar moment: the living entity does not remain within itself, and neither do metaphysical categories remain closed and compartmentalized. This is borne out by Jonas's insistence that the mixture of categories that is the organism calls for more than a merely agnostic acknowledgement. A 'descriptive abstention', or metaphysical neutrality as to the relation between the two dimensions of life, can only be accomplished if the two fields of phenomena, the mental and the physical, 'are closed in themselves at least *qua* phenomena and do not transcend themselves by their own contents'; but

> our living body constitutes that very self-transcendence in either direction and thereby makes the methodological epoché founder on its rock. [The body] must be described as extended and inert, but equally as feeling and willing.[42]

The living organism is excessive and transgressive, a reproach to dualism and its offspring. In regarding the living body, thought cannot bracket or postpone the issue of the real relation of mental and physical. The problem of life is the 'constant disturbance' of metaphysical solutions which accept a mind-matter divorce, for '[i]n the body, the knot of being is tied which dualism does not unravel but cut'.[43] As Milbank employs it, the notion of participation enshrines just this perpetual impossibility of secure demarcation. What is disturbed is the attempt to fix boundaries within finitude. Jonas expresses this with his claim that any successful ontology, able to meet the challenge of the living body, must move entirely beyond the mutual exclusion of either-or.

> Thus the organic body signifies the latent crisis of every known ontology. . . . As it was first the body on which, in the fact of *death,* that antithesis of life and nonlife became manifest whose relentless pressure on thought destroyed primitive panvitalism and caused the image of being to split, so it is conversely the concrete unity manifest in its *life* on which in turn the dualism of the two substances founders, and again this bi-unity which also brings to grief both

41. Kathryn Tanner uses these terms in relation to models of divine transcendence; *God and Creation in Christian Theology: Tyranny or Empowerment?* (Minneapolis: Fortress Press, 2005), 36ff.

42. *Phenomenon*, 18.

43. *Phenomenon*, 25.

alternatives branching off from dualism, whenever they – as they cannot help doing – enlarge themselves into total ontologies.[44]

For Jonas this 'bi-unity' is the defining quality of the living body from a metaphysical point of view. The organism indeed faces dissolution in death. But its aliveness and inwardness, its feeling and responding, its purposefulness and self-concern, its automotive activity are intransigently resistant to reduction. In any theory which is ontologically monochrome, organic life stands as the reproachful exception.

> The living body that can die, that has a world and itself belongs to the world, that feels and itself can be felt, whose outward form is organism and causality, and whose inward form is selfhood and finality; this body is the memento of the still unsolved question of ontology: 'What is being?' and must be the canon of coming attempts to solve it.[45]

For Jonas it is by a grasp of the living organism that thought unlocks the world as a whole, because it forces thinking to a surrender of mutually isolable metaphysical realms, or the possibility of true opposites within reality; and since the body alive is the world at its most immediate, in first-hand undeniability, there is no bypassing of this surrender. This is why the 'middle' that ontology must seek is 'the *living* middle'. It is not the middle *simpliciter* that stands at the centre of thought but the middle *vivans*. To theologies of the suspended middle, Jonas has something decisive to say: the most suspended middle is the living, and it is here that ontology itself is inscribed *in nuce*. 'Pure' mind and 'pure' matter by themselves are naked, for

> life does not bear distillation; it is somewhere between the purified aspects – in their concretion. The abstractions themselves do not live. [. . .] The dualistic antithesis leads not to a heightening of the features of life through their concentration on one side, but to a deadening of both sides through their separation from the living middle.[46]

The manner in which an organism occupies this middle is taken up in a more technical key when Jonas turns to the specifically biological subjects of evolution and metabolism as ways into the nature of life. The ontological character of life is absolutely concrete: it manifests itself in the life of the organic body in time.

---

44. *Phenomenon*, 19.
45. *Phenomenon*, 19.
46. *Phenomenon*, 22. Strachan Donnelley ('Hans Jonas, the Philosophy of Nature, and the Ethics of Responsibility', *Social Research* 56 (1989): 635–57, 645) and others want to interpret Jonas as a monist, but passages such as this indicate that Jonas wants to go beyond monism and dualism.

The legitimacy of anthropomorphism

Jonas's defence of anthropomorphism or animism is a central part of his vitalistic agenda: life has such a fundamental commonality with us that we must see in it our own 'shape', we must attribute to nature the spirit, the *anima*, that we know in ourselves. This is the epistemological ground of the vitalism he represents: we are more than justified in seeing life in the terms of our own experience of consciousness; we are actually compelled to see it this way, and our attribution to all life of the inwardness which we ourselves experience is the only responsible way of viewing it. For the reality of the living body can only be known by propriobodily extrapolation. A prohibition on anthropomorphic reasoning makes it impossible to give an account of causality and teleology, and so mechanistic materialism cannot meet the needs of the physical sciences, even though it seems at first sight to be answering directly to their requirements. As ever, for Jonas, the living body is at the centre; it is its extrusion, the inadmissibility of its felt experience in the world, which leads mechanistic materialism and idealism alike to the anathematization of cause and purpose.

For Jonas, a metaphysics which outlaws anthropomorphism and zoomorphism makes the world unintelligible. '[H]uman subjectivity loses its experiential, self-validating credentials' and is denied 'a foothold in efficacious reality'; if mind and matter are conceived as substances sharing no continuity, causal interaction between them is inconceivable.[47] The loss of subjectivity leads to the loss of intention, purpose and all the other properties of mind by which it impacts (and is impacted by) the material. The valid place of subjective experience *in nature* is lost, either as delusion (materialism) or as efficacious only in a circular and self-referring sense (idealism). Observing the crisis this causes, and pursuing the metaphysical possibilities of placing felt experience within and not outside nature, plays a central role in Jonas's metaphysics of the organic and is a key step in his restoration of teleology as an inner-natural reality, not a fictive superimposition by epiphenomenal mind.

By withdrawing consciousness from the body into a metaphysically separate sphere, as in metaphysical dualism, our knowledge becomes merely perceptive, and the world truly external. We no longer possess that first-hand experience of cause, namely 'force and action in self-performance', the experience of effort, resistance, action and reaction, which we feel immediately in our bodies.[48] Total externalization, in materialism, and total reduction to consciousness, in idealism, make the phenomenon of causation completely inaccessible. Thence arises inevitably the position of Hume as Jonas reads him, for whom all possibility of an

---

47. Donnelley, 'Hans Jonas, the Philosophy of Nature, and the Ethics of Responsibility', 639ff.

48. *Phenomenon*, 20–1.

'inner connection', a real relation between external events and bodies, is merely arbitrary and speculative, and so 'causality . . . becomes a fiction'.[49]

Milbank's adoption of the Humean critique of cause resembles Jonas here. Jonas's defence of anthropomorphic reasoning resonates with the Milbankian critique of representationalist rationality: what is in question is the notion of the mind as a discretely interior and bounded phenomenon. Milbank's own brand of realist constructivism, or constructivist realism, which he claims to inherit from Vico, Hamann, Jacobi and others, can be seen as an extended retrieval of anthropomorphic reasoning: we make the world up, and this is what the real is. There appears to be a divergence in that Milbank gives a realist status to 'fictioning', while for Jonas 'fiction' is genuinely illusory. Milbank denies the kind of reading of Hume Jonas assumes, using Hume instead to back up just the kind of principled anthropomorphism that Jonas is pursuing. But the divergence is only apparent. Jonas's point is that we are entirely justified in assuming, broadly speaking, that what is true of us is true of the world; for Milbank, this is fictioning (even if, for him, this is not all that fictioning is), and this is (Milbank's) Hume's real point.[50] Milbank and Jonas are equally opposed to the substantial separation of body from thought which makes every operation of the body in the world, and every perception of movement and effect in other objects, senseless. Jonas's distinctive angle is his view of the underlying problem: it is not so much the elimination of mind from nature but the elimination of life itself, life as alive rather than life as dead, that destroys causation: '[G]eneral causality loses in intelligibility what the elimination of life was meant to secure for it in terms of scientific knowledge.'[51] In this way Jonas indicates the extent to which, for him, 'mind' and 'life' are synonyms.

This brief comparison points up the inappropriateness of reading Jonas as a naturalist. Strachan Donnelley, for example, is right to see the restoration of reality and efficacy to human thought, and a valid epistemic role to human subjectivity, as a vital step for Jonas.[52] But he does not make clear the crucial role this plays in Jonas's analyses of Darwinism and metabolism, nor does he recognize the connection between this restoration and Jonas's option for anthropomorphism. He fails to make the link, which Jonas does very insistently, between denying a central role to subjectivity – including causal efficacy and epistemic reliability –

---

49. *Phenomenon*, 21.

50. 'Even though [Hume] takes it that we are but part of natural causation, he says that the best clue to the nature of latter lies within our own self-experience. . . . [W]ithin ourselves the experience of our own consecutive causal action is a matter or feeling, habit and imagination. One might say that we are led according to a consistent pattern to 'make ourselves up'. [It is] in terms of our experience of willing that we must try to decipher causality. . . . [I]n nature herself there must reside something analogous to 'will'. It follows that the primacy of feeling in Hume entails also a species of vitalism' (Milbank, 'Hume Versus Kant', 280).

51. *Phenomenon*, 21.

52. Donnelley, 'Hans Jonas, the Philosophy of Nature, and the Ethics of Responsibility', 644.

and the exclusive association of anthropomorphism with fictional construals of the world; nor does he observe the crucial claim Jonas makes for a type of animism as the foundation of our belief in the world's order and intelligibility. One suspects that this is because Donnelley, like other commentators, wishes to present Jonas as propagating monistic naturalism.[53] This is a view which the critical examination of Jonas below contends with as failing to note the tensions and *aporias* within Jonas's philosophical biology. Jonas has implicitly defended a kind of 'fictioning' in his conception of cause, purpose and inwardness: our thinking and feeling and projecting of ourselves into the world is not just 'making stuff up' in the vacuous sense but gives us a clue to what reality is like. But Jonas does not follow the logic of this defence by concluding to a realism of narrative, despite having implicitly acknowledged the narrative shape of any understanding which chooses, in a way which must remain always finally inscrutable, to begin its story either with life or with death. Failing to conclude to a primacy of narrative, Jonas's anthropomorphism, the keystone of his epistemology, remains only half complete. This point will be significant in the critical examination of Chapter 7.

As for Milbank, one of Jonas's chief targets is Kant, an agenda which is particularly clear in his discussion of causation. Only bodily life, 'in the actual interplay of its self-feeling powers with the world, can be the source of the "idea" of force and thus of cause',[54] and so Kant's location of causality as a category of pure understanding cannot be sustained. Only the experience of 'living force' in the body's action and reaction gives us notions of cause and effect; the mind can generate only reason and consequence – which are relations of form – not action and causation, which can only arise from bodily experience. The basis of this experience is the sensation of effort in the body as it meets the resistance of the material environment and undergoes the impact of the environment upon itself. In this experience are both 'extensive outwardness' and 'intensive inwardness' at once, which are equally indelible aspects of myself, and from which I build up a picture of 'a world of force and resistance, action and inertia, cause and effect'.[55] So causality is not an *a priori* 'but the universal extrapolation from the propriobodily prime experience into the whole of reality', rooted in the self-transcendence of the organism reaching out into space and forward into the future, continuing itself into the world with its actions.[56] Causality is thus 'a finding of the practical, not of the theoretical, self, of its activity, not of its perception'.[57] Hume is correct in his recognition that causality is not met with in perception, for force 'is not a datum, but an "actum" humanly present in effort'; and 'effort is surely not a percept'.[58]

53. Donnelley, 'Hans Jonas, the Philosophy of Nature, and the Ethics of Responsibility', 644ff.

54. *Phenomenon*, 22.

55. *Phenomenon*, 23.

56. *Phenomenon*, 23.

57. *Phenomenon*, 23.

58. *Phenomenon*, 25.

In his exploration of this theme, Jonas makes the strong claim that all knowledge, including the most basic empirical operations of physical science, hinges on whether inference from felt experience to world is valid, which is to say, on the question of the legitimacy of anthropomorphism, of taking the living body of our first-hand experience as the only adequate model for our interpretation of the world.[59] Here he supports the classical understanding of the ontological microcosmism of the human being, this time expressed in such a way that an incipient personalism seems to be suggested: we can only interpret the world as self-aware subjects who project their subjectivity into 'exterior' reality. He modifies phenomenology decisively in the direction of ontology: only a personalistic epistemology which takes the felt experience of the human person as the legitimate basis of entering and grasping the world of things has any chance at ontological coherence. If anthropomorphism is as absolutely inadmissible as modern science takes it to be, *skepsis* will conquer knowledge, description will conquer explanation, matter will conquer form.[60] The minded body just is our way of knowing the world. Once its evidence is disallowed from informing our understanding, notions such as cause and purpose are forfeit and the expectation of the world's intelligibility must be abandoned. Against this, Jonas supports anthropomorphism as the true epistemology in the strongest possible terms. Although he does not term this a 'vitalism', it begs such a gloss, because it invites human beings to take their experience of aliveness as hermeneutically central.

Jonas is also sympathetic with the animism of human prehistory. Belief in causation is, in a certain sense, an act of animistic faith, because animism is simply the projection into the world of certain human qualities. Anthropomorphism is an animistic expectation that the world will be characterized by the qualities and properties of our own lives and felt experience. The perception of causation is an interpolation of an experienced effort and impact into the world remote from

---

59. *Phenomenon*, Appendix 1: 'Causality and Perception', 26–33.

60. For Jonas, this constitutes a fundamental critique of the epistemological project of modernity, and therefore of contemporary scientific self-understanding. The extension of the experience of the self in the world into the whole of reality, which occurs in the extrapolative attribution of causation to physical events remote from my own body, is foreign to modern thought. 'The struggle against teleology is a stage in the struggle against anthropomorphism which by itself is as old as Western science' (*Phenomenon*, 36). If causation and purposefulness are primarily phenomena of the felt body and are extrapolated to the world on this basis, the result of anthropomorphism's exclusion is the anathematization of causation and teleology, prohibitions which are 'not an inductive result but an *a priori* prohibition of modern science' (*Phenomenon*, 34). Without causation and teleology, nothing can really be accounted for: 'the very idea of explanation has evaporated with the completion of the anti-anthropomorphic movement in epistemology' (*Phenomenon*, 37). Ratzinger seems to be evoking the same point, counterintuitively as Hanby says, in arguing that the sciences have actually renounced the search for truth (*Introduction to Christianity*, 57–66, 77).

ourselves, a superstition of sorts, which projects our felt experience and by doing so discovers the world to be intelligible. In Jonas's view Hume was right to judge it 'objectively' groundless, in the sense that he perceived that it is from our own minds and bodies that cause becomes apparent, not from the world considered 'in itself'.

So Jonas opts for animism over mechanism, for a world alive over a world dead, in order to save cause, explanation, the life of organisms and the world as a whole. Rejecting the validity of felt experience for the interpretation of the world results in the collapse of the project of understanding, which is what has occurred in contemporary scientism in its abandonment of the ambition to really know and be able to explain objects and their relations. Thus, if Darwinism is taken as a mechanistic reduction of life to non-life, it destroys itself as an explanatory project. Hanby expresses his own project in a similar way: to save the world that science intends to explain, in which process science itself is saved from terminal incoherence.

Hanby uses Jonas in support of his bid for a recovery of a primacy of form, and particularly to underline the impossibility of undermining intelligence and at the same time expecting that intelligence credibly to perform the work of demonstrating its own unintelligent origins. For Hanby too the self-referential incoherence that results from denying the evidence of our own mindedness is crucial in the assault on scientism. But Jonas goes beyond Hanby in his analysis of the living organism which elevates non-human life to contiguity with the human life, and thus implicitly supporting a full vitalism: the *entire* permeation of material life by mind. He is more interested in the *intrinsic* dignity of aliveness as such, whatever its form, and although a defence of its intelligibility is important, ultimately his concern is the solidarity of all the living. He defends a spiritual and moral unity of the living world which Hanby's account does not repeat, and this difference is explained by the fact that the latter is primarily concerned to defend intelligibility, while Jonas wants to defend the meaningfulness of life as such: beyond being merely intelligible to us, it has purpose, self-concern and inwardness on its own account. Thus, although Jonas has made anthropomorphism epistemically central, the outcome of that anthropomorphism is a re-contextualization of human existence: suddenly we are not the only bearers of inwardness, purpose or self-concern, and our solidarity with the living presses on our self-awareness.[61] This becomes apparent in Jonas's treatment of metabolism, one of the two biological 'facts' which he analyses. The other is Darwinism, or common descent; the next two sections treat Jonas's analyses of these.

---

61. Jonas does not, however, defend biotic egalitarianism, as his straightforward attribution of unique moral and ethical centrality to human beings in *The Imperative of Responsibility* indicates. Donnelley considers the question of animal ethics in relation to Jonas in 'Bioethical Troubles: Animal Individuals and Human Organisms', *The Hastings Centre Report* 25 (1995): 21–9.

Turning the tables: Darwinism as vitalism

Jonas reads Darwinism as the decisive undoing of Cartesianism: '[E]volutionism undid Descartes' work more effectively than any metaphysical critique had managed to do.'[62] He approaches it dialectically, but his reading highlights Darwinism's narrative character: it is a story which can be told in different ways, and in the telling life is interpreted and given a meaning. In one version of the story, life is simply non-life arranged in a particular formation: this is Darwinism as mechanism. In the other version, life is truly life and becomes the hermeneutic for unlocking existence as a whole.

Darwinism is in one sense remarkably successful in its elimination of any non-material, non-mechanistic element in the production of living organisms, but in this very success it falls prey to the fatal contradiction of the monistic project. Having rejected the dualistic metaphysics in which a transcendent realm, or a nonphysical principle or substance, could be called on to account for the presence of mind and consciousness, the new ontology has to deal with these phenomena in the only terms it has allowed to remain, namely the material. Jonas has argued that materialism creates an insuperable problem for itself by depriving itself of the resources to respond comprehensively to the awkward fact that bodies are not only extended in space; they are also living, feeling, purposeful and, in some cases, thinking and reflecting. When metaphysical dualism is rejected, the phenomena for which it formerly accounted now press painfully on materialistic premises that can account for them only by reduction: what appears to be x is really y.[63] Rather than really accounting for the depth, complexity and difference of life, in particular the phenomenon of minded life, these are denied. But dualism too came at a heavy price, namely the sleight of mind involved in avoiding the living body's transgression of the available categories. Descartes's division of reality into the two isolable substances of *extensa* and *cogitans* was crucial for the development of the natural sciences in allowing them to bracket out the latter, relegating it to an alternative idiom of explanation and securing the empirical as a self-contained field of enquiry, comprehensible fully on its own terms. Cartesian dualism legitimated methodological materialism within a model which retained an intelligible place for mind. But once severed from the sustaining metaphysical dualism of its origins, scientific materialism, now ontological rather than methodological, 'became an absurdity'.[64] A metaphysical dualism such as Descartes's, which maintained 'the mutual causal unrelatedness

---

62. *Phenomenon*, 57.

63. 'Saving the appearances' is a key concern of Radical Orthodoxy: 'Curiously, perhaps, it is immanence that is dualistic and tends to remove the mysterious diversity of matter in assuming that appearances do not exceed themselves.' Milbank, Pickstock and Ward, 'Suspending the Material', 3.

64. *Phenomenon*, 55.

of the two orders of being',[65] was always bound to collapse because it cannot accommodate the way these two orders have a real relation in the living body; they are indissolubly intertwined and self-transcending, one into the other. Various contorted philosophical solutions, such Leibnizian occasionalism and other forms of psychophysical parallelism, were attempted to preserve the causal unrelatedness of the two orders, but such extremes were a sign of the profundity of the challenge dualism faced.

Only metaphysical dualism sustained science in its methodological neutrality as to the question of the relation, since the body as living, feeling, purposing and so on was one of its own proper objects. Descartes propped up this neutrality by restricting the problem of consciousness to the human realm; non-human beings were automata with the appearance of purpose, pain, pleasure, awareness and so on, while being wholly describable as machines. In this way he contracted the metaphysical enigma of the mind-body relation down to one gland in the human brain where it was, at least, well-contained and did not spill over into the organic realm as a whole.

The absurdity of this dualism is inherited by its philosophical offspring, which keep everything, including the organic, in only one metaphysical container. The absurdity, for Jonas, is twofold: it consists first in refusing to allow the most undeniable evidence of all, the evidence of myself, to count for anything, and secondly, in its failure to acknowledge the most obvious characteristic of the organic realm, namely its striving for existence and fulfilment, its willing of itself.[66] The denial of the living organism as a site in which mind and body really meet and interact with one another was equally a flagrant denial of our own first-hand knowledge of psychophysical events: when I will to move my arm, it does move; when I feel hunger, my body moves to eat. In the most general terms, I experience an inward appetition for the continuance of my life which effects my physical actions. In this sense dualistic metaphysics, and the speculation which succeeded it, has a certain 'violence': we are coerced into rejecting our common-sense understanding and literally undeniable acquaintance with ourselves and the world of objects we inhabit: '[n]ever had the rift between reason and immediate knowledge been so great.'[67]

The great change of metaphysical fortunes, from mechanism to vitalism, occurs with a surprisingly simple conceptual leap. Once one takes into account the evidence of inwardness and subjectivity of one's own mind, Darwinism works the other way.

> In the hue and cry over the indignity done to man's metaphysical status in the doctrine of his animal descent, it was overlooked that by the same token some dignity had been restored to the realm of life as a whole. If man was the relative

65. *Phenomenon*, 55.
66. *Phenomenon*, 61.
67. *Phenomenon*, 62.

of animals, then animals were the relatives of man and in degrees bearers of that inwardness of which man, the most advanced of their kin, was conscious in himself. Thus . . . the province of 'soul', with feeling, striving, suffering, enjoyment, extended again, by the principle of continuous gradation, from man over the kingdom of life.[68]

Inwardness is 'coextensive with life'.[69] A mechanistic account of the organic which is cognizant only of its outward, physical, extended properties cannot do justice to the whole. If human beings are in continuity with the organic history from which they emerged, if the whole is a kind of continuous gradation, how could mind be wholly unprefigured and unanticipated, absolutely discontinuous from what preceded it? The postulation of such an absolute break has been excluded by Darwinism. The various facets of inward existence are not quantifiable, not describable in physical terms; appetition is not the same as physical momentum, nor is the drive for self-preservation identical to inertia.

Jonas's analysis of Darwinism overcomes the isolationism of both Descartes's *cogito* and Heidegger's *Dasein*.[70] These ontological islands have been submerged in the democracy of evolutionary origins; or rather, to reverse the metaphor, all life has been raised to contiguity with human *psyche*. Jonas is close here to Milbank's defence of (what Milbank sees as) Hume's fundamental point about knowledge, which, he suggests, is continued in the twentieth century by Bergson.

> [T]rue Humean 'empiricism' suggests that the route to know the exterior realm is not to *represent* it, *or* to grasp it *a priori*, but rather to *think with it*, on the assumption that the way things 'go' inside us may well be the best clue as to how everything else in reality sustains itself. All thought therefore, again in the longterm wake of Hume, is fundamentally *sympathy*.[71]

The question remains, however, what sense can be made of attributing mind or inwardness to non-human organisms, and here Jonas comes into his own. His claim that inwardness is coextensive with life is the key contention of *The Phenomenon of Life* and begs elucidation and justification, requiring him to engage with the whole kingdom of life including lower animals, plants and even protozoa. It calls for the identification of the common property of the living which would be the seat or root of inwardness. For Jonas, this common and most basic feature, analysis of which reveals the minded nature of all living things, is metabolism.

68. *Phenomenon*, 57.
69. *Phenomenon*, 57.
70. Levy, *Hans Jonas*, 56.
71. Milbank, 'Immanence and Life', 22.

Metabolism: The biology of freedom

Jonas says modestly that he has brought the reader only to 'the threshold' of a philosophical biology,[72] but his analysis of metabolism provides the fundaments of such an enterprise. Organic life exhibits qualities of freedom, inwardness and self-transcendence, which arise from the distinction between form and matter which obtains as a result of metabolism. Jonas argues directly from biological to metaphysical facts, making an implied assault on the so-called naturalistic fallacy. By emphasizing the transition from phenomenal to ontological individual identity, he indicates that phenomenology taken by itself, taken non-ontologically, is insufficient. Consideration of the living opens phenomenology to metaphysics, for life raises form to a level above phenomenal appearance; it raises it to the level of being. Organic life is necessarily metaphysical and requires a metaphysical as well as a physical science to grasp it. His analysis also implicitly invites an understanding of organismic life as narratival: it unfolds in time through its desire to perpetuate itself in being. This underlies Jonas's interpretation of organismic self-transcendence, which occurs not only outward in space but also forward in time.[73]

Metabolism is the exchange of matter and energy between an organism and its environment in which the organism's material constituents are constantly cycled through it and replaced. The living form of the organism is sustained by this exchange. In the process of exchange, the organism's form becomes distinguishable from its matter; the organism persists in its distinctive identity through the exchange of its material components with its environment. If it were to become statically identical with its material components it would be dead, in the sense that its metabolism would have ceased to function. But although its form is distinguishable from its matter, the organism's metabolic character places it in a relationship of extreme dependence upon the physical environment. It is caught in a paradoxical dialectic between freedom and necessity: in the very moment of being liberated from total coincidence with form, the organism gains both sovereignty and indigence. The self-identity of the organism introduces

---

72. *Phenomenon*, 92.

73. When he turns briefly to the question of the nature of an organism as a biological reality, Milbank stresses similar themes to those we shall find Jonas exploring: 'What makes this individual *biological* in nature? The answer must have to do both with the inner inertial drive to organic self-development, and the drive to reproduce within certain regular parameters' ('Immanence and Life', 13). Milbank is here discussing the question of the level at which natural selection operates, an issue in which the *aporias* of biological understanding are readily apparent, since it inevitably raises the question of what it is that seeks to survive; what is the subject of survival. This leads naturally to 'a nakedly teleological construal of the biological individual (granting it a kind of "quasi-intention")', (13). While Milbank adverts to these questions briefly, they are employed to the end of demonstrating the inadequacy of a purely immanent account of biological change.

an element of heterogeneity into the otherwise homogeneous uniformity of non-living matter; it becomes isolable from its environment, gaining a sense of singleness and distinction which it must constantly reassert in order to continue as itself. Thus is invented 'the world' as an object, as an experienced reality that is distinct from the self, a world 'in which, by which, and against which' the organism must maintain itself.[74]

Jonas notes that there are some mathematically analysable objects familiar to the physical sciences which seem to share this property, namely waves, which from moment to moment are comprised by different particles, and yet maintain a distinctive identity through time. In the case of waves, physics does recognize a form 'with a cognitive significance of its own' distinct from matter.[75] But an object such as a wave, although possessing a cognizable form, is nevertheless not more than the sum of its parts; in fact its parts must completely account for every aspect of its form. Mathematically, an equation must be able to demonstrate a complete equivalence between a wave's matter and its formal structure. Physical scientists can argue that the same applies to a living organism: the seeming continuity of a single living form is an abstraction, an apparent identity which is no more than the identity of the particles whose collective motion really constitutes the motion of the individual they comprise. On this view, the organism 'must appear as a function of metabolism, rather than metabolism as a function of the organism': the organism is the consequential object, not the causal subject, of the metabolic process.[76] '[T]he apparent sameness and individuality of the organic whole will resolve itself' into an incidental coincidence of factors and forces; its outward character as 'a self-related autonomous entity' would then appear 'as purely phenomenal, that is, fictitious'.[77]

It is precisely this sort of reductive analysis that, in Jonas' view, is unable to do justice to the real properties of organisms. The distinction of form from matter means that organismic life must be described in terms of inwardness as well as outwardness. Organisms affirm, in the sense of actively pursuing, their own existence: 'existence affirmed is existence as a concern'.[78] The mathematical-mechanical analysis of the organism 'misses the decisive point – the point of life itself: its being self-centered individuality, being for itself and in contraposition to all the rest of the world'.[79] This 'contrapositionality' indicates the incipient agonism of Jonas account, for the organism is itself only as pitted against the world.

Life is characterized by 'active self-integration', which yields an ontological and not merely phenomenological meaning to the term 'individual' (used

74. *Phenomenon*, 83.
75. *Phenomenon*, 77.
76. *Phenomenon*, 78.
77. *Phenomenon*, 78.
78. *Phenomenon*, 4.
79. *Phenomenon*, 79.

biologically).[80] While in the case of waves and similar physical event-structures, their seeming wholeness and distinctness can be argued to be a phenomenon merely of our sensuous perception and not of their inherent being, in the case of a living organism there is something else there: not just continuance through time but active self-continuation; not just inertia but appetitive persistence in being. An organic being is constantly involved in saying 'yes' to its own existence. In the living organism,

> nature springs an ontological surprise . . . an entirely new possibility of being: systems of matter that are unities of a manifold, not in virtue of a synthesizing perception whose object they happen to be, nor by the mere concurrence of the forces that bind their parts together, but in virtue of themselves, for the sake of themselves, and continually sustained by themselves. . . . [F]orm for once is the cause rather than the result of the material collections in which it successively subsists.[81]

> The introduction of the term 'self', unavoidable in any description of the most elementary instance of life, indicates the emergence, with life as such, of internal identity.[82]

The language of selfhood, self-concern and neediness may seem unduly loaded and anthropomorphizing. But Jonas uses his terms advisedly: for satisfaction or frustration to be able to pertain to the organic, for appetition and satiation to make any difference to an organism, there must be a quality of felt selfhood, resulting from a living organism's 'supreme concern' with 'its own being and continuation in being'.[83] We are compelled to speak of inwardness or subjectivity pertaining to organismic existence as such, no matter how faint. Organismic identity is decisively not inertia but 'perpetual self-renewal through process' – a deliberate and sentient pursuit of continuance of self.[84] Whereas, for a material entity, continuity is detected in the persistence of a substratum, a traceable 'path', the constant transformation of its material constitution means that the continuity of a living body cannot be identified in this way; there is, in fact, no external referent of continuity. There being no solid and enduring external material identity, on the basis of morphological observation we spontaneously acknowledge that an organism's identity is internal and formal, an acknowledgement based on the first-hand experience of the living body that every human observer possesses; a 'pure Mathematician' could not make such an inference, being bodiless.[85] Just as in the case of causality, only an animistic interpolation from lived experience, an

---

80. *Phenomenon*, 79.
81. *Phenomenon*, 79.
82. *Phenomenon*, 82.
83. *Phenomenon*, 84.
84. *Phenomenon*, 79.
85. Jonas deals with the 'pure Mathematician' at some length, demonstrating his incapacity to grasp the reality of the body without first-hand experience of it.

inference from our own bodily life, allows us to make sense of the stable identity of organisms through time and space.[86] An organism's form is, in contrast to non-metabolizing entities, an 'essential', 'real' and 'efficacious' factor in its existence;[87] having been, in the case of the lifeless, an abstract if useful notion, distinct from matter only phenomenally, in an organism form gains concrete reality over against its constitutive material components and, in Jonas's language, attains to causative status: in the case of a living thing, its form *causes* its being as the distinctive thing that it is. 'Form [is] the essence, matter the accident.'[88]

It is through this arising of individuality in an ontological sense, the arrival of form as a real and efficacious presence on the ontological scene, that 'the venture of freedom[,] by which a form maintains its identity through the change of its matter', begins.[89] Jonas's use of the term 'freedom' indicates something prior to reflectivity, choice, decision or theoretic awareness. Freedom really arises on the biological plane. In metabolizing, an entity comes into a relation with its body; it becomes possible for its body to become an 'other' to it. In contrast to the self-identity of matter, which is inertly itself without any deliberate act of self-continuation, whose duration is 'mere remaining, not reaffirmation'[90] and whose cognizability is wholly external, in its acquisition of autonomous form an organism gains an identity which is 'mediate and functional'[91] through the 'perpetual turnover of constituents'.[92] An organism must 'exert' itself to live. For the freedom of form with respect to matter, of self with respect to world, is dialectical in the sense that it is attended by a like-for-like increase in necessity. The metabolic process, while enabling the distinction of organism from material environment, also introduces it to a precarious dependence on that environment for the substance(s) necessary for life: at the most basic level, nutrition, but the dependence complexifies and intensifies with every gain in organization. 'Thus the sovereignty of form with respect to its matter is also its subjection to the need of it', for a metabolizing organism can never rest with the sum of stuff which makes it up but is always striving through and depending on the necessary transformations of its constitution; it suffers an 'indigence' which is 'foreign to the self-sufficiency of mere matter'.[93] This dependence turns the organism outward towards the world in

86. '[T]his is the advantage – perennially disowned or slandered in the history of epistemology – of our "having", that is, being, bodies. . . . [I]t is by interpolation of an internal identity alone that the mere morphological (and as such meaningless) *fact* of metabolic continuity is comprehended as an incessant *act*; that is, continuity is comprehended as self-continuation' (*Phenomenon*, 82).

87. *Phenomenon*, 80.

88. *Phenomenon*, 80. The classical influences on Jonas are readily apparent here.

89. *Phenomenon*, 106.

90. *Phenomenon*, 81.

91. *Phenomenon*, 81.

92. *Phenomenon*, 82.

93. *Phenomenon*, 84.

active self-concern, its needy seeking of satisfaction a direct result of its autonomy, producing 'a dialectic of needful freedom'.[94] This neediness of the organism, its 'indigence' in comparison to non-living matter, indicates a certain pathos that is proper to the organic realm. Life has a poverty that the non-living will never suffer, a poverty of fragility and precariousness, of being dependent on what it can never control, which is the world outside itself. This is a poverty in which dependence and constraint increase in direct proportion to independence and freedom; there is no increase of freedom without a concomitant increase in limit and exposure.

Metabolism stimulates the arrival of 'world' as 'a horizon of co-reality', a meaningful, pressing and necessary objective context of life.[95] The distinction of form from matter thus results in a constant referral beyond the body to the world as something both foreign and potentially assimilable to the self; the organism's need drives it to transcend itself towards the world both spatially and temporally. The organism is thus in an inherently tensional state of both exceeding and preserving the self, producing in every form of life a horizon of transcendence.

> The great contradictions which man discovers in himself – freedom and necessity, autonomy and dependence, self and world, relation and isolation, creativity and mortality – have their rudimentary traces in even the most primitive forms of life, each precariously balanced between being and not-being, and each already endowed with an internal horizon of 'transcendence'.[96]

The self-transcendence of life generates sensitivity, responsiveness, affectivity – a range of modes of reactivity to the world, now experienced as outward and different from the self, but inalienably important to the organism's self-continuance. The world as it were sets off the self by contrast. The combination of inwardness and reactivity parallels the paradox of needful freedom: the organism is self-centred, appetitively preoccupied with its own continuance and satisfaction, but by this very fact driven into various modes of urgent relation with the world now perceived as 'external', as other to the self, impinging on it as something separate. The affecting object is taken in to the affected subject, becoming a presence within it and not just outside it, and so affectation becomes absorption and interiorization: thus the isolation of organism is overcome by a newly intimate relationship with objects, objects which are experienced as 'objective' for the first time in the 'subjective' awareness of the organism. Self-transcendence brings the world into the very being of the organism, both physically through metabolic processes, such as respiration, and also in terms of perceptive assimilation of environments. In both respects the organism's identity becomes a mediate one; it is not a given static being but a relational dynamic being, constantly involved in the mediation of its environment.

94. *Phenomenon*, 84.
95. *Phenomenon*, 84.
96. *Phenomenon*, ix.

Self-transcendence means that the organism must entertain 'a horizon, or horizons, beyond its point-identity'.[97] There are both spatial and temporal horizons: the physical environment and the co-presence of objects within that environment, towards which the organism reaches and which impinge on its subjectivity; and the imminence of the future into which the organism continuously reaches to satisfy the moment's want, which comprises 'not [just] outer presence, but inner imminence'.[98] Orientation to the future is more fundamental than memory's retention of the past, because of the dominant role played by appetition in the life of the organism: 'future is the dominant time-horizon opening before the thrust of life, if *concern* is its primary principle of inwardness'.[99] It is this which explains 'the teleological or finalistic nature of life', its dynamic forward-oriented character which is caused in the first place by the independence of an organism's identity as form from its matter, rather than the result of a particular physical structure; thus the teleological character of life is of a metaphysical, not just a physical, nature.

Jonas's emphasis on the superior and indubitable authority of the subjective is married firmly to a claim for the intrinsic orientation of the subjective towards the objective, via the arising of world as a horizon of co-reality which, as soon as the subject becomes aware of itself, has impinged as object on the subject's space. This marriage is important for Jonas's epistemology, which is founded on a rejection of Cartesian subjectivism and its heirs, placing the sensory reception of the world in prime epistemological position, entailing an understanding of the organism as a mediatory being, neither enclosed in subjectivity nor reducible to exteriority, alive in a world of objects which impinge on it but with which it remains in precarious, self-aware distinction. Jonas's castigation of ontological dualism is mirrored, therefore, by his cautious use of the traditional phenomenological emphasis on the way things appear to the subject, by which he moves the subject decidedly out of its own zone while showing how that movement accentuates the individuality of the organism. In this way he makes some tentative and implicit moves towards an epistemology beyond subjectivity and objectivity. This resonates with some of the theological concerns familiar from the first two chapters of this book.

The organism's inwardness and spatio-temporal self-transcendence generate that self-concern which is the root of teleological behaviour, but this can only be recognized if epistemic centrality is granted to our 'inside' knowledge of ourselves. The only way we can see seeming external purposiveness as manifesting an underlying real purposiveness and self-concern is via the evidence of our own subjectivity. Without the ability to infer, from external manifestation of purposiveness, the existence of an inwardness behind or within that manifestation, no 'life' can be recognized, only mechanism.[100] To a purely external

97. *Phenomenon*, 85.
98. *Phenomenon*, 85.
99. *Phenomenon*, 86.
100. Milbank picks up on the same point: '[O]ne cannot stop asking exactly what it is that in some sense seeks to survive and to increase, or simply to sustain an inertia beneath

physicochemical description, life does not appear at all, for the organism appears as just another physical object: 'In the fullness of success this [method] would result in the disappearance of life as such.'[101]

A non-teleological approach which tries to understand an organismic arrangement with no finalistic reference is, in Jonas's view, never going to understand the organization in question. The fact that the finalistic element will not be detectable by mathematical or physical measurement shows the inadequacy of quantitative epistemology, not the non-existence of finalistic factors in physical organization. An eye is detectable by physicochemical analysis, but seeing is not; an ear, but not hearing; a finger, but not touching. And yet these functions are not incidental to the structure of these organs, but formative of them, and this teleological character is also true of the organism as a whole, which is structured for particular functions. We cannot deny the

> purposiveness of organism as such and its concern in living: effective already in the vegetative tendency, awakening to primordial awareness in the dim reflexes, the responding irritability of lowly organisms; more so in urge and effort and anguish of animal life endowed with motility and sense-organs; reaching self-transparency in consciousness, will and thought of man: all these being inward aspects of the teleological side in the nature of 'matter'.[102]

Jonas uses Aristotelian terminology to express himself on this point: the *causa materialis* and the *causa efficiens* cannot encapsulate the reality of an organism. Without realist reference to a *causa formalis* and the dreaded *causa finalis*, the organism itself does not appear but is replaced by an incomprehensible confluence of forces and factors which cannot be cognized as an individual, by which analysis the human thinker too disappears to herself. A teleological account of organismic structure and function is not an alternative form of description of the biological sphere; it is necessary to do justice to the evidence, which includes our own felt inwardness as a correlate to our external expressions of purposiveness. The form of an organism is indelibly linked to its function, and both are necessary for understanding the organism as a whole. 'There is no organism without teleology; there is no teleology without inwardness; and: life can be known only by life.'[103]

The nature of organic purposiveness is illuminated by the non-comparability of organisms with machines. Jonas denies that the inflow-outflow of a machine could be considered equivalent to the metabolic process, for '[t]he exchange of matter with the environment is not a peripheral activity engaged in by a persistent core:

variety? Why are there any consistent living things at all? For if variation were more absolute, if no continuities in growth and reproduction were readily discernible, then there would be no reason whatsoever to speak of "life" in any sense' (Milbank, 'Immanence and Life', 14).

101. *Phenomenon*, 88.

102. *Phenomenon*, 90.

103. *Phenomenon*, 91.

it is the total mode of continuity (self-continuation) of the subject of life itself'.[104] Machines do not 'participate' in the exchange; 'their substance is not involved in the transformations which the fuel undergoes.'[105]

Discussing the way in which the concept of purpose is used by cyberneticians in relation to machines, Jonas notes that in their usage, by 'purposeful' is understood action directed to an end in the sense of an end state, the outcome of a process. In this sense of the term, cybernetic constructions such as missiles might be described as purposeful, suggesting that purpose is extricable from the context of biological life and so can be reducible to mechanism. Jonas, however, adopts Aristotle's distinction between the ending of a motion or change, which is the situation or condition in which the action or entity comes to rest, and the intrinsic *end* which is the positively discerned purpose of a motion or change. Taking the cybernetician's 'purpose' as the final condition in which something comes to rest, one would have to say – and here Jonas draws attention again to the pervasiveness of the ontology of death – that the 'purpose' of all organic life is death, since this is the end to which all life tends. One would more generally have to say that the purpose of all physical organization in the universe is entropy. Jonas recognizes that this is not the conclusion the cyberneticians are aiming at, but it is nevertheless the inevitable conclusion of a notion of purpose which has abandoned its original meaning 'as the *propositum*, that which someone sets *before* himself as the whereto of his action'.[106] For this understanding of purpose, a bearer of purpose is required; but since each cybernetical part, by itself, is not purposeful, rather the cybernetical entity is only claimed to be purposeful if taken as a whole, then the machine would have to possess a wholeness, identity or selfness, so as to be justifiably called *bearer*. But a machine does possess such a wholeness; if any one of its mechanical parts were replaced by a human operator, we all immediately know that the apparent purposiveness of the machine is localizable in the human operator. Why, then, should the purposiveness migrate to the whole machine once that human operator is replaced by a mechanical part? Nor, by analogy with human sense organs and information receptors, can feedback mechanisms such as we see in cybernetic constructions replace purposiveness. For a person does not act on sense receptors in a purpose-driven way except in light of a purpose which provides the context for received information to be put to use in a particular direction.

> The feedback combination of a receptor-effector system (which an organism indeed is among other things) lends itself to purposive action precisely if and when it is *not* a mere feedback *mechanism* – that is, if the two elements are not coupled directly, but if interposed between them there is will or interest or concern.[107]

104. *Phenomenon*, 76.
105. *Phenomenon*, 60.
106. *Phenomenon*, 115.
107. *Phenomenon*, 120.

Jonas treats cybernetics in order to reinstate finalistic teleology as conceptually indispensable, irreplaceable by accounts of action and behaviour that would like to maintain the appearance of purposiveness in non-teleological terms.

> This amounts precisely to saying that purposive behaviour requires the presence of purpose. That statement is no mere tautology, for cybernetics is an attempt to account for purposive behaviour without purpose, just as behaviourism is an attempt at a psychology without the 'psyche', and mechanistic biology a description of organic processes without 'life'.[108]

These reductions remain terminally duplicitous insofar as the explainer himself never comes 'under the terms of his doctrine': '[h]e considers behaviour, except his own; purposiveness, except his own; thinking, except his own'.[109]

The restoration of a notion of purpose distinct from feedback mechanisms and automatization necessitates once again the idea of the good as an essential element in the interpretation of behaviour, insofar as purposive behaviour arises from identifying and acting towards a desired end. Mechanistic interpretations of organic life reduce it to sentience and motility, neglecting that distinctive and unique property of the metabolizing, namely need, from which arises what Jonas calls 'emotion': the diverse expressions of desire, fear and appetition which characterize metabolic existence.[110] Only in the context of the recognition of such needs as intrinsic to organic being can the notion of purpose, and thence the proper place of the good, be retrieved as essential to the understanding of life. In this world a notion of goods, and consequently the possibility of *the* good, cannot be dispensed with; it arises spontaneously from biological existence.

Jonas's project in *The Phenomenon of Life* is a rejection of attempts to explain meaning in terms of the meaningless, life in terms of the lifeless. He defends the common-sense world, in which there is life and mind, as the real world, inviting us deeper into it on precisely the terms in which it presents itself. Jonas's world is a 'face-value' world, which is just as it seems to be: teeming with lives, meanings, purposes, filled with a striving multitude yearning for life.

The next and final chapter opens a critical perspective on the account of life Jonas has given, beginning with an overview of what his philosophical biology has achieved. Christian theology regards as exemplary Jonas's attention to biological phenomena, seeing in it that 'infinite exact study of the natural world'[111] which honours creatures as mediations of God and recognizes in his philosophical biology that 'shift' in our understanding of the world by which we know God.[112]

---

108. *Phenomenon*, 120.
109. *Phenomenon*, 124.
110. *Phenomenon*, 126.
111. Milbank, 'The New Divide', 30.
112. Milbank, 'Foreword', 13.

With Jonas, Christian theology 'will not suppress the testimony of life'.[113] But it also sees, in Jonas's philosophical biology, life's witness against secular reason which Jonas himself still suppresses. For all his brave affirmations, life for Jonas remains a deathly struggle, though it never ceases valiantly to assert itself in the face of emptiness. In Christian theology alone are Jonas's ambitions fully realized: in the end, there is only life.

113. *Phenomenon*, 1.

Chapter 7

LIFE AFTER ALL

A THEOLOGICAL VITALISM

This chapter suggests that in Jonas's philosophical biology we can see the shape of the Christian narration of finitude, which enables a fuller development of a Christian theological vitalism, while also undertaking a prophetic disruption of Jonas's vitalism, both with respect to its method and its content. It considers the significance of a theological vitalism for understanding the prevalence of conflict and death in the natural world.

Jonas as vitalist

Although Jonas uses the term only to describe the ancient world views whose demise he wistfully records, his position about the nature of organic existence can be regarded as a vitalism.[1] But this vitalism is not simply a retrieval of archaic philosophy. Jonas seeks a creative integration, not a return to positions which have now become untenable.

Jonas's vitalism consists in a number of linked propositions about life which we have seen him defend. He arrives at vitalism through an analysis of biological data combined with an epistemic defence of anthropomorphic reasoning. Darwinism and metabolism are the key biological facts which, taken together with our self-experience, indicate 'the essential specificity of organic being'.[2] Darwinism shows the contiguity with every rung of the organic ladder with ourselves. Metabolism indicates the priority of an organism's formal identity over its matter, constituting an incipient selfhood or subjectivity which transcends any given physical constitution. Specifically, Jonas's vitalism is an account of life as precarious, concerned self-continuation in freedom, characterized at every level by inwardness and self-transcendence.[3] Biological facts are always also psychic.

---

1. Richard Wolin, one of Jonas's more perceptive critics, describes Jonas's philosophy of life as a metaphysical vitalism (*Heidegger's Children*, 124).
2. *Phenomenon*, 1.
3. Levy, *Hans Jonas*, 46–7.

Life testifies against every form of dualism: it is itself the answer to nihilism, overcoming the reductive metaphysical options of modernity by acting as the solvent of inadequate ontologies. It occupies an irreducible ontological middle, the 'between' of minded matter, material freedom. Inherently purposive, life generates value: teleology and a notion of the good are intrinsic to biology.[4] Jonas's vitalism seeks to find in life the ultimate and overriding good, and to affirm it as the final and unsurpassable value in spite of its mortal and threatened character.

Although Jonas's vitalism is in continuity with many historic themes of classical vitalist thought, its taking of the biological as its central locus is quite distinctive among modern vitalisms. While both Jonas and Bergson employ a phenomenological approach, Bergson's appeal to intuition, rather than discursive method or scientific analysis, contrasts with Jonas's emphatic enquiry into biological facts 'scientifically' conceived.[5] His *élan vitale* is reminiscent of spiritualizing vitalisms which regard the essence of life as transcending biological reality.[6] In contrast, Jonas's vitalism is unabashedly biological. While repudiating a narrow physicalism, it does not invoke immaterial causes but remains in determined fidelity to the metabolic life of the organism. This characteristic of Jonas's vitalism turns the conversation away from the spectres of ghostly substances and mystifying postulations which have haunted vitalism, and which still make philosophers who today explore a coextensivity of life with consciousness avoid using the term.[7]

4. Value and disvalue are not, then, properties only of the human sphere. They arise from nature itself, which thereby shows her deepest character. The full significance of this is only spelled out in *The Imperative of Responsibility*, in which Jonas explains that '[r]eality or nature is one, and testifies to itself in what it *allows* to come forth from it' (69), but it is already foreshadowed in certain comments in *The Phenomenon of Life* in which Jonas reflects on what life implies about the nature of matter; life is a potency of matter, a latent power of material being itself: matter's 'bare, inertial determination' is 'dormant, as yet unawakened freedom' (24).

5. Agata Bielik-Robson is surely mistaken in her suggestion that for both Bergson and Jonas 'nature' is a fundamentally regressive context characterized by repetitive regularity ('Taking Life Out of Nature: Jewish Messianic Vitalism and the Problem of Denaturalisation', in *Radical Orthodoxy: Annual Review I*, ed. Neil Turnbull (Eugene, OR: Wipf & Stock, 2012), 180–98, 183), at least as far as *The Phenomenon of Life* is concerned.

6. Contemporary vitalists mostly trace their lineage to Bergson; Michael Weintsein, for example, eschews an overidentification of life with biological reality (Justin Mueller, 'This Flesh Belongs to Me: Michael Weinstein and Max Stirner', in *Michael A. Weinstein: Action, Contemplation, Vitalism*, ed. Robert Oprisko and Diane Rubenstein (London: Routledge, 2015), 55–76, 56).

7. As in Evan Thompson's comprehensive work, where it is a glaring absence; *Mind in Life: Biology, Phenomenology and the Sciences of Mind* (Cambridge, MA: Harvard University Press, 2007), 224. But Thompson's philosophy of biology is intriguingly congruent with Jonas's, emphasizing the interiority and intentionality of biological existence at every level. David Storey, *Naturalizing Heidegger: His Confrontation with Nietzsche, His Contributions to*

Jonas's vitalism and Christian theology

What use is such a vitalism for Christian theology? It is tempting to pick up Jonas's analysis as a kind of natural philosophy and put it to work for a theological purpose. This would be to treat it as an *ancilla theologiae*, providing a kind of philosophical account of life that is taken up by theology in an extrinsic manner, rather as an industry might put to use a particular piece of technology. But the foregoing chapters questioned just this approach.[8] Philosophical or scientific accounts of the world cannot be cut and pasted into the Christian story like a clause in a sentence. Jonas's account of life is already theological. The Christian task is to notice the theology already at work there, and hospitably to welcome and/or prophetically to disrupt it according to the logic of its own narrative of peace.

At this point a methodological matter with which we are now familiar needs to be raised again, this time with a more definite application which will be tested in the performance. In the discussion of theological methodology to which we have circled back repeatedly throughout this work, it has been considered that no absolute starting point can be discovered, nor can a distinction between knowledge 'from above' and 'from below' be maintained practically, since the two are irresolvably mutually implied one by the other. For this reason, the boundaries between the Christian disruption of Jonas and the recognition of the truthfully theological character of his philosophical biology, the boundaries between the Christian narrative and knowledges of the world that do not explicitly inhere in that narrative, cannot be established absolutely, in the same way that there cannot be a secure mutual isolation of reason from faith or nature from grace. It is therefore impossible to provide a universalizable norm for prophetic disruption and hospitable reception, other than the norm which is the narrative of peace itself. This approach is supposed to be evident in the discussion which follows, in which there has been an attempt, perhaps not successful, to avoid any covert relapse into notions of what is known by 'nature' and what is shown by 'revelation', 'philosophy' versus 'theology', etc. The reiteration of the account of knowledge and being we have defended in this study is meant to stand against such a relapse. Notions of 'Christian narrative' and 'scientific knowledge/physical nature' are not meant to set

Environmental Philosophy (New York: SUNY Press, 2015), 194–202, suggests a convergence between Jonas and Thompson.

8. I am here taking the view that the notion of philosophy, or indeed science, as *ancilla theologiae* presumes the kind of extrinsicist picture that I have objected to in previous chapters. This is not to say that there might not be a way of parsing this tradition more fittingly for what has been defended. The notion of natural science as an *ancilla theologiae* has been pursued by some recent authors, such as Alister McGrath; see James Dew, *Science as the Ancilla Theologiae: A Critical Assessment of Alister E. McGrath's Scientific Theology from an Evangelical Philosophical/Theological Perspective* (PhD diss., Southeastern Baptist Theological Seminary, 2008).

up an ontological or epistemological dualism but are rather used always to resist such interpretation.

To the ready objections that will once again arise here, it is crucial to admit on the one hand that the tension this sets up is severe and on the other that, according to the view we have taken, this tension characterizes knowledge and existence as such; it runs through Milbank's account from start to finish. Transcendence is so transcendent that it is hyper-immanent; immanence is so suspended that it can only be grasped as transcendence. The Christian narrative alone is true; but that narrative finds all language and action to be revelatory. There are 'two cities'; but there is only one reality. This tension needs to be admitted quite openly as intrinsic to the paradox which Milbank, off the back of the *nouvelle théologie*, has attempted to develop. All one can say at this point is that if one rejects this irresolvability as untenable in principle, on the basis of (to caricature) neo-scholastic-style rationalism or Barthian-style fideism, then the following account will not stand, since it is unable to draw a fixed line between finding that finitude of itself shows infinitude and finding that only by the Christian narrative is finitude discoverable as unbounded – identifying an 'outside' to the Christian narrative (there are two cities) and the impossibility of an outside (there is neither pure reason nor pure immanence). The mystery of an outside without an outside is surely, to speculate, explicated only by an account of the nature and presence of death and conflict, since it is in the *nihil* of these alone that an 'outside' to the harmonious difference of God's peace occurs. It is not accidental, then, that a concern with death and conflict dominates the remainder of the discussion.

To give a rudimentary sense of this, what are some of the ways Christian theology, in its hospitable moment, recognizes its own logic in Jonas's account? Jonas puts biological life at the centre of ontology. This is Christianly narrated as the poetic character of bodily existence: it discloses more than itself; it is conjecture, ontology from below. Jonas argues that the life of the body is irreducible to matter or spirit: it defeats metaphysical boundaries. This is Christianly narrated in terms of participation, in which unity and difference of being are equally maintained without loss. Jonas sees life as defying disciplinary capture; it escapes univocal description. For the Christian this expresses its inherently theological character. Jonas finds life to be coextensive with mind, free, purposeful, self-transcending; he finds that it generates value. The Christian narrates this in terms of the freedom, purpose and transcendence of God, and the Good which God is, in which creatures participate. Jonas says that what is distinctively human belongs in some way to life as a whole; the Christian says all reality is personal. Jonas shows that all of life has a fundamental solidarity in inwardness, freedom, purposiveness, self-transcendence. The Christian narrates this as the unity of cosmology and theological anthropology: human mind and self-awareness do not drastically separate us from non-human life but rather represent an intensification of something realized to different degrees throughout life taken as a whole, from amoeba to primate. In this hospitable mode, Jonas can be taken as a theologian in good standing, as it were; one who has told a story about life that shows forth in some mode the shape of the Christian narrative; an extrapolation of a trajectory intrinsic to the Christian story which reveals new perspectives unseen or underemphasized; a telling which in some way shows the story more clearly to itself. The chief of these is Jonas's regard of every organism, even the most primitive, as a conscious subject with purposes, concerns, agendas of its own. This can prompt a deeper thinking of the Christian story which articulates more comprehensively the place and value of every living creature, each one's inestimable dignity as a bearer of inwardness, in solidarity with human beings.[9]

But the ontological ultimacy of life narrated as resurrection, as peace, disrupts Jonas's philosophical biology by exposing the conflictual elements in his account, recognizing these as theological and bringing to bear on them the Christian alternative. Following the shape of the scheme pursued in this book, a need for both ontological and epistemological disruption can be discerned, while recognizing the fundamental unity of these dimensions. With regard to the latter, although Jonas's philosophy shows life's irreducibility to non-life, its trespassing over metaphysical boundaries and its evasion of conceptual containment, it does not fully narrate the lack of closure characterizing both life and science. That requires a metaphysics of participated transcendence which explains life as ontologically ultimate even as embodied and material, and, consequently, knowledge of that life as in principle unfinishable and never exhaustive. With regard to the former, it does not narrate life and the knowledge of that life as peaceful, and this is abundantly clear in the element of Jonas's treatment which perpetuates conflict at the heart of life, and which is traceable to his existentialist loyalties: life is life only as over-against-death.

In this way a theological vitalism will answer to persistent concerns that Christianity perpetuates a violent and exclusive anthropocentrism. Bennett frames this familiar worry specifically in terms of wrong uses of vitalism, suggesting that vitalism has been put to work *against* the overall integrity and aliveness of matter and of the world *in toto*, diminishing the value of non-human life and material

---

9. Much more could be said about the connections between the vitalism and animism of Jonas's philosophical biology and the Christian panentheism which Milbank espouses. Jonas senses the depth of an organism's life which Milbank, after Eckhart, articulates in a frankly pantheist manner: '[T]he created soul (and, indeed, the Augustinian "seminal reason" of every created thing) is identical with the uncreated deity' (John Milbank and Slavoj Žižek, *The Monstrosity of Christ*, 189).

Christianity's opposition to animism can be overstated: 'Perhaps Christianity chased the gods and sprites away, or forced them to assume different forms, but it never did so entirely. And, after all, Paul never suggested that the elemental powers or ethereal principalities were illusions; he merely claimed that they had been made subject to Christ. The author of Colossians even seems to say that they have now been reconciled to God' (David Bentley Hart, 'Of Hills, Brooks, Standing Lakes and Groves . . .', http://www.firstthings.com/web-exclusives/2010/10/hellipof-hills-brooks-standing-lakes-and-groveshellip, accessed 17 February 2016).

Mark Wallace has explored Christian animism more systematically in *Finding God in the Singing River: Christianity, Spirit, Nature* (Minneapolis: Fortress Press, 2005).

reality in general. Jonas's philosophical biology presents itself as the apposite response to these concerns: a valuation of life is used to elevate, not to denigrate, both within the realm of the living and in the cosmos as a whole, by dissolving dualism. But Bennett's concern that vitalism seems repeatedly to be allied to violent political projects is worryingly borne out by Jonas. The burden of a theological vitalism, then, would be to narrate vitalism precisely in opposition to violence.

The next section reviews these disruptions by observing some ways in which *The Phenomenon of Life* is characterized by unresolved tensions, which commentators gloss over but which themselves point towards the insufficiency of Jonas's account taken as 'pure' philosophy. We begin first with one more tangential to our concerns here, namely the metaphysical grounds for Jonas's treatment of form, which leads into the more substantive epistemological and ontological issues.

A metaphysics of form

Levy is right to observe that one of the remarkable metaphysical aspects of Jonas's philosophy of life is that he seems to unite contraries: while maintaining the primacy of form over matter in the organic realm, he fully espouses Darwinism, which is usually taken to signify the dissolution of fixed essences.[10] This uniting of seeming contraries without losing the distinctive qualities of those contraries is one of the things that makes Jonas's philosophy of life receptive to narration by the kind of Christian metaphysics defended in this study. Levy misses the point, however, when he tries to resolve this apparent contradiction by attributing to Jonas a claim for 'relative constancies and intrinsically necessary conditions of survival' which are compatible with Darwinian flux.[11] Jonas's response to Darwinian nominalism is, in the order of the book, his analysis of metabolism which reveals a primacy of form. He never clearly reconciles the high place he wishes to give to a causative, teleological understanding of form on the basis of a philosophical analysis of metabolism, with the denial of fixity of species as sustained in traditional Darwinism. Levy avoids this tension, but it is a central aspect of the metaphysical problematic Jonas sets up and relates directly to his rejection of dualism. Jonas's construal of form is only reconcilable with Darwinian evolution if dualism can be overcome by the post-dualistic ontological synthesis he calls for, by which being and becoming, time and eternity, fixture and flux may be conceived not as alternatives or opposites, nor as merely compatible in a flat sense, but as mysteriously more-than-compatible in a unity which comprehends difference. Christian theology contends that this post-dualistic synthesis would look something like a theological notion of participation: the kind of difference that God is, the difference that names the relation between Creator and creation, makes difference and union directly and not inversely proportionate.

10. Levy, *Hans Jonas*, 57.
11. Levy, *Hans Jonas*, 58.

The issue is highlighted by the question of Jonas's relationship to Aristotle. Although Levy is in a certain sense correct in claiming that 'Jonas's conception of science is hardly Aristotle's', and that 'if anything in Aristotle is untenable today, it is his natural scientific understanding of the universe as a complex of essential unchanging substances',[12] this is an insufficiently nuanced response to the clear Aristotelian leanings of Jonas whose prioritization of form as an '*essential*', '*real*', '*efficacious*' factor in an organism's existence is nothing if not metaphysically realist.[13] It is untrue, then, to say that Jonas is in *no* sense a neo-Aristotelian.[14] It is more convenient for metaphysically naturalist commentators to see Jonas's Aristotelianism as qualified and subordinate, because it minimizes the *aporia* which result from Jonas's metaphysical realism. There is an unwillingness to engage with the frank sympathies towards classical teleology and realist ontology in *The Phenomenon of Life*. This is perhaps understandable given that while Jonas evinces these sympathies, he does not directly address their metaphysical implications, nor the structures that would be needed to support them.[15] Jonas's lack of theological readers has contributed to this blind spot in commentary. What is needed is a readership which will take his metaphysical proclivities at face value and run with them, bringing to them a narrative which reconciles metaphysical realism with change and time, which can support finalism while respecting finite causation. It just such a running-with that the participative metaphysics of Christian theological reasoning makes possible. This could involve the kind of strong metaphysics of form which we saw Hanby defending in the previous chapter.[16] Jonas's moves towards a high teleology and an emphasis on the priority of form over matter are in danger of being question-begging in the absence of an ontology to underwrite them. On the kind of narrative we have defended in

12. Levy, *Hans Jonas*, 58.

13. *Phenomenon*, 80; my italics.

14. Levy, *Hans Jonas*, 58.

15. Jonas's theology, heavily influenced by Whitehead and process theism, is surely inadequate for sustaining the sort of metaphysics he would need to support, for example, finalism, or formal realism. Robert Neville discusses Jonas's relationship to process thought in more depth: 'More on Jonas and Process Philosophy', in *The Legacy of Hans Jonas: Judaism and the Philosophy of Life*, ed. Hava Tirosh-Samuelson and Christian Wiese (Boston: Brill, 2008), 511–18. Jonas had an appreciative but critical relationship with Whitehead; see *Phenomenon*, 95ff.

16. This raises the well-known problems concerning nominalism and the debate around the fixity of species which are tangential to our concerns here, but it is an important debate impinging directly on the kinds of metaphysical concerns which hover behind Jonas's philosophical biology. I do not pursue in this section, for reasons of space, the larger question of the extent to which Hanby's use of a metaphysics of form complements or departs from Jonas's approach, and how directly it may answer to some of the concerns I raise in this section. But the larger metaphysical canvas Hanby defends will surely allow for a more defensible account of formal reality and final causation.

this study, a metaphysics based on a creation conceived as an intrinsic and not extrinsic relation is a frontrunner for such an ontology.

The previous chapter discussed the tensions that arise between this kind of metaphysical approach and the narratival model of Milbank; there a pragmatic and heuristic role for a dialectical metaphysics was suggested. One might think that Hanby's type of metaphysical approach, in which metaphysics appeared normative over narrative, is a more appropriate theological framework in which to approach Jonas. I suggest, however, that Jonas's philosophical biology rather points towards and begs narrative explication. This comes by means of, and not in spite of, Christian theology taking up question of the role of formal identity.

For Jonas, life is basically self-assertion in the face of non-life. An organism is constituted by a certain self-regard, even in the most primitive biological form. This reflexivity and incipient selfhood, which Jonas identifies with life itself, makes narration – the sense of the organismic self as *having* a story, as being through time with a stake in its own unfolding – characteristic of life itself. This is one of the more intriguing and undeveloped aspects of Jonas's treatment of life: as embodied self-concern in time, each life is inherently a conducting of its own story of being, a constant recuperation of its beginning and anticipation of its ending. The affirmation of life which Jonas expresses and calls for in his philosophical biology, and ultimately in his ethics, points towards that affirmation which is the biological truth of each organism as it pursues its own existence. His finding of the physical and mental aspects of this pursuance to be inextricable only reinforces this: life is desire, and formal identity is used not so much to sustain a metaphysical realism as it is to underwrite life as self-assertion. Just as it was argued that Hanby's normative and universal metaphysics must be subordinate to a primacy of story, Jonas's language of form is subordinate to the story of that form's precarious self-perpetuation in the face of the constant threat of non-being. It is the sense of having a bounded self which seeks a future in a world that is not oneself that Jonas's language of form invites. This is characteristic of vitalism: life is construed as having a will that is immanent to it. It is not merely the automatic operation of blind process but a determined pursuance of existence, a forceful expression of a subject's longing for life. In this way the narrative content of Jonas's treatment begins to emerge: life is not only metaphysically but also temporally suspended in a between, by the horizons of beginning and ending, origin and dissolution.

Thus Jonas's use of a dialectical method as his primary mode of analysis is in some tension with his picture of life. This is not only at the level of organismic being – life itself – but equally in his account of the knowledge of life, which remains genealogical. Jonas explains the fundamental role of organic existence in showing the impossibility of a closed scientist account of reality through its inherent exceeding of its own boundaries, and so indicates that life's beginning and ending must be beyond the horizons of conceptual control, but this 'beyond' is not narrated. In this, although he has demonstrated the incapacity of scientist frameworks for a total grasp of the phenomenon of life, he has not securely put it beyond scientist capture, for a framework of pure immanence is always susceptible to circumscription and thus to (in principle) total explanation. As a vitalism which remains immanent, it cannot help seeing life as dualistically evasive of closure in a bad sense: as opposed to the representable, and as 'beyond physical science', which problematically degrades knowing, representation and materiality. According to Wolin, this tendency to a certain irrationalism would be ominously typical of German vitalism.[17]

The next section pursues this point by considering the ambiguous moral and political implications of Jonas's agonism; here, the concern is Jonas's need of prophetic disruption by a reason that transcends mere rationalism and so is able to overcome a dualism of knowable-unknowable. The category of the speculative and uncircumscribable, as Milbank employs it, is precisely not meant to evacuate attempts at representation but rather to underwrite them as indefinable, that is, as not confinable to finitude. It does not follow that they wholly evade finite description. This would be part of the point the last chapter attempted to make: Milbank's account of *poesis* is suggestive of a high view of scientific knowing, not a derogatory view. Biology's knowing of life is dignified and not destroyed by an understanding of noetic acts as poetic. Simply to show life's irreducibility to physical or noetic constituents is not adequate, since it still suggests that the physical and the noetic are somehow an alternative to the spiritual and apophatic, rather than being modes of the transcendent and unsayable, and unconceivable without them. Life as irreducible to matter is not what transcendent vitalism should seek, for this allows matter to remain 'mere'. Narration in the terms of the Christian story would rather be a 'making strange' in which these terms mean more and not less than they did; not a mystification which puts the term beyond conceptual explication but a setting of that term against a horizon which opens up possibilities of intelligibility predicated on an infinite depth.

This leads to a consideration of Jonas's implicit contention that a vitalism can be dialectically demonstrated by the analysis of scientific data and of competing metaphysical options, as he seems to presume. It has been said that he fails to provide a means of narrating science's lack of closure, which the vitalism he moves towards seems to call for. He regards himself as pursuing a 'phenomenology' of life, but pure phenomenology is (on the Milbankian view) impossible; ontology

---

17. 'In German *Geistesgeschichte*, vitalism has an ambiguous legacy. Historically it has been employed as an intellectual weapon in the struggle against the (Western) idea of "reason".... [L]ife' connoted a dimension of "experiential immediacy" that was purportedly superior to the intellect's more abstract musings. In the German context, the ideological thrust of this standpoint is unmistakable. As Herbert Schnädelbach has remarked: 'If the later history of life-philosophy is so little known . . . this is chiefly because life-philosophy is branded with the stigma of irrationalism and of being a precursor of fascism. . . . [T]he "heroic realism" of Bäumler, Krieck and Rosenberg, which was considered to be the official philosophy of National Socialism, was inspired by the traditions of life-philosophy after Nietzsche' (Wolin, *Heidegger's Children*, 124).

is always implicitly invoked, and description always exceeds the merely 'evident' towards the speculative and the conjectural.[18]

Attempting to identify the point of disagreement between vitalists and mechanists, one author ruefully concludes that the difference is not so much a difference within a single discourse as a difference between worlds of discourse, what he calls 'universes' or 'horizons' of discourse.[19] 'A universe so conditioned may well be called *one's* universe, as distinguished from *the universe . . .* the relations established within one universe cannot be assumed to hold within

18. '[T]he idea that we can have a "pure" phenomenology, describing appearances only in terms of appearances, of "how things show themselves" . . . is quite simply impossible. For every description, in order to be a description and not simply a mute regarding, has to describe what appears in terms of something *other* than what appears' (Milbank, 'The Grandeur of Reason', 389).

19. The reflections of Edgar Singer, an early twentieth-century commentator on the vitalist-mechanist debate, are so apposite that they are worth quoting at length:

'During the course of the last century it has grown increasingly clear that not all the issues with which an experimental science can be faced are experimental issues. If there were no other ground for this belief, history itself would force upon us some such conviction. For there are differences of opinion dividing men today that have divided men from the earliest times recorded, and in every one of the ages in between the self-same issue will have involved in dissension, not an occasional disputant here and there, but all the best thinkers in all the known sciences of their day. Yet at no time has either party to such strifes been in possession of facts ignored by the other; for had this been the case, the ignorant party must ere now have been driven from the field by the force of the facts it ignored. It is fair to suppose that an issue which has come no nearer to solution as century after century added its contribution to the store of human knowledge, cannot depend for its decision on any information to be looked for from the centuries to come.

But if the matter of dispute in such interminable strifes is not, never has been, never can be one whose decision turns on a question of fact, on what can the decision turn? It would be easy to answer that in all cases in which an issue has proven itself perennial, the matter of difference is not indeed one of fact, but of conception. And all history would seem to confirm this opinion, for throughout its length, the speech of either party to such enduring discords is witness to the fact that to each the conceptions of the other were inconceivable, the thoughts of the other unthinkable. The only trouble with this answer would be that it raised a question more difficult to resolve than any it pretended to answer. *Why* should it be impossible for one intelligence to grasp the world or another, both having before them the same range of facts?' (Edgar A. Singer, 'Beyond Mechanism and Vitalism', *Philosophy of Science* 1, no. 3 (1934): 273–94, 273–4).

Singer's framing of the vitalist-mechanist controversy is as follows: either everything in nature is 'structural', which is the mechanist view (the 'Democritean' position), or some things in nature are non-structural in nature, which is the vitalist view (the 'Aristotelian' position) ('Vitalism', 275). For just the reasons discussed in this section, this kind of account remains too dualist.

another.'[20] Previous chapters argued that there is a choice of narratives which is fundamentally aesthetic and not rationally derivable in the sense of 'pure' reason. With this in mind, it can be contended against Jonas that vitalism cannot be dialectically established; although the biological 'facts' may be considered to disclose its truth, they cannot be adduced so as to make any other conclusion impossible. It is a particular strength of Jonas's account, though, that it indicates how this undecidability or indeterminateness might be considered as intrinsic to life as such: the way one perceives and interprets the world of life is itself a decision of desire, a response in freedom which is always directed to the perpetuation of life. It is not simply a moral or ontological imperative that life be narrated in a certain way; it is an epistemological inevitability, because its nature as peace or conflict is not manifest, but calls for a beginning and an ending to be given it, a beginning and ending which never could be 'discovered', for they are over the horizon. In light of this beginning and ending, life will be seen to be a certain sort of thing, rather than another; it will be seen as death (notwithstanding that it may have the appearance of aliveness) or it will be seen as life – all the way down. It is seeing life as death that Jonas resists, but he surely has not secured the alternative, which is seeing life as life. That will be the concern of the next section.

These considerations provide a guide for how Jonas's philosophical biology is to function in the approach taken by this study. His dialectical approach is problematic only insofar as it is thought to be the ultimate mode of demonstration. It cannot be used to 'settle the facts'; nor can we say that 'the evidence' forces a vitalistic agenda upon us. Vitalism needs to be acknowledged as a narrative choice. But it is aesthetic, not arbitrary, because the metaphysics of transcendence within which a home for Jonas is made, which regards no fact as singularly self-explanatory or self-contained, holds that facts 'speak for themselves' in a narrative of what is given, what is made, the true *factum*. Of course, the very notion of a 'fact' in the modern and colloquial sense already contains a narrative which is contrary to the narrative of orthodoxy, because it imagines an inert and self-evident given, rather than the dynamic gift of creation which mysteriously participates in its own making.

Jonas's philosophical biology cannot, therefore, be an apologetic tool – powerful because 'natural' and untarnished by explicit Christian faith; it cannot be an unstoried argument which establishes for the non-believer Christianity's own claims about life, a biology-as-natural-theology. There is nothing self-sufficient or self-explanatory about life being what it is; nothing is 'obvious', apart from its being told or shown in a certain way. Jonas has his role as a 'theologian' not because he shows what anyone properly observing biological truths must necessarily conclude but because his so-called philosophical biology indicates what Christian theology might look like as biology, what kind of approach a theology-as-biology might take: it might read organisms in just the way Jonas has, and I am suggesting that it do so. It may function as a biology-as-natural-theology in the apologetic

---

20. Singer, 'Beyond Mechanism and Vitalism', 280.

sense only to the extent that it invites us to regard the living organism in a certain way, and once we do so, we see the force and fittingness of this way. But it is an invitation, not a dialectical proof. And this is apparent on Jonas's own grounds, for although he uses the term, there are no 'facts' for him in the discrete Cartesian sense; there are only lives, and being and truth are apparent only to life, to that which is alive. The living, metabolizing organism is the locus of it all.

It is thus in answer to both ontology and epistemology that the Christian narration of life presents itself as the apposite framework for and completion of all that Jonas wants to say about life, as well as finding in it a biology which expresses its theology, its narrative, with perhaps a quite fresh and new disclosure of the dignity of the organism which was yet always anticipated by the story so far.

Refusing death and conflict

The most urgent disruption concerns the role of death and conflict in Jonas's philosophical biology. On this matter the interrogation must be more incisive. This disruption is critical not only in the relation to Jonas himself but more generally in the attempt by Christian theology to take up for its own the term 'vitalism'. The ambiguous moral and political dimensions of vitalism have been mentioned; this section considers Jonas's own problematic entanglement in these ambiguities. By addressing and disrupting them there, Christian theology questions a secular vitalism.

Most readings of Jonas fail to grasp with any seriousness the contrast he sets up between the primal ontology of life and the modern, mechanistic ontology of death. The 'ontology of death' and 'ontology of life' is stark vocabulary and must be seen to govern his call for a post-dualistic ontological synthesis. This is the most fundamental of the *aporia* which mark Jonas's thought: he votes absolutely for life, at the same time as saying that primitive panvitalism could not survive the realization of mortality.[21] The reluctant admission that death must be allowed to qualify life stands in unresolved tension with the underlying desire to see life as the ontological ultimate. Although his genealogical narration insistently opts for a primacy of life in its repudiation of mechanistic ontologies of death, it is nevertheless characterized by a pained consciousness of the nullity of death, against which, in dramatic contrast, the adventure of life is set as a constant 'no' to non-being and dissolution. It is by this that Jonas defines the individual organism as a coherent entity, and it is the real burden of his metaphysics of form: an organism's metabolic existence just is the affirmation of its own being over against nothingness. With this agonistic, existentialist model of life, it will always remain in the shadow of death; the ontology of death will always maintain the upper hand, a fact Jonas does not admit anywhere in the pages of *The Phenomenon of Life* but which vitiates the defence of life's irreducibility to non-life. How could Jonas protect the absolute

21. *Phenomenon*, 19.

reality of life, which is to say, the victory of the ontology of life over the ontology of death which he calls for in his genealogies of modern metaphysics, without asserting the ontological ultimacy of life? Its irreducibility to mechanism alone cannot establish this ultimacy, and nor can an ethic of affirmation of life that is not grounded in a story which makes life alone finally real. As an ethic of affirmation without an ontology of affirmation, it has an ineliminable element of irony. Only a metaphysic which takes as fundamental the ultimate extinction of death by life, not contingently but because life is that which is alone real and true, and from which the whole universe must be constituted, would be able to establish securely the sort of vitalism Jonas reaches towards. This would be vitalism not as an ethic, nor as an analysis of the organism as exceeding its physical constituents, but as the story of being itself. Jonas wants to say that life is irreducible not only to matter but also to non-life: the terms of non-life can never adequately capture the reality of life. But the irreducibility of life to matter and to non-life is secured only by a narrative in which life somehow names reality itself.

The decisive role of death in constituting the organism in the world, defined by the constant threat of non-being, accords central place to conflict in Jonas's account: life becomes, fundamentally, struggle. Such an agonism is perhaps to be expected in an author with existentialist heritage; Jonas may be unintentionally perpetuating Heidegger's philosophical and political entanglements. But it calls for the deepest disruption of Jonas's philosophy of biology, as it pertains to the theme most central to the narrative we have been defending, namely peace. It is also determinative of the success of Jonas's project on its own terms, since it concerns the way in which he succeeds or fails in resisting nihilism.

Jonas's imagining of deity, marked by the need for a post-Holocaust theodicy, substantiates the suspicion that he is propounding a profoundly conflictual ontology. He postulates, in mythic mode, a powerless and ultimately contingent deity: a God who grows in the growth of creation, who discovers himself in the development of life, and in which God himself is both beneficiary and victim of the human finale to the evolutionary story: the distinctive significance of the human being is in the 'awesome impact of his deeds on God's destiny'.[22] Without pursuing detailed exposition of Jonas's explicit engagements with a concept of God,[23] it can be noted that it excludes the narration of life as peace insofar as the divine is itself complicit in the conflict and competition which is embodied life.[24] In this process-

---

22. Jonas, *Phenomenon*, 277.

23. Engagement with this aspect of Jonas's thought is thin on the ground: 'Jonas' contributions to post-Holocaust theology are among his most important writings, yet they represent the aspect of his work that is probably least known and understood' (Wolin, *Heidegger's Children*, 129).

24. Which is not for a moment to say that Jonas's theology is of no worth, nor that it is unfruitful for Christian theological engagement. For a perceptive and sympathetic treatment, with particular attention to its character as an expression of Jonas's identity as a German Jew, see Hans Henrix, 'Powerlessness of God? A Critical Appraisal of Hans

inflected theology, suffering is part of the harmony which fulfils God.[25] This is just what we would expect from Jonas's philosophical biology, in which it is the very conflictuality of organic existence that produces its most distinctive characteristics and is the context in which its inwardness, freedom and self-transcendence can be apprehended: it is the sense of precariousness, of freedom conceived as over-against-death and nothingness, that defines the forward striving of the embodied organism and its self-transcendence in time and space.

Competition as the fundamental value of life is a typical theme of evolutionary thought in general and occupies much of the rhetoric around the moral or spiritual significance of evolution. Process-influenced treatments of God are common responses to this problematic. Jonas's later work gives evidence that his critical analysis of Darwinism has not prevented him from absorbing its underlying agonism and perpetuating this in his conception of life: 'encroaching on other life is *eo ipso* given with belonging to the kingdom of life. . . . In simple words: *to eat and be eaten is the principle of existence*.'[26]

One can anticipate in defence of Jonas the counterproposal of a Nietzschean-type view: simply to affirm life, in the very teeth of its inherent conflictuality and precariousness, is the grandest 'Yes' to life that can be imagined; it is and must be enough.[27] But the contention here pursued is that Jonas reaches towards something for which he has not the story: an account of life in which life itself has the last word. This is contended not from an impossible outside but by Christian theology, which welcomes and disrupts in the name of peace. From the view of that peace, an affirmation of life will only appear to be an affirmation if behind it there hovers an unshakeable bleakness about the deathly constitution of reality itself. For Nietzsche, modern nihilism is rooted in the disorientation which results from the death of God: our values no longer have a metaphysical purchase but hang nauseatingly in mid-air.[28] This highlights the point: the present critique of Jonas is not making the naïve proposal that Christianity somehow 'proves' the values that

Jonas's Idea of God After Auschwitz', http://www.jcrelations.net/Powerlessness_of_God_ _A_Critical_Appraisal_of_Hans_Jonas___s _Idea_of_God_after_A.2198.0.html, accessed 10 January 2016.

25. 'The ever more sharpened keenness of appetite and fear, pleasure and pain triumph and anguish, love and even cruelty – their very edge the deity's gain. Their countless, yet never blunted incidence – hence the necessity of death and new birth – supplies the tempered essence from which the Godhead reconstitutes itself. . . . [C]reatures, by merely fulfilling themselves in pursuit of their lives, vindicate the divine venture. Even their suffering deepens the fullness of the symphony' (*Phenomenon*, 277).

26. Hans Jonas, 'Responsibility Today: The Ethics of an Endangered Future', *Social Research* 43, no. 1 (1974): 77–97, 78.

27. See Bernard Reginster, *The Affirmation of Life: Nietzsche on Overcoming Nihilism* (Cambridge, MA: Harvard University Press, 2009): 'Nietzsche regards the affirmation of life as his defining philosophical achievement', 2.

28. Reginster, *The Affirmation of Life*, 54ff.

Jonas wants to defend and that without this validation they remain unjustified. They are indeed unjustified and cannot be proved. It is also not suggesting that Christianity extrinsically supplies the metaphysical framework within which Jonas's philosophical biology can believably say what it wants to say. It is suggesting that Jonas's own narrative, admitted or not, simultaneously gives voice to the Christian story and fails to express the Christian story, and that only the narrative of creation, redemption and *eschaton* will do to recognize, affirm and complete these elements of Jonas's conception of life. What counts is not metaphysical establishment from the ground up but a narrative location that is more suspension than foundation. This is emphatically a post-Nietzschean construal of meaning insofar as it has accepted a fundamental groundlessness of values, in the sense of a 'common ground' on which a universally transparent rational structure could be constructed. But it views this suspension not as negative unknowability but as a revelation of the character of reason as graced, and of reality itself not as fundamentally impatient of being seen and known but rather as a hypervisible plenitude.

The religious awareness expressed in Jonas's choice of the vocabulary of life and death is important in showing that he grasps the moral ladenness of the biological language of life and death; and it also bears out the sense that the option for life is, for him, the profoundest affirmation of all that is sacred.

> Jonas was an able student of the long history of thought – Christian, Gnostic, and philosophical – that turned the Jew into a figure for the flesh. This history taught him that the defense of Judaism was therefore a defense of life itself. It is no accident that the first words of *The Phenomenon of Life* were written in 1944, two decades before its actual publication, while Jonas was fighting for the 'Jewish Battalion' on the battlefields of Italy: 'It is in the dark stirrings of primeval organic substance that a principle of freedom shines forth for the first time.' For Jonas, the Jews and organic life were bound together in one common love, in one destiny.[29]

For Jonas the dignity of human beings – and during much of his life the Jew was a type for the *mere* human being, the human being with nothing else to recommend it but humanness – was bound up with respect for life as such, not merely human life. This in itself is one of the most significant features of Jonas's account: he recognizes that the value of the human and the value of life itself cannot be extricated from one another. There is a fundamental moral solidarity of life itself. This is the concern, differently expressed, by Milbank and the *nouvelle théologie*: if true meaning can be attained only by plucking the human out from the world at large, the battle for

---

29. David Nirenberg, 'Choosing Life', Review of *Memoirs: Hans Jonas*, in *The New Republic Online*, 6 November 2008, https://newrepublic.com/article/64504/choosing-life, accessed 27 June 2017. A fundamental solidarity between human and non-human life taking the concrete shape of the Jewish people is an intriguing theme for further development.

meaning has been lost. If a downgrade of one is the necessary basis for the upgrade of the other, the equation remains nihilistic in spirit.[30] But the embrace of the kind of absolute oppositionality which characterizes Jonas's treatment of life and death undermines this very project. It perpetuates that dualism which allows there to be true opposites in being. Jonas's pained awareness that death must qualify life, that panvitalism cannot ultimately succeed the realization of ultimate annihilation for the living, unsettles his stubborn option for the vital over the mechanical.

Biology is indeed a theology; this is particularly apparent in the unity of Jonas's 'doctrine of God' (a doctrine which in his account appears more as effect than cause of his account of life) with his account of life itself. The theology that is operative in Jonas's account is feeding a conflictual narrative at both these levels: the divine and the natural. This global conflictuality is in keeping with vitalism's history as summarized above: it 'normally has implicit notions of power or struggle'.[31] In the mode of existentialist self-concern with which Jonas reads the self-transcendence of life, life remains most fundamentally a form of self-assertion, not donation, and so is ultimately captive to a binary logic. Consequently, one must submit that as a philosophical biology Jonas's conception of life remains trapped within dualism – the very dualism he sought, in his philosophical biology, to avoid. If so, it fails on its own terms; for although he shows biology's own evasion of any kind of substance dualism and the monisms which spring from it, the more fundamental dualism of being versus non-being, life versus death, peace versus conflict remains the operative hermeneutic and is not transcended; even God is drawn into it. And so after all, on Jonas's reading, life does not escape nihilism. Jonas turns out, somewhat surprisingly, to be residually but perniciously Darwinian, or even Nietzschean.

If this seems like an extreme conclusion, it is borne out by Wolin's observation that in Jonas's political thought the key incentive for the establishment of human society is '*fear*—fear of a violent death'.[32] Wolin finds disturbing Jonas's defence

---

30. Failure to recognize just this point has disastrously stymied Christian engagement with increasingly pressing ethical questions about non-human life. It is embarrassingly evident that 'animals' are generally mentioned in Christian theology only negatively, to highlight the unique and pre-eminent characteristics of human beings. This gives everything away, for it secularly imagines value as fundamentally competitive, as though human dignity somehow depends on the lack of dignity of everything else. Until Christian language about non-human creatures attains to a truly Scriptural practice – in which animals possess the inestimable majesty of participating in the order of redemption – non-Christian thought will continue to monopolize the whole issue, since at this point it is non-Christian thought that takes 'animals' seriously as moral objects.

31. Lash, 'Life (Vitalism)', 323; though it should be noted that Lash appears to have a slightly more dogmatic conception of vitalism as a fixed tradition, in contrast to Normandin and Wolfe.

32. Wolin, *Heidegger's Children*, 122.

of political autocracy, expressed in 'nightmarish' thought experiments about appropriate forms of government:

> The gist of Jonas' political philosophy is contained in an ominously titled section of *The Imperative of Responsibility*, 'The Advantage of Total Governmental Power'. His indebtedness to the antidemocratic prejudices of Plato's doctrine of the philosopher-king – prejudices that also seduced Heidegger . . . is palpable. Jonas openly praises the advantages of autocracy – for example, the fact that 'the decisions from the top, which can be made without prior assent from below, meet with no resistance . . . in the social body'. . . . Jonas's willingness to contemplate seriously the merits of political autocracy is disconcerting.[33]

Wolin recognizes the centrality of Jonas's philosophical biology in supporting and motivating his political thought. Jonas's proximity to Darwin is key: he characterizes biological life

> as essentially a competitive struggle for survival. By taking nature and biology as his normative points of departure . . . Jonas is led to anticipate the worst from humanity, rather than to expect the best. [This] element of resignation implicit in Jonas's metaphysical vision cannot help but affect his approach to ethics.[34]

In Jonas it is clear that conceptions of biological life are determinative of conceptions of society, God, nature and meaning altogether. This indeed is the point of Jonas's analysis of life: it holds the keystone in a world view. To narrate life-as-conflict rather than life-as-peace decides the whole character of an ontology as well as a politics. Conversely one might say that in a conception of biological life one can see crystallized a picture of existence as a whole. In Jonas one sees distilled the effects of reading life outside of that narrative of peace which tells the beginning as unrivalrous donation and the end as difference in harmony. Wolin sees in Jonas the consequence of this reading of life: autocracy in politics and resignation in one's expectation of the human. In a story of life as over-against-death, there is not hope but survival, and life in society is containment of the inevitable rather than a realism tempered by the patient expectation of divine peace.

Wolin's concerns about Jonas's vitalism are intriguing from the point of view of the present critique. He observes several linked *aporia* in Jonas's use of the life theme. He worries that the 'vitalist sanctification of "life" as an ultimate good' elevates mere survival over the truly good life.[35] The attribution of subjectivity and inwardness to all of life seems in some sense a demotion of the human, an eradication of distinctively human goods – an odd aping of Darwinism's own uninflected flattening of our cultural hierarchies. The reading of metabolic life

---

33. Wolin, *Heidegger's Children*, 126, 129.
34. Wolin, *Heidegger's Children*, 122.
35. Wolin, *Heidegger's Children*, 124, 121.

as free seems, to Wolin, to do something disturbing to freedom; it naturalizes it, rendering it too close to harsh necessity. An organism does not have a choice, after all; if it is to live, it must metabolize.[36] What is being said about human freedom if it is essentially continuous with that 'freedom' which is the spontaneous and automatic operation of a biological imperative – the freedom of an amoeba? One of Wolin's most serious charges against Jonas is that he consistently avoids the real challenge of the fact-value gap; seeking to root ethics in biological life, Jonas remains in denial of what Wolin takes as the unavoidable reality: you cannot get an ought from an is.[37]

Jonas might say to Wolin that he has put the cart before the horse; the whole point is an elevation of life as a whole, not a degradation of the human. But the critique remains valid insofar as there is no *a priori* reason within Jonas's scheme for reading it this way – a problem only because the fundamental reference point for what life is remains immanent. This underlines the need prophetically to disrupt and hospitably to situate Jonas's vitalism in a Christian narrative. Survival remains the measure of life-under-death, and a reigning Darwinian agonism, no matter how surreptitious, will necessarily make biology a perilous framework on which to hang truth and meaning, no matter how adroitly one reads 'freedom' and 'transcendence' into the biological facts. To return to Wolin's point, if nature is harsh necessity because causally circumscribed, and freedom is in some sense located outside of the limit which is nature, then to be natural is indeed to be 'mere', and to locate freedom in such a nature would be offensive to the distinctively human good. But the identification of the solidarity of all life is a demotion only if immanence is presumed. In a hierarchy suspended from an infinite transcendence, the lower participates in the higher without limiting or containing it. On this kind of picture, 'freedom' does not consist in liberation from material constraints, since matter has at no stage been opposed to consciousness, and nature has never been conceived as 'separate' from the human so as to be able to debase it by association.

Wolin perhaps has not quite taken on board the unresolved tension between the two moments in Jonas's own treatment: the recognition that biology intrinsically escapes its own limits, simultaneous with the sense that biology is the fundamentally threatened and exclusively finite context in which all our human goods and freedoms ambiguously unfold. But the kinds of problems Wolin observes in Jonas – the question of the relation of 'is' and 'ought', and the meaning of naturalizing the human – draw directly towards Christian theology's narration of nature and life, which decisively overcomes the separations between the human, the natural and the good which dog Jonas's vitalism in spite of his attempts to use biological facts to overcome them. To be naturalized is no insult unless nature is but poor, bounded finitude. Indeed, Jonas's touching regard of life's poverty, its indigence, becomes sinister if that indigence is solely the reflection in life's eye of the always-intensifying fear of loss and scarcity. Peaceful narration would not erase

36. Wolin, *Heidegger's Children*, 121.
37. Wolin, *Heidegger's Children*, 124.

that indigence but simply render it innocent: the blessed yearning and inherent incompleteness of the creature in time.

Vitalism will not attain to that comprehensive vision which puts itself beyond the pernicious dichotomies of nature and the human, necessity and freedom, biology and morality, not to mention the terminal dichotomy of death and life, apart from the suspension of nature from transcendence. This is enabled only by that deeper rejection of opposites in being which is the Christian story. Here is the prophecy in the Christian reception of biology's 'theology': the Christian narrative will give rise to a conception of life, just as it has in Milbank's terms a conception of 'society', which will not dwell parallel to scientific or philosophical accounts, seeking isolated points of overlap, common ground or contradiction. Rather, it makes a disruptive difference to the use of these terms in the whole of a scientific discourse by showing their proper home in the story of the world created, redeemed and sanctified by God. In that world life is not predicated on conflict. This is theology as a biology, as a story of what organic existence is. Although it is interrogative and critical with respect to the conflictuality of Jonas's account, it is not at cross-purposes with it *tout court*. On the contrary: the present treatment has attempted to demonstrate that this is really the fundamental direction of Jonas's exposition of metabolism and Darwinian descent, as it is the underlying orientation of the metaphysical story he tells. But it is a direction and a story that cannot be sustained in the absence of a narrative of creation, redemption and *eschaton*. In this story the effects of death, violence and conflict are apprehended, and seen to be tragically pervasive, but are not allowed an ontological presence: they do not define life. Rather Christian theology remains committed to narrating life as ontologically fundamental and so as peace: hope and expectancy of peace are what characterize life's encounter with death, violence and conflict. To be peace without contrast, life cannot, in its most fundamental character, be over against anything at all; death must be the parasite, the latecomer, and life simply the self-engendering, self-explicating, self-authenticating truth.

The residual dualism of Jonas's account of life is the result of a metaphysical framework which remains immanent, if ambiguously so. It was said above that the realist thrust of Jonas's account of organismic existence is not grounded in a story of what makes an object 'real' in the first place, a fact underlined by his theism which is more transcendental than transcendent: God remains an object within the domain of time and change, and a spectating one at that. Nor does his account of the intrinsic purposefulness of organic being, his description of life as desire, find a response, an echo, in his ontology. The teleology he observes in organismic existence remains unexplicated and unnarrated. And so, while his account of life as prophetic for ontology shows life's irreducibility to its physical constituents, the irreducibility remains limited in scope: it may not be mechanistically reducible, but it remains reducible to being-over-against-death, trapped within a scheme of opposites. This is the more fundamental kind of reduction which is inescapable in the terms of immanence, for life remains a merely relative reality: what it is is still pinned to a contrast with what it is not. Although life transcends its physical and temporal conditions both outward in space and forward in time, this 'outwards' and 'forwards' remain captive, notwithstanding that their permeation by transcendence is traceable in life's exceeding of ontological categories.

This brief critical reception of Jonas as a theologian has attempted to situate his philosophical biology in the narrative of orthodoxy, within which alone the theological character of both life and knowledge can be comprehensively and peacefully affirmed. The next step, fully to elaborate a transcendent vitalism according to Christian orthodoxy, is a thesis in itself. But it has been suggested that Jonas's own thinking on this subject can be both prompt and substrate for such narration. To substantiate this further the next section considers in speculative outline one of the prospects opened up by a theological vitalism, which would comprehend and secure Jonas's philosophical biology. It is, arguably, the single most important of all the agenda generated by a theological vitalism, since it concerns the reality of 'life' itself.

Naming 'natural evil'

It is likely that, presented with the Christian narration of life as peace, most observers of the natural world – scientists or laypeople –will reject it simply on grounds of ludicrousness. How could the Christian narration of life be a 'biology' when it appears to inhabit a fantasy world in which lions lie down with lambs and life has nothing to do with death?[38] Biological reality is a nightmarish scene of destruction, decay, waste and suffering, and the terrible 'discovery' of modern evolutionary theory is that these are necessary for the emergence of life itself. After the protests considered above about the illegitimate trespass of theology into the remits of professional scientists, this would appear as a terminal stumbling block to the presentation of Christian theology as a biology. It seems like the views adopted by so-called creationists: closing their eyes to 'the facts' in favour of a risible biblically derived tale of their own devising which ignores agreed biological data. These data include the reality of omnipresent death, to which Jonas's philosophical biology at least has the honesty to attempt a courageous response. The issue is a crucial one and demands the undertaking of a further project to discern how the Christian narration of peace can meaningfully engage with the narrative of the origins and evolution of life regnant in modern biology.

---

38. Milbank records responses of this nature to the first edition of *TST*, saying that one critic ascribed to him 'a kind of blithe wilful Maytime optimism' (*TST*, xv). His answer supports the direction that the argument of this section takes with respect to the biological world: the criticism 'entirely ignores my Pauline insistence on the utter fallenness and demonic captivity of the current world. Only with strenuous difficulty, only indeed as a form of Christian *gnosis* – which Paul yet dared to proclaim in the public forum – are we able to discern the hidden realm of real peaceful being that cosmic evil obscures from our view.'

A brief review of some common responses to this issue highlights how crucial the contribution of a theological vitalism might be. Some authors simply adjust the narrative of orthodoxy to include a necessary element of death and suffering, involving the divine itself in that necessity.[39] Others subject Christianity to an evolutionary paradigm as the determinative criterion of its narrative.[40] Mahoney sees two moments in Christianity's response to post-Darwinian biology. The first, practised by scientist-theologians such as Alister McGrath, John Polkinghorne and Arthur Peacocke, is an apologetic project to justify Christian belief in light of the discovery of evolution. The second, his own project, is to allow evolutionary thought to impact Christianity in a positive, not merely defensive, way, reshaping the meaning of central tenets of Christian faith such as original sin, incarnation and atonement. Mahoney reinterprets Christian dogmas in the light of evolutionary truths to produce an 'evolutionary theology'.[41] Other authors such as Philip Clayton, John Cobb and John Haught have followed similar paths.[42] Theodicy for non-human suffering has drawn on these kinds of accounts.[43]

The rejection of the real beginning of the story of creation in a divine peace, from which a catastrophic departure occurred, is a common feature of these accounts. It is an understandable response to moral and historical embarrassment over traditional formulations of an Adamic fall. This move may seem attractive, but it is terminal. The consequence of erasing a real fall is that conflict becomes endemic and innate, and peace merely fabricated and contingent; struggle and death assume a defining and necessary place in 'nature'.[44] The natural world emerges and fulfils its purposes by means of divinely ordained conflictual process

---

39. Not unlike Jonas. See, for example, Christopher Southgate, *The Groaning of Creation: God, Evolution and the Problem of Evil* (Louisville: Westminster John Knox Press, 2008).

40. A prominent example is Jack Mahoney, *Christianity in Evolution: An Exploration* (Georgetown: Georgetown University Press, 2011).

41. See Mahoney, *Christianity in Evolution: An Exploration*, Public Lecture delivered at Gresham College, 1 December 2011, http://www.gresham.ac.uk/lectures-and-events/christianity-in-evolution-an-exploration, accessed 17 March 2015.

42. See, for example, John Haught, *Deeper Than Darwin: The Prospect for Religion in an Age of Evolution* (Cambridge, MA: Westview, 2003) and Philip Clayton and Zachary Simpson, eds., *Adventures in the Spirit: God, World and Divine Action* (Minneapolis: Fortress, 2008).

43. Southgate, *The Groaning of Creation*, represents the most developed version of this. Denis Edwards, *Partaking of God: Trinity, Evolution and Ecology* (Collegeville, MN: Liturgical, 2014), uses a patristic approach to end up in a broadly similar place with regard to divine sharing in evolutionary change and suffering.

44. Southgate invokes a kind of Leibnizian argument that evolution was the 'only way' God could have made the goods this world exemplifies (Southgate, *The Groaning of Creation*, 29).

beginning not in peace but in chaos, and God becomes active agent and/or helpless patient of violence.[45]

Two partial responses to this problematic from the grounds of orthodoxy are the 'problem of good' response and the contesting of the Darwinian hermeneutic. The first stipulates that the recognition of evil as evil depends on the prior and normative reality of the good, and so even to acknowledge such a thing as evolutionary 'evils' commits one to goodness as what is real, and 'evil' as measurable only by contrast to this norm.[46] Inherent in the expression of the problem is a sense of the applicability of a language of 'evil' to natural events. The second capitalizes on the neglected co-presence of cooperation with competition in evolutionary process as articulated by modern biology.[47] By themselves, however, these approaches do not acknowledge the scale of the scandal which is the incomprehensible pervasiveness and seeming necessity of natural evil that modern biology indicates. A full response can be made only through a vigorous doctrine of the fall, which would allow death to be recognized as evil, not as good in disguise, and to be acknowledged as catastrophically pervasive to the point of sabotaging creation.[48] Conflict and suffering are, on this view, intruders which do not belong to nature. This is clearly called for by Paul in his letter to the Romans (8.20ff.), but the recognition of the nature of creation's 'subjection' requires more detailed articulation. Such an articulation might require a retrieval of the doctrine of the angelic fall; the presence of death in non-human nature both

45. Quentin Smith puts the problem with distressing clarity: 'Not long ago I was sleeping in a cabin in the woods and was awoken . . . by the sounds of a struggle between two animals. Cries of terror and extreme agony rent the night, intermingled with the sounds of jaws snapping bones and flesh being torn from limbs. . . . A clearer case of a horrible event in nature, a natural evil, has never been presented to me. It seemed to me self-evident that the natural law that *animals must savagely kill and devour each other in order to survive* was an evil natural law and that the obtaining of this law was sufficient evidence that God did not exist' ('An Atheological Argument from Evil Natural Laws', *International Journal for Philosophy of Religion* 29, no. 3 (1991): 159–74, 159, quoted in Southgate, *The Groaning of Creation*, 5, italics original).

46. Conor Cunningham takes this line in his too-brief discussion of the issue in *Darwin's*, 288f.; he does not allow this worry the force it deserves.

47. See, for example, Sarah Coakley's 2012 Gifford Lectures, 'Sacrifice Regained: Evolution, Cooperation and God', http://www.giffordlectures.org/lectures/sacrifice-regained-evolution-cooperation-and-god, accessed 27 June 2017). This approach is helpful insofar as it engages with what biologists themselves say and do, but it can only take one so far: cooperation may be important, but that the process is predicated upon death and waste remains unarguable.

48. The approach taken by David Bentley Hart, *The Doors of the Sea: Where Was God in the Tsunami?* (Grand Rapids: Eerdmans, 2011), especially Chapter 2. Regrettably he does not consider the question on the larger canvas of organismic death and suffering altogether (as opposed to human tragedy).

temporally and spatially discontiguous from human life calls for something like this.[49] A cosmology in which intellectual being is cardinal in the whole of creation becomes, perhaps counterintuitively, the best way of giving dignity to the whole natural order, by protesting its travails in terms of its subjection to intellectual powers tragically twisted by sin.[50]

49. Southgate has no patience for this approach, which he calls the 'mysterious fallenness' position. He quotes Keith Ward approvingly: an Adamic fall must 'seem a very unrealistic view to anyone who accepts some form of evolutionary theory and accepts that much evil is an inevitable consequence of such a world' (Keith Ward, *Rational Theology and the Creativity of God* (Oxford: Wiley-Blackwell, 1986), 203). For Southgate, to posit a 'mysterious fallenness' and attribute it to angelic goings-on is pitifully ungrounded speculation.

The question is whether the price of speculatively positing an angelic fall is greater than the price of making goods parasitic upon evils. For the real cost of the latter is a denial that evolutionary evils are true evils. In conversation with Southgate on this point, he posed the question: What is it that the defenders of a privative view of evil are so afraid of losing? The answer is, as Charles Mathewes explains in his defence of Augustine's account of evil, that 'evil is quite literally *not good*' (Charles Mathewes, *Evil and the Augustinian Tradition* (Cambridge: Cambridge University Press, 2001), 92, italics original). It is evil as genuinely evil, and good as truly good, that is at stake. Perhaps one wants to deny then that evolutionary evils are true evils (as surely Southgate must). But then one must answer to the experience of Quentin Smith as quoted above.

A theological vitalism responds to this kind of problematic by insisting (a) that our instinct that the horrors of nature are real evils, really regrettable, really undesirable, is a trustworthy one; and (b) that such evils in some way contradict what 'nature' fundamentally is and is about; what it is from and what it is towards. There is no belying the formidable explanatory challenge that this generates. But a theological vitalism would find that challenge preferable to any concession on either of the two points. Indeed, it would actively insist on a position of 'mysterious fallenness'. For 'evil offers no purchase for reflection; it is wholly frictionless to thought'; 'it cannot be thought at all' (Mathewes, *Evil and the Augustinian Tradition*, 237). A theological vitalism will take as its starting point that 'the basic character of the world is found in a love that cannot be explained from the perspective of the world' (Mathewes, *Evil and the Augustinian Tradition*, 237). It would defend and apply an account of nature's evil as precisely *un*-natural, and of God as the judge of all the living.

50. Milbank poses the question: 'the awareness of dynamic processes within nature is greatly increased by the discovery of biological evolution, which renders life a more unstable and violence-dominated process. Within a post-evolutionary climate, the traditional question of theodicy becomes much intensified: what can justify this endemic *agon* within life itself[?]' ('Sophiology', 6). In the context of discussing Bulgakov's response to evil in the natural world, he says: 'For Bulgakov, this collective and historical aspect of fall and salvation extended also to the natural world.' Uncompromisingly and rightly, citing *Wisdom* 1.13, 'God made not death', he insisted that for the Wisdom literature and then clearly for the New Testament death is no part of the original divine order. In league with death and

It is just here that Christian orthodoxy sees in Jonas what it needs to say about nature, while immeasurably expanding it. In Jonas's recognition that life generates value, that it necessitates a notion of the good, is articulated the pervasiveness of the moral. This is the Christian truth of the involvement of all nature in the drama of salvation: there is no non-moral nature, no nature to which notions of 'good' and 'evil' do not in some way apply. In Jonas's account of the organism is expressed the recognition of every creature as a moral object; as Milbank says, the moral intrudes everywhere there is desire.[51] 'Natural' events are not ones we witness as outsiders, comfortably certain that they occur in a moral vacuum. We are permitted no indifference. Natural events participate in some way in the drama of innocence and guilt, peace and violence, which characterize reality as such. This makes profound sense of our ineliminable tendency to describe nature in moral terms: the cuckoo mother killing the chicks of the 'robbed' parents by ejecting them from the 'stolen' nest. This is not a carte blanche for whatever type of anthropomorphization we happen to favour. It is simply an affirmation of the fact that we do not experience nature as morally vacuous. That we, as human observers, do not experience nature as an amoral reality is largely ignored by naturalistic accounts (it is hived off as an automatic 'sympathy' or 'biophilia'). Our distress at the innocent suffering of animals, the waste and destruction wrought by nature's multiple upheavals, is a spontaneous recognition of the moral solidarity of the living, however complex it is to parse that solidarity.

The point is that a theological vitalism, which recognizes life as coterminous with mind, equips us to frame the moral and intellectual character of life as such. This opens the possibility of understanding how it could be that an estrangement of intellectual being from God could influence the whole natural order in what otherwise appears an incomprehensibly total way. The solidarity of life in inwardness, freedom and self-transcendence allows the affirmation of its solidarity in sin and in redemption: non-human creatures are equally agents and victims of sin and participants in the drama of salvation (as some Christian literature recognizes).[52] Just as every organism is a perpetrator, direct or indirect, of the

---

in opposition to life, are 'blind necessity, unintelligible raging elements' besides 'deadened mechanism, iron fate' ('Sophiology', 39, quoting Bulgakov, *Philosophy of Economy: The World as Household*, trans. Catherine Evtuhov (New Haven: Yale University Press, 2000), 68–76). Milbank goes on to speculate that since 'Creation only subsists through hypostatic beings, angels and humans . . . when they refuse the supreme gift of intellectual life, all life falters and is impaired' ('Sophiology', 40).

51. *TST*, 361.

52. Rowan Williams explores this dimension of C. S. Lewis's thought in *The Lion's World* (Oxford: Oxford University Press, 2012). Commenting on the role of animals in the Narnia Chronicles, Williams asks: '[W]hat if you had to make conversation with nonhuman partners? To make friends with them?' (26). It would mean at least that 'the moral world is not exclusively human and that obligations and relationships are not restricted to intra-human affairs' (22). Lewis's use of animal players shows how 'the key role of human beings

deaths of others, so every organism is a victim of others' need to live. This is already evident in the human sphere; a theological vitalism illuminates it everywhere in the world of life.

We have arrived at a curious inversion of Jonas's philosophical biology. Death and conflict are not elided in the Christian narration of the world of life but given even greater prominence, precisely as scandalous perversions of the ontological priority of life; because they are not allowed to be hermeneutically determinative, their status as intruders whose presence cannot be accommodated is all the more serious. The fall will be articulated not simply as the interruption of life by death but the rendering of life perversely dependent on loss, waste and decay; the seeming necessity of evolutionary evils for the emergence of evolutionary values, and thus the apparent parasitism of good upon evil, will be articulated as the ultimate signature of evil itself. Indeed, a theological vitalism will perhaps regard this as its single most urgent task: to articulate how life could be so incomprehensibly disturbed and seemingly defeated in the biological world we inhabit.

Concluding Part III: Biology against secular reason

The philosophical biology of Hans Jonas illuminates the nature of the organism as ontologically and epistemically uncontainable. Attending to the concrete lives of organisms in time, as the sciences of life describe them in terms of Darwinism and metabolism, Jonas shows the organism as prophetic for ontology, overcoming metaphysical boundaries and witnessing against metaphysical dualisms and the nihilisms they sponsor. Jonas's patient analysis of biological 'facts' has the shape of a theological reading of finitude.

At the same time, this study has sought to show that the life of the organism, and the 'scientific' knowledge of it, cannot testify in this way as a free-floating 'given'. Jonas fails to establish the primacy of life he so urgently seeks, because he places it absolutely, and not merely contingently, under death. Remaining within a primarily dialectical paradigm, he cannot secure life beyond scientistic capture. Only the Christian narrative of creation and *eschaton*, and the analogical ontology expressing it, finds life to be what is ultimately real, and to be peace.

in the moral cosmos is only intelligible when we see that human beings are always already embedded in their relations with the non-human world and that their moral quality is utterly bound up with this. . . . To be invited to see trees and rivers as part of the 'people' of Narnia, and to have to ask what proper and respectful relations might be between a human and a talking beast is to be jolted out of a one-dimensional understanding of human uniqueness or human destiny under God. To be human is to be with the non-human world' (24–5). (Some Narnians mock Aslan for being a mere *Lion*. But Aslan is not embarrassed by his animality: 'Touch me. Smell me. Here are my paws, here is my tail, these are my whiskers. I am a true Beast' (C. S. Lewis, *The Chronicles of Narnia* (London: HarperCollins, 2011): 299.)

This study has called the view that Christian theology takes of life a 'theological vitalism'. It has argued that theological vitalism is a regard of life as prophetic for ontology; as epistemically uncontainable; as coincident with peace; and as ontologically ultimate. The first two proposals represent the hospitable recognition of Jonas's philosophical biology as truthfully theological; the second, prophetic disruptions of Jonas's philosophical biology as falsely theological. It has been suggested that such a vitalism is both continuous and discontinuous with previous vitalisms: continuous in its regard of life as an ultimate good, and in its embrace of life's defiance of conceptual capture; discontinuous in its disruption of the narratives of power, tensioned flux and negative unknowability which have typically characterized secular vitalisms.

This theological vitalism invites us to recognize a total solidarity of life.[53] It calls for a reverence for life as such, not merely human life, as a participation in the divine life, originating in and destined for divine peace. It shows a way to affirm

---

53. David Abram, *The Spell of the Sensuous: Perception and Language in a More Than Human World* (New York: Vintage Books, 2007), is a fine contemporary expression of this agenda. Abram draws on Merleau-Ponty's phenomenology, combined with extensive engagement with indigenous animistic traditions of Indonesia and elsewhere, to explore how human beings can resume a real communication with the 'more-than-human' world. Abram is dismayed at the idea of pristine 'interior' in the human subject, which he connects to 'the loss of our ancestral reciprocity with the animate earth. . . . [W]hen the generative earth is abruptly defined as a determinate object devoid of its own sensations and feelings, then the sense of a wild and multiplicitous otherness (in relation to which human existence has always oriented itself) must migrate, either into a supersensory heaven beyond the natural world, or else into the human skull itself – the only allowable refuge, in this world, for what is ineffable and unfathomable' (10). Abram operates in explicit criticism of Christian failures to comprehend a solidarity in the world of life (*Sensuous*, 8, 15, 94, 253–4) and takes a one-dimensional view of the tradition – though the theologian sympathetic to Milbank's genealogy will perhaps concede to the charge as far as much of Christian 'modernity' is concerned. Particularly striking in light of Pickstock's *After Writing* is Abram's critique of the alphabetization propagated hand in hand with Christian mission: 'Only as the written text began to speak would the voices of the forest, and of the river, begin to fade' (254).

The theologian would find much to 'disrupt' in Abram's approach. But a theological vitalism should be able to bring into its house of peace the sheer *communicativeness* of the living world that he eloquently witnesses to. His treatment of the theme is an exemplary instance of that 'making strange' which Milbank calls for, applied to the world of life; he emphasizes simultaneously our kinship with the 'more-than-human' world and its un-domesticable otherness.

An appreciation of the living qualities of landscape will also be important. Belden Lane, *The Solace of Fierce Landscapes* (Oxford: Oxford University Press, 2007), is an admirable call for Christians to recover a sense of the aliveness of place. So-called bioregionalism is an aspect of contemporary ecological ethics which calls for Christian theological attention (see, for example, Brian Campbell, 'The Power of Place', in *Grounding Religion: A Field*

the biological knowledge of organisms without placing this knowledge in an impossible 'outside' to theology, manifesting the two moments of judgement and welcome in Christian theology's approach to the sciences of life. In this way, the work has comprehended theology, science and life and defended a regard of each as possessing the highest dignity.

Guide to the Study of Religion and Ecology, ed. Whitney Bauman, Richard Bohannon and Kevin O'Brien (Oxford: Routledge, 2017), 94–114).

CONCLUSION

THEOLOGY, SCIENCE AND LIFE

Prevailing conceptions of 'life' have a profound influence on culture, politics and human self-image. They dominate public and scientific discourse about nature, ecology, environment and the meaning of human being. To be prophets to this age, Christians must know how to tell their story as decisive for all discourse about life. Otherwise Christianity appears as a set of isolable values or beliefs which, having no compelling account of what life is, awaits the authoritative deliverances of the sciences, to which are added its own pale colourings of ethical or religious sentiment. But Christian theology does not ice a cake which is first made by the sciences.

This book opened with the posing of a question: Can theology be 'master' even of biology in the twenty-first century? It has answered this question with a heavily qualified 'yes' – a 'yes' which evacuates that 'mastery' of any dominating or coercive power, giving that term a content which is no more and no less than peace. Theology's unique competence is to narrate Christianity's peace, again and again, in all the voices of human knowledge.

The relation of theology to the disciplines has been approached from both sides. On the one hand, every discipline is poetic and conjectural in its constitution. Each one is implicitly theological, and so the theologian is obliged to attend generously to its deliverances. On the other, Christian theology, which narrates the being of every creature as uncoerced and unrivalrous gift, questions all violent and competitive ontologies, and any disciplines founded on them. Theological narration saves difference from nihilistic conflict and dissolution by narrating it in terms of the transcendent harmony of infinitely realized difference which is God. Far from collapsing disciplinary difference into itself, theology conducts a 'making strange' in which the peculiarity of a discourse and its objects is protected and enhanced.

Organic life testifies to the impossibility of self-contained immanence and secular reason. Biology shows itself as always intrinsically theological; and theology shows itself as a biology, a narrative reasoning about life which cannot be confined to 'religious' or 'transcendent' subject matter. Christian theology discerns, with Hans Jonas, an ontological irreducibility of life in biology's knowledge of it and sees in biological 'facts' an inwardness, freedom, subjectivity and purposiveness inherent in organismic existence. Organic life tells against ontological dualisms, which sponsor nihilism by locating meaning in an 'elsewhere' which finally evaporates into nothing. Theology 'will not suppress the testimony of life'[1] but finds in every organism the witness to its own story of being. At the same time, telling the story of life's free creation in innocence, its subjection to violence and death, and its restoration to the peace of God, Christian theology prophetically announces life's final reality over death and its coincidence with peace.

I have called these considerations a 'theological vitalism', a usage which intends to disrupt the mystifying spiritualisms and tensioned flux which characterize the history of that term, inflecting it fully with the content of Christianity's own narrative. A *theological* vitalism proclaims not a negative unknowability of life, nor an ontologized struggle for survival in which death and conflict define what life is, but the profoundest affirmation that is possible: as a participation in the life of God, life is finally real and fundamentally peaceful. In such a vitalism, knowledge of life 'from below' and 'from above' is inextricable, appearing indistinguishably from the organism itself and from the Christian *mythos*.

Where does all this leave the practice of Christian theology, with whose scope this book opened? The theologian has come to rest rather far from her original starting place in Milbank's claim for theology's mastery. In a certain sense, she ends up not with 'mastery' but a curious lack thereof. Rather than 'lording it' over the disciplines, she ends up having no specialism 'of her own', no peculiar field of competence over which she can claim an expert's authority.

There is a salutary lesson in modern theology's lamented loss of confidence: it is inescapably an oddity in the contemporary university and intellectual scene, which has rightly, if in perversely triumphal manner, spotted that theologians are not specialists in anything.[2] The error is to assume that the only alternative status for theology is that it is simply a 'fantasising about the void'.[3] For though this lack of specific competence may seem to be bad news for 'professional' theologians, that impression is based on the mistaken conception that theology has somehow 'lost' the ground it used justly to occupy. For theology to occupy 'a' ground was always a travesty of its vocation. The authority 'left to' theologians remains most comprehensive authority of all: the narration of divine peace. This is a project which always proceeds by speaking of creatures in the right way, telling the right stories about creatures, and is 'never unambiguous'.[4]

---

1. *Phenomenon*, 1.

2. Cf. Richard Dawkins' comment: 'I'm not an expert in "theology". There's nothing in "theology" to be expert about', https://twitter.com/richarddawkins/status /631856937127256064, accessed 3 February 2016); elsewhere Dawkins quotes Thomas Jefferson: '[A] professorship of Theology should have no place in our institution', quoted in Gary Keogh, *Reading Richard Dawkins: A Theological Dialogue with New Atheism* (Minneapolis: Fortress Press, 2014), 24.

3. Milbank, 'Theology and the Economy of the Sciences', 39.

4. Milbank, *WMS*, 3. *In principle* this is the remit of any Christian; indeed, perhaps the most 'well-qualified' person for this task is the saint (John Chryssavgis, ed., *Speaking the*

To be a 'theologian' is therefore to assume the daunting responsibility of becoming fluent in multiple discourses and disciplines.[5] Practically, this is surely best accomplished by undertaking to gain credible proficiency in one discipline above all. The natural sciences should claim the apprenticeship of more theologians, and theologians should more commonly pursue higher qualifications in natural science than they presently do. And if the thesis defended here can be made to stand, life science should claim a lion's share, for it is 'life' that tells the meaning of the whole.[6] It should not need saying that this is absolutely *not* the same imperative as that frequently intended by those who call for 'religious people' to 'listen more' to scientists, implying by that a slavish fawning of theology over science in which theologians scamper to keep up with the latest scientific research and hastily manoeuvre to agree with it. Christian theology recognizes no 'valid points of view outside the theological'.[7]

This book has deliberately been framed in the form of a proposal, rather than a watertight 'case' which triumphantly sweeps all objections before it. This approach was elected not only as a gesture of humility and a realistic assessment of the possibilities of a single volume. More fundamentally, it is an attempt, faltering no doubt, to enact what has been defended: speaking in the voices of the disciplines, Christian theology does not shut down or silence alternative voices and conducts no unimpeachable dialectic demonstration. It is an unfinishable project of generous attention to creatures, an enquiry which acknowledges no boundaries, no starting point and no finishing point. In that enquiry, that which is alone indispensable is alone insisted upon: the peace of God as the final truth and the ultimate reality.

I stipulated at the start of the book that I am unsure whether Milbank's position is the 'right' one, but that I would adopt a deliberately sympathetic approach to bring out the distinctive strength and character of his approach. The intention was selectively to use Milbank in a specific way, rather than to establish a thesis about him per se. The critique of Milbank has therefore been a partial one. To interrogate him more comprehensively and externally is an equally important task. Certain internal tensions in Milbank's account of reason beg scrutiny, particularly the relationship of language to the real, for although Milbank seems to hold to their complete convergence, he at the same time recognizes a resistance which

---

Truth in Love: Theological and Spiritual Exhortations of Ecumenical Patriarch Bartholomew (New York: Fordham University Press, 2011), 362).

5. Not even mentioning the spiritual obligations they assume; see, for example, Gavin D'Costa, 'On Cultivating the Disciplined Habits of a Love Affair, *Or* on How to do Theology on Your Knees', *New Blackfriars* 79, no. 925 (1998): 116–36.

6. And also, pragmatically, because biotechnology is likely increasingly to dominate human meanings and decisions in developed societies. The gravity of the questions it poses cannot be overstated. The engagement that is required will be ineffective unless theologians, and Christians generally, more confidently tell their *own* story of life in the mode of life science itself.

7. Milbank, 'Radical Orthodoxy: Twenty-Four Theses', thesis 5.

meets our narratives, a constraining orientation to something 'beyond'. Does he successfully unite his 'theological objectivism' with his historicist relativism? As Milbank himself indicates, it is Blondel who holds the key to this union. Whether Blondel can bear that weight calls for further study.

The engagement with biological science represented here is an invitation to a larger project of patient theological listening to, and robust interrogation of, contemporary life science. Far from being the 'soft' science, reducible to physics and chemistry, in the vision outlined in this book biology recovers the integrity of its object and becomes a discourse about reality itself.[8] The capture of the 'theology-biology' conversation by narrow apologetic questions to do with design and evolution misses a deeper opportunity to look searchingly at biology's world-picture and to ask how theology is already operating there.

I have attempted only the most speculative outline of a theological vitalism. The notion requires extensive unpacking and scrutiny. It must be parsed in the terms of Christian tradition, with particular attention paid to metaphysics and the doctrine of God, especially pneumatology; it is above all as *Vivificantem* that Christians profess the Holy Spirit.[9] Most fundamental would be a scriptural exegesis,

---

8. It may seem that there must be less metaphysically expensive ways of 'saving' biology's standing as a discipline, and indeed most biologists, although physicalists, are not reductionists in the sense of thinking their science is identical to physics and chemistry. But Alex Rosenberg is surely right in arguing that physicalism ultimately arrives at a total reign of reductionism (*Darwinian Reductionism: Or, How to Stop Worrying and Love Molecular Biology* (Chicago: University of Chicago Press, 2006). (For Rosenberg, however, this does not entail the dissolution of biology as a discipline, for biological systems are so complex that the reduction probably cannot be conceptually achieved; it simply means that biology is the most 'instrumental', the least 'real', of the natural sciences; Rosenberg, *Instrumental Biology*.) As one of Rosenberg's reviewers advises ruefully, the choice really is either physicalism or 'spookiness': 'Over the last twenty years and more, philosophers and theoretical biologists have built an antireductionist consensus about biology. We have thought that biology is autonomous without being spooky. While biological systems are built from chemical ones, biological facts are not just physical facts, and biological explanations cannot be replaced by physical and chemical ones. . . . [But Rosenberg] argues that we can show the paradigm facts of biology – evolution and development – are built from the chemical and physical, and reduce to them. Moreover, he argues, unpleasantly plausibly, that defenders of the consensus must slip one way or the other: into spookiness about the biological, or into a reduction program for the biological. People like me have no middle way. Bugger' (Kim Sterelny, review of Rosenberg, *Darwinian Reductionism*).

Certain philosophers of science may prove important partners here such as Evan Thompson, *Mind in Life*, or Thomas Nagel, *Mind and Cosmos* (Oxford: Oxford University Press, 2012).

9. A Mariological dimension also calls for exploration, since it is Eve who is 'the mother of all living' (Genesis 3.20, NRSV).

examining how the term 'life' functions, semantically and philosophically, as the subject of salvation history as a whole and in relation to the person of Christ.

Perhaps most importantly of all, the implications for Christian practice ought to be dramatic. If there is a deep ontological continuity in organic life, the casual disregard which too often characterizes the human relation to the non-human, whether organism or ecosystem, is more than simply senseless self-destruction. It is an offence against the order of things, a blasphemy against the life in which all life participates.[10] The Christian rehearsal of tiringly univocal conceptions of life, as in 'the sanctity of life' and 'the culture of life', is not good enough. 'Life' must be allowed a purchase beyond the human. Without the attribution of an intrinsic dignity to the organic per se, it is not just the existence of the human, but her value, that is inescapably threatened. To elevate the human by demoting the non-human is not just moral idiocy; it is also philosophical stupidity. It is time to stop defining the importance of the human by using the non-human as negative traction. Created value is not a zero-sum game.

It may be that the vistas indicated in this short conclusion, and this book itself, appear grandiose and overweening, not to say unrealistic. What are the chances that 'the public square' will ever take such reflections remotely seriously? Of the many failings of this study, I take complete and regretful ownership. But for its scope and aspiration, apology would be misplaced. The grandeur of Christian theology seems ludicrous only because its falsity is generally assumed. If true, its project, no matter how demanding, is neither arrogant nor excessive. It is simply fitting to the story its vocation is ceaselessly to tell.

This text can perhaps only be rightly completed by acknowledgement of the almost entire absence from its pages of its only really essential player: the person of Jesus himself. He features little in *Theology and Social Theory*, despite the template for its narrative and rhetoric that his life is.[11] To make his person explicit in relation to the concerns set forth here is an important task for future projects such as I allude to in this conclusion. But this work, albeit implicitly, has always been about him. For he was 'in the beginning' and 'in him was life'.

10. A theological vitalism would particularly draw attention to the lives of plants, pitifully ignored by philosophy and theology alike, but whose distinctive intelligence is now being recognized (Tony Trewavas, 'Plant Intelligence: An Overview', *BioScience* 66, no. 7 (2016): 542–51. See also Stefano Mancuso and Alessandro Viola, *Brilliant Green: The Surprising History and Science of Plant Intelligence* (Washington: Island Press, 2016).

11. A fact not missed by critics; for example, Coles, 'Storied Others and Possibilities of *Caritas*', 350, note 5.

BIBLIOGRAPHY

Abram, David. *The Spell of the Sensuous: Perception and Language in a More Than Human World*. New York: Vintage Books, 2007.

Arbib, Michael and Mary Hesse, eds. *The Construction of Reality*. Cambridge: Cambridge University Press, 1986.

Ayala, Francisco, and Robert Arp, eds. *Contemporary Debates in Philosophy of Biology*. Contemporary Debates in Philosophy. Oxford: Wiley-Blackwell, 2010.

Barnes, Stephen. 'Reconciling Augustine and Aquinas: An Introduction to Radical Orthodoxy's Postmodern Theology'. *Studia Universitatis Babes-Bolyai, Theologica Catholica Latina* 1 (2009): 15–26.

Bauerschmidt, Frederick. 'The Word Made Speculative? John Milbank's Christological Poetics'. *Modern Theology* 15 (1999): 417–32.

Baum, Gregory. *Essays in Critical Theology*. Kansas City: Sheed and Ward, 1994.

Beilik-Robinson, Agata. 'Taking Life Out of Nature: Jewish Messianic Vitalism and the Problem of Denaturalisation'. In *Radical Orthodoxy: Annual Review I*, edited by Neil Turnbull, 180–98. Eugene, OR: Wipf & Stock, 2012.

Bennett, Jane. *Vibrant Matter: A Political Ecology of Things*. Durham, NC: Duke University Press, 2010.

Blanchette, Oliva. 'Blondel's Original Philosophy of the Supernatural'. *Revista Portuguesa di Filosofia* 49, no. 3 (1993): 413–44.

Blanchette, Oliva. *Maurice Blondel: A Philosophical Life*. Grand Rapids, MI: Eerdmans, 2010.

Blanchette, Oliva. 'Rationale for a Catholic Philosophy'. *Revista Portuguesa di Filosofia* 60, no. 2 (2004): 329–48.

Blondel, Maurice. *L'Action, Essay on a Critique of Life and a Science of Practice*. Translated by Oliva Blanchette. Notre Dame, IN: University of Notre Dame Press, 1984.

Boersma, Hans. 'Radical Orthodoxy and the Rejection of Boundaries'. *Pro Ecclesia* 15, no. 4 (2006): 418–47.

Boermsa, Hans. 'Theology as Queen of Hospitality'. *EQ* 79, no. 4 (2007): 291–310.

Boyer, Pascal. *Religion Explained: The Evolutionary Origins of Religious Thought*. New York: Basic Books, 2001.

Brachtendorf, Johannes. 'Orthodoxy without Augustine: A Response to Michael Hanby's *Augustine and Modernity*'. *Ars Disputandi* 7 (2007): 297–304.

Brooke, John Hedley, and Geoffrey Cantor. *Reconstructing Nature*. Oxford: Oxford University Press, 1998.

Brown, Malcolm. *After the Market: Economics, Moral Agreement and the Churches' Mission*. Oxford: Peter Lang, 2004.

Bulgakov, Sergei. *Philosophy of Economy: The World as Household*. Translated by Catherine Evtuhov. New Haven, CT: Yale University Press, 2000.

Burwick, Frederick and Paul Douglass, eds. *The Crisis in Modernism: Bergson and the Vitalist Controversy*. Cambridge: Cambridge University Press, 1992.

Caeymaux, Florence. 'The Comprehensive Meaning of Life in Bergson'. In *The Science, Politics and Ontology of Life-Philosophy*, edited by Scott Campbell and Paul Bruno, 47–64. London: Bloomsbury, 2013.

Caldecott, Stratford. 'Is Life A Transcendental?' *Radical Orthodoxy: Theology, Philosophy, Politics* 1 (August 2012): 188–200.

Campbell, Brian. 'The Power of Place'. In *Grounding Religion: A Field Guide to the Study of Religion and Ecology*, edited by Whitney Bauman, Richard Bohannon and Kevin O'Brien, 94–114. Oxford: Routledge, 2017.

Campbell, Scott, and Paul Bruno, eds. *The Science, Politics and Ontology of Life-Philosophy*. London: Bloomsbury, 2013.

Castree, Noel. *Making Sense of Nature*. Oxford: Routledge, 2013.

Chryssavgis, John, ed. *Speaking the Truth in Love: Theological and Spiritual Exhortations of Ecumenical Patriarch Bartholomew*. New York: Fordham University Press, 2011.

Clayton, Philip and Zachary Simpson, eds. *Adventures in the Spirit: God, World and Divine Action*. Minneapolis: Fortress Press, 2008.

Coakley, Sarah. Gifford Lectures 2012, 'Sacrifice Regained: Evolution, Cooperation and God'. http://www.giffordlectures.org/lectures/sacrifice-regained-evolution-cooperation -and-god, accessed 27 June 2017.

Conway-Morris, Simon. *The Deep Structure of Biology: Is Convergence Sufficiently Ubiquitous to Give a Directional Signal?* Pennsylvania: Templeton Foundation Press, 2008.

Cooper, Gregory. *The Science of the Struggle for Existence: On the Foundations of Ecology*. Cambridge: Cambridge University Press, 2003.

Cox, Christoph. *Nietszche: Naturalism and Interpretation*. Berkeley, CA: University of California Press, 1999.

Crick, Francis. *Of Molecules and Men*. Seattle: University of Washington Press, 1966.

Cunningham, Conor. *Darwin's Pious Idea: Why the Ultra-Darwinists and Creationists Both Get It Wrong*. Grand Rapids, MI: Eerdmans, 2005.

Cunningham, Conor. 'Natura Pura, the Invention of the AntiChrist: A Week With No Sabbath'. *Communio* 37 (2010): 243–54.

Cunningham, Conor. 'Trying My Very Best to Believe Darwin, or, The Supernaturalistic Fallacy: From Is to Nought'. In *Belief and Metaphysics*, edited by Conor Cunningham and Peter Candler, 100–40. London: SCM, 2007.

D'Costa, Gavin. 'On Cultivating the Disciplined Habits of a Love Affair, *Or* on How to do Theology on Your Knees'. *New Blackfriars* 79, no. 925 (1998): 116–36.

D'Costa, Gavin. *Theology in the Public Square: Church, Academy and Nation*. Oxford: Blackwell, 2005.

Daniels, John. 'Not the Whole Story: Another Response to John Milbank's *Theology and Social Theory*, Part I'. *New Blackfriars* 82 (2001): 188–96.

Daniels, John. 'Not the Whole Story: Another Response to John Milbank's *Theology and Social Theory*, Part II'. *New Blackfriars* 82 (2001): 224–40.

Dawkins, Richard. 'The Descent of Edward Wilson'. Review of *The Social Conquest of Earth*, by E. O. Wilson. *Prospect*, June 2012. http://www.prospectmagazine.co.uk/ magazine/edward-wilson-social- conquest-earth-evolutionary-errors-origin species, accessed 1 February 2017.

De Lubac, Henri. *The Mystery of the Supernatural*. Translated by Rosemary Sheed. New York: Crossroad, 1998.

De Lubac, Henri. *Theological Fragments*. Translated by Rebecca Howell Balinski. San Francisco: Ignatius, 1989.

De Lubac, Henri. *Theology in History*. Translated by Anne Englund Nash. San Francisco: Ignatius, 1996.

De Marko, Donald and Benjamin Wiker. *Architects of the Culture of Death*. San Francisco: Ignatius, 2004.

Deane-Drummond, Celia. 'Who on Earth Is Jesus Christ? Plumbing the Depths of Deep Incarnation'. In *Christian Faith and the Earth: Current Paths and Emerging Horizons in Ecotheology*, edited by Celia Deane-Drummond, Denis Edwards, Sigurd Bergmann and Ernst Conradie, 31–50. London: Bloomsbury, 2014.

Deane-Drummond, Celia, Denis Edwards, Sigurd Bergmann and Ernst Conradie, eds. *Celia Christian Faith and the Earth: Current Paths and Emerging Horizons in Ecotheology*. London: Bloomsbury, 2014.

Dennett, Daniel. *From Bacteria to Bach and Back: The Evolution of Minds*. London: Allen Lane, 2017.

Depew, David and Bruce Weber. *Darwinism Evolving: Systems Dynamics and the Genealogy of Natural Selection*. Cambridge, MA: MIT Press, 1997.

Dew, James. *Science as the Ancilla Theologiae: A Critical Assessment of Alister E. McGrath's Scientific Theology from an Evangelical Philosophical/Theological Perspective*. PhD diss., Southeastern Baptist Theological Seminary, 2008.

Dewan, Lawrence. 'On Milbank and Pickstock's *Truth in Aquinas'*. *Nova et Vetera* 1, no. 1 (2003): 199–212.

Di Paolo, Ezequiel. 'Hans Jonas, The Phenomenon of Life'. http://users.sussex.ac.uk/~ezequiel/dipaolo-jonas.pdf, accessed 5 January 2016.

Dilley, Stephen. 'Nothing in Biology Makes Sense Except in Light of Theology?' *Studies in History and Philosophy of Biological and Biomedical Sciences* 44 (2013): 774–86.

Doak, Mary. 'A Pragmatism Without Plurality? John Milbank's "Pragmatic" New Christendom'. *Contemporary Pragmatism* 1, no. 2 (2004): 123–35.

Donnelley, Strachan. 'Bioethical Troubles: Animal Individuals and Human Organisms'. *The Hastings Centre Report* 25 (1995): 21–9.

Donnelley, Strachan. 'Hans Jonas, the Philosophy of Nature, and the Ethics of Responsibility'. *Social Research* 56 (1989): 635–57.

Driesch, Hans. *The History & Theory of Vitalism*. Translated by C. K. Ogden. London: Macmillan, 1914.

Dupré, Louis. *Passage to Modernity: An Essay in the Hermeneutics of Nature and Culture*. New Haven, CT: Yale University Press, 1993.

Edwards, Denis. *Partaking of God: Trinity, Evolution and Ecology*. Collegeville, MN: Liturgical, 2014.

Endean, Philip. *Karl Rahner and Ignatian Spirituality*. Oxford: Oxford University Press, 2001.

English, Adam. '"Science Cannot Stop With Science": Maurice Blondel and the Sciences'. *Journal of the History of Ideas* 69, no. 2 (2008): 269–92.

Evernden, Neil. *The Social Creation of Nature*. Baltimore: John Hopkins University Press, 1992.

Ferré, Frederick. 'On Making Persons: Philosophy of Nature and Ethics'. In *The Legacy of Hans Jonas: Judaism and the Philosophy of Life*, edited by Hava Tirosh-Samuelson and Christian Wiese, 493–502. Boston: Brill, 2008.

Flanagan, Kieran. *The Enchantment of Sociology: A Study of Theology and Culture*. London: Macmillan, 1996.

Flanagan, Kieran. 'Sublime Policing: Sociology and Milbank's City of God'. *New Blackfriars* 73 (1992): 333–40.

Flanagan, Kieran and Peter Jupp, eds. *Postmodernity, Sociology and Religion*. London: Macmillan, 1996.

Foster, David and Joseph Koterski, eds. *Two Wings of Catholic Thought: Essays on Fides et Ratio*. Washington, DC: Catholic University of America Press, 2003.

Fraser, Mariam, Sarah Kember and Celia Lury, eds. *Inventive Life: Approaches to the New Vitalism*. London: Sage, 2006.

Gallie, Walter. 'Essentially Contested Concepts'. *Proceedings of the Aristotelian Society* 56, no. 2 (1956): 167–98.

Gilbert, Scott and Sahotra Sarkar. 'Embracing Complexity: Organicism for the 21st Century'. *Developmental Dynamics* 219 (2000): 1–9.

Gould, Stephen Jay. *Rocks of Ages: Science and Religion in the Fullness of Life*. New York: Ballantine, 1999.

Greco, Monica. 'On the Vitality of Vitalism'. *Theory, Culture & Society* 22 (2005): 15–27.

Grumett, David. *De Lubac: A Guide for the Perplexed*. London: Bloomsbury, 2007.

Grummett, David. 'Radical Orthodoxy'. www.research.ed.ac.uk/portal/files/14269984/radical_ orthodoxy.docx, accessed 9 May 2017.

Haffner, John. 'Post-Metaphysical Faith in the Philosophy of Charles Taylor'. MA Thesis, Queen's University Ontario, 1998.

Hanby, Michael. *Augustine and Modernity*. London: Routledge, 2003.

Hanby, Michael. *No God, No Science: Theology, Cosmology, Biology*. Oxford: Wiley-Blackwell, 2013.

Hankey, Wayne. 'Between and Beyond Augustine and Descartes: More Than a Source of the Self'. *Augustinian Studies* 32 (2001): 65–88.

Hankey, Wayne. 'The Postmodern Retrieval of Neoplatonism in Jean-Luc Marion and John Milbank and the Origins of Western Subjectivity in Augustine and Eriugena'. *Hermathena* 165 (1998): 9–70.

Hankey, Wayne. 'Why Philosophy Abides for Aquinas'. *Heythorp Journal* 42, no. 3 (2001): 329–48.

Hankey, Wayne and Douglas Hedley, eds. *Deconstructing Radical Orthodoxy: Postmodern Theology, Rhetoric and Truth*. Aldershot: Ashgate, 2005.

Haraway, Donna. *Modest–Witness@Second–Millennium.FemaleMan–Meets–OncoMouse: Feminism and Technoscience*. London: Routledge, 1997.

Haraway, Donna. *Simians, Cyborgs, and Women: The Reinvention of Nature*. London: Free Association Books, 1991.

Hart, David. *The Doors of the Sea: Where Was God in the Tsunami?* Grand Rapids, MI: Eerdmans, 2011.

Hart, David. 'Of Hills, Brooks, Standing Lakes and Groves . . . '. http://www.firstthings.com/web- exclusives/2010/10/hellipof-hills-brooks-standing-lakes-and-groveshellip, accessed 17 February 2016.

Hauerwas, Stanley. 'On Keeping Theological Ethics Theological'. In *Against the Nations: War and Survival in a Liberal Society*, edited by Stanley Hauerwas, Chapter 2. Notre Dame, IN: University of Notre Dame Press, 1992.

Hauerwas, Stanley. *Resident Aliens: Life in the Christian Colony*. Nashville: Abingdon, 2014.

Haught, John. *Deeper Than Darwin: The Prospect for Religion in an Age of Evolution*. Cambridge, MA: Westview, 2003.

Hedley, Douglas. 'Should Divinity Overcome Metaphysics? Reflections on John Milbank's Theology and Social Theory and Confessions of a Cambridge Platonist'. *Journal of Religion* 80, no. 2 (2000): 271–98.

Hein, Hilde. 'The Endurance of the Mechanism-Vitalism Controversy'. *Journal of the History of Biology* 5 (1972): 155–88.

Hein, Hilde. 'Mechanism and Vitalism as Meta-Theoretical Commitments'. *Philosophical Forum* 1 (1968): 185–205.

Hemming, Laurence. 'Quod Impossible Est! Aquinas and Radical Orthodoxy'. In *Radical Orthodoxy? — A Catholic Enquiry*, edited by Laurence Hemming, 76–93. Aldershot: Ashgate, 2000.

Hemming, Laurence. 'Radical Orthodoxy's Appeal to Catholic Scholarship'. In *Radical Orthodoxy? — A Catholic Enquiry*, edited by Laurence Hemming, 76–93. Aldershot: Ashgate, 2000.

Henning, Brian and Adam Scarfe, eds. *Beyond Mechanism: Putting Life Back Into Biology*. Lanham, MD: Lexington Books, 2013.

Henrix, Hans. 'Powerlessness of God? A Critical Appraisal of Hans Jonas's Idea of God After Auschwitz'. http://www.jcrelations.net/Powerlessness_of_God A_Critical_Appr aisal_of_Hans_Jonass_Idea_of_God_after_A.2198.0.html, accessed 10 January 2016.

Henry, Michel. *I Am The Truth: Toward a Philosophy of Christianity*. Translated by Susan Emanuel. Stanford, CA: Stanford University Press, 2003.

Herdt, Jennifer. 'Alasdair MacIntyre's "Rationality of Traditions" and Tradition-Transcendental Standards of Justification'. *Journal of Religion* 78, no. 4 (1998): 524–46.

Hittinger, Russell. 'The Coherence of the Four Basic Themes of Catholic Social Doctrine: An Interpretation'. In *Pursuing the Common Good: How Solidarity and Subsidiarity Can Work Together*, Pontifical Academy of Social Sciences, *Acta* 14. Vatican City, 2008.

Hollerich, Michael. 'John Milbank, Augustine, and the "Secular"'. *Augustinian Studies* 30 (1999): 311–22.

Hollon, Bryan. *Everything Is Sacred: Scriptural Exegesis in the Political Theology of Henri De Lubac*. Eugene, OR: Cascade Books, 2009.

Horan, Daniel. *Postmodernity and Univocity: A Critical Account of Radical Orthodoxy and John Duns Scotus*. Minneapolis: Fortress Press, 2014.

Hull, David and Michael Ruse, eds. *The Cambridge Companion to Philosophy of Biology*. Cambridge: Cambridge University Press, 2007.

Huttinga, Wolter. *Participation and Communicability: Herman Bavinck and John Milbank on the Relation Between God and the World*. Amsterdam: Buijten et Schipperheijn Motief, 2014.

Hyman, Gavin. *The Predicament of Postmodern Theology: Radical Orthodoxy or Nihilist Textualism?* London: Westminster John Knox Press, 2001.

Insole, Christopher. 'Against Radical Orthodoxy: The Dangers of Overcoming Political Liberalism'. *Modern Theology* 20 (2004): 213–41.

Janz, Paul. 'Radical Orthodoxy and the New Culture of Obscurantism'. *Modern Theology* 20 (2004): 363–405.

John Paul II. *Evangelium Vitae*. London: Catholic Truth Society, 1995.

Jonas, Hans. 'Change and Permanence: On the Possibility of Historical Understanding'. *Social Research* 38 (1971): 498–528.

Jonas, Hans. *The Gnostic Religion: The Message of the Alien God and the Beginnings of Christianity*. Boston, MA: Beacon Press, 2001.

Jonas, Hans. *The Imperative of Responsibility: In Search of an Ethics for the Technological Age*. Chicago: University of Chicago Press, 1985.

Jonas, Hans. *The Phenomenon of Life: Toward a Philosophical Biology*. Evanston, IL: Northwestern University Press, 2001.

Jones, Donna. *The Racial Discourses of Life Philosophy: Négritude, Vitalism, and Modernity.* New York: Columbia University Press, 2010.

Jonas, Hans. 'Responsibility Today: The Ethics of an Endangered Future'. *Social Research* 43, no. 1 (1974): 77–97.

Kaufman, David. 'One of The Most Relevant Thinkers You've Never Heard Of'. Review of *The Life and Thought of Hans Jonas Jewish Dimensions,* by Christian Wiese. *Forward, The Jewish Daily,* 17 October 2007. http://forward.com/articles/11826/one-of-most -relevant-thinkers-you-ve-never-heard/, accessed 2 February 2013.

Keogh, Gary. *Reading Richard Dawkins: A Theological Dialogue with New Atheism.* Minneapolis: Fortress Press, 2014.

Kerr, Fergus. 'Rescuing Girard's Argument?' *Modern Theology* 8, no. 4 (1992): 385–99.

Kerr, Fergus. 'Simplicity Itself: Milbank's Thesis'. *New Blackfriars* 73 (1992): 305–10.

Kucer, Peter. *Truth and Politics: A Theological Comparison of John Milbank and Benedict XVI.* Minneapolis: Fortress Press, 2014.

Lane, Belden. *The Solace of Fierce Landscapes.* Oxford: Oxford University Press, 2007.

Lash, Nicholas. 'Where Does Holy Teaching Leave Philosophy? Questions on Milbank's Aquinas'. *Modern Theology* 15, no. 4 (1999): 433–45.

Lazier, Benjamin. 'Overcoming Gnosticism: Hans Jonas, Hans Blumenberg, and the Legitimacy of the Natural World'. *Journal of the History of Ideas* 64 (2003): 619–37.

Levy, David. *Hans Jonas: The Integrity of Thinking.* Missouri: University of Missouri Press, 2002.

Lewis, Clive S. *The Chronicles of Narnia.* London: HarperCollins, 2011.

Logan, Pat. *Policing the Sublime: Tradition and Transformation. Report of a Seminar with John Milbank, 5–7 July 1995.* Anglican Association for Social Responsibility, 1995.

Long, Stephen. 'Radical Orthodoxy'. In *The Cambridge Companion to Postmodern Theology,* edited by Kevin J. Vanhoozer, 126–46. Cambridge: Cambridge University Press, 2003.

Lubarsky, Sandra. 'Jonas, Whitehead and the Problem of Power'. In *The Legacy of Hans Jonas: Judaism and the Philosophy of Life,* edited by Hava Tirosh-Samuelson and Christian Wiese, 397–418. Boston: Brill, 2008.

MacDonald, Paul. *Christian Theology and the Secular University.* Oxford: Routledge, 2017.

Mader, Mary-Beth. 'Modern Living and Vital Race: Foucault and the Science of Life'. *Foucault Studies* 12 (2011): 97–112.

Mahoney, Jack. 'Christianity in Evolution: An Exploration'. Public Lecture delivered at Gresham College, 1 December 2011. http://www.gresham.ac.uk/lectures-and-events/ christianity-in- evolution-an-exploration, accessed 17 March 2015.

Mahoney, Jack. *Christianity in Evolution: An Exploration.* Georgetown: Georgetown University Press, 2011.

Mancuso, Stefano and Alessandro Viola. *Brilliant Green: The Surprising History and Science of Plant Intelligence.* Washington, DC: Island Press, 2016.

Marenbon, John. 'Aquinas, Radical Orthodoxy and the Importance of Truth'. In *Deconstructing Radical Orthodoxy: Postmodern Theology, Rhetoric and Truth,* edited by Wayne Hankey and Douglas Hedley, 49–64. Burlington, VT: Ashgate, 2005.

Margolin, Ron. 'Hans Jonas and Secular Religiosity'. In *The Legacy of Hans Jonas: Judaism and the Philosophy of Life,* edited by Hava Tirosh-Samuelson and Christian Wiese, 231–58. Boston: Brill, 2008.

Markham, Ian. 'Postmodern Christian Traditionalism?' Review of *Theology and Social Theory: Beyond Secular Reason,* by John Milbank. *First Things,* January 1992. http://

www.firstthings.com/ article/1992/01/002-postmodern-christian-traditionalism, accessed 13 May 2016.

Martin, David, John Orme Mills and William S. F. Pickering, eds. *Sociology and Theology: Alliance and Conflict*. London: Harvest, 1980.

Melle, Ullrich. 'Responsibility and the Crisis of Technological Civilization: A Husserlian Meditation on Hans Jonas'. *Human Studies* 21 (1998): 321–42.

Milbank, John. 'Afterword: The Grandeur of Reason and the Perversity of Rationalism: Radical Orthodoxy's First Decade'. In *The Radical Orthodoxy Reader*, edited by John Milbank and Simon Oliver, 367–404. London: Routledge, 2009.

Milbank, John. *Beyond Secular Order: The Representation of Being and the Representation of the People*. Oxford: Wiley-Blackwell, 2014.

Milbank, John. 'Culture, Nature and Mediation'. http://blogs.ssrc.org/tif/2010/12/01/culture- nature-mediation/, accessed 6 June 2017.

Milbank, John. 'The Double Glory, or Paradox Versus Dialectics: On Not Quite Agreeing with Slavoj Žižek'. In *The Monstrosity of Christ: Paradox or Dialectic*, edited by Creston Davis, 110–234. Cambridge, MA: MIT Press, 2009.

Milbank, John. 'Enclaves, or Where is the Church?'. *New Blackfriars* (1992) 73: 341–52.

Milbank, John. 'The End of Dialogue'. In *Christian Uniqueness Reconsidered: The Myth of a Pluralistic Theology of Religions*, edited by Gavin D'Costa, 174–91. New York: Maryknoll, 1998.

Milbank, John. 'Faith, Reason and Imagination: The Study of Theology and Philosophy in the Twenty- First Century'. http://theologyphilosophycentre.co.uk/papers/Milbank_StudyofTheologyandPhilo sophyinthe21stCentury.pdf, accessed 24 June 2014.

Milbank, John. 'Fictioning Things: Gift and Narrative'. *Religion and Literature* 37 (2005): 1–35.

Milbank, John. 'The Future of Love: A Reading of Benedict XVI's Encyclical *Deus Caritas Est*'. In *The Future of Love: Essays in Political Theology*, edited by John Milbank, 364–70. Eugene, OR: Cascade Books, 2009.

Milbank, John. 'Hume Versus Kant: Faith, Reason and Feeling'. *Modern Theology* 27, no. 2 (2011): 276–97.

Milbank, John. 'Invocation of Clio'. *Journal of Religious Ethics* 33 (2005): 3–44.

Milbank, John. 'Life, or Gift and Glissando'. *Radical Orthodoxy: Theology, Philosophy, Politics*, 1 (2012): 121–51.

Milbank, John. 'The New Divide: Romantic Versus Classical Orthodoxy'. *Modern Theology* 26, no. 1 (2010): 26–38.

Milbank, John. 'Only Theology Saves Metaphysics: On the Modalities of Terror'. http://www.theologyphilosophycentre.co.uk/papers/Milbank_OnlyTheologySavesMe taphysics.pdf, accessed 11 June 2016.

Milbank, John. '"Postmodern Critical Augustinianism": A Short Summa in Forty-Two Responses to Unasked Questions'. In *The Radical Orthodoxy Reader*, edited by John Milbank and Simon Oliver, 49–61. London: Routledge, 2009.

Milbank, John. 'The Programme of Radical Orthodoxy'. In *Radical Orthodoxy? — A Catholic Enquiry*, edited by Laurence Hemming, 33–45. Aldershot: Ashgate, 2000.

Milbank, John. 'Radical Orthodoxy: Twenty-Four Theses'. In *Radical Orthodoxy? — A Catholic Enquiry*, edited by Laurence Hemming, 33–45. Aldershot: Ashgate, 2000.

Milbank, John. *The Religious Dimension in the Thought of Giambattista Vico, 1668-1744*. Lewiston, NY: Edwin Mellen Press, 1991-2.

Milbank, John. 'Sophiology and Theurgy: The New Theological Horizon'. http://theologyphilosophy centre.co.uk/papers/Milbank_SophiologyTheurgy.pdf, accessed 12 March 2015.

Milbank, John. 'The Soul of Reciprocity Part One: Reciprocity Refused'. *Modern Theology* 17, no. 3 (2001): 335–91.

Milbank, John. 'The Soul of Reciprocity Part Two: Reciprocity Granted'. *Modern Theology* 17, no. 4 (2001): 485–507.

Milbank, John. 'Stanton Lecture 2: Immanence and Life'. http://theologyphilosophycentre.co.uk/papers/Milbank_Stanton Lecture2.pdf, accessed 8 June 2016.

Milbank, John. 'Stanton Lecture 5: Participated Transcendence Reconceived' http://theologyphilo sophycentre.co.uk/papers/Milbank_StantonLecture5.pdf, accessed June 8 2015.

Milbank, John. 'Stanton Lecture 6: The Habit of Reason'. http://theologyphilosophycentre.co.uk/papers/Milbank_ StantonLecture6.pdf, accessed 20 May 2014.

Milbank, John. 'Stanton Lecture 8: The Surprise of the Imagined'. http://theologyphilosophycentre.co.uk/papers/Milbank_StantonLecture8.pdf, accessed 12 March 2015.

Milbank, John. *The Suspended Middle: Henri de Lubac and the Debate Concerning the Supernatural*. Grand Rapids, MI: Eerdmans, 2005.

Milbank, John. 'The Theological Critique of Philosophy in Hamann and Jacobi'. In *Radical Orthodoxy: A New Theology*, edited by John Milbank, Catherine Pickstock and Graham Ward, 21–37. London: Routledge, 1999.

Milbank, John. *Theology and Social Theory: Beyond Secular Reason*. Oxford: Wiley-Blackwell, 2005.

Milbank, John. 'Theology in the Economy of the Sciences'. In *Faithfulness and Fortitude: In Conversation with the Theological Ethics of Stanley Hauerwas*, edited by Mark Nation and Samuel Wells, 39–59. Edinburgh: T&T Clark, 2000.

Milbank, John. 'What Lacks Is Feeling: Hume Versus Kant and Habermas'. In *Faithful Reading: New Essays in Theology in Honour of Fergus Kerr OP*, edited by Simon Oliver, Karen Kilby and Thomas O'Loughlin, 1–28. London: T&T Clark, 2012.

Milbank, John. *The Word Made Strange: Theology, Language and Culture*. Oxford: Blackwell, 1997.

Milbank, John and Simon Oliver, eds. *The Radical Orthodoxy Reader*. London: Routledge, 2009.

Milbank, John and Simon Oliver. 'Theologians in Conversation: Radical Orthodoxy'. http://www.youtube.com/watch?v=LRemJU5mTPc, accessed 13 October 2014.

Milbank, John and Catherine Pickstock, eds. *Truth in Aquinas*. London: Routledge, 2001.

Milbank, John, and Aaron Riches. Foreword to *Theurgy and the Soul: The Neoplatonism of Iamblichus*, edited by Gregory Shaw, v–xviii. Kettering, OH: Angelico Press/Sophia Perennis, 2014.

Milbank, John, Catherine Pickstock and Graham Ward. 'Suspending the Material: The Turn of Radical Orthodoxy'. In *Radical Orthodoxy: A New Theology*, edited by John Milbank, Catherine Pickstock and Graham Ward, 1–20. London: Routledge, 2002.

Mills, William. *Church, World and Kingdom: The Eucharistic Foundation of Alexander Schmemann's Pastoral Theology*. Mundelein, IL: Hillenbrand Books, 2012.

Mir, Amene. 'A Panentheist Reading of John Milbank'. *Modern Theology* 28, no. 3 (2012): 526–60.

Morris, Theresa. *Hans Jonas's Ethic of Responsibility: From Ontology to Ecology*. New York: State University of New York Press, 2013.

Mueller, Justin. 'This Flesh Belongs to Me: Michael Weinstein and Max Stirner'. In *Michael A. Weinstein: Action, Contemplation, Vitalism*, edited by Robert Oprisko and Diane Rubenstein, 55–76. London: Routledge, 2015.

Myers, Ben. *Christ the Stranger: The Theology of Rowan Williams*. London: Bloomsbury T&T Clark, 2012.

Nagel, Thomas. *Mind and Cosmos: Why the Materialist Neo-Darwinian Conception of Nature Is Almost Certainly False*. Oxford: Oxford University Press, 2012.

Nelson, Eric. 'Biological and Historical Life: Heidegger Between Levinas and Dilthey'. In *The Science, Politics and Ontology of Life-Philosophy*, edited by Scott Campbell and Paul Bruno, 15–30. London: Bloomsbury, 2013.

Neville, Robert. 'More on Jonas and Process Philosophy'. In *The Legacy of Hans Jonas: Judaism and the Philosophy of Life*, edited by Hava Tirosh-Samuelson and Christian Wiese, 511–18. Boston: Brill, 2008.

Nichols, Aidan. *Conversation of Faith and Reason: Modern Catholic Thought from Hermes to Benedict XVI*. Gracewing: Leominster, 2009.

Nichols, Aidan. 'Non Tali Auxilio: Not By Such Help'. *New Blackfriars* 73 (1992): 326–32.

Nirenberg, David. 'Choosing Life', Review of *Memoirs: Hans Jonas*. In *The New Republic Online*, 6 November 2008. http://www.powells.com/review/2008_11_06.html , accessed 23 January 2013.

Normandin, Sebastian and Charles Wolfe, eds. *Vitalism and the Scientific Image in Post-Enlightenment Life Science, 1800–2010. History, Philosophy and Theory of the Life Sciences Series, Volume 2*. London: Springer, 2013.

Oliver, Simon. 'Introducing Radical Orthodoxy: From Participation to Late Modernity'. In *The Radical Orthodoxy Reader*, edited by John Milbank and Simon Oliver, 3–27. London: Routledge, 2009.

Oliver, Simon. *Philosophy, God and Motion*. London: Routledge, 2005.

Oyama, Susan. 'Biologists Behaving Badly: Vitalism and the Language of Language'. *History of Philosophy of the Life Sciences* 32 (2010): 401–23.

Packham, Catherine. *Eighteenth-Century Vitalism: Bodies, Culture, Politics. Palgrave Studies in the Enlightenment, Romanticism, and Cultures of Print*. Basingstoke: Palgrave Macmillan, 2012.

Pickstock, Catherine. *After Writing: On the Liturgical Consummation of Philosophy*. Oxford: Wiley-Blackwell, 1997.

Pickstock, Catherine. 'Duns Scotus: His Historical and Contemporary Significance'. *Modern Theology* 21 (2005): 543–74.

Pickstock, Catherine. 'Radical Orthodoxy and the Meditations of Time'. In *Radical Orthodoxy? – A Catholic Enquiry*, edited by Laurence Hemming, 63–75. Aldershot: Ashgate, 2000.

Pollard, Sam. 'If God Is Real, What Difference Does He Make? Recognising the Interpretative Key to Reading Stanley Hauerwas in Response to Nicholas Healy's (Very) Critical Introduction'. Unpublished paper, 2015.

Porter, Jean. 'Openness and Constraint: Moral Reflection as Tradition-guided Inquiry in Alasdair MacIntyre's Recent Works'. *Journal of Religion* 73 (1993): 514–36.

Portier, William. 'Twentieth Century Catholic Theology and the Triumph of Maurice Blondel'. *Communio* 38 (2011): 103–37.

Prusak, Bernard. 'Cloning and Corporeality'. In *The Legacy of Hans Jonas: Judaism and the Philosophy of Life*, edited by Hava Tirosh-Samuelson and Christian Wiese, 315–43. Boston: Brill, 2008.

Ratzinger, Joseph. *Introduction to Christianity*. San Francisco: Ignatius, 2004.

Reginster, Bernard. *The Affirmation of Life: Nietzsche on Overcoming Nihilism*. Cambridge, MA: Harvard University Press, 2009.

Richardson, Graeme. 'Integrity and Realism: Assessing John Milbank's Theology'. *New Blackfriars* 84 (2007): 268–80.

Roberts, Richard. *Religion, Theology and the Human Sciences*. Cambridge: Cambridge University Press, 2002.

Roberts, Richard. 'Transcendental Sociology? A Critique of John Milbank's *Theology and Social Theory Beyond Secular Reason*'. *Scottish Journal of Theology* 46, no. 4 (1993): 527–36.

Rosenberg, Alex. *Darwinian Reductionism: Or, How to Stop Worrying and Love Molecular Biology*. Chicago: University of Chicago Press, 2006.

Rosenberg, Alex. *Instrumental Biology: Or the Disunity of Science*. Chicago: University of Chicago Press 1994.

Ruse, Michael. *Darwin and Design: Does Evolution Have A Purpose?* Cambridge, MA: Harvard University Press, 2003.

Sarkar, Sahotra and Anya Plutynski, eds. *A Companion to the Philosophy of Biology*. Blackwell Companions to Philosophy. Oxford: Blackwell, 2008.

Schindler, David. 'The Given As Gift: Creation and Disciplinary Abstraction in Science'. *Communio* 38 (2011): 52–102.

Schubert-Soldern, Rainer. *Mechanism and Vitalism: Philosophical Aspects of Biology*. Edited by Philip Fothergill, translated by C. E. Robin. London: Burns & Oates Ltd., 1962.

Shakespeare, Steven. *Radical Orthodoxy: A Critical Introduction*. London: SPCK, 2007.

Shortt, Rupert. *God's Advocates: Christian Thinkers in Conversation*. London: Darton, Longman & Todd, 2005.

Singer, Edgar. 'Beyond Mechanism and Vitalism'. *Philosophy of Science* 1, no. 3 (1934): 273–94.

Skrbina, David. *Panpsychism in the West*. London: MIT Press, 2005.

Smith, James. *Introducing Radical Orthodoxy: Mapping a Post-Secular Theology*. Grand Rapids, MI: Baker, 2004.

Smith, James. 'Radical Orthodoxy: A Select Bibliography'. http://www.virgo-maria.org/ Archives- CSI/2005/CSI-2005-07-05-AngliCampos-Radical%20Orthodoxy-bibliography-2004-06-1.pdf, accessed 26 June 2017.

Soskice, Janet. *Metaphor and Religious Language*. London: Clarendon, 1985.

Southgate, Christopher. *The Groaning of Creation: God, Evolution and the Problem of Evil*. Louisville: Westminster John Knox Press, 2008.

Spassov, Spas. 'Metaphysics and Vitalism in Henri Bergson's Biophilosophy: A New Look'. *Analecta Husserliana* 52 (1998): 197–206.

Sterelny, Kim and, Paul E. Griffiths, eds. *Sex and Death: An Introduction to Philosophy of Biology*. Science and Its Conceptual Foundations Series. Chicago: University of Chicago Press, 1999.

Storey, David. *Naturalizing Heidegger: His Confrontation with Nietzsche, His Contributions to Environmental Philosophy*. New York: SUNY Press, 2015.

Tanner, Kathryn. *God and Creation in Christian Theology: Tyranny or Empowerment?* Minneapolis: Fortress Press, 2005.

Taylor, Charles. 'Closed World Structures'. In *Religion After Metaphysics*, edited by Mark Wrathall, 47–68. Cambridge: Cambridge University Press, 2003.

Taylor, Charles. *Philosophical Arguments*. Cambridge, MA: Harvard University Press, 1995.

Taylor, Charles. *A Secular Age*. Cambridge, MA: Harvard University Press, 2007.

Taylor, Charles. *Sources of the Self*. Cambridge, MA: Harvard University Press, 1989.

The New English Bible. Cambridge: Cambridge University Press, 1961.

Theokritoff, Elizabeth. 'The Vision of Maximus the Confessor: That Creation May All Be One'. In *The Wiley-Blackwell Companion to Religion and Ecology*, edited by John Hart, Chapter 17. Oxford: Wiley- Blackwell, 2017.

Thompson, Evan. *Mind in Life: Biology, Phenomenology and the Sciences of Mind*. Cambridge, MA: Harvard University Press, 2007.

Thomson, Alan. *Culture in a Post-Secular Context: Theological Possibilities in Milbank, Barth, and Bediako*. Eugene, OR: Pickwick Publications, 2014.

Tirosh-Samuelson, Hava and Christian Wiese, eds. *The Legacy of Hans Jonas: Judaism and The Phenomenon of Life*. Boston: Brill, 2008.

Trainor, Brian. 'Why Augustine did, and Milbank didn't quite, get it right'. *New Blackfriars* 93 (2012): 524–43.

Trewavas, Tony. 'Plant Intelligence: An Overview'. *BioScience* 66, no. 7 (2016): 542–51.

Triffett, Brendan. 'Plurally Possessed: Gift and Participation in the Theo-ontology of John Milbank'. PhD diss., University of Tasmania, 2011.

Troster, Lawrence. 'Caretaker or Citizen: Hans Jonas, Aldo Leopold, and the Development of Jewish Environmental Ethics'. In *The Legacy of Hans Jonas: Judaism and the Philosophy of Life*, edited by Hava Tirosh-Samuelson and Christian Wiese, 373–96. Boston: Brill, 2008.

Tudge, Colin. *The Secret Life of Trees: How They Live and Why They Matter*. London: Penguin, 2005.

Turner, Denys. *Faith, Reason and the Existence of God*. Cambridge: Cambridge University Press, 2004.

Turner, J. Scott. 'Biology's Second Law: Homeostasis, Purpose and Desire'. In *Beyond Mechanism: Putting Life Back Into Biology*, edited by Brian Henning and Adam Scarfe, 183–205. Lanham, MD: Lexington Books, 2013.

Turner, J. Scott. *The Extended Organism: The Physiology of Animal-Built Structures*. Cambridge, MA: Harvard University Press, 200

Turner, J. Scott. *The Tinkerer's Accomplice: How Design Emerges from Life Itself*. Cambridge, MA: Harvard University Press, 2007.

Vogel, Lawrence. Foreword to *The Phenomenon of Life: Towards a Philosophical Biology*, edited by Hans Jonas, xi–xxii. Evanston, IL: Northwestern University Press, 2001.

Vogel, Lawrence. 'Natural Law Judaism?: The Genesis of Bioethics in Hans Jonas, Leo Strauss, and Leon Kass'. In *The Legacy of Hans Jonas: Judaism and the Philosophy of Life*, edited by Hava Tirosh- Samuelson and Christian Wiese, 287–314. Boston: Brill, 2008.

von Balthasar, Hans Urs. *The Glory of the Lord: A Theological Aesthetics V: The Realm of Metaphysics in the Modern Age*. Translated by O. Davies et al. Edinburgh: T&T Clark, 1991.

Wallace, Mark. *Finding God in the Singing River: Christianity, Spirit, Nature*. Minneapolis: Fortress Press, 2005.

Ward, Graham. 'In the Economy of the Divine: A Response to James Smith'. *Pneuma: Journal of the Society for Pentecostal Studies* 25 (2003): 118–19.

Ward, Graham. 'John Milbank's Divina Commedia'. *New Blackfriars, New Blackfriars* 73 (1992): 311–18.

Wiese, Christian. *The Life and Thought of Hans Jonas: Jewish Dimensions*. Tauber Institute for the Study of European Jewry Series. New Hampshire: University Press of New England, 2010.

Williams, Rowan. *The Edge of Words: God and the Habits of Language*. London: Bloomsbury, 2014.

Williams, Rowan. *The Lion's World*. Oxford: Oxford University Press, 2012.

Williams, Rowan. 'Saving Time: Thoughts on Practice, Patience and Vision'. *New Blackfriars* 73 (1992): 319–26.

Wilson, Edward O. *The Meaning of Human Existence*. New York: Liveright, 2014.

Wilson, Edward O. *Sociobiology: The New Synthesis*. Cambridge, MA: Harvard University Press, 1975.

Wohlleben, Peter. *The Hidden Life of Trees: What They Feel, How They Communicate*. Canada: Greystone, 2016.

Wolin, Richard. *Heidegger's Children: Hannah Arendt, Karl Lowith, Hans Jonas, and Herbert Marcuse*. Princeton, NJ: Princeton University Press, 2015.

INDEX

Page numbers followed with 'n' refer to footnotes.

Printed in the USA
CPSIA information can be obtained
at www.ICGtesting.com
LVHW020257040824
787202LV00001B/91